Jesus Christ
at the Encounter
of World Religions

FAITH MEETS FAITH

An Orbis Series in Interreligious Dialogue

Paul F. Knitter, General Editor

In our contemporary world, the many religions and spiritualities stand in need of greater intercommunication and cooperation. More than ever before, they must speak to, learn from, and work with each other, in order to maintain their own identity and vitality and so to contribute to fashioning a better world.

FAITH MEETS FAITH seeks to promote interreligious dialogue by providing an open forum for the exchanges between and among followers of different religious paths. While the series wants to encourage creative and bold responses to the new questions of pluralism confronting religious persons today, it also recognizes the present plurality of perspectives concerning the methods and content of interreligious dialogue.

This series, therefore, does not want to endorse any one school of thought. By making available to both the scholarly community and the general public works that represent a variety of religious and methodological viewpoints, FAITH MEETS FAITH hopes to foster and focus the emerging encounter among the religions of the world.

Already published:

Toward a Universal Theology of Religion, Leonard Swidler, Editor
The Myth of Christian Uniqueness, John Hick and Paul F. Knitter, Editors
An Asian Theology of Liberation, Aloysius Pieris, S.J.
The Dialogical Imperative, David Lochhead
Love Meets Wisdom, Aloysius Pieris, S.J.
Many Paths, Eugene Hillman, C.S.Sp.
The Silence of God, Raimundo Panikkar
The Challenge of the Scriptures, Groupe de Recherches
    Islamo-Chrétien
The Meaning of Christ, John P. Keenan
Hindu-Christian Dialogue, Harold Coward, Editor
The Emptying God, John B. Cobb, Jr. and Christopher Ives, Editors
Christianity through Non-Christian Eyes, Paul J. Griffiths, Editor
Christian Uniqueness Reconsidered, Gavid D'Costa, Editor
Women Speaking, Women Listening, Maura O'Neill
Bursting the Bonds?, Leonard Swidler, Lewis John Eron, Lester Dean, and
    Gerard Sloyan
One Christ—Many Religions, Stanley J. Samartha
The New Universalism, David J. Krieger

FAITH MEETS FAITH SERIES

Jesus Christ at the Encounter of World Religions

Jacques Dupuis, S.J.

Translated from the French by
Robert R. Barr

ORBIS BOOKS

Maryknoll, New York 10545

The Catholic Foreign Mission Society of America (Maryknoll) recruits and trains people for overseas missionary service. Through Orbis Books, Maryknoll aims to foster the international dialogue that is essential to mission. The books published, however, reflect the opinions of their authors and are not meant to represent the official position of the society.

This is a translation of *Jésus-Christ à la rencontre des religions*, © 1989 by Desclée, Paris.
Translation copyright, © 1991 by Orbis Books
Published by Orbis Books, Maryknoll, New York 10545
Printed in the United States of America
All rights reserved

Library of Congress Cataloging-in-Publication Data

Dupuis, Jacques, 1923-
    [Jésus-Christ à la rencontre des religions. English]
    Jesus Christ at the encounter of world religions / Jacques Dupuis ;
translated from the French by Robert R. Barr.
      p. cm. — (Faith meets faith)
    Translation of: Jésus-Christ à la rencontre des religions.
    Includes bibliographical references and index.
    ISBN 0-88344-724-X — ISBN 0-88344-723-1 (pbk.)
    1. Jesus Christ—Person and offices. 2. Christianity and other
religions. 3. Christianity and other religions—Hinduism.
4. Hinduism—Relations—Christianity. 5. Jesus Christ—Hindu
interpretations. I. Title. II. Series
BT205.D87   1991
232—dc20   91-7840
                                      CIP

Contents

A Note on Orthography

The problem of rendering non-Western systems of writing into Roman letters for English and other modern European languages is notoriously difficult. Joining many publishers who do not insert diacritical marks for words such as the Sanskrit *Śūnyatā*, this book also omits them.

Scholars and others who know languages such as Sanskrit, Pali, Arabic, or Japanese do not need the diacritical marks to identify words in their original written form. And persons who do not know these languages gain little from having the marks reproduced. We recognize that languages employing different orthographic systems have a richness and distinctiveness that *are* partially conveyed by the orthographics of diacritical marks. And while we do not wish to be part of flattening out the contours of our linguistically plural globe, the high cost of ensuring accuracy in using the diacritical marks does not justify reproducing them here.

Foreword

Jesus Christ at the Encounter of World Religions owes its origins to an encounter that took place in midsummer 1980. The author was at that time Professor of Dogmatic Theology at the Jesuit Faculty of Theology of New Delhi and editor of *Vidyajyoti: Journal of Theological Reflection*. Since then he has departed Asia for Rome, where he continues his teaching of theology at the Gregorian University and where he is editor of *Gregorianum*.

A theologian of the West, a Francophone Belgian Jesuit who was formed in the tradition of his order, then worked long years in India, steeped in the blessings and hazards of Christian mission, offers us, in these pages, a response to the fundamental question that has concerned him throughout his life: the encounter of the mystery of Jesus Christ with the great religious traditions of humanity.

The subject is one of importance, and the partner in dialogue well selected. The subject is the *relationship between the mystery of Christ and other religions*. The author's investigation of this relationship has a twofold objective. He not only seeks to take a position, from a Christian viewpoint, with regard to diverse ways to God, which other religions appear to be, he likewise seeks to reveal the light the confrontation of world religious traditions sheds on Christian faith itself.

Admittedly, such an undertaking, while rather broadly accepted today, is relatively recent with theologians. True, it is traditional with them to practice a dialogue with *philosophy*: Neoplatonism, Aristotelianism, German idealism, and so on. Long is the list of the partners Christian faith has found here. It is clear, furthermore, that since their birth in the contemporary era — and beginning with history — the human sciences have opened up a whole new space to faith for debate, criticism, and in some instances, mutual enrichment. But until very recently, who in theology was really concerned with a comparable attitude toward world religions? Did it not seem that dialogue among world religions — apart from pastoral (or mission) considerations — was likely to be fruitless and therefore to be relegated to the status of an ancillary enterprise? But why should it have seemed so evident that other religions — with a richness at once spiritual, ethical, and speculative — should be less qualified for dialogue with Christian faith and theology than nonreligious intellectual and philosophical schools of thought having far less in common with religious traditions as such?

True, the reason for this comportment on theology's part was that it sought to bestow the honor of a dialogue upon partners operating in its own Western cultural heritage. But it is precisely elsewhere than in Europe and North America that the great living religions are to be found. Thus, it was only when sufficient attention was paid to the other continents *in their difference and otherness* that there arose both the opportunity and the interest, indeed the urgency, of an encounter with the worldviews, and, more broadly, the various currents, that characterize these religions.

But now a considerable diversity has appeared. Latin America, which had been profoundly marked by Christianity for centuries, developed a confrontation with the currents and combats of political and economic liberation. Analogously, Africa has often tended to place more importance on approaches to inculturation, in which ethnology, ethnolinguistics, ethnopsychology, the study of rituals, and so forth, took precedence over a properly religious approach. It is actually in Asia, then, that the religious traditions as such have come to be the principal partners in the dialogue with Christian theology.

The interest of the reflection proposed to us by Jacques Dupuis derives precisely from the encounter with such a partner. But we must further specify who this partner is.

With towering religions like Hinduism and Buddhism, Taoism, Confucianism, and Shinto, Asian religious traditions are extremely varied. The fact remains, however, that chiefly in India and with Hinduism have dialogues with Christian faith been initiated. In devoting the first part of his work to presenting us with numerous varied readings of the figure of Christ, as these have been practiced in the Indian context, the author gains a twofold advantage. Not only does Fr. Dupuis demonstrate the appropriateness of the partner that he has selected from among all those who could have been chosen; he also furnishes his readers with sufficiently rich material to show them the breadth of the debate begun, and what is really at stake.

One point must be emphasized, as it sums up the whole. The following pages constitute a work on *christology*, and not on Christianity in general. The author serves notice that he means to practice his theology within the Christian faith. He holds that Jesus Christ is the only Savior of the entire world. At the same time, he forthrightly acknowledges that he thereby faces a series of formidable problems, which, in his second part, he addresses with method and rigor through the use of three levels of investigation.

He first addresses the problem of the manner in which Jesus Christ reaches those whom he saves outside the Christian way. More precisely, he asks what role the non-Christian religious ways are equipped to play in their devotees' access to the salvation secured for them by Jesus Christ alone.

The question then becomes how, in that case, the aspects of "uniqueness" and universality, both of which have now been ascribed to Jesus Christ, are reconcilable. Once again, the author finds it incumbent to explain more precisely how the spatiotemporal historical unicity of Jesus and the universal dimension of the *Christ* professed *in him* by Christian faith interrelate. The author devotes to these major christological points the two decisive chapters of his work.

The last stage of his task is to identify the principles of an interreligious dialogue capable both of throwing light, in a useful way, on the evangelizing practice of the church, and of evolving into a "theology of dialogue" worthy of the name. To Fr. Dupuis, then, we are all indebted for a superb, challenging, and readable analysis of the issues facing christology as the Christian Faith seeks to understand itself in the context of world religious plurality.

JOSEPH DORÉ

Jesus Christ
at the Encounter
of World Religions

Introduction

Two debates hold center stage in theology today that seem assured of a position of importance in the years to come. They are the discussions concerning liberation theology, whose particular currency is in the countries of the third world, and secondly, discussions on a Christian theology of the religious traditions of humanity, in which the Asian and African continents are particularly involved. The scenario of theological debate has considerably evolved, then, in these last years. The burning issues now touch first and foremost the life of the continents and churches of the third world. The rapid geopolitical evolution of the planet, characterized by what has been called, correctly enough, the "irruption" of the third world and the "third church,"[1] is not without its repercussions on the theological agenda of the churches.

It is the second burning question of contemporary theology that the present volume seeks to address. Shortly, we shall have the opportunity to paint a compact panorama of the current debate on the question. By way of an introduction, it would seem desirable to explain the perspective in which we shall place ourselves, establish the method that our study will adopt, and cite some of the crucial questions to which we must attempt to seek an answer.

OVERALL PERSPECTIVE

The title of this book—*Jesus Christ at the Encounter of World Religions*— points to the series of problems with which we shall be dealing. It will not be superfluous to explicate the terms of that title.

First of all, we shall be dealing not with a comparative history of religions, and still less with a phenomenology or philosophy of religions, but precisely with a *theology* of religions. Between the latter and the others is all the distance that separates theology, a reflection on faith, from positive science or philosophy. Thus, we shall not be observing, evaluating, or comparing religious phenomena with the objective detachment that is claimed for positive science. Obviously such an approach cannot levy any absolute value judgment regarding the "uniqueness" or superiority of any religious tradition. To the eyes of the science of comparative religions, each tradition can only be "unique" in its way—that is, different and original—without any of them being able to claim absolute superiority over all the others.

1

With the religion of Christ, then, as with the other traditions, science will endeavor to detect its specificity, which it will find in the originality of the gospel.

Our approach is different. Being theological, it commences with faith and develops in faith. We are aware that faith comports, if not its prejudices, at least its presuppositions. We accept and assume these, as guides in our theological discourse. This does not mean that questions are either thrust aside or resolved a priori. It does mean that we address them from a point of departure in a faith commitment—here, the commitment of Christian faith in Jesus Christ.

"Jesus Christ," our title reads, precisely. This indicates an essential of our own purpose. We are not concerned solely with the Jesus of history, not even the Jesus of history as rediscovered by contemporary exegesis with such renewed assurance now that the dispute over the quest for this Jesus has been laid to rest. Nor are we interested solely in the Christ of faith or the cosmic Christ, which, in separation from the Jesus of history, would run the serious risk of being reduced to a principle or an abstraction. Our concern is precisely with "Jesus Christ," that is, with Jesus of Nazareth who died and was raised—with that crucified one of whom the apostolic kerygma tells us that, in raising him from the dead, "God has made him Lord and Christ" (Acts 2:36). He it is who, first and principally, is the object of Christian faith.

Primarily, then, we are concerned—and we shall have occasion to underscore this on a later page—not with Christianity or with the church, and still less with Christendom, but, very precisely, with Jesus Christ, the center of Christian faith. Let us recall, in this connection, the "hierarchy of truths" of which the Second Vatican Council spoke (*Unitatis Redintegratio*, no. 11), which it constructed in function of differing relationships of truths to the foundation of the Christian faith. This foundation is the person and mystery of Jesus Christ, in function of which everything else, including the church and its mission, must be conceived and to which it is ordered. The Jesus Christ event is the fundamental mystery. All else is derived.

Next, we shall be treating the encounter of Jesus Christ, the center of Christian faith, with world religions. At first we hesitated, uncertain which of two formulations to adopt for our French title: "Jesus Christ *at the encounter of* the religions," or "*the encounter of Jesus Christ with* the religions." ("Jésus-Christ *dans* la rencontre des religions," or "Jésus-Christ *à* la rencontre des religions.") The first choice connoted the current historical context of the encounter and interaction of the various religious traditions, and directly posed the question of the originality of Jesus Christ and Christianity in this new context. It suggests that Jesus Christ goes forth to meet other religions. It raises the question of the place of interreligious dialogue in Christian mission as the obligatory foundation of a theology of religions. At all events, our purpose is to elucidate, from and in faith, the mutual relationship between Jesus Christ and the religious traditions of humanity.

Let us further remark that, throughout this study, the expression *non-Christian religions* will be constantly and sedulously avoided. That this appellation is seen as offensive today is not simply a matter of passing taste. It is founded in theology. The expression defines others by what they are not — even though we may be determined to understand them as "anonymous Christians" — rather than by what they are and say that they are. We seem to be refusing them their own identity as others, in their irreducible specificity, by imposing upon them a title that asserts of them one thing only, namely, that they are not us. In so doing, Christianity seems to be establishing itself as an a priori, absolute norm — whereas actually Christianity is only one of the religious traditions of humanity among others. Once more we perceive — and we shall return to this explicitly below — the importance in a Christian theology of religions of positing a living faith in Jesus Christ — not Christianity as such — as the point of departure for its reflection.

A TOPIC OF CURRENT IMPORTANCE

The topic concerning us is not altogether new; it is actually, in a sense, as old as Christianity itself. Did not the apostolic church, particularly Paul, see the need to situate the Christian message they proclaimed in its rapport with the faith of Israel, on the one hand, and the Greek "pagan" religious world on the other (cf. Acts 17:19–34)? The theme has gained new importance and urgency, however, in today's context of religious pluralism. For the moment, we need only offer a brief overview of some of the main coordinates of this new context.

First of all comes the new knowledge we possess today of the other religious traditions and consequently the new awareness, in East and West alike, of humanity's multireligious context. Add to this the fact of the daily coexistence of various traditions, the result of the day-to-day commingling of populations through modern means of communication. It has become a commonplace today to observe that the world has been reduced to the size of a "big village." In this global village, whose population today surpasses five billion, the total Christian proportion seems to be diminishing, while Islam enjoys continuous growth. And if we direct our gaze toward Asia, especially India, which has given birth to Hinduism and Buddhism, Christianity, with the exception of the Philippines, finds itself constituting a ludicrous minority: in India, today, it represents 2.5 percent of a population of more than 800 million. And what shall we say of China?

In this context, is it realistic or even theologically possible to think — as we thought we had to in the past, on the basis of Matthew 28:19 — that the whole world is concretely called to profess Christianity in an explicit way? Or ought we rather to rethink, theologically, the relationship of the religious traditions of humanity to the mystery of Jesus Christ? The question is all the more obvious because of the fact that, far from showing any signs of decline, these other traditions are experiencing a genuine revival today. Not only are they still the source of inspiration that feeds the religious life of millions of their adherents; they are likewise seeing a movement of expansion. Not to mention a mission-minded and often militant Islam, we need only think of the attraction exerted today in the West by the so-called mystical religions, especially Hinduism and Buddhism. While thousands of Westerners, especially the young, journey to India each year in quest of religious experiences Christianity has apparently denied them, Hindu ashrams and Buddhist monasteries are built in Western countries, attracting no insignificant number of devotees. What theological significance are we to assign to these unprecedented phenomena? In an era dubbed "post-Christian" by some, how are we to evaluate theologically, from a Christian viewpoint, this fascination for Eastern spirituality and mysticism that "post-Christians" themselves evince? If, as we have said, the subject of the relationship between the Christian mystery and humanity's religious traditions is an old one, it is nonetheless also new, as the facts show.

As we know, the question was rendered moot by the Second Vatican Council, and we must by no means overlook the fact that the last council was the first in the history of the church to speak of other religions in a positive way. The Declaration "On the Relations of the Church with the Non-Christian Religions," *Nostra Aetate*, especially exhorts Christians to recognize the positive values presented in other traditions and enter into a relationship of dialogue (*colloquia*) and collaboration (*Nostra Aetate*, no. 2) with their adherents. We shall have to return to the texts of the council that deal with our subject and attempt to determine their precise scope, attributing to the council neither more nor less than what it meant and said. For the time being, let us be content simply to note the climate of openness that prevails and the call for dialogue issued by the council. In inviting Christians to dialogue with other religions, as it does most explicitly in the conclusion of the Pastoral Constitution, *Gaudium et Spes* (nos. 92–93), the council was answering the call issued by Pope Paul VI in his encyclical, *Ecclesiam Suam*, which was published during the council itself. The Pope had sketched four concentric circles, inviting Christians to enter into a dialogue at all four levels: within the church itself; with other Christians; with "non-Christians"; and with nonbelievers. With Paul VI and the council, then, interreligious dialogue received its credentials. We shall have to return to these sources and ask what place this dialogue holds in the evangelizing mission of the church.

A QUESTION OF METHOD

It will be important to offer something of an explanation of the method that will guide the present work. That our endeavor will be, as we have already clearly indicated, resolutely theological, does not automatically solve the methodological problem. To be sure, theologians still agree that theology is "faith in search of understanding" —*fides quaerens intellectum.* We begin with faith, then, and there we remain at every step. But with this point established, it remains to ask what role we assign, in this initial faith, to the living experience of an intersubjective relationship, and what other role to objective enunciations of the content of faith. Again, we must know the nature of the process that leads from faith to theology. The question we broach, then, requires that we make a choice between the received theological method, called "deductive," and the one gaining favor today, which we may call "inductive."

It must be acknowledged that Western theologians, even the most popular, who have concerned themselves with a Christian theology of religions have most often adopted a purely deductive method. They begin with certain statements in the New Testament that they judge to be clear and indisputable in their meaning, then they ask what Christian faith can grant the other religious traditions. Do the premises of revelation authorize the ascription to these traditions of a positive meaning and value in God's plan of salvation? Going a step further, do these premises permit Christians to look upon these traditions as actual ways of salvation—not parallel ways to that opened by God in Jesus Christ, surely, but genuine ways of salvation nonetheless, in virtue of some relationship they might enjoy with the Christian way?

The reaction to an exclusively deductive method, an aprioristic one, and as such necessarily inadequate, has arisen, as might be expected, in the churches in which coexistence with other religious traditions is an integral part of daily life, as in India, where the great world religions mingle on a daily basis. Indeed, in recent times, even in the West—as there, too, religious pluralism has gradually become a daily reality—theologians have been found to champion a resolutely inductive method in this material. One begins with a praxis of interreligious dialogue among the various traditions—lived, on either side, in one's own faith, as is fitting—and theological conclusions concerning the relationship of these traditions follow as "second act." Let us note, in passing, the analogy with the method underlying liberation theology, precisely as a new method of the *actus theologicus*: Gustavo Gutiérrez insists on the priority of a liberative praxis over theological discourse, which of its very nature follows in second place.[2] Similarly, where the relationship between the Christian mystery and the religious traditions of humanity is concerned, priority belongs to the praxis of the interreligious dialogue as obligatory foundation of a theological discourse. The a priori operation, we hear, must be replaced by an a posteriori operation.

What are we to think of all this? At issue is the hermeneutic problem itself. Obviously the datum of faith and the living context of religious pluralism must be brought together. There are two possible routes to this encounter: the deductive and the inductive. While legitimate in itself, the deductive operation nevertheless has its congenital limits. It is based on principles, and so is in danger of remaining abstract, of not really encountering the concrete reality of other religious traditions, just as the inductive operation, based as it is on the praxis of dialogue, has its own limits. Whether by ineffectuality or hesitancy, it may fail to attain its goal: theological conclusions that harmonize with the Christian datum.

In a situation such as this, the indicated methodology would seem to be a combination of the deductive and inductive methods. Their reciprocal movement would ensure the indispensable encounter between the datum of faith and the living reality of pluralism. Paul F. Knitter labels this approach the "global theological method" and describes it as follows, applying it to the subject with which we are concerned:

> Any viable method of theology will have to make use of two sources — Christian tradition (scripture and its living interpretation through history) and human experience (which includes both thought and praxis). Both these sources must be listened to openly and honestly; both must be brought into a mutually clarifying and mutually criticizing correlation.
>
> Applying the two-source approach to a method for a theology of religions, we must recognize that a Christian understanding of and approach to other religions cannot be fashioned only from the fabric of Christian beliefs. We will want to start with what the Bible or the official statements of councils have to say about other religions. And what we find must be taken seriously. But no final conclusions as to the value or the truth of other traditions can be reached until our Christian "data" is brought into relationship with a concrete knowledge (theory) and experience (praxis) of other religions.[3]

With a view to guaranteeing this obligatory encounter of Christian datum and praxis of dialogue, we must insist on the role of dialogue as the necessary foundation of a theology of religion because of its frequent omission in the past and the need to reestablish a balance between the two sources. From a point of departure in the praxis of the dialogue, the inductive operation is immediately immersed in the concrete religious experience of others. This is its strength and its irreplaceable contribution. Here too, of course, limitations are immediately in evidence, and we must subject these limitations to an attentive examination. Faith itself, by definition, is a commitment of the whole person. To what point is it possible, as dialogue seems to require, to enter into the religious experience of another and make it one's own? If it is true that the very authenticity of dialogue demands that one's own faith never be "bracketed," what reception is it possible to accord the religious faith of another? We shall return to this, especially to ask whether it is theologically intelligible and humanly honest to regard and style oneself a Hindu-Christian. Can one person share two whole and entire religious faiths?

For the moment, we need only notice that the operation that seems indicated is the one that combines both the deductive method—one's own faith not being called into question—and the inductive method—involving an encounter of the other believer, insofar as possible, in the concrete reality of his or her own actual religious experience.

Finally, let us raise one more problem, to which we shall likewise have to return later. This bears on the concept just evoked of the Hindu-Christian or Buddhist-Christian. If it seems theologically indefensible and concretely impracticable to bear within oneself the integrality of two distinct religious faiths—often opposed and contradictory, even in essential elements—does it not follow that the concept of a universal or world theology of religions, common to the various religious traditions and developed by them in concert, will likewise be utopian and vain?[4] It is one thing, by virtue of the interreligious dialogue practiced on the level of the spirit, to enter as far as possible into another's experience and perspective and to share, insofar as one can, the worldview of that other. It is another thing entirely to share the faith commitment and the coexistence thereupon ensuing of two seemingly contradictory faiths in the furthest depths of oneself. It is something else again to pretend to construct a universal theology that would transcend Christian theology and lay claim to universality.

To return to the title of this book in light of the preceding clarifications: Clearly what is at stake here is a *Christian theology* of religions. It is of the very nature of theology, as a reflection on faith, to constitute a specific particular vision and to address first of all those who share the same perspective. A recent author has written quite to the point: "Christian theology is the theology that is held by the Christian tradition, Muslim theology is the theology that is held by the Muslim tradition, and so on."[5] In seeking to transcend the specificity of one's own faith, we risk reducing, or even emptying, the content of that faith. The task to be executed is, on the contrary, to show forth the universality of the particular itself. Bringing to light the universality of the Jesus Christ event will be one of the important goals of this volume.

Indeed, as our title indicates, it is essentially with Jesus Christ and christology that we shall be dealing throughout these pages—but with christology in a context of the current pluralism of religious traditions and their interaction through interreligious dialogue. Need we cite the revival of theological interest in christology that has held the ascendancy in recent years, after the preference of the immediate postconciliar phase for ecclesiological investigations? This was entirely as might have been expected. Even during the council and after its end, Paul VI explained that an understanding of the mystery of the church—the immediate object of the work of the council—had ineluctably led to a consideration of the mystery of Christ.[6] Theology has had the same experience since the council. However, with all the abundance of christological output in recent years, rare are the works that concern themselves explicitly and with some degree of development with situating the mystery of Christ in the larger context of the religious traditions of humanity. Meanwhile, the numerous works recently devoted to the theology of religions, whatever their particular orientation — any of the various approaches we shall presently be taking into account — generally agree on the importance of the christological question for an ultimate determination of their own material. Here that question will be, from the outset and at every step, the core and focus of our considerations.

As for other religious traditions, we shall generally be forced to lump them together. We shall not be able to make the constant distinctions among them that we ought ideally to make. This limitation is partly deliberate and partly imposed by the limits of the author's own competency,[7] but it is important to take note of it from the outset. Surely not all religions actually have the same theological meaning in the divine plan of salvation nor can all be gathered up pell-mell and placed on the same footing in an interreligious dialogue. One must accord a unique place at least to Judaism, by reason of its singular rapport with the economy of salvation effected in Jesus Christ by the God of Israel. Likewise one must distinguish the monotheistic religions, which a terminology now classic calls prophetical, from the mystical religions of Asia such as Hinduism and Buddhism. However, despite inevitable distinctions, general questions retain a valid meaning as well. It is perfectly legitimate, theologically, to pose the general question of the salvific value of the "other" religious traditions and of the existence or nonexistence of an obligatory relationship with the mystery of Christ in view of the salvific value we have learned to acknowledge in them today. This is but one example of the general questions a Christian theology of religions will have to ask vis-à-vis other religious traditions.

Still, we shall take care not to fall into abstractions under the weight of our generalizations. To this end, we shall be making concrete topical references to different traditions. More importantly, we hope to escape the pitfalls of abstraction by situating the Christian theology of religions in relation to the properly christological stepping-stones of a particular religious tradition.

The tradition (or traditions) of Hinduism lend themselves to this project perhaps better than any other, and thus constitute an evident choice here. Long theological and christological reflection has culminated in the recognition in the Hindu tradition of what has rightly been called the "unbound Christ"[8] — Christ detached from Christianity and the church. The "Indian renaissance," it has been arrestingly observed, has in its own way genuinely "acknowledged" Christ.[9] The knowledge and recognition of Jesus Christ by Hindu tradition (however partial) constitutes an important theological locus that we must exploit to its depths if the Christian theology of religions that we have in view wishes to avoid an absolute apriority bereft of all relation to reality. Hinduism is all the better qualified to serve as a basis for encounter and dialogue because it possesses — doubtless as no other religious tradition, and in virtue of independent sources — concepts of God and God's personal manifestation in the world which, despite important differences, are nevertheless surprisingly akin to the essence and core of Christian dogma. The *trimurti*, for example, or, even more, God conceived of as *saccidananda* (being, thought, bliss), are akin to the Trinity revealed in Jesus Christ, as the concept of *avatara* (descent, manifestation) is reminiscent of the Christian concept of incarnation.

Facts of this sort call for theological interpretation. Are we dealing with presentiments of the twofold mystery manifested decisively in Jesus Christ, presentiments attributable to a personal revelation or manifestation on the part of God in the sacred history of the nations, however fragmentary such a manifestation may be in comparison to the decisive word uttered by God in Jesus Christ? Explicit recourse to Hindu tradition will enable us to escape abstraction and to rest, to some extent, a Christian (and christological) theology of religions on elements of encounter and a certain praxis of dialogue that in some sort date from ancient times but in other respects are recent and current. A rapid survey of the scope and sequence that we propose to observe in this book will enable us to demonstrate our intent more explicitly.

SCOPE AND SEQUENCE OF THIS WORK

Part one bears the general title, Stepping-Stones of a Tradition. This title refers to the stepping-stones to a christological theology of religions that reside in Hindu tradition.[10] First we examine the "unbound" Christ as "recognized" by Hinduism (chapter one). This furnishes elements for dialogue and poses questions to theology.

Chapter two takes up certain elements of this first encounter and seeks to determine the points of contact between Jesus Christ and the Hindu *yoga* tradition. On a deeper level, it sets Christianity and Hinduism in a dialogic relationship in their most profound and most mystical elements: the Upanishadic experience of *advaita* (nonduality), culmination of the experience of God in Hindu mysticism, and the religious experience of Jesus Christ (Jesus' own experience of God as his Father, into which the Christian is invited to enter in turn).

A concrete study follows: Chapter three traces in broad strokes the experience of Hindu mysticism as undergone (to a depth perhaps never attained before) by a Hindu-Christian monk named Abhishiktananda (Dom Henri Le Saux). The writings of Abhishiktananda, especially those published posthumously, constitute a stunning testimonial to an experience that raises serious, inescapable problems for a theology and christology of religions.

On the basis of these first data of a bilateral dialogue with Hinduism, chapter four extends the discourse to religious traditions in general, as evaluated and understood in Christian theology. Here we take up the classic question of the purpose of the incarnation (*Cur Deus homo?*), situating it in the broader context of a religious pluralism in which the traditional response may well seem scandalous and unacceptable. We then review the various fundamental perspectives and attitudes represented in the recent abundant literature on the theology of religions. We must make a choice among these contrasting attitudes; however, we must justify our choice theologically.

Part two, entitled Christ, One and Universal, addresses the christological and theological problems raised by today's religious pluralism and the praxis of the interreligious dialogue. Here our first task will be to situate in one salvation history the various covenants struck by God with the nations, followed by the decisive divine covenant with the whole of humanity in Jesus Christ (chapter five).

But if God's covenant in Jesus Christ extends to all humanity, does it do away with all previous covenants, whose regime of salvation will thereby be cancelled and abolished? This is the question taken up in chapter six: Is there salvation today without the gospel? More precisely, do the other religious traditions have salvific value for their millions of adherents, so that they can be regarded theologically as ways of salvation? If they have, then what relationship do they maintain with the mystery of Jesus Christ if it is true, as the New Testament seems to understand, that all salvation is in Jesus Christ, the universal mediator?

Chapter seven pursues the same question, but this time respecting the divine revelation contained in the religious traditions of humanity. Can we, from a Christian theological point of view, acknowledge in the sacred books of these traditions a word addressed to human beings by God, of which Christians themselves can take advantage, even in the presence of the deci- sive word uttered by God in Jesus Christ? In order to answer this question, we shall appeal to the economy of the Spirit, an economy that must be recognized to be universal.

The christological question has underlain all of these chapters. However, we must now approach it anew by posing once more, in the context of religious pluralism, the old, but always current, problem of the Jesus of history and the Christ of faith (chapter eight). This context requires an old question to be asked in a new dimension, one which actually renders it more radical; and we must seek an adequate solution to it in this new context.

Chapter nine approaches the crucial christological question of the nov- elty and originality of Jesus Christ, as well as that of his oneness and universality, which, without suppressing his historical particularity, never- theless transcends it. Thus we return to the theme of chapter four, in which we had already posed the question of the "meaning" of Jesus Christ in the divine plan of salvation.

Thus having completed the circle, we hope to have shown that in a Christian theology of religions, christocentrism and theocentrism go hand in hand; indeed, they are inseparable. There can be no Christian theo-

centrism without christocentrism; but neither can there be a genuine christocentrism that will not at the same time be theocentric. We must likewise
recall that, in the single economy of salvation, the deeds of the Son and
the Spirit are themselves relational and interdependent. Christ was filled
with the Holy Spirit in order to communicate that Spirit, and it is by the
work of the Spirit that the historical event of Jesus Christ remains contemporary. In a theology of religions, as in any other domain of Christian
theology, there can be no christology without a pneumatology; nor can there
be a pneumatology without a christology.[11] Thus we see that the Christic
mystery is indivisible from the trinitarian.

In the two remaining chapters, we shall reflect on the interreligious
dialogue with which a theology and christology of religions cannot dispense.
The praxis of dialogue, still new in the church, calls for serious theological
reflection that will oblige its practitioners to transcend, as passé, no small
number of received traditional conceptions. Our first task will be to determine the place and role of the interreligious dialogue in the overall evangelizing mission of the church (chapter ten). Finally we shall attempt to
develop the elements of a theology of dialogue, keeping account of both
its demands and its promises (chapter eleven).

We hear much of "inculturation" today, even (and correctly), in the area
of faith and doctrine, where its requirements are so formidable and so
delicate. Doctrinal inculturation, however, can be misunderstood. It can be
thought of as a purely transcultural transposition or translation of doctrinal
content from one cultural idiom to another. This would reduce doctrinal
inculturation to an abstract, ultimately fruitless enterprise.

Contextualization would be a better word. To contextualize the *actus
theologicus* — to "do theology in context" — is to conceive theology as a hermeneutics.[12] We have already suggested this in speaking of the encounter
between the datum of faith in Jesus Christ and today's living reality of
religious pluralism and interreligious dialogue — the encounter of text and
context. At the end of this book, by way of a conclusion, we plan to suggest
certain orientations calculated to promote an inculturated, contextual christology of religions. While it is true that a universal theology seems to be
unreachable and utopian, given the specific demands of each religious faith,
it is no less true that there is no such thing (or no longer is such a thing)
as a universal Christian theology that would be valid for all times and places.
Now, on two of the three continents of the third world and the "third
church" — in Africa, and even more so in Asia — the coexistence of Christianity with other religious traditions is a primary, essential component of
the context in which the hermeneutic theological act must be performed.
Thus an African or Asian christology can no longer (if indeed it ever could)
dispense with a serious reflection on "the encounter of Jesus Christ with
the religions." How we may contextualize christology from a point of departure of the interreligious encounter and dialogue is the question to which,
at the terminus of our journey, we hope to have sketched an answer.

PART I

Stepping-Stones
of a Tradition

1

The "Unbound" Christ
Acknowledged in Hinduism

We may say that Christianity and Hinduism have had an unprecedented encounter during what has become customary to refer to as the Indian Renaissance, or the age of Neo-Hinduism. The nineteenth century and first part of the twentieth are shot through with various movements and individual personalities who, at varying depths, entered into contact with Jesus Christ and his message. True, most often this contact was established by the intermediary of Christian groups not under Catholic obedience, whether of an evangelical cast, or on the contrary, of a liberal tendency. This must be taken into account in any analysis and evaluation of the fruits of the encounter.

M. M. Thomas has spoken of the acknowledgment of Christ by the Indian Renaissance—while being careful to specify in each case and for each author the particular tenor of this acknowledgment.[1] S. J. Samartha describes the Christ acknowledged by Neo-Hinduism as an "unbound" Christ.[2] By this he means, first of all, that, while many attach themselves to the person of Jesus Christ, they usually detach that person from the institutional church, which, in their eyes, screens the Christian message from view. If they are willing to recognize a church made up of disciples of Jesus, then the highly organized, hierarchical form historically taken by that group, as well as its covenant with Western culture (that is, with the colonial powers) and the foreign character it has adopted, present an obstacle to the Hindu "response."

The Christ acknowledged by Hinduism is often a churchless Christ. For that matter, the Christ acknowledged by Hinduism is often a Christ delivered from the encumbrances of numerous "bonds" with which he is laden by traditional Christianity—whether it be a matter of applauding his message while rejecting the Christian claim to his person, or of receiving him as one divine manifestation among others in a catalog of divine descents (*avatara*) as varied as it is extensive. One realizes from the outset that the

15

encounter between Christ and Hinduism, viewed in its historicity, has raised ecclesiological and christological problems that are stumbling blocks even today.

The intent of this chapter is first to take account, in their main lines, of the principal currents that have marked the historical encounter between Jesus Christ and Neo-Hinduism. Here we shall distinguish a number of different categories characterizing various attitudes or "responses" to the person of Jesus Christ.[3] Our second step will be to sketch a rapid outline of the various models of the personhood of Jesus as developed by the protagonists of Neo-Hinduism. This will be a question of setting forth the most characteristic approaches to that personhood that the encounter with Jesus Christ has occasioned among them. A third section will then take up the material thus expounded and attempt to identify, first with respect to each model previously examined, and then in more general terms, the challenges posed to ecclesiology and christology by the "response to the unbound Christ."

An important observation: We have no intention of rehearsing, even briefly, the history of an Indian theology or christology of the era that concerns us. We propose rather to analyze, in sweeping lines, the encounter between Hinduism and the person of Jesus Christ, with the specific aim of indicating the challenge that this encounter has raised in the past and continues to raise today.

We shall not directly examine, except by way of exception, Christian theologians such as P. Chenchiah (1886–1959), V. Chakkarai (1880–1958), and A. J. Appasamy (1891–1976), who, during the period under examination, have for their own part sought to respond to the questions posed, suggesting, with varying felicitousness, an Indian ecclesiology and christology. This work, begun by the pioneers of inculturation, is pursued today in the broader framework of contextualization. We shall touch on this at the end of the book.

The challenge posed by the encounter of Neo-Hinduism with the person of Jesus Christ will serve as our particular but concrete basis for the theological and especially christological problems raised by religious pluralism and the interreligious dialogue.

VARIOUS RESPONSES TO THE PERSON OF JESUS CHRIST

"Response," wrote S. J. Samartha, "is a complex attitude involving cultural, psychological and theological factors, and in trying to describe [the Hindu response to Jesus Christ] one should be careful to avoid generalisations and oversimplification of the issues."[4] Nevertheless, he thinks general attitudes can be ranged under three broad categories:

• There are those who respond to Christ *without a commitment* to him. Nuances vary here, but this is the most widespread attitude. It is usually accompanied by a thoroughgoing disregard for the church.

- Next there are those who respond to Christ *with a commitment* to him, but to him alone, and *in the context of Hinduism* itself, while they either remain indifferent to the church or entirely reject it.
- Finally there are those whose response to and commitment to Christ lead them to enter the church openly through baptism, but who, *within the communion of the church*, address it severe *criticisms*.[5]

H. Staffner likewise distinguishes three categories, which, without coinciding precisely with those of Samartha, are nonetheless rather closely related to them.[6] They are the following, and they correspond to the three respective parts of our study.

- There are Hindus for whom the social teaching of Christ serves as an inspiration, but without involving a personal commitment to him. Mahatma Gandhi is an eminent, but not solitary, example.
- There are Hindus who are intensely committed to Christ, but to whom it seems impossible to enter any of the existing churches, such as Keshub Chunder Sen.
- Finally, there are Hindus who have become Christians but insist that they have remained Hindus. That is, they continue to lay claim to Hinduism as well. The best-known case is that of Brahmabandhab Upadhyaya.[7]

We must not expect to be able to apply these categories too rigidly, nor must we exaggerate their scope. The reality is more complex, and the nuances among the various positions are very marked. One might, for example, be exercised by the absence of a personal commitment to Jesus on the part of Mahatma Gandhi. But that depends on what we understand by personal commitment. True, there was no religious engagement in the sense of a Christian faith. But Jesus certainly became a source of inspiration, even religious inspiration, for the Mahatma's social and political action, while it was not the only religious inspiration. On the other hand, some have cast doubt on Upadhyaya's fidelity to Christianity in the period of his political involvement and his disputes with the official church. Thus the above-cited categories must be handled with care.

However, they are basically valid. They have the merit of describing the basic attitudes in question. They assert something fundamental about the reality of the encounter between Jesus Christ and Hinduism. It is perfectly possible for Hinduism to integrate Jesus into its vision of the world and reality—to assimilate him—without necessarily involving faith in Jesus Christ as Christianity understands that faith. It is equally easy for Hinduism to separate faith in Jesus Christ, as a profession of being his disciple, from commitment to or acknowledgment of the community of disciples that is the church. In this basic sense, the categories listed above are themselves revelatory of theological problems—christological and ecclesiological problems—raised by the encounter of Jesus Christ and the protagonists of Neo-Hinduism.

While already implicitly mentioned in the above categories, one group deserves special attention because of its basic approach. That approach consists in the construction of a personal synthesis of Christianity and Hinduism. M. Maupilier has devoted to this group a study entitled *Les mystiques hindous-chrétiens*.[8] Maupilier calls the members of this group "Hindu mystics of Jesus Christ"—Hindu-Christian *sannyasi* or *sadhu*. There were such during the period that concerns us, most often solitaries, and there are today. The best known is Brahmabandhab Upadhyaya, whom we have already mentioned. These Hindu-Christian *sannyasi*, delivered from all attachments through complete asceticism, had no intention of renouncing anything of their rooting in faith in Jesus Christ, Son of God and Savior, and lived their lives of discipleship in an often tense relationship with, and sometimes apart from, the churches supposed to represent him. Maupilier writes:

> Hindu-Christians, in their time, were the unintentional witnesses of the fact that the Spirit awakens the entire reality of Jesus Christ without any of the distortions and wounds inflicted upon him by the "churches" that would present him in channels that bound, deviate from, or diminish their Source.[9]

Thus the Hindu-Christian mystics of yesterday and today figure as the symbol of the dramatic encounter, so frequently unsuccessful, even confrontational, between Jesus Christ and Hinduism. They, more than anyone else, show us the urgency of the theological problems they have lived as a personal drama: Are Christianity and Hinduism compatible as culture and as faith? Are true encounter and conviviality—that is, mutual contribution and enrichment—possible? Is it theologically possible to be a Hindu-Christian? At what price? The question cannot be avoided.

HINDU MODELS OF JESUS CHRIST

It scarcely comes as a surprise that during that period of the encounter between Jesus Christ and Hinduism with which we are concerned, Hindu partners should have constructed a number of different models of the object of their encounter. Various hermeneutics were at play, with different authors building their respective interpretations of Jesus on the basis of their own personal experience, but also in function of the presuppositions of their personal viewpoints and the limits of their sources of information. There is a variety of Hindu christologic models, whose most typical and most important traits we shall now attempt to highlight.

Without wishing to thrust distinctions beyond their actual content and utility, it seems that we might, with a view to clarity in our discourse, distinguish the following christologic models: the Christ of the Sermon on the Mount and the Beatitudes; the Christ of personal devotion or *bhakti*; Christ as the end-point of humanity's self-development and evolution;

Christ the self-manifestation of the divine in the world; Christ the *yogi*; the Christ of the mystical experience of *advaita* (nonduality). We might characterize these various approaches, respectively, as moral, devotional, philosophical, theological, ascetic, and mystical. For the sake of concretion, we shall present our rapid description of each of these christologic models through the eyes of a particular author who seems sufficiently representative of that particular approach.

Mahatma Gandhi's Jesus of the Beatitudes

The moral (that is, the ethical) character of the Jesus of Mohandas K. Gandhi (1869–1948) must not be understood in a pejorative sense. We know how deeply the teaching of Jesus, especially the Beatitudes of the evangelical discourse that contain in programmatic fashion the doctrine of the Reign of God (Matt. 5:1–12), influenced the thought and activity, even the political activity, of the Mahatma in the two essential components of that activity: *satyagraha* (the search for truth) and *ahimsa* (nonviolence). Not in the sense that these essential attitudes were drawn directly from the gospel of Jesus without root in the Asian religious traditions of Hinduism and Buddhism, which Gandhi cherished as his own religious heritage, but rather in the sense that Gandhi saw these fundamental religious values as singularly represented in Jesus' teaching and realized in exemplary fashion in Jesus' life and activity.

As for the person of Jesus, while the Mahatma was deeply attached to him, his attachment never became a personal commitment of faith as a Christian understands this commitment. For Gandhi, Jesus was a model to imitate and an inspiration with which to be fired. In other words, Jesus was one of those singular human beings (among others) in whom one inescapably recognizes a manifestation of the Truth that is very God. But Gandhi never rejected his deep roots in Hindu tradition, and tradition made it impossible for him to go further. True, Jesus was a divine manifestation; but he was only one among others, and hence could not be called Son of God in a "unique" fashion. Still less could one call him "God" in proper terms.

As for the church, while crediting it with certain positive elements, Gandhi also criticized it as he thought appropriate. Christians generally seemed to him to be rather poor disciples of their master. But was not discipleship the essential—that is, the unique—function of mission? When the gospel was lived, it propagated itself; nothing more was necessary. Steeped to the quick in conversion understood as continuous conversion to the Truth that is God, Gandhi was never able to understand Christian mission as the effort to convert human beings to the church, which he regarded as an unseemly "proselytism." What was important was the search for Truth along one's path, in whatever religious tradition one happened to be travelling. It was a matter of each one's personal sincerity and loyalty to the authentic identity of his or her religious tradition. As all religions were rooted in faith in the same God, all were of equal value, while each was specially adapted to its own people.

Gandhi desired mutual understanding and collaboration among the various religious traditions. Let Hindus become better Hindus, Muslims better Muslims, and Christians better Christians. Such was the road that would lead independent India, once it had obtained its *swaraj* (own government), to harmony among the various religious communities. It was for this community harmony that Gandhi appealed with his whole heart and soul. It was for this that he gave his life.[10]

Mahatma Gandhi's Jesus can thus be legitimately regarded as representative of the Hindu model that we have called the Jesus of the Beatitudes. In the titles of respective chapters they devote to the Gandhian model of Jesus, M. M. Thomas and S. J. Samartha make use of similar expressions: "Jesus, the Supreme *Satyagrahi*," and "Jesus Christ, the Ideal *Satyagrahi*." Such is the central place of the search for the divine Truth in the figure of Jesus as Gandhi understood him. We cannot concern ourselves here with a development of the various aspects of this concept. We must rest content with a succinct reference to writers who have treated our subject more directly. First and foremost let us cite Gandhi himself.

For Gandhi, the Sermon on the Mount contains the whole of Jesus' teaching, which is summed up in the principle of nonviolence. Jesus' own life, and his suffering inspired by love, is the perfect example of this, and yet the principle contained in the gospel teaching matters more than the historical person of Jesus who incarnates it. It would be true without him. Gandhi writes:

> The message of Jesus, as I understand it, is contained in His Sermon on the Mount. The Spirit of the Sermon on the Mount competes almost on equal terms with the *Bhagavadgita* for the domination of my heart. It is that Sermon which has endeared Jesus to me.[11]

> Though I cannot claim to be a Christian in the sectarian sense, the example of Jesus' suffering is a factor in the composition of my underlying faith in non-violence, which rules all my actions, worldly and temporal. Jesus lived and died in vain, if he did not teach us to regulate the whole of life by the eternal Law of Love.[12]

> I may say that I have never been interested in a historical Jesus. I should not care if it was proved by someone that the man called Jesus never lived, and that what was narrated in the Gospels was a figment of the writer's imagination. For the Sermon on the Mount would still be true to me.[13]

The important thing for Gandhi is not the historical Jesus, and still less the interpretation of his person such as Christian faith conceives it. For

Gandhi, the crucial thing is that Jesus is born in us by the imitation of his cross as the gospel inculcates that cross. Thus, Gandhi addresses Christians:

> God did not bear the Cross only nineteen hundred years ago, but He bears it today, and He dies and is resurrected from day to day. It would be poor comfort to the world, if it had to depend upon a historical God who died two thousand years ago. Do not then preach the God of history but show Him as He lives today through you.[14]

Thomas's observation, then, is well-taken:

> Against this background any idea of a unique place for the Person or work of Jesus Christ in the moral and spiritual progress of mankind is ruled out. Gandhi is prepared to consider Jesus Christ as one of the many teachers and prophets of mankind, and even as one of the many names and incarnations of God, but without giving his divine nature, his atoning deed or his mediation between God and mankind any uniqueness.[15]

And to cite Gandhi himself:

> It was more than I could believe that Jesus was the only incarnate Son of God and that only he who believed in him would have ever-lasting life. If God could have sons, all of us were his sons. If Jesus was like God, or God himself, then all men were like God and could be God Himself.[16]

Gandhi's theology of religions goes hand in hand with his Hinduizing interpretation of Jesus Christ. Its basic principle is the equality of all religions. This equality flows from the unfathomable character of the one God, who, even when self-revealed in an indefinite number of varied forms, remains beyond all manifestation. It follows, then, that all religions will ceaselessly develop toward a more plenary realization of Truth. Thus, no religion can lay claim to a monopoly on divine revelation. On the contrary, all must practice mutual respect and tolerance.

He writes: "The soul of religion is one, but it is encased in a multitude of forms."[17] Indeed, Gandhi is convinced that "If a man reaches the heart of his own religion he has reached the heart of the others too. ... [They all] converge to the same point. ..."[18] He is convinced, then, that he may render equal homage to Jesus, Muhammad, Krishna, the Buddha, and others. For that matter, all religions are imperfect, as all bear the mark of human frailty and have need of moral correction and regeneration; but all are likewise in the process of growing, in quest of the fullness of the Truth that they must pursue together.

At this point we may be permitted to draw attention, following Thomas, to the "reinterpretation of Christianity" proposed by Gandhi. Having posited the essence of Christianity in the Sermon on the Mount, understood as the principle of nonviolence of which Jesus is the symbol, Gandhi is led to reject what he calls "orthodox Christianity" and to interpret Christianity in function of his own perception. For Gandhi, "not christology but ethics as the means to Truth constitute fundamental Christianity."[19] All else is superadded. It follows that "God and Christianity can be found also in institutions that do not call themselves Christian."[20]

At the end of his study, Thomas refers to the way in which certain Christians, more or less familiar with Gandhi, have reacted to his interpretation of Jesus and Christianity. The opinion, at once sympathetic and critical, of E. Stanley Jones, the evangelist and theologian who had known Gandhi personally, is particularly enlightening. In the book that he devotes to him, Jones writes that Gandhi "was a Hindu by allegiance and a Christian by affinity," and adds: "The Mahatma was a natural Christian rather than an orthodox one."[21] He explains his precise meaning:

> The Mahatma was influenced and moulded by Christian principles, particularly the Sermon on the Mount. . . .
> In the practice of those principles he discovered and lived by the person of Christ, however dimly and unconsciously. . . . But he never seemed to get to Christ as a Person.[22]

And to Gandhi himself Jones writes: "You have grasped the principles but you have missed the Person. . . . May I suggest that you penetrate through the principles to the Person and then come back and tell us what you have found."[23]

That is, in concentrating on the ethics of the Sermon on the Mount, the very essence of Christianity, Gandhi had missed the Christian sense of the person of Jesus as God's decisive revelation and redemptive deed, which is at the center of Christianity. Thomas's evaluation is in substantial agreement with that of E. Stanley Jones. He writes, in a more explicit way:

> The crucial issue in the theological debate between Christians and Gandhi is whether the historical Person of Jesus Christ is an essential part of the Christian kerygma, or whether his significance for the life of mankind was exhausted by being accepted and assimilated as the supreme symbol of the principle of redemptive love. . . . There is an either/or decision which is to be taken between the orthodox and Gandhian approaches to catholicity, one which bases itself ultimately on the principles of the Sermon on the Mount, and the other which bases itself on the Person of Christ as the divine deed of reconciliation between God and man and among men, to whichever living religions and secular faiths they belong. . . . This does not mean that Christianity should set Christian principles and the Person of Christ in oppo-

sition to one another, but rather seek to move through the principles to the Person.[24]

Keshub Chunder Sen's Christ of Bhakti

The Christ of Keshub Chunder Sen (1838–1884) must be regarded as being mainly under the sign of *bhakti*, personal devotion. Of all of the religious reformers of Neo-Hinduism, none has placed such fervent, emotional accents on an understanding of the person of Jesus as has Keshub. Enthusiastically he reminds his readers that Jesus is an Asian, a fact calculated to recommend him to the affection of his Indian compatriots and to enable them to understand him better than the West, which has dressed him up in European clothing:

> Was not Jesus Christ an Asiatic? Yes, and his disciples were Asiatics. ... In fact, Christianity was founded and developed by Asiatics and in Asia. When I recollect on this, my love for Jesus becomes hundredfold intensified: I feel him nearer to my heart, and deeper in my national sympathies.[25]

Jesus is no stranger to the Indian people, then. It is most regrettable, indeed contradictory, Keshub laments, that Indian Christians have largely adopted a foreign, Western culture.[26]

Keshub waxes lyrical in his expressions of devotion to Jesus. Here are a few examples: "My Christ, my sweet Christ, the brightest Jewel of my heart, the Necklace of my soul! For twenty years I have cherished him in my miserable heart! ..."[27] "None but Jesus ever deserved this bright, this precious diadem, India; and Jesus shall have it."[28]

We need not imagine, however, that the paeans pronounced by Keshub Chunder Sen in the framework of Brahmo Samaj and the Church of the New Dispensation, which he founded,[29] contain only sentiments wafting aloft and devoid of any theological underpinnings. We have already referred to the first of a long series of addresses entitled "Jesus Christ: Europe and Asia" (1866). The two most important, from the point of view that interests us here, are entitled, "India Asks: Who Is Jesus Christ?" (1879) and "That Marvellous Mystery: The Trinity" (1882). There Keshub develops what we might call a trinitarian christology, which, while independent of historical Christian tradition and often ambiguous, is well worthy of our attention. Indeed, it surprises us at times with the pertinence of its discourse to theological discussion on the mystery of Jesus Christ and its relation to other religions.

Keshub summed up his christology as a "doctrine of the divine humanity." He knows that "it is not Christ's humanity that is a stumbling block in your [the Indians'] way, but his so-called divinity."[30] It is this that he seeks to clarify with a response to the question of his title: "Who Is

Jesus Christ?" First he declares: "Christ struck the key-note of his doctrine when he announced his divinity before an astonished and amazed world in these words: 'I and my Father are one.' "[31] He then explains that Christ is "as a transparent crystal reservoir in which are the waters of divine life. . . . The 'medium' is transparent, and we clearly see through Christ the God of truth and holiness dwelling in him."[32] This transparency of Jesus to God is manifested in Jesus' total self-abandonment to God and perfect asceticism. Thus his life was "rooted in the Divinity," says Keshub, and he could rightly assert his oneness with God.

Keshub attempts to understand and explain the preexistence of Jesus as Son. Jesus preexists in God as a divine idea that was later incarnated in Jesus to teach us filiation:

> How then, and in what shape, did he exist in heaven? As an Idea, as a plan of life, as a predetermined dispensation yet to be realized, as purity of character, not concrete but abstract, as light not yet manifested . . . In fact Christ was nothing but a manifestation on earth, in human form, of certain ideas and sentiments which lay before in the Godhead. . . . Thus it is that Christ existed in God before he was created. There is an uncreated Christ as also the created Christ, the idea of the son and the incarnate son drawing all his vitality and inspiration from the Father. This is the true doctrine of incarnation. Take away from Christ all that is divine, all that is God's, no Christ remains.[33]

This text is an important one. It shows both Keshub's effort to understand the mystery of Christ in terms of the culture and religious tradition of Hinduism and the ambiguity of that effort. Below we shall see the consequences for the mystery of the Trinity. For now, let us observe that, in the same address, Keshub explicitly intends to establish a point of contact between the mystery of Christ and that of the divine filiation of humanity, on the one hand, and on the other, the religious experience of Hinduism— the Vedantine theory of a mystical identification with the divine (which he designates, surely erroneously, as pantheism): The mystery of Christ shows that what is at stake is an active union of will with, and communion with, God. However, it is through Hindu tradition that India will discover Christ. Keshub writes:

> Christ's pantheism is a pantheism of a loftier and more perfect type. It is the conscious union of the human with the Divine Spirit in truth, love and joy. The Hindu sage . . . seeks unconscious absorption in his God. . . . But Christ's communion is active and righteous. . . . Christ's pantheism is the active self-surrender of the will. It is the union of the obedient, humble and loving son with the Father. In Christ you see true pantheism. And as the basis of early Hinduism is pantheism,

you, my countrymen, cannot help accepting Christ in the spirit of your natural Scriptures.[34]

The term "pantheism" is doubly misleading in this context. *Advaita* — even in its Vedantine form, where many distinctions are to be made — does not in itself mean pantheism. Still less may one qualify the Christian mystery as pantheism. Despite these imperfections of language, however, one sees what Keshub means to suggest: The Christian mystery of communion transcends the Hindu mystique of identification, while the latter nevertheless moves toward the former.

The address entitled "That Marvellous Mystery: The Trinity" makes the connection between christology and the mystery of God. It represents Keshub's ultimate theological position on these points. Keshub sees Christ, as "divine humanity," emerge from God the Trinity at the end of the creation process. He writes:

> The Logos was the beginning of creation and its perfection too was the Logos — the culmination of humanity in the Divine Son. We have arrived at the last link in the series of created organism. The last expression of Divinity is Divine Humanity. Having exhibited itself in endless varieties of progressive existence the primary creative force at last took the form of the Son in Christ Jesus.[35]

The process of creation does not terminate, however, with the humanity of Christ, in which the divinity dwells. A further stage of the process is the extension of the filiation of Christ to all human beings: "The problem of creation was not how to produce one Christ, but how to make every man Christ. Christ . . . was 'the way.'" This is the deed of the Holy Spirit — hence what Keshub calls "the complete triangular figure of the Trinity," which includes the whole economy of creation and salvation:

> The apex is the very God . . . the Supreme Brahma of the Vedas. Alone, in his own eternal glory He dwells. From him comes down the Son, in a direct line, an emanation from Divinity. Thus God descends and touches one end of the base of humanity; then running all along the base permeates the world and there by the power of the Holy Ghost drags up degenerated humanity to Himself. Divinity coming down to Humanity is the Son; Divinity carrying up humanity to heaven is the Holy Ghost.[36]

It is easy to establish a parallel between the christological and trinitarian positions of Keshub and the classic heresies rejected by the church in the age of the first councils. Keshub has not escaped the imputation, among other things, of Arianism and "unitarianism" or modalism. Moreover, it is scarcely possible to overlook the relevance for today's theological debate of certain utterances of this Hindu theologian of Christianity, such as, for example, his express concern—reminiscent of Teilhard de Chardin—to situate the doctrine of the divine humanity in the context of the process of creative evolution. Equally striking is his preoccupation with providing the mystery of Jesus Christ with an access to the religious tradition of Hinduism.

This leads us to a further clarification of how Keshub conceives the relationship between the Christian mystery and other religions, Hinduism in particular. For Keshub, not only can Hinduism serve as a medium through which to present an "Eastern Christ" to India; Hinduism actually conceals within itself values and truths that, in Jesus Christ, find their fulfillment and perfection: "In accepting him . . . you accept the spirit of a devout *yogi* and loving *bhakta*, the fulfilment of your national prophets and scriptures. . . ."[37] And again: "I repudiate the little Christ of popular theology, and stand for a greater Christ, a fuller Christ, a more eternal Christ."[38]

Despite certain assertions of his earlier years which seem to suggest the equal truth of all religions, Keshub's profound, ultimate conviction, according to discerning interpreters,[39] clearly seems to be that Jesus Christ represents the "standard" by which all other religions are to be evaluated. He has not envisaged, like certain other representatives of Neo-Hinduism—S. Radhakrishnan, for example—the emergence of a "universal religion" based on the equality of all established religious traditions, in which the very idea of a decisive intervention of God in history loses its meaning and dissolves into thin air. Rather he saw the church of the "New Dispensation" as seeking "the Christocentric harmony of religions in general and of Hinduism and Christianity in particular." Parekh concludes:

> Keshub's chief service, not only to Hinduism but to the world, lies in the fact that he in his life and experience affiliated the mystic consciousness of the Hindu race to the Christ ideal.[40]

The Christ of Neo-Vedantine Philosophy: Sarvepalli Radhakrishnan

The clearest example of this model of Hindu interpretation of Jesus Christ is that of Dr. Sarvepalli Radhakrishnan (1888–1975). A philosopher by profession, Radhakrishnan strove to construct a synthesis of Western philosophy with Eastern thought, especially as found in the Vedanta, which he interpreted in a modernizing fashion not entirely free of the influence of various currents of Western thought. Once he had become president of the independent Indian republic (1962–1967), his ideas exerted a redoubled influence on the Indian intelligentsia.

Radhakrishnan is the symbol of a philosophical approach to the mystery of Christ. That doctrine is rethought in function not only of a Neo-Vedantine interpretation of Hindu *advaita*, but also of an evolutionistic humanism having connections with Western idealism. The teaching of the *avatara*, or divine manifestations, then becomes a symbolic expression of humanity's faith in the power of the spirit that penetrates both itself and the entire cosmos. Radhakrishnan rejects the popular notion of personal, individual "incarnations" (*avatara*), replacing it with that of an evolutive process through which humanity gradually realizes its potentialities: God is not born as a human being once in time; rather, humanity gradually gives birth to God in its midst by a process of self-realization. Radhakrishnan writes:

> [The *avatara*] are the moulds into which the seeking soul tries to cast itself, that it might grow towards God. What has been achieved by one man, a Christ or a Buddha, may be repeated in the lives of other men.[41]

Elsewhere Radhakrishnan writes, in rather polemic fashion, apropos of Christians' historical Jesus: "A suffering God — a deity that wears a crown of thorns — will never be able to satisfy the religious soul."[42]

Let us review, in more systematic fashion, the principal elements of Radhakrishnan's Neo-Vedantine interpretation of Christ and the relationship between Christianity and other religions, especially Hinduism. The work that bears on our subject more than any other is entitled *Eastern Religions and Western Thought*.[43]

The important thing to remember is that the Neo-Vedantine interpretation of Christ presented by Radhakrishnan rests in the matrix of a cosmic evolutionism, according to which "the germ of divinity is in each of us." "Salvation" consists in delivering oneself from all ties to the unreal values that dominate us, by contemplation of the mystery of the divinity present within us.

In this framework, Jesus is best understood as "a mystic who believes in the inner light, . . . ignores ritual and is indifferent to legalistic piety."[44] As for the "secret of the cross," whose realistic, morbid Christian view is rejected by this author, here one must see "the abandonment of the ego, identification with a fuller life and consciousness. The soul is raised to a sense of its universality."[45] Thus Christ becomes one symbol among others of evolution toward the spirit for which humanity is destined. The "resurrection," the "Reign of God," the "eternal life" that, in the Christian schema, are regarded as the human being's destiny, must be reinterpreted in terms of Hindu faith before they can deliver their true spiritual reality. All human beings are destined for a passage "from the darkness of selfish individualism to the light of universal spirit, . . . from slavery to the world to the liberty of the eternal."[46]

The life of Jesus has a symbolic value: It is not to be interpreted as a simple historical event. What is important is not the historical person of Jesus but the "Christhood" symbolized by that person:

Christ is born in the depths of spirit: we say that he passes through life, dies on the Cross and rises again. Those are not so much historical events which occurred once upon a time as universal processes of spiritual life, which are being continually accomplished in the souls of men. . . . Christhood [is] an attainment of the soul, a state of inward glorious illumination in which the divine wisdom has become the heritage of the soul.[47]

On the basis of this idealistic, dehistoricizing view of the mystery of Christ, drawn from advaitine Vedantism, Radhakrishnan interprets both the history and development of primitive Christianity and the relationship between Christianity and Hinduism. His interpretation of the Jesus of the New Testament is shot through with gnostic and Neoplatonic views that display a kinship with the teaching of the Upanishads and primitive Buddhism: "The insistence on the neo-platonic idea of the *Logos* is so great as to reduce the human life of Jesus to a mere illusive appearance." Paul especially "warns us against over-estimating the historical instead of looking upon it as the symbol of metaphysical truth. . . ."[48] The struggle between a dogmatic and a spiritualistic interpretation extends all through the post-biblical tradition, Radhakrishnan insists. A historicizing dogmatism, he thinks, must be transcended if Christianity hopes to "regain universality."

Perhaps Christianity, which arose out of an Eastern background and early in its career got wedded to Graeco-Roman culture, may find her rebirth today in the heritage of India.[49]

This last citation indicates the direction in which Radhakrishnan will now turn in order to give an account of the relationship among the various religions, especially between Christianity and Hinduism. He preaches a "universal religion, of which the historical religious faiths are but so many branches." But let us see what he means by this. For Radhakrishnan, all historical religions are but different forms of the true religion of the spirit; they do, however, represent different stages of realization. True, they are essentially one; still, the *Vedanta* is the pinnacle, for the *Vedanta* is not "*a* religion, but religion itself, in its most universal and deepest significance."[50] Why? Because it discovers the "formless" Divine in the various forms of religion. As for Christianity, it must evolve in the direction of a transhistorical mystique. This mystique "is indifferent to all questions of history. . . . A temporal and finite symbolism cannot be regarded as unique, definitive, and absolute."[51] "The different creeds are the historical formulations of the formless truth."[52]

Expressing his definitive views on the subject concerning us in a passage entitled, "Fragments of a Confession," Radhakrishnan reaffirms the universality of the experience of God as expressed in different ways by the various religious traditions. It is on the basis of this "religion of the spirit" that communion among the various religions becomes possible:

> The world is seeking not so much a fusion of religions as a fellowship of religions, based on the realization of the fundamental character of man's religious experience. ... The different religious traditions clothe the one Reality in various images and their visions could embrace and fertilise each other so as to give mankind a many-sided perfection. ... [The religious traditions] all ... represent different aspects of the inward spiritual life, projections on the intellectual plane of the ineffable experiences of the human spirit.[53]

The human being's evolution toward spiritual illumination represents the "unchanging substance" of the religions.

> [This unchanging substance is] the eternal religion behind all religions, this *sanatana dharma*, the timeless tradition; ... it is our duty to get back to this central core of religion. ... Our historical religions will have to transform themselves into the universal faith or they will fade away.[54]

As we see, at this point Radhakrishnan's thought is invested with a certain ambiguity that his critics, especially his Christian critics, have not failed to remark.[55] At times, he seems to regard all religions of equal value and calls for a spiritual communion among them with all his heart on the basis of the return of each to the eternal religion, that of the spirit. At other times, however, the *sanatana dharma*, capable of embracing all religions, seems identified with Neo-Hinduism in its Vedantine form. In particular, it embraces Christianity, which it summons to a self-purification from its historicist, dogmatic tendency.

In either case, however, Radhakrishnan rejects, as some of his critics observe,[56] that which constitutes the essence of Christianity and the basis of its universality: the Jesus Christ event understood as God's decisive intervention in human history and universal redemptive act. Christian universalism is based on the unicity of Jesus Christ. By contrast, Vedantine universalism is founded on a spiritual experience, which is actually an individual matter. In the last analysis, the equality of all religions, as well as the "unique" value of any one of them, is likewise a matter of faith. Surely one must see that Christianity and *Vedanta* differ at their very foundations: the nature of God and the human being, spiritual fulfillment, and the method of arriving at the latter.

Thomas's final verdict coincides substantially with the foregoing appraisal. While giving Radhakrishnan all due credit for seeking to infuse a "new humanism" into the classic structure of *advaita*, he doubts that Radhakrishnan "has succeeded in the task of giving ultimate reality to the

personal God who is 'the Absolute humanized,' and ultimate spiritual significance to 'the human world and its values.' "[57] Hence his temptation to
separate Christianity from its original essential foundation—the domain of
the personal and historical. In effecting this divorce, Radhakrishnan, who
rejects the Christian position that Christianity is the fulfillment of the truths
and values contained in Hinduism, in fact reverses this position, making
the mystique of *advaita* the crown precisely of Christianity. "It is essential
that both Hindus and Christians recognize the similarity of the foundational
dogmas and the a priori nature of the choice between them."[58] The choice
is a matter of faith.

The Christ Avatara *of Swami Akhilananda*

It would seem justifiable to characterize the model of Jesus Christ proposed by Swami Akhilananda (1894–1962) as theological. This model
employs several theological concepts that are basic to Hinduism, despite
the fact that it is addressed primarily to Westerners. It was in the United
States, where he lived for many years spreading the message of Sri Rama-
krishna, that Swami Akhilananda published his book entitled *The Hindu
View of Christ*.[59] His use of theological categories has the purpose of showing
that Christ has already been given an authentic interpretation in the framework of Hindu religious tradition. The principal concepts employed by this
author are those of Christ-*yogi* and Christ-*avatara*. The latter appears to be
more central, although in the Swami's interpretation and in actual fact both
concepts are connected and interdependent.

Christ appears first and principally as an *avatara*. Obviously we are
speaking of but one divine "descent" among others. Still, this particular
descent is especially opportune and meaningful, since it took place "at the
most propitious moment . . . for showing the world of that time the way of
religion."[60]

Let us observe at once, however, that in the mind of Akhilananda, as
with numerous modern Hindu theologians, the notion of *avatara* is accom-
modated simultaneously to the classic *bhakti* worship and to the Neo-Hin-
duist philosophy of *advaita*. This, as we shall presently see, explains
Akhilananda's conjoint application of the concepts of *avatara* and *yogi* to
Christ.

For Akhilananda, an *avatara* is an utterly illuminated soul, one enjoying
full awareness of its divine identity. Again, let us observe that there is an
important difference between a saint and an *avatara*. The saint, through
long intellectual and spiritual discipline that puts to flight all mental "super-
impositions" (*adhyasa*), must attain to the realization of supreme identity
with the *Brahman*. By contrast, the *avatara* is free of all such shackles from
the very outset and lives in this divine consciousness permanently. Such
was Christ, whose entire life was spent on the supreme level of spiritual
experience that the Upanishads express in two great aphorisms (*maha-*

vakya): *Aham brahmasmi* ("I am the Brahman" — *Brhadaranyaka Upanishad* 1.4.10) and *Tattvamasi* ("You are That [the Brahman]" — *Chandogya Upanishad* 6.8.7). Jesus expresses this in analogous terms in the gospel according to Saint John: "I and the Father are one" (see John 10:30). At this level, awareness of the self disappears. "Even though, at times," Akhilananda writes, "the term 'I' is used in a very exalted sense, beneath this 'I' is to be found an awareness of the 'Thou'—that is, the Father, or the Absolute."[61]

Let us enter upon a somewhat broader analysis of Akhilananda's christology. Akhilananda's basic concern is with an interpretation of the person and work of Christ in the framework of the religious categories of Hinduism. His purpose is to show not only that Christ can be at home in India, but more than this, that he has already in fact been appropriated by Hinduism. Christ must be regarded as "Eastern," Akhilananda insists. Christ's teaching is Eastern, as is his life-style. Indeed, he exemplifies in his person the Hindu ideal of the perfection to be attained, the Hindu ideal of self-actualization.

It is here that Akhilananda applies the double concept of *yogi* and *avatara*. Jesus' words are interpreted in a yogic way. According to Akhilananda, the genuine *yogi* is the one who can declare in truth: "I am the Self; I am the Brahman." Such is Jesus, who exemplifies in his person the three classic ways that lead to God: *jnana yoga*, or the way of knowledge; *bhakti yoga*, or the way of loving devotion; and *karma yoga*, or the way of responsible action. The most exalted way, however, is the way of knowledge. Only a person who has undergone the experience of the oneness in which all duality vanishes can say in all truth, as Jesus does, "I and the Father are one." Has Jesus learned the *yoga* technique, then? No, the Swami tells us; as an *avatara*, he need not submit to the schooling of any master.[62]

The concept of the *avatara*, then, is more pregnant for an understanding of the person of Jesus than is that of the *yogi*. Jesus is a divine manifestation, an "incarnation of the divine love in human form."[63] Not that Jesus is the only incarnation; there are others. No "uniqueness," then, no "finality" or ultimacy whatsoever, can be claimed for him. Akhilananda sets forth the Hindu concept of the *avatara*:

> According to the Indian standpoint, an incarnation is a person who is thoroughly established in the All-Loving Being, who has no trace of cosmic ignorance, who is completely illumined (namely, who has direct knowledge of God and consequent understanding of the world process), and who understands the meaning and value of historical events.[64]

According to the traditional understanding of Hindu theism—to put it more clearly than the Swami does—the *avatara* is a divine "descent" (from the root *tr*, "to come," with the prefix *ava*, "downward") to the world, a manifestation of the supreme *Brahman* in human form. The purpose of this descent is to establish or reestablish *dharma* (right, law, religion) in the world and to destroy *adharma* there. The basic text for the concept of the *avatara* in Hindu theism is to be found in the *Bhagavad-Gita* (4.5–10, especially 6–8), where Krishna declares to Arjuna:

> Unborn though I am, though my Self is unchangeable,
> though I am Lord of Beings—
> in joining myself to the [material] nature (*prakrti*)
>   that is mine,
> I come to be [in time] by my own creative energy
>   (*sambhavamy atmamayaya*) [v. 6].
> For, each time that law and the right (*dharma*) are
>   in abeyance,
> and impiety (*adharma*) rears its head,
> I engender myself [on earth] (*atmanam srjamy aham*) [v. 7].
> For the protection of the good and the destruction
>   of malefactors,
> and to reestablish right (*dharma*),
> I come to be (*sambhavamy*), from age to age [v. 8].

The Hindu theologians of the classic *Vedanta*, such as Shankara and Ramanuja, and after them, Chaitanya and Jiva Goswami, have interpreted the concept of the *avatara* and its principal source, just cited, in different ways. We cannot enter into this detailed discussion. Suffice it to say that, while Krishna surely represents the Absolute (conceived as a personal God along classic *bhakti* lines), his earthly manifestation in human form is never conceived as a personal, genuine insertion into human history. Krishna is not sprung from our race, nor does he suffer for our salvation. He is a human being in appearance only, not in reality. His human manifestation is a disguise. It is as if he wished to seem to be what his transcendence prevents him from condescending to become in reality. In Christian terminology, the doctrine of the *avatara* is both docetist and gnostic. The *avatara* lacks the realism and historicity implied in the Christian concept of incarnation.

J.A. Cuttat is correct, then:

By no means do Hindus believe that their God, in showing himself to Arjuna with the human traits of his companion at arms Krishna, has really assumed our frail nature, including our body, and has actually suffered as a human being properly "incarnate." For the Hindu, Vishnu has only donned the *appearance* of a human being. He has never ceased, in his transcendence of the latter, to remain pure God, unaffected by our vicissitudes.[65]

As P. Johanns, responding to Sarvepalli Radhakrishnan's challenge as we have reported it above, wrote somewhat polemically:

Krishna is the God who has never borne on his shoulders the guilt of the world and the consequences of its sins—the God that could not be fully in earnest about our salvation, since it was all a play which cost him nothing.[66]

Akhilananda, for his part, is concerned to show that the essential characteristics of the *avatara* are verified in Jesus. At first, Jesus' historicity seems to pose no problem for Akhilananda. He accepts the principal events of the life of Christ, attributing a special importance to his cross and resurrection. But he interprets the latter as *"symbolical*, standing for certain universal principles."[67] Thus the cross is a symbol of divine love and forgiveness. It need not be seen as a unique event in the history of humanity. In the last analysis, what Jesus' cross and resurrection signify is that only renunciation can lead to unchangeable eternal life. The resurrection shows that the awakening to God can raise the human being to the level of spirit. It shows the superiority of spirit to flesh.

None of this is without interest. However, we must admit that it practically evacuates the theological density of both the Jesus Christ event in history and his "mysteries." There is no longer any question of the Christian view of an actual, decisive divine intervention in history. We are dealing with a symbol—an eminent one, it is true—of the supreme experience of the consciousness or illumination in which knowledge of God can issue. Is a gnosticizing interpretation the inevitable price to be paid for any attempt to transpose the christologic mystery into a Hindu key? The question must be asked, but this is not the place to attempt to answer it.

In the meantime, we may subscribe in substance to S. J. Samartha's verdict on the Christ of Akhilananda. Samartha observes first that in this portrait, Jesus loses his originality—loses what makes him different. A "pale, anemic" Christ emerges. His oneness with the Father is a union of will and intention; it goes no deeper than that. As for the two theological concepts Akhilananda employs, neither of them, as he conceives them, can give an adequate account of the mystery of Christ. The concept of the *avatara* mocks the historical and the ontological. That of the *yogi* reduces Jesus to a searcher for salvation and liberation (*moksa*) through an interior discipline—a pilgrim in quest of the supreme experience of nonduality (*samadhi*). When all is said and done, both concepts are too limited to be predicated of the person and work of Jesus Christ. Is the crucial question not the meaning of the person of Christ in his relation to God and human beings?

The Yogi *Christ of Manilal C. Parekh*

We have already encountered the concept of the *yogi* as applied to the person of Jesus Christ in our examination of the *avatara* Christ of Swami Akhilananda. Manilal C. Parekh (1885–1967), however, especially in his last book, *A Hindu's Portrait of Jesus*,[68] develops the theme rather more broadly. Indeed, we may consider ourselves authorized to regard this author as a protagonist of the Hindu model of Jesus as an ascetic or *yogi*.

This, of course, is again a Hindu model. True, Parekh accepted baptism in the Anglican communion, out of what he regarded as considerations of honesty for anyone who would profess to be a disciple of Jesus—a line of reasoning that we cannot take time to explore further here. The fact remains, however, that he understood his discipleship as that of a Hindu. He was convinced that the Hindu mentality led to the discovery of the authentic Jesus better than the established churches could. Parekh writes:

> It is very significant that the discovery of the true Jesus as distinguished from that of the Western Churches and Missions, is largely due to the Hindu mind. The Hindus as a race have been gifted with the spiritual faculty which separates the things of the spirit from those of the flesh. With the help of this faculty they have succeeded in separating the kernel of Christianity from the husks thereof.[69]

And, even more clearly, in an address entitled "Jesus Christ and Christianity": "The more I am a Hindu, the more I am a disciple of Christ, and the more I am a disciple of Christ, the more I am a Hindu."[70] Again we recall the revealing title of the book mentioned above. We are indeed dealing with a "Hindu portrait of Jesus," and Parekh's portrait is that of a *yogi*.

Here let us recall, very briefly, the meaning of *yoga*. We may begin with the term itself. *Yoga* comes from the root *yuj*, to harness, to yoke, but also to join, to unite. The adept at *yoga*—that is, the *yogi*—as J. Filliozat tells us, is one who has brought the senses and thinking "under the yoke," and thus is fully in tune with reality.

As Patanjali himself describes it in the *Yoga-sutras*, *yoga* consists in "preventing thought (*citta*) from taking various forms (*vrtti*)." The goal pursued by *yoga* is the same as that to which the way of knowledge (*jnana-marga*) leads: concentration of thought, and through this the self-realization that transcends the subject-object duality. The true *yogi* is one who is established in his or her real Self. The means employed in *yoga*, however, are different: they are more like spiritual exercises and disciplines.

It is scarcely necessary to enter upon a detailed examination of the eight parts or "members" of which *yoga* is composed according to Patanjali's *Yoga-sutras*. It will be more useful to observe that *yoga* comports three distinct levels, among which classical *yoga* (unlike *hatha yoga*, which insists almost exclusively on psychophysiological techniques, the first level) gives precedence to the two higher levels: *dhyana*, meditation or fixation of thought, and *samadhi*, ecstasy or pure consciousness. The three levels of *yoga* can be characterized as constituting, respectively: the outer envelope, composed of manifold psychophysiological exercises; the backbone, consisting of mental exercises, meditation, and concentration; and finally the soul, that is, instasy or attainment of pure consciousness, and through this, the spiritual experience: the vision of light, the experience of God.

In order for *yoga* to be authentic, the highest level, which is its deliberately sought end, must inspire, inform, as tendency, the entire undertaking. The goal of *yoga* is the spiritual experience of God. Is this what Manilal C. Parekh means by *yoga* when he applies it to Jesus?

We must confess that the ascetical view of Jesus as a *yogi* in Neo-Hinduism is lacking in depth and disappoints with its superficiality. Parekh does distinguish two kinds of souls who betake themselves to the pathway of *yoga*: those who undergo a lengthy process of self-realization through the practice of *yoga* and those who are naturally (at times even from the beginning) in full possession of their yogic power. Jesus, according to Parekh, belongs to this second category: He is an "extraordinary *yogi*," having extraordinary powers (*siddhi*) at his disposal, as his miracles evince, especially his transfiguration and his resurrection. However, Jesus never makes use of his powers to his own benefit and advantage. He uses them only in favor of others. And indeed, do not Patanjali's *Yoga-sutras* (III, 37) warn us that the *yogi* must never seek or pursue these extraordinary "powers" for himself, at the risk of compromising his spiritual progress? The powers are not the goal of *yoga*; they turn out to be rather peripheral, incidental phenomena. Once sought for themselves, they become an obstacle to self-realization.

This observation is correct and important. It also bears witness to our author's sympathy for the *yogi* Jesus. But the Neo-Hindu approach it represents is nonetheless disappointing. It misses the essential. On the one hand, while Parekh insists that Jesus does not use his yogic powers to his own advantage, these extraordinary powers mean too much to Parekh. The authentic meaning of Jesus' miracles is not brought out. Rather it is falsified. Secondly, in making Jesus a *yogi* who achieves his complete self-realization naturally from the outset, Parekh denies him any genuinely human history, any progress, any development in self-awareness and self-realization. Paradoxically, the an-historical interpretation of Jesus as *yogi* is akin to certain Christian interpretations current just a few decades ago but abandoned today precisely on account of their an-historicism. Christology today insists on Jesus' genuine humanity and human history.

It will scarcely be necessary to rehearse the details of these christological counterfeits. We need only remind ourselves how a Jesus wearing a costume of superhuman perfections had become such an unapproachable ideal for us, precisely in proportion as these qualities were extraordinary. In ascribing to him altogether gratuitously a perfect, full, and fulfilled human knowledge—the ultimate beatific vision of God—we denied, at times unconsciously, that he might have known the least struggle or crisis, that he could have been tempted, that he could and did choose the particular manner of achieving his destiny and responding to his mission. Only a shadow remained of Jesus as a historical human being.

We must disavow all such forgeries and return to the real Jesus, a human being genuinely engaged in a history he lived as his own, just as the gospel tradition testifies. We must restore to him his true human freedom, a freedom woven of choices, commitments, and doubts. We must return to him his true human consciousness, a consciousness capable of progress and development. Only then will Jesus be able to appear to human beings, themselves engaged in the world and history, as an inspiring, attractive model. Only then shall we be able to see in him—to borrow Parekh's expression, but using it in a new sense—an "extraordinary *yogi*."

If the Neo-Hindu concept of the *yogi* Jesus disappoints where the historicity of his humanity is concerned, it is no less faulty with respect to his divine identity. As we have already stated, an advaitine Neo-Hinduism, with its concept of self-realization by an experience of identification with the Divine, is found in various Hindu interpretations of Jesus Christ, including that of the *yogi* Jesus. It is marked by a basic incapacity to account for the original, unique interpersonal communion between Jesus and his Father.

It remains only to provide a rapid sketch of Parekh's way of conceiving the relationship between Christianity and Hinduism and the broader relationship among the various religious traditions.

For Parekh, to be a Christian consists in sharing with Jesus the awareness of "a new relationship between God and man, which is expressed by the term 'the Fatherhood of God.' " He writes:

> Jesus has opened the door to such consciousness and communion under divine favour and guidance and it should be the proudest privilege of any man, of whatever race and creed, to follow him in this Holy of Holiest. This is the Kingdom of God and none other. It belongs to all, if only they would come to it with a proper attitude. It is not the monopoly of so called Christians alone: rather whosoever have this consciousness are Christians.[71]

Christianity and Hinduism are not, then, two antagonistic, incompatible poles. On the contrary, writes Parekh: "To me, to be a Hindu was to be a true disciple of Christ, and to be a true disciple of Christ meant to be more a Hindu. . . ."[72] This conviction that he could be more Christian by holding aloof from established Christianity led Parekh to sever all ties with the church. Just as discipleship does not depend on membership in the church, so neither has the church any title to a monopoly on evangelization. To evangelize consists of spreading the knowledge of Christ. It consists of helping others to become his disciples, which does not imply adherence to an official Christian community. After all, to be a Christian "meant to put on the mind of Christ, to enter into Christ's religious consciousness."[73] Thus Parekh finally comes to conceive an interior Christianity, open to all and everywhere present—perhaps an anticipated version, in a way, despite differences, of the "unknown Christ of Hinduism," to which we shall return later. However this may be, for Parekh not only can one be Jesus' disciple wherever one may be, but no dislocation, no shift is required for it:

In order that discipleship might grow among Hindus and others in this land it is essential that the disciples should remain where they are, i.e. in their own respective communities.[74]

This Christianity, whose reduction to the consciousness of the Parenthood of God guarantees its universal presence, is assimilated by Parekh to what he finally calls the *Bhagavata Dharma*. He explains the latter as follows:

As I see it all religions who believe in God can be counted as Bhagavata Dharma. For if we hold that whoever believes in Bhagavan and worships him is a Bhagavata, we can surely say with conviction that all religions who believe in God are merely different forms of the one Bhagavata Dharma. In this way I include in it Christianity, Judaism, Islam, Zoroastrianism and all the religions which believe in God. It is in this sense that I use the term. . . .[75]

In the last analysis, then, the various religions are only different forms of a basic belief in God. This belief constitutes the essence of religion, which is expressed in different ways in Indian tradition, in Christianity, and elsewhere.

We may be permitted to conclude, with H. Staffner, that Parekh's Hindu portrait of Jesus Christ—and, we may add, his theology of religions—are rather disappointing. "Parekh lacked the enthusiasm of Keshub and fell far short of Brahmabandhab Upadhyaya in a thorough grasp of the Christian faith."[76] It is to the last named that we now turn our attention.

Christ in Advaita Mysticism: Brahmabandhab Upadhyaya

Bhawami Charan Banerji (1861–1907), as he was named at birth, was from his youngest years one of the most brilliant members of the Brahmo Samaj. In 1891 he passed from the Church of the New Dispensation founded by his friend Keshub Chunder Sen to the Anglican communion, where he received baptism; that same year he joined the Roman Catholic Church. Soon after, he donned the saffron robe of the Hindu *sannyasi* and became a "Catholic *sannyasi*." It was then that he adopted the monastic name under which he would be known henceforward: Brahmabandhab ("Friend of God") Upadhyaya.

Henceforward his energy would be devoted to the quest for a truly indigenous expression—today we should say "inculturated" expression—in an Indian religious context, of the Christian faith and message. In other words, he sought to harmonize Hinduism and Christianity, taking each in all its purity, and thereby help "lead India to the faith." To this end, he founded a periodical called *Sophia*, whose editor he was, and then another called *The Twentieth Century*. To his mind, the effort to which he devoted himself comported four elements: the integration of the Indian social structure into the Christian way of life; the foundation of an Indian Christian monastic order; the use of the categories of the *Vedanta* in Christian theology; and the acknowledgment of the Vedas as a preparation for the gospel in India analogous to the place of the Old Testament in the West.[77] There can be no doubt of the considerable influence of his pioneering work, even if, as so often happens, his ideas had to be taken up by others later in order to bear genuine, lasting fruit.

In justification of our use of the term *mystical* for the model of interpretation of Jesus Christ and the Christian mystery proposed by Upadhyaya, we might list the following characteristics. Upadhyaya's model is founded first of all on a deep personal experience of the person of Jesus the Son of God, who becomes at once his *guru* and his friend. To objections to the divinity of Jesus, he replies: "One may believe or not believe that Christ is the Son of God; but there is not the shadow of a doubt that Christ claimed to be the Son of God."[78] One might also examine his profession of monk, or "Catholic *sannyasi*," which, as we shall presently see, led him to understand and express Jesus Christ in terms of the Hindu mystical experience of *advaita* —without succumbing to the monistic Vedantine tendencies of the Hindu theologians. We might also stress the spiritual and theological quality of his writings, especially the hymns (in Sanskrit) he dedicated to the mystery of the Trinity as *saccidananda* (being-thought-bliss) and to the Son as *vac* (logos, Verbum, Word).[79]

However, we shall concentrate here on a sketch of Upadhyaya's christology, especially in relation to the Hindu religious and mystical tradition — and in so doing, attempt to clarify his conception of the uniqueness of the person and work of Jesus vis-à-vis other religions, especially Hinduism.

For Upadhyaya, only *sannyasi*, or monks steeped in the contemplative tradition of India, could ever succeed in presenting India with the mysteries of the Catholic faith in a convincing way. Hence his project of founding a group of contemplative, itinerant Hindu-Catholic monks. He wrote: "The ancient land of the Aryans is to be won over to the Catholic faith; and who can achieve the conquest but Hindu-Catholic *sannyasi*, inspired with the spirit of the ancient monks?"[80]

Their task will be to place Hindu philosophy at the service of the Christian message in such a way as to attire that teaching in an Indian garment. The *Vedanta* will then render to the Catholic faith in India the service that Greek philosophy rendered in Europe. That the *Vedanta* contains errors cannot be cited as an insuperable obstacle to this process of assimilation. Plato and Aristotle contained errors, as well, and first the Fathers of the Church, and then St. Thomas Aquinas, had to make judicious use of them.

Nor, for that matter, does Upadhyaya intend to prioritize any particular philosophical system in the accomplishment of this work of inculturation of the Christian message. Like the Greek Fathers themselves, and Origen in particular, he intends rather to be eclectic, choosing the concepts he finds best suited to his goal, knowing perfectly well that concepts perfectly adapted a priori to the task are nowhere to be found. Christianity transforms what it assimilates. Thus, these Hindu-Christian monks will be able to synthesize what the "metaphysical genius" of Indian tradition has produced and the "eternal truths" contained in Jesus Christ and taught by the church.

An important observation remains to be made upon what has just been stated. It would be false to think that Upadhyaya draws exclusively and relies blindly on the theological interpretation of *advaita* such as it had been developed by Shankara, the most prestigious representative of the *Vedanta*. On the contrary—to cite merely one example, though an important one—he denounces the Shankarian doctrine of *maya* as a characterization of the universe in relation to the *Brahman*, understood as illusion and nonbeing. *Maya* must be reinterpreted, in the sense of the contingency and ontological density of created being, which must necessarily serve as the foundation for the Christian mystery. In sum, the true source of an osmosis between Hinduism and Christianity will be found less in the theologico-philosophical systems of the *Vedanta*, which incline either toward monism or dualism, than in the original religious experience of *advaita* or non-dualism, which is pure theism. Thus the task consists in building up a Christian *advaita*. Upadhyaya means to be a Roman Catholic advaitine.

Thus the necessary preparation for a correct understanding of the Christian message in an Indian context is a correct knowledge of God. That knowledge must be of such a nature as to permit an interpersonal relationship between the Absolute and the contingent, the Infinite and the finite, God and created humanity. Upadhyaya finds such a concept of God in Vedic theism. In a study entitled "Vedic-Christian Theology," he writes:

> Whatever may be the theology of the Vedas they are, from cover to cover, surcharged with the idea of a Supreme Being, who knows all things, who is a personal God, who is father, friend, nay even brother to His worshippers, who rewards the virtuous, punishes the wicked, who controls the destinies of man. . . .[81]

Then he goes on to see in Vedic monotheism the equivalent of the Jewish monotheism of the Old Testament. He concludes that the Vedas, in an Indian context, serve as a parallel to the Old Testament and represent in the same context an initial divine revelation serving as evangelical preparation for the mystery of Jesus Christ. The conversion of India to Christ must therefore occur by way of a return to Vedic theism. This step will consist in "form[ing], as it were, a natural platform upon which the Hindu taking their stand may have a view of the glorious, supernatural edifice of the Catholic religion of Christ."[82] "The primitive [Hinduism] and the new [Christianity] are linked together as root and trunk, base and structure, as outline and filling."[83] Despite Upadhyaya's use of the antithetical "natural" and "supernatural," the parallel he establishes between the Vedas and the Old Testament raised, and answered in the affirmative, the question of a divine revelation in the sacred books of Hinduism — a question to which we shall have to return below.

In his "A Brief Outline of Christianity," in the periodical *Twentieth Century*, Upadhyaya begins with the divine destiny of the human being as created by God and elevated by grace, and moves from there to the fall and the need for salvation and restoration. At the heart of his thought, as constituting the essence and center of Christian faith, we find the mystery of the triune God, the incarnate Word, and the condescending "re-union" between God and humanity.[84]

Upadhyaya had already studied the mystery of the Trinity conceived in terms of *saccidananda* (being-thought-bliss), and we have cited the hymn that he dedicated to that Trinity. The concept was not without direct foundation in the advaitine and Vedantic tradition. Upadhyaya was aware, however, that if the analogy was valid, in transposing it to the mystery of the divine life revealed in Jesus Christ, it would be necessary to endow it with a new, deeper signification. "Being" (*sat*) would represent the Father as ultimate source of the divine life; "thought" (*cit*) would be the inner Word, or begotten Son; and "bliss" (*ananda*), the Spirit, or source of life.

In an essay entitled "The Incarnate Word," Upadhyaya further develops the mystery of the Trinity, especially the mystery of the eternal and incarnate Son:

> God begets in thought His infinite self-image and reposes on it with infinite delight while the begotten self acknowledges responsively His eternal thought-generation. . . . The Infinite, Eternal God who recognises His own Self reproduced in Thought is the Father; and the same God who is the Begotten Image of Divinity, who acknowledges the Father in Reason, is the Logos, the Son. . . . The eternal, intellectual act of Divine generation and the correspondence which binds the Father and his Logos-Image in the Spirit of Love completes the life of God and makes it self-sufficient. Revelation has given us a fore-glimpse of the inner life of God. . . . We Christians believe that the Logos, the Eternal image of the Father, became incarnate, that is united Himself to a human nature, created and so adapted as to be wedded to Divinity. . . .[85]

Upadhyaya now attempts to express the doctrine of the Incarnation and the two natures of Christ in terms familiar to Hinduism. It will scarcely be necessary to enter upon a detailed examination of the philosophical and rather technical terms he employs in his account of the integrity of Christ's human nature, which is "presided over by the person of the Logos himself and not by any created personhood (*aham*)."

> In the God-man, the five sheaths (*kosa*) [composing the human nature] are acted upon direct [sic] by the Logos-God and not through the medium of any individuality. The Incarnation was thus accomplished by uniting humanity with Divinity in the person of the Logos. This incarnate God in man we call Jesus Christ.[86]

Let us note, in this text, Upadhyaya's concern both for dogmatic precision and for a transposition into philosophical concepts borrowed from the *Vedanta*. It has been observed, and justly, that Upadhyaya's christology is not without traits resembling one of the patristic solutions to the christological problem: In taking its point of departure in the assumed humanity, it is akin to the so-called *Logos-Anthropos* christology.[87]

We may now give a brief account of the manner in which, from a point of departure in his personal experience and commitment, Upadhyaya conceives of the relationship between Hinduism and Christianity. We have already taken note of his deliberate profession of Hindu-Catholic monk and Roman Catholic advaitine. We have pointed out that his objective was to bring India to the Christian faith, which he thought only such a profession could accomplish. Upadhyaya resented the European theological monopoly, which he regarded as cultural domination. In order to be free of the same, one must build a Christian-Hindu theology from the ground up. The symbiosis between Hinduism and Christianity that he thought to be making in his own life seemed smooth enough. An important and oft-cited text sums up his thought on this subject. We here transcribe only the essentials:

> By birth we are Hindus and shall remain Hindu till death. But as *dvija* (twice-born) by virtue of our sacramental rebirth, we are Catholics, we are members of the indefinable communion embracing all ages and climes. . . . In short we are Hindus so far as our physical and mental constitution is concerned, but in regard to our immortal souls we are Catholics. We are Hindu Catholics.[88]

If being Hindu-Christian seemed to raise no problem in the mind of Upadhyaya, the reason is that Hinduism represented in his eyes a culture rather than a religious faith. Like any other culture, however radical a purification it might require, it was basically compatible with the Christian message. The essential thing about Hinduism was the observance of certain social customs. It did not involve the acceptance of a clearly defined creed. Thus belief in Christ could present no obstacle to his maintaining his ties with the Hindu community; in other words, he might remain a Hindu. In the text mentioned above, he writes: "The more strictly we practice our universal [Catholic] faith, the better we grow as Hindus."[89] He asks:

> Do we really believe in Hinduism? The question must be understood before it can be answered. Hinduism has no definite creed. . . . The test of being a Hindu cannot therefore lie in religious opinions.[90]

Rather, it is a question of a spirit, with which Upadhyaya says he is "fully imbued," and to which he means to remain faithful. Hindu-Christians are Hindus in their customs and habits, their observance of caste and social distinctions, their way of thinking. They are Christians by their faith in Jesus Christ.

Let us note in passing that Upadhyaya raises an important question here that we must return to later. Is it true that Hinduism is reducible to a culture without a religious faith of its own and that this is the reason, as Upadhyaya seems to think, that justifies one's being a Hindu-Christian? Would a like symbiosis be completely unthinkable if it were a matter of two religious faiths? The question is a real one. Upadhyaya seems to suggest it himself. After all, when he speaks of the Vedas—and, we might add, of the Hindu tradition generally, despite certain weaknesses, which he combats—as an "evangelical preparation" or even a divine revelation, he is no longer positing the justification for being a Hindu-Christian in terms of a synthesis between culture and faith. He is speaking of a symbiosis between two religious faiths. Indeed, the distinction between nature and the supernatural that Upadhyaya applies to the relation between Hinduism and Christianity is contradicted by certain deeper convictions of his. A like distinction would undercut any possibility of the action of divine grace within the Hindu tradition as such. Perhaps we must conclude that Upadhyaya is less than perfectly clear in his own mind on the relationship between Hinduism and Christianity. Notwithstanding, he is surely one of the most important pioneers of Indian Christianity.

CHRISTOLOGICAL CHALLENGE OF THE ENCOUNTER BETWEEN HINDUISM AND CHRISTIANITY

We have briefly presented six christological models of interpretation that seem to characterize Neo-Hinduism. We have cited the ethical, the devotional, the philosophical, the theological, the ascetic, and the mystical models. Obviously these designations have no more than an operational value. The various models overlap rather than being mutually exclusive. Thus, for example, the model that has been called theological was partially dependent on the Jesus-*yogi* concept, which has been found more explicitly in the so-called ascetic model. Analogously, the model proposed by Upadhyaya that we have called mystical is akin to Keshub Chunder Sen's devotional model, although it surpasses it in depth.

We must also insist that the six models we propose make no pretense whatever of exhausting the list of ways in which modern Hinduism has reacted to and interpreted the person of Jesus Christ. Acknowledgment of and response to its unbound Christ is characterized, in the Indian Renaissance, by as many nuances as it has authors. We have had to be selective here. Still, the six models that we have proposed seem sufficiently characteristic, and the authors chosen to illustrate them seem to be their most authentic representatives. It remains to show, briefly, the challenge or challenges posed to Christianity today by the historical encounter with modern Hinduism and its various ways of interpreting Jesus Christ.

In the six models expounded above, we have seen a Hindu theology of Christianity or, to be more precise, a number of Hindu christologies. What have they to say to a Christian theology of religions or, more precisely, to Christian christology in the framework of the Hindu-Christian dialogue and more generally in the framework of religious pluralism?

Our identification of the challenge or challenges will necessarily involve, on the one hand, our taking a position from the viewpoint of our own faith in order to identify the "stepping-stones" to the mystery of Jesus Christ contained in the Hindu models of his work and person. But this will also mean being scrupulously attentive to the questions that we shall be asked — questions to which we shall not likely have ready-made answers. Here we shall be making two rapid sketches at once. First we shall attempt to identify the principal challenge implied in each of the christological models expounded above. Then we shall ask ourselves in a more general way, what fundamental challenge seems to be posed by the various Hindu christologies to Christian christology and theology.

Mahatma Gandhi's ethical model of Jesus permits him to see, in the Jesus of the Sermon on the Mount, the perfect symbol of nonviolence. In this sense Jesus is a manifestation of the Truth that is God. Whether or not Jesus is personally God is a meaningless question here. Even his historicity is ultimately without importance: Were he not to have existed, the message attributed to him by the gospel would be no less real. Implicitly, then, but radically, we are dealing here with the problem of the Jesus of history and demythologization.

The devotional model of Jesus proposed by Keshub Chunder Sen culminates in Keshub's doctrine of the divine humanity. When all is said and done, Jesus' oneness with God comes down to a moral union between Jesus and the God he calls his Father. His preexistence is that of a "divine idea" that must become actualized in him. Surely Keshub's christology sins by default vis-à-vis the christological and trinitarian dogmas of the church, and he has been accused of Arianism, modalism, and unitarianism. Indeed, his concern to bring Jesus into the evolutionary process of humanity, of which Jesus would constitute the pinnacle, leads him to regard Christianity as the crown of Hinduism. Here, then, is the thesis (to which we shall return) of the fulfillment in Jesus of the religious traditions of humanity. But by this very fact, the question of the theological foundation of this thesis arises.

The philosophical model of Jesus, whose most authentic representative is S. Radhakrishnan, suffers from the ineptitudes that, from a Christian theological viewpoint, one can lay at the doorstep of both a Western idealistic philosophy and an evolutionistic Neo-Vedantism. The notion of *avatara* as applied to Jesus has been divested of the meaning it originally had in the classic Hindu *bhakti* movement (where it refers to a divine manifestation), and reduced to a symbolic expression of the evolutionary process of humanity toward its self-realization. The various religions constitute distinct, ultimately equivalent, manifestations of this process, all based on a universal religion. Here we have the problem of human history as a vehicle of divine interventions, and of a dialogue between God and humanity in the face of evolutionistic reductions of a gnostic tenor. Here we likewise have the question of the pluralism of religious traditions, their originality, their theological meaning, and their reciprocal relationship.

The theological model of Jesus propounded by Akhilananda implements first and foremost the Hindu concept of *avatara*. Akhilananda employs it to assimilate Jesus' religious experience to that of identification with the *Brahman* in a transcendence of all duality, the experience of which the Upanishads speak. Furthermore, not even in the classic sense of divine manifestation can the concept of *avatara* of itself imply the notion of a personal, decisive engagement of God in the history of human beings. Hindu *avatara* does not mean "Incarnation" in the Christian sense. For Akhilananda, Jesus is ultimately the symbol of an advaitine mysticism that gives the historical and the ontological short shrift. Here we have the central problems of the originality of Jesus' religious experience and of the concreteness of the Jesus Christ event as God's decisive intervention in history.

The ascetical Jesus-*yogi* model, as developed by M. C. Parekh, is disappointing despite the author's sympathy for his model. Jesus, the extraordinary *yogi*, is not the only begotten, veritable Son of God. Indeed the extraordinary nature of Jesus' *yoga* renders his humanity unhistorical. He ultimately appears as a symbol of the siblingship of God with humanity. Being a Christian now means entering into a consciousness of the divine filiation, the common possession of all religions. The various religions are ultimately equivalent, representing various forms of one faith in God. Once more called in question here are: the authenticity of Jesus' humanity and the unique character of his divine filiation; and, by way of consequence, the originality of Christianity, which, once reduced to its spirit, can be said to be everywhere present. To what extent must we see here an anticipated version of the "unknown Christ of Hinduism"?

The mystical model of Jesus Christ developed by Brahmabandhab Upadhyaya is scarcely lacking in christological depth, as we have seen, either with regard to the christological mystery itself or the trinitarian mystery from which the other is inseparable. Together these two mysteries constitute the essence and center of the Christian mystery itself, which Upadhyaya means to present to his compatriots in terms of the contemplative and philosophical tradition of India. Upadhyaya is the pioneer when it comes to posing the problem of "inculturation" in the most delicate and most demanding of all its dimensions — the doctrinal. He poses the problem of the value of the sacred books of Hinduism as divine revelation and evangelical preparation. Further, he raises the problem of the hyphenated Christian — in this case, the problem of the legitimacy of being a Hindu-Christian — a problem that can never more be sidestepped in the context of interreligious dialogue.

At the termination of this series of inquiries, we are doubtless struck both by the seriousness of the questions we have broached and by their currency for today's christological discussion. Hinduism is a redoubtable interlocutor indeed in the interreligious dialogue. In the area of christology in particular, Hinduism surely seems to pose all the questions of a religious pluralism. As we shall presently see, these questions are often the same as those of recent christological discussion; but the context of religious pluralism and dialogue invests them with a new, more radical dimension.

Were we to attempt to formulate the challenge posed to Christianity by its historical encounter with renascent Hinduism, of which the questions cited above, apropos of different Neo-Hindu christological models, are various partial expressions, we might do so as follows. The challenge is the one posed by the mysticism of an an-historical interiority of identification to the mystery of a God personally involved in the history of human beings with a view to awakening communion. The challenge or challenges have a repercussion on a basic question: Is the Christian mystery bound up with a view of the world and history, a worldview, a *Weltanschauung*, apart from which that mystery is not only unintelligible but objectless? Or is it not so bound up? In other words, do the presuppositions of Christian faith in and of themselves imply a specific, irreducible view of reality proper to that faith, while Hinduism presupposes a different, equally specific and irreducible view? Concretely, does not Christianity suppose a sense and density of history that Hinduism not only does not require but positively excludes? The issue is an important one, and there will be no evading it. It comes down to a dilemma: Can or cannot the Christian message accommodate itself to all cultures? Or do there exist in cultures certain elements, perhaps essential ones, that are hermetically sealed and impenetrable to the Christian message?

2

Hindu and Christian Christologies: Doctrines in Dialogue

In its own way, the Hindu renaissance has "acknowledged" Jesus Christ. We have even spoken of a Hindu christology. Without claiming to be exhaustive, and admitting that our systematization is somewhat oversimplified, we have attempted to distinguish six different models. They do not all have the same weight in the Hindu-Christian dialogue, nor have they the same meaning for a Christian theology of Hinduism. The philosophical model, for example, while somewhat akin to the idealistic christology of certain Western philosophers, exhibits little affinity with the Christian interpretation of the Jesus Christ event.

The intent of the present chapter is to initiate a dialogue between Hindu christology and Christian christology—and thus between the "unbound" Christ of Neo-Hinduism and Christ as Christian faith has traditionally understood and interpreted him. From the side of Christian interpretation, we shall not prioritize the dogmatic formulas of the christological councils, the differences between the christological positions of established theological schools, or viewpoints taken in contemporary christological discussion. Transcending all of these divergencies—which a theological, christological pluralism present in the New Testament itself renders perfectly legitimate—our point of reference will be the fundamental christological faith that is common to the churches and communities that call themselves Christian and merit that name by their faith in that Jesus of Nazareth whom God has made Lord and Christ (Acts 2:36) by raising him from the dead, and in whom he has reconciled (2 Cor. 5:19) the world with himself—that is, Jesus Christ, the Son of God and universal Savior.

From the side of Hindu christology, we must make a choice. Our dialogue cannot be conducted in terms of all the models expounded in the foregoing chapter. This would mean prohibitively extensive developments

46

of those models—developments which would be repetitive, since the models at least partially overlap.

Having to make a choice, we could have chosen, in order to initiate the dialogue, the Hindu *avatara* model on the one side, and the Christian model of the Incarnation on the other. We could then have developed the material that we have merely touched upon in the foregoing chapter: the consistent divergency between the Hindu concept of *avatara*, as interpreted throughout the Hindu tradition—despite various understandings of the same in other respects—and the Christian notion of incarnation consistent in the Christian traditions of the great churches, although there, too, various theological developments have not been lacking, nor are they lacking today.

Briefly, the contrast is between a divine manifestation in human form and a personal involvement on the part of God in the history of human beings, whose nature and concrete condition God actually shares. The contrast between these two conceptions is at the heart of the distinction between Hinduism and Christianity. This cannot be denied. For that matter, it has been dealt with time and time again, and there could scarcely be any need of rehearsing it here.[1]

We must also notice, at least in passing, that despite unquestionable formal differences between the two concepts, the Hindu notion of *avatara* represents one of the most promising stepping-stones to the Christian mystery. It is not without significance that, on the subject of the two mysteries that constitute the essence and center of Christianity—the trinitarian and the christological—Hindu tradition offers striking analogues: the concept of God as *saccidananda* (being-thought-bliss) on the one hand, and on the other, that of *avatara*. Apropos of the latter, here Christian theology is constrained to acknowledge the expression of the innate aspiration of the human being to enter into contact with the Infinite at the human level: That is to say (since a like contact can only come by the free initiative of God), the expression of the human being's inborn desire for a human manifestation of God in his and her regard—an expectancy of, a waiting for, incarnation (or, to use Karl Rahner's expression), a "christology in expectancy." Is not the devotee of Krishna or Rama closer to the mystery of Jesus Christ than the idealist philosopher of human evolution toward a superconsciousness? The "religiousness" of Athens, manifested to the eyes of Saint Paul in the worship of images (Acts 17:23–31)—to be distinguished from idolatry—was itself closer to the mystery of Jesus Christ than was Greek philosophy (Plato, for example) for which the notion of incarnation was unthinkable, contradicting as it did the transcendence of God. Can we go further and see in the Hindu doctrine of *avatara* not only a stepping-stone in human beings to the mystery of Christ, but a first approach of God toward them, an initial manifestation of God setting them on the road to Jesus Christ, an "evangelical preparation" by way of an anticipatory revelation? This is not the place to attempt to answer this question. We shall return to it later.

In order to get the dialogue between Hindu christology and Christian christology, in the sense indicated above, underway, we shall concentrate especially on two themes or models of Hindu christology: the ascetic model of Jesus-*yogi* and the theme of the Jesus of the mystical experience of *advaita*, which is employed, with various nuances, by more than one Hindu current of christological interpretation.

This choice is not arbitrary: It is based on renewed interest in these themes today. We know the interest evoked today by the idea and practice of Christian *yoga*. We may wonder whether, in spite of the weaknesses of the Hindu model of Jesus-*yogi*, we may not recognize the authenticity of the idea of Jesus at the origin of a Christian *yoga*. How? The theme of the mysticism of *advaita* so often identified with Jesus' religious experience, as in John 10:30, "I and the Father are one," calls for important clarifications with a view to an altogether clear identification of the originality of Jesus' filial consciousness, that obligatory fundament of any Christian christology.

Our aim is clarity in the dialogue. The similarities and analogies are undeniable. Far from denying them, we must attribute to them the value of stepping-stones. The differences that emerge from the encounter are no less basic; we must acknowledge them in all forthrightness. Only then will the dialogue serve as a Christian theology's foundation for the relationship between Christianity and Hinduism in their various components.

JESUS AT THE ORIGIN OF CHRISTIAN *YOGA*

It may seem risky, even superficial, and rather tinged with a spirit of syncretism, to present Jesus as a *yogi* and to make him the model or actual origin of a self-styled Christian *yoga*. We might wonder whether there is not actually a profound, even irreducible, opposition between *yoga* and Christian practice. Is not the mental void for which *yoga* strives incompatible with the Christian experience? Is not the yogic concentration on the "I" irreducible to the prayer addressed to God as a "Thou"?

The question is a real one, and important. However, the opposition may well be more apparent than profound. To be sure, *yoga* strives for the transformation of awareness, but it aims at an authentic spiritual experience. This experience is an experience of God. One must unhesitatingly acknowledge that God can be encountered in the depths of oneself as well as in the events of history. The encounter with God in history is more characteristic of the so-called prophetic religions, especially of Christianity. That taking place in the depths of oneself, at the source of the self, is more typical of the mystical Asian religious traditions.

When we speak of *yoga*, it is important to see that its goal is really to attain a pure awareness of that "Self" that is actually God. The experience of the self, the high point of psychic activity that the human being attains by concentration, is the substrate of the authentic mystical experience, or the experience of God—provided, of course (and this is crucial), the means do not become an end in themselves (as occurs with idolatry). Where *yoga* is concerned, this means that the soul cannot be satisfied with its "self" and its concentration on itself; it must move beyond itself, to plunge into the very abyss of God. Such is the price of the authentic spiritual experience.

Here the word of the gospel comes to mind: "The man who loves his life loses it, while the man who hates his life in this world preserves it to life eternal" (John 12:25). Or again, "He who seeks only himself brings himself to ruin, whereas he who brings himself to nought for me discovers who he is" (Matt. 10:39). We find only what we seek: self or God. *Yoga* may not be deprived of its authentic goal.

Swami Abhishiktananda issues a warning to the adepts of a Christian *yoga*, without any smugness, to the following effect: The means cannot be turned into an end with impunity. He writes:

> Yoga, being a technique, inevitably suffers the fate of all techniques, whether physical, psychical, social or religious. The technique tends to attract more and more attention to itself; mere means are in danger of being valued for their own sake to the detriment of the end which is primarily sought. Thus the dangers of yoga should not be underestimated.[2]

Thanks to these initial clarifications and warnings, we shall be better disposed, as Christians, to ask ourselves in what sense one may speak of Jesus as a *yogi* and see him at the origin of a Christian *yoga*. We need not here rehearse the notion of the classic doctrine of *yoga* as a spiritual discipline. We have already cited its various levels and its orientation toward the authentic experience of God (see chapter one). Perhaps, however, we ought to ask of what Jesus we are speaking when we place him at the origin of Christian *yoga*.

The question may sound strange unless we recall that we are dealing with Jesus of Nazareth, who, nearly two thousand years ago, lived an authentic, genuine human life. After all, it is because he is as authentically human as ourselves that Jesus has meaning for us and can be our model.

There is scarcely any need of reviewing the recent history of the hermeneutics of the gospel tradition in an effort to show that, despite the paschal interpretation coloring the events of the gospel accounts, access to the historical Jesus is not closed off to us. Jesus' personality, the singular traits of his person, his choices, his commitments, his practice, and through them, his very consciousness are sufficiently accessible to us.

Indeed, it could not have been otherwise. After all, it is to Jesus that the whole of Christian tradition has laid claim, lo, these two thousand years, and we know better today that what that tradition tells us on the subject of Jesus himself could not, when all is said and done, have been founded on anything but his own understanding and witness. The Christian phenomenon would be inexplicable without its foundation on the historical Jesus, the obligatory fundament of all authentic Christian tradition. It is this prepaschal Jesus that we propose to place at the origin of Christian *yoga*. Let us explain what we mean.

We have shown the weaknesses of the Hindu model of the *yogi*-Jesus. Concretely, we have said that it errs by a twofold impotence: It gives an inadequate account of Jesus' divine filiation; and Jesus' humanity—clothed in extraordinary powers—is unreal and unhistorical. The second shortcoming, let us point out, is as pernicious as the first. It is the historical Jesus, then, as the apostolic tradition affords us a glimpse of him, that we are concerned to follow here. We shall ask ourselves whether the traits that make the true *yogi*, as defined above, are verified in him. Does one discover in Jesus the three levels of *yoga* that we have characterized as outer wrapping, backbone, and soul of *yoga*? And especially, what spiritual experience constitutes this soul? What concrete end draws Jesus, informing, as it must, all his asceticism and concentration?

Jesus' Yoga

The opening of Mark's gospel will place us on the right track. There, in an astonishing sequence in the space of a few verses, it is given to us to discover the various elements of the *yoga* that Jesus practiced. In a programmatic summary, Mark tells us that no sooner was Jesus baptized by John in the waters of the Jordan than "he saw the sky rent in two and the Spirit descending on him like a dove. Then a voice came from the heavens: 'You are my beloved Son. On you my favor rests.' At that point," Mark continues, "the Spirit sent him out toward the desert. He remained in the wasteland forty days, put to test there by Satan" (Mark 1:10–13).

Matthew specifies that Jesus was led into the desert by the Spirit to be tempted, and that he fasted for forty days and forty nights, after which he was hungry (Matt. 4:2).

Then Mark comes back in, telling us that Jesus then "appeared in Galilee proclaiming the good news of God: 'This is the time of fulfillment. The reign of God is at hand! Reform your lives and believe in the gospel!'" (Mark 1:15). Immediately, we are told, Jesus calls disciples, and they follow him. He is to be a *guru* (Mark 1:16–20). Immediately, once more, his teaching is accompanied by cures and miracles. He is a wonder-worker (Mark 1:21–28).

Ascetic, prophet, and itinerant preacher, thaumaturge: This is how Jesus appears from the outset of his ministry. Obviously the portrait is incomplete. The person of Jesus is proposed to us from the beginning, although many personal traits will later enhance the account. Let us take note of some of them, returning to them later in order to discover their meaning and scope.

Jesus prays to the God who has sent him and upon whom he depends.

As we read the gospel account, we see that every decision, each of the choices he must make in function of the accomplishment of his mission, is accompanied, or rather preceded, by a prayer to the God he calls his Father. Jesus is infinitely attentive to others. His life is a pro-existence: We rightly define him as the "person for others." His miracles are all directed toward others, while he himself, in the desert, has refused to make use of his power for his own advantage. That is, he refuses comfort, prestige, and power. He is altogether absorbed by his mission.

Jesus centers his whole attention and energy on one essential: the Reign of God, which he not only announces and proclaims, but inaugurates through his actions and words—or more precisely, which God inaugurates through the human life of his envoy, as well as by his death and resurrection. All of Jesus' parables focus on the Reign of God. He tells us how God establishes it among us and how it grows. All of his miracles are there to show us that the Reign is already present and active, transforming human beings and the world, toppling the power of evil and inaugurating a new order of relationships among human beings and between human beings and God.

Jesus has an acute awareness of the mission he has received from God. It matters little whether or not he personally employed the messianic titles placed in his mouth or applied to him by the gospel tradition. The striking thing is that the most decisive, profound datum is also the best attested: Jesus' consciousness is essentially one of divine filiation. He knows that he is the Son of God his Father, in a unique, ineffable relationship. We might say that, under the astonished and doubtless uncomprehending gaze of his disciples, he makes of this unspeakable filial relationship his very life. He translates it into human terms of intimacy, calling his Father God "Abba," as the gospel tradition explicitly reports. Jesus' filial consciousness is the key to his authentic mystery.

We have said nothing of the astounding page of the gospel on which Jesus appears transfigured on Mount Tabor. Nor have we spoken of the torment of the cross—prefigured by his baptism, as Jesus himself attests. Nor have we considered the resurrection, precisely prefigured by that strange transfiguration, and for his disciples the true point of departure for faith in Jesus Christ.

In the meantime, what has been said is perhaps already enough by way of background for a consideration of our original question: that of Jesus as *yogi*. Without forcing things, but admitting that Jesus has his own, unique style, we may be permitted to recognize, in the traits underscored above, the three levels or dimensions of *yoga*: It is equally clear that the wellspring of the whole is what we have just referred to as Jesus' filial consciousness. Thus we may list, for the sake of verification and order, the three successive levels in question.

At the level of asceticism and the psychophysiological techniques that have been called *yoga*'s envelope or wrapping, the gospel almost casually mentions that Jesus fasted, or that he prayed at moments of choice and decision, to bring his human will into conformity with that of the God who had sent him. The temptation in the desert symbolizes the spiritual combat being waged within him and investing him with kinship with our own frailty. The temptation account in Luke's gospel ends with a strange notation: "When the devil had finished all the tempting he left him, to await another opportunity" (Luke 4:13). That opportunity will be the time of agony in the garden of Gethsemane, where, in tears and prayer, in anguish and darkness, Jesus will seek the will of his Father, suddenly become astonishingly obscure. Even more, it will be the moment of his cry of affliction on the cross—an affliction, to be sure, which becomes abandonment to the hands of the Father to whom the gospel tells us he surrenders his spirit. It is abundantly clear, then: Jesus has known weakness, and it is in this weakness that he is closest to us. He has practiced asceticism and has experienced genuine spiritual combat.

At the level of concentration, we must say that, in his words and deeds, in his life and his death, Jesus is altogether centered on the Reign of God, which he preaches and which is inaugurated in him—indeed, which is identified with his very person. The Reign of God, the new order personally established by God in the world of human beings—this good news to the poor—is Jesus' sole concern and sole thought. All his words, all his deeds refer to it, his whole preaching, all his parables. Of this reign that God inaugurates in his envoy, all of Jesus' miracles are an integral part, anticipatory signs and firstfruits. In them, the Reign of God already triumphs over the powers of evil, transforming the world and human relations.

This relationship between Jesus' miracles and the establishment of the Reign of God is very clearly indicated by Jesus himself. To the disciples of John the Baptist, come to question him on his mission, he replies: "Go back and report to John what you hear and see: the blind recover their sight, cripples walk, lepers are cured, the deaf hear, dead men are raised to life, and the poor have the good news preached to them" (Matt. 11:4–5). These miracles that transform the body are an integral part of the good news that is the inauguration of the Reign of God on earth. This is even clearer in the gospel episode that reports the controversy between Jesus and the Pharisees over the expulsion of demons: "If it is by the Spirit of God that I expel demons, then the reign of God has overtaken you" (Matt. 12:28). In Jesus' deeds, the Reign of God is not only near, it is already present in our midst, transforming bodies and liberating souls. After all, in the last analysis, Jesus himself is the Reign of God present and operative among human beings as Jesus states, according to Luke's gospel, in the synagogue of Nazareth where he is invited to do a liturgical reading.

When the book of the prophet Isaiah was handed him, he unrolled the scroll and found the passage where it was written:

"The spirit of the Lord is upon me;
  therefore, he has anointed me.
He has sent me to bring glad tidings to the poor,
  to proclaim liberty to captives,
Recovery of sight to the blind
  and release to prisoners,
To announce a year of favor from the Lord."

Rolling up the scroll he gave it back to the assistant and sat down. All in the synagogue had their eyes fixed on him. Then he began by saying to them, "Today this Scripture passage is fulfilled in your hearing" (Luke 4:16–21).

The Reign of God on earth is himself. Upon this Reign he centers his whole attention and his whole thought, as well as all his discourse and activity. The Reign of God is the fixed point of his concentration, the backbone of his *yoga*.

And yet we must go deeper. Surely the Reign of God is the fixed point of his concentration and activity, but this fixed point has an ulterior source. Here we touch on the deepest level of the mystery of Jesus—on what constitutes the soul of his *yoga*. We are confronted with Jesus' awareness of his relation to God his Father and of his own identity as Son. We have already remarked that this consciousness transcends everything the messianic titles borrowed from the Old Testament could have said, and indeed say in New Testament christology, to express Jesus' functions with regard to human beings. Beyond all that, it is a matter of his personal relationship with God. But, as we have noted, Jesus' personal consciousness with respect to God is essentially filial, and this filial relationship, as the gospel testifies, is marked by an unspeakable intimacy, which no single term can adequately render. "Abba" itself is a term at least partially successful in expressing this relationship.

We find a related formula, intended likewise to express the depths of Jesus' consciousness, in the Gospel of John, namely the absolute formula, "I am" (*Ego eimi*, John 8:24,28, 8:58, 13:19), which in the Greek Septuagint translation recalls the way in which God had been revealed to Moses in the Book of Exodus as "I am who I am"; "I shall be with you as the one who is" (see Exod. 3:14). We may also mention the oft-cited formula that John places on the lips of Jesus: "I and the Father are one" (John 10:30).

Below, we shall return to this formula, in which, as we have already observed, some have seen, in a Neo-Hindu climate, the expression on Jesus' lips of the supreme experience he has of his identity with the *Brahman*: *Aham brahmasmi; tattvamasi* ("I am the *Brahman*; you are that," *Brhadaranyaka Upanishad* 1.4.10). Thus, we are told, Jesus is a *jivanmukta*, a soul liberated in this very life in that it has arrived at the experience of identity with the *Brahman*, which is also the experience of total self-realization. On the contrary, as we shall show later in this chapter, we must read here the singular experience that Jesus has of God as his Father, in which the values of a radical oneness, far from excluding those of an interpersonal communion, combine with them, in a mutual appeal. It is this that constitutes the irreducible reality of Jesus' religious experience. It is also at this level and at this depth — that of Jesus' personal consciousness — that what we have called the soul of his *yoga* is to be discovered.

Toward Christian Yoga

Resisting all temptations to the contrary, we have sought from the outset to emphasize the artless authenticity of the humanity of a Jesus "like unto us in all things save sin" — or as Paul rather crudely puts it, "born of a woman" (Gal. 4:4). A member of our race, he assumed our human condition and walked with us in our history. However, having set out to discover the *yoga* he lived, we find ourselves having arrived, through what we have agreed to call the wrapping and the backbone of *yoga*, at its soul, that is, this unique, ineffable awareness of Jesus of being the Son of God. With this consciousness, we have finally come to the threshold of the most profound mystery, where Jesus and God are but one. That is to say, Jesus' *yoga* issues in a foundational experience of which that of the greatest mystics is but an analogical, distant approach. In Jesus' case, we are forced to the absolute degree of both oneness, and the personal. In this sense the soul of his *yoga* is unique and inimitable.

It is no less the model of Christian *yoga*, however, even if the latter can never hope to reproduce its archetype. Jesus the Christ is the model of being a Christian, that is, of discipleship. He is also its perfect accomplishment and end. Christian *yoga*, in other words, is entirely centered on the person of Jesus. Through techniques and concentration, it invites us to enter into Jesus' filiation vis-à-vis our Parent, in the movement by which he comes from his Parent and returns there. It invites us to enter into the filial consciousness of Jesus himself, which makes us cry out, "*Abba*, Father" (see Rom. 8:15). Such is the soul of Christian *yoga*. But we must add: this is possible only in faith. Faith and not techniques must be at the center of any *yoga* that would style itself Christian.

Thomas Matus makes an important point when he observes:

> It is faith that is essential; all else is auxiliary. Yoga belongs to the order of optional means, even though it has its own intrinsic end, which, in the concrete situation, can be made to coincide with the ultimate end of the Christian: loving union with God through Jesus Christ in the Holy Spirit. In this sense, a Christian understanding of yoga means the perception of the Christian end in all the means employed and experiences had throughout the yogic quest.[3]

Matus concludes:

> For the Christian, this means that Jesus Christ becomes the model both of the spiritual journey and of its goal ... In other words, the one, true yogi is Jesus. His life, His mysteries, His Person *are* the Christian's yoga.[4]

THE CONSCIOUSNESS OF CHRIST
AND THE EXPERIENCE OF *ADVAITA*

Let us now take up the second theme that we have regarded as essential to a dialogue between Neo-Hindu christology and Christian christology. We have already made a brief reference to its interest and importance. In order to appreciate that importance, however, we must have a clear picture of the problems of interpretation that underlie it.[5]

First, let us recall that every religious tradition, including the Christian tradition, must be perceived and understood in its historical context. Jesus is heir to a particular religious and cultural legacy. However novel his message, however unprecedented its presentation, it is nonetheless tied to the mental categories and models of thought of a Hebrew culture and to the worldview that prevailed in the Semitic regions of his time. And the New Testament witness to the ancient faith in Jesus Christ is likewise dependent on the culture or cultures from which it took its rise.

This twofold fact would seem to lead to a twin conclusion. First, to the question, "Who do you say that I am?" there cannot be one Christian answer valid for all times and intelligible in all places. Secondly, the originality of Jesus' self-awareness cannot be defined or determined as easily as has sometimes been supposed. After all, just as the content of faith and the formulation expressing it cannot be neatly relegated into two perfectly airtight compartments, so also it is impossible to extract Jesus' self-consciousness from the manifold elements of the Hebrew idiom in which he himself expressed it as if we were dealing with some pure, incorporeal form.

And yet in the last analysis the identity of Jesus Christ must be based on Jesus' own awareness of that identity, as well as on its revelation by himself through his words and deeds over the course of his earthly existence. The apostolic faith in Jesus Christ can be supported by the apostles' and disciples' paschal experience only if the latter is itself based on the testimony of the prepaschal Jesus. Thus, a penetration of Jesus' self-consciousness, or, equivalently, his experience of God, is an indispensable theological task, without which it would be impossible to do justice to the identity of Jesus as understood by Christian faith. The originality of this state of "awakening to God" as experienced by Jesus, and the singularity of his consequent self-awareness, must become the object of explanations and elucidations.

The task is all the more necessary and urgent in our particular context, where our concern is to establish a dialogue between Jesus' and others' experiences of God. The genuine character of their difference has often been too casually glossed over. According to a widespread interpretation among representatives of Neo-Hinduism—precisely the interpretation that we are considering here—Jesus must be regarded as a *jivanmukta*: a self-actualized soul. Thus Jesus is imaged as one fully awake to his own identity with *Brahman*. His words in the Gospel of John, "I and the Father are one" (John 10:30), are understood as expressing the equivalence, although in a different mental context, of Hindu mysticism's decisive experience of *advaita*: *Aham brahmasmi.*[6] Certain Christian interpreters are even inclined to think that the difference between the self-consciousness of Christ and the experience of *advaita* would be mainly a question of context and language.[7] What, then, is the relationship between Jesus' self-awareness and the experience of *advaita*? This point must be clarified.

Do Jesus' self-consciousness and the experience of *advaita* coincide— although expressed differently, as we should expect, since they arise in philosophical views and conceptions of the world that issue from different cultures? Or must we maintain that there is a radical difference between what Jesus experienced and what was experienced by the sages of the Upanishads? The answers we give to these questions will naturally raise other questions, and these will be relative to our life today. If, as we shall see, the experience of God proper to Christians is a participation in the religious experience of Jesus himself, then the relationship between the Christian experience and that of *advaita* must be conceived along the lines of the considerations into which we shall now enter concerning Jesus' religious consciousness.

Jesus' Awareness

From the outset, we must recall that Jesus' consciousness cannot be evaluated strictly from a point of departure in the direct evidence of his own testimony, without reference to the paschal experience and the apostolic faith. The testimony of the prepaschal Jesus—without which, as has been stated above, the paschal faith would not have had an adequate foundation—has received, in the writings of the New Testament, a certain coloration, precisely from this paschal faith. Having discovered, in their paschal and pentecostal experience, their master's true identity, the apostles and disciples have rethought, reinterpreted, and sometimes reexpressed the actual testimony of Jesus about himself. Of all of the writings of the New Testament, it is the Gospel of John that is composed to pierce most deeply into the human psychology of Jesus as the Incarnate Word and reveal this psychology to the believer. Jesus' consciousness in the New Testament expression, of course, can be approached and discovered only through the eyes of the apostolic faith. It likewise follows that a reflection on faith can help us to a certain extent to go beyond the formulation given in the writings of the New Testament in our attempt to understand Jesus' consciousness.

Jesus' consciousness—as we have already stated—is essentially filial. Nothing is more central in Jesus' religious experience than his relation to God as his "Father." This God who is Parent is the Yahweh of the Jewish religious tradition, the God of the Covenant, known and familiar to Jesus' hearers. The concept of Father as applied to Yahweh is not unknown to the Old Testament, which describes God's fatherly attitude toward the chosen people (cf. Exod. 4:22). But in Jesus' consciousness, Yahweh's parenthood takes on an altogether new meaning, a meaning bound up with the relationship to Yahweh that Jesus himself experienced. Its filial nature vis-à-vis God is unique in its kind, and is of a distinct order: Jesus is the Son (Mark 3:11), the very Son of God (Mark 12:6), the Only-Begotten (John 1:14).

There is no better indication of the claim for the unique nature of Jesus' divine filiation, perhaps, than the familiar term of address "Abba," preserved by the gospel witness (Mark 14:36) in its original Semitic form by which Jesus addresses God his Father. This word, which Jewish tradition used in family relationships, when addressed to God implies a familiarity and an intimacy with God never before so denoted. This image, then, functions to portray Jesus' lived experience and revelation of his proper unique divine filiation. The "hymn of jubilation" (Matt. 11:25-27) is further testimony. It expresses the unique relationship that faith sees binding Jesus to God as Son to the Father. It shows that there is a mystery of the Son as there is a mystery of the Father, indeed that the Father and the Son are one and the same mystery. Saint John sums this up when he says: "He [Jesus] called God his own Father, making himself God's equal" (John 5:18).

This claim of unique filiation implies that between Yahweh-Father and Jesus-Son there is at once a distinction and a unity. The distinction is evident, and scarcely calls for explanation. Jesus refers to the Father as if he is addressing another, someone he praises, someone to whom he prays. But the other side of the coin—the unity side—bestows on Jesus' religious consciousness its specific character—*Jesus referring to the Father with a familiarity never before conceived or attested*. What Jesus reveals of the mystery of God could not be explained by an extraordinary knowledge of the scriptures. It was not something learned. It was something that flowed out of the living experience of a unique intimacy. If, as the gospel testifies, no one had ever spoken as Jesus did (cf. John 7:46), the reason why is that no other human experience of God was comparable to his. John's Gospel offers us certain glimpses of this oneness between Father and Son: "I and the Father are one" (John 10:30). From this unity in "being," this reciprocal immanence (10:38, 14:11, 17:21), results a mutual acquaintance (10:15), a mutual love (5:20, 15:10), a common action—what Jesus accomplishes, the Father accomplishes in him (5:17).

In a commentary on the relationship uniting Jesus and his Father as formulated in John's Gospel, Raymond E. Brown writes:

> It will be noted that all these relationships between Father and Son are described in function of the Son's dealings with men. It would be the work of later theologians to take this gospel material pertaining to the mission of the Son ad extra and draw from it a theology of the inner life of the Trinity.
>
> Returning to [John] x 30, we find that the unity posited there also concerns men; for just as the Father and Son are one, so they bind men to themselves as one — "that they may be one, even as we" (xvii 11).[8]

It does not serve our purpose here to pursue the process of theological development to which Brown alludes, which progresses from the "economy" of the manifestation of God in the human Jesus to the "theology" of the intratrinitarian relation between Father and Son. The "functional christology" of the New Testament — which directly concerns the relationship between Jesus, the human being sent by God, with the Father who has sent him — suffices to justify an important conclusion, which we may formulate as follows: *Jesus' relationship with God is an "I-Thou" relationship of Son with Father.* The two elements of this relationship — distinction (Son-Father) and unity ("are one") — together constitute the originality and specificity of the experience of God that Jesus lived. This is so eminently true that no other category seems even remotely capable of expressing this singular relationship. In Jesus' experience, he is not the Father but between him and his Father the communication of likeness, indeed the oneness, are such that they call for expression in terms of a Father-Son relationship.

Jesus' consciousness of this unique relationship with God his Father is doubtless best manifested in his prayer. However, it finds expression in everything constituting his religious life — his obedience and his submission to the will of the Father, the sacrifice he offers when he surrenders his spirit into his Father's hands. Jesus' entire religious life is centered on the person of the Father. When he prays and worships, when he supplicates or implores, the orientation of his entire human spirit to the Father is so profound that it is evidently rooted beyond the sphere of the human. His sense of total dependence vis-à-vis the Father surely seems a human echo of a deeper origin with regard to him. In the "economy" of Jesus' prayer, the "theology" of his person is transposed to the key of human awareness. The mystery of Jesus is the mystery of the Son as displayed in humanity, but without being exhausted there.

Thus, Jesus' human life and condition are a human expression of the mystery of the Son of God. In this way his human words are the human expression of the divine Word. Jesus not only addresses to human beings words received from God as the prophets did — he is himself the Word of

God made flesh. The reason why God's self-revelation in Jesus is decisive and ultimate is that in his human consciousness Jesus experiences the mystery of the divine life which he personally shares. This transposition of the divine mystery into human consciousness permits its expression in human language. In Jesus, then, the revelation of this mystery is qualitatively different, since in the biblical record he is himself the Son of God, who expresses himself and elucidates his divine parentage in human terms. This revelation is central and normative, in the sense that no one is capable of communicating to human beings the mystery of God with greater depth than does the Son himself, who has become a human being. Jesus brings the word because he is the Word.

However, even this revelation remains limited, incomplete, and imperfect. First of all, no human consciousness, not even that of God become a human being, can comprehend or contain the divine mystery. Human words, were they to be pronounced by Godself, must fail to exhaust God's reality. Furthermore, to this inescapable, intrinsic limitation affecting the revelation of God in Jesus Christ must be added a specific limit due to the particular idiom in which Jesus actually expressed himself—the Aramaic spoken in his time. This shows that the "fullness" attributed to the Christian revelation must be qualified and correctly understood. That fullness must be sought not in the written word of the New Testament, but beyond it in the person and life of Jesus himself, who is the Word addressed to human beings by the Father.

Experience of Advaita

On the basis of what we have said, it is clear that Jesus' human awareness is crucial for the theological understanding of the mystery of Christ according to the Christian faith. Jesus' awareness as portrayed in diverse ways in scripture manifests the originality and unique character of his experience of God. It is also the human source of the divine revelation which takes place in him. In Hindu mysticism, the experience of *advaita* likewise occupies a central place and it is this that authorizes its comparison, from a number of viewpoints, with the consciousness of Jesus. But before there can be an exchange of views at any depth on these two experiences of God, we must describe at least in its main lines the experience of *advaita* itself.

Traditionally, two formulae, which we have already recalled, serve to express the heart of the experience of *advaita*, both taken from the Upanishads: *Aham brahmasmi* (*Brhadaranyaka Upanishad* 1.4.10), and *tattvamasi* (*Chandogya Upanishad* 6.8.7). The latter is contained in the instruction Svetaketu receives from his father. The text, based on that of R. C. Zaehner, is the following.

> In the beginning this [universe] was *Brahman* alone,
> and he knew [him]self (*atman*) in truth,

saying: I am *Brahman* [*aham brahmasmi*].
And thus he became the all.
The gods, whichever they are, who became aware of
   this,
likewise became the [all].
Thus it [was] with seers (*rsi*) and men. . . .
This remains true even today.
Whoever knows that he is *Brahman* becomes this
   whole [universe].
The very gods have no power to reduce him to non-
   being,
   for he becomes their own Self.
         (*Brhadaranyaka Upanishad* 1.4.10)[9]

My dearest child, all of these creatures [here] have Being as their
root, Being as their place of repose, Being as their foundation. . . .
   My dear boy, I have already explained to you how each of these
substances (*devata*) [itself] becomes threefold when it enters into the
sphere of the human.
   My dear boy, when a man dies, his voice is absorbed (*sampad*) into
mind, his mind into breath, his breath into light-and-heat, and the
latter into the highest substance. This finest essence, the whole universe possesses as its Self. Behold the Real. Behold the Self. That
you are (*tattvamasi*), *Svetaketu*! (*Chandogya Upanishad* 6.8.7).[10]

At the root of the experience of *advaita* resides an inner, tireless search
for the awakening to Self. Following the experience and teaching of Sri
Ramana Maharshi, Abhishiktananda describes it as follows:[11]

The mind then realizes more and more its inability to say: "I am this
or that; I am this person or that person." For in the very moment at
which the thought appears that I am this or that, this person or that
person, then this manifestation with which I have automatically tried
to identify myself in the flow of consciousness has fled away from
me—but *I* continue. Sensory and psychic experience flow on in a
steady stream which nothing can stop, being part of that constant
succession of change which is the nature of the cosmos. While this
flow continues endlessly, I myself abide, *I am*, in an unchanging present. All things pass, change, *panta rhei*; but as for me, *I am*. What am
I? Who am I? There is no answer except the pure awareness that *I
am*, transcending all thought.
   "I am," and there is no need for me to strive in order to find this
"I am." I am not an "I" searching for itself. . . . All that a man has
to do is simply to allow himself to be grasped by this light which
springs up from within, but itself cannot be grasped.[12]

The experience of *advaita*, to which the tireless quest for the inner self leads, may be described, it would seem, as an entry, or better, assumption, into the knowledge that the Absolute has of itself, and thus as a view of being literally from the viewpoint of the Absolute. From the special viewpoint of this absolute awareness, all duality (*dvaita*) vanishes, since the Absolute alone is absolutely, is One-without-a-second (*ekam advitiyam*). From this viewpoint, the universe, and history, have no absolute meaning (*paramartha*): their existence pertains to the domain of the relative (*vyavahara*), God's *lila* (God's play in creation). At the awakening of the experience of *advaita*, the ontological density of the finite seer itself vanishes. The awakening to absolute awareness leaves no room for a subjective awareness of self as finite subject of cognition: there remains only the *aham*-("I"-) awareness of the Absolute in the epiphenomenon of the body (*sariram*): *Aham brahmasmi*.

If this description is correct, then it is evident that the experience of *advaita* implies a radical evanescence of all that is not the Absolute. When the consciousness of the absolute *Aham* emerges in the seer, the latter is submerged in it. "Who knows and who is known?" asks the *Upanishad*. Henceforth it is no longer a finite "me" who—regarding God and regarded by God—contemplates and addresses a prayer to God. What abides is the awakening of the one who knows to the subjective consciousness of the Absolute itself. And it is not an objective knowledge of the Absolute by a finite me. In the process of illumination, the human "me" gives way to the divine *Aham*. Such is the radical demand of *advaita*.

The Ego of Jesus and the **Aham** *("I") of* **Advaita**

"I and the Father are one"—"You are That"—"I am Brahman." These experiences seem at first glance to be entirely different. Jesus' words express the awareness of a distinction in unity, the experience of an interpersonal relationship whose two poles (distinction and oneness) are inseparable constituents: Jesus is not the Father, but he *is* one with him. The citations from the *Upanishads*, on the contrary, express an awareness of an absolute identity, in which all distinction has disappeared. At the awakening of self-realization, only the consciousness of the absolute *Aham*, the *atman-Brahman* identity, abides. On the one side, Jesus is humanly conscious of being one with God his Father; on the other, the consciousness of the finite "me" gives place to the consciousness of the infinite Self, identical with the *Brahman*. On one side, the Word of God becomes humanly aware of itself in the human consciousness of Jesus; on the other, an awareness of the divine *Aham* invades and submerges the subjective consciousness of the finite self.

Jesus' relation to the Father is an "I-Thou" relationship, that "primordial word," as Martin Buber calls it, that expresses communion.

How powerful, even overpowering, is Jesus' I-saying, and how legitimate to the point of being a matter of course! For it is the I of the unconditional relation in which man calls his You "Father" in such a way that he himself becomes nothing but a son. Whenever he says I, he can only mean the I of the holy basic word that has become unconditional for him.[13]

And, Buber continues, this unconditional relationship of Jesus to the Father expressed by the primordial word "I-Thou" cannot be reduced to the relationship of the I with the Self, as certain representatives of the study of comparative religion are inclined, it would seem, to suppose:

> The Gospel according to John . . . is really nothing less than the Gospel of pure relationship. . . . The father and the son, being consubstantial—we may say: God and man, being consubstantial, are actually and forever Two, the two partners of the primal relationship. . . . All modern attempts to reinterpret this primal actuality of dialogue and to make of it a relationship of the I to the self or something of that sort, as if it were a process confined to man's self-sufficient inwardness, are vain and belong to the abysmal history of deactualization.[14]

That the distinction between Jesus and the Father is an irreducible component of Jesus' experience is altogether certain in the scriptural record. But just as central to that experience in important New Testament strata is his oneness with the Father—a unity not solely due to his mission, but founded, in the last analysis, on being: Jesus and the Father are one, nonduality, *advaita*. The "I" of Jesus' gospel words, while they establish the distinction from the "Thou" of the Father, also implies unity with him. Ultimately, this "I" does not mean, properly speaking, that a human person called Jesus is related to God as to a Father, but rather that the Son-of-God-become-a-human-being is posited in relation with his Father.

As we see, the "I am *Brahman*," the *Aham brahmasmi*, of the *Upanishads*, finds its truest application, paradoxically, precisely in Jesus. In him this proposition becomes literally true, and acquires a new meaning: it proclaims Jesus' union with the Father, a union whose foundation is beyond the human condition. More precisely, it expresses Jesus' personal awareness of belonging, along with the Father, to the sphere of the divinity. Applied to Jesus, the *Aham brahmasmi* then seems to correspond to Jesus' "absolute" *ego eimi* in the Gospel of Saint John: "I am" (cf. John 8:24,28, 8:58, 13:19). As we know, these words are taken from the Septuagint translation of Exodus 3:14. In the original Hebrew of Exodus 3:14, the revelation of the name YHWH connotes God's "being with" Moses and his people, in fidelity to his promises. In the Greek version, by contrast, the connotation is more metaphysical—Yahweh is "the one who is." In the Gospel of John, the absolute *ego eimi* can take on both nuances: in Jesus *Em-manu-el*, God is "with us" in a decisive way, and at the same time Jesus is the one who, along with the Father, belongs to the sphere of the divine; the one who is, and consequently is capable, in an acquired human consciousness, of declaring in all truth: "I am," *aham brahmasmi*.

One can think, then, that Jesus' consciousness of his personal communion with the Father in the *advaita* of the divinity is the crown and fulfillment of the intuition of the seers of the *Upanishads*. After all, this intuition stretches the human mind to the limit — and beyond — of what it is capable of experiencing and of expressing in words. Perhaps we might say that Jesus' human consciousness resolves the insurmountable antinomy to which the experience of *advaita* leads — the antinomy between the values of absolute oneness, on the one hand, and the values of personal communion on the other. At least we can assert that Jesus' awareness of his relationship with the Father is the supreme realization of *advaita* in the human condition — a realization, indeed, that even the seers of the *Upanishads* did not foresee or describe.[15] Abhishiktananda is very clear on this point:

> The experience of the Absolute to which India's mystical tradition bears such powerful witness is all included in Jesus' word: "My Father and I are one." All that the Maharshi, and countless others before him, knew and handed on of the inexorable experience of non-duality, Jesus also knew himself, and that in a pre-eminent manner. We need only refer to his words: "He who has seen me has seen the Father" (John 14:9). Whatever the Father does, he does through the Son; whatever the Son does, it is the Father doing it through him. And yet, at the very heart of all this, there remains the "face-to-face" of the Son and the Father.
>
> The conclusion is inescapable: the experience of Jesus includes the advaitic experience, but it certainly cannot be reduced to the commonly accepted formulation of that experience.[16]

Meanwhile, concerned as we may be to emphasize the notion that Jesus' awareness brings the experience of *advaita* to an unexpected fulfillment, we must likewise ascribe all due importance to the absolute quest for *advaita*, which helps us purify our understanding of Jesus' communion with his Parent: this communion is unique, and simply irreducible to the measure of the interpersonal relationship among human beings.[17] Jesus' awareness of his union with his Father is human, but it is a human awareness of communion in divinity. While it finds its most perfect realization in the mystery of Christ, the experience of *advaita* also helps us discover new depths in that same mystery. It is in this sense that Swami Abhishiktananda could say, in all truth, that the study of the *Upanishads* helps us pierce more deeply into the mystery of the Lord revealed to us in the Gospel of John when he writes:

That mystery which had first been glimpsed by the rishis is now revealed by St John in all its splendour, seen in the clear light of the Word and in the depth of the Spirit. . . .

It was as though we had returned from the *Upanishads* to the Bible with eyes miraculously unsealed, with eyes accustomed to the depths, capable of a wholly new penetration into the mystery of the Lord. . . .[18]

Christian Consciousness and the Experience of Advaita

We have confronted the experience of *advaita* with the human consciousness of Jesus himself. Now we shall briefly compare it with the religious awareness of the Christian. This will require a short description of the Christian experience of God and identification of its specific character.

The specificity of the Christian experience of God resides in the experience of the mediation of Jesus Christ.[19] The proposition that the human Jesus is the sole mediator between God and humankind (cf. 1 Tim. 2:5), not merely an intermediary, means in theology that divinity and humanity have become so inseparably united in him that in his human condition we encounter very God: "Who has seen me, has seen the Father" (see John 14:9). The Christian lives the experience of God not only *by* but *in* the human condition of Jesus, whose face is the human face of God.

When we attempt to describe this same reality from the standpoint of subjective awareness, we must say that in the Christian the experience of God consists in sharing the religious consciousness of Jesus Christ himself, and concretely, his consciousness of his divine filiation. Just as Jesus' own religious consciousness was essentially filial, so is it with that of the Christian. Just as Jesus was entirely centered on the Father, so are we called to be, for we have received from him a spirit of sonship in which we cry out: "Abba, Father" (cf. Rom. 8:15).[20] The New Testament evinces beyond a doubt that Christians of the apostolic era addressed God, the Father of Jesus, using the term of familiarity employed by Jesus himself. Thus they expressed their conviction of having entered with him into a new and intimate filial relationship with God. To participate in Jesus' religious experience is to have a conscious part in his filiation vis-à-vis the Father: "The proof that you are sons is that God has sent the Spirit of his Son into our hearts, who cries: 'Abba! Father' " (see Gal. 4:6).

This participation in the divine filiation of Jesus constitutes such an enormous claim that, when we reflect upon it, we are tempted to reduce it to a pious metaphor. Theology has developed distinctions here which, partially necessary and useful though they be, have often contributed to the weakening of this Christian truth. Is one who lives under the regime of faith, who is subject to the law of the flesh, in any position to aspire to a share in Jesus' divine filiation? All attempts to attenuate the reality of the Christian experience have their origin in a "high christology" inclined to underestimate the authentic humanity of Jesus and the depth of his identification with our earthly condition. If Jesus' filiation seems beyond our reach, it is because Jesus himself has become a stranger to us. It is urgent, therefore, to recover the meaning of Jesus' true humanity and likeness to us. Jesus lived his divine filiation in our human situation, thereby showing in his own existence that the divine filiation is not beyond the possibilities of our condition. In particular, he lived his divine filiation as a commitment of himself that did not exclude, but rather comported, the risk—and the certitude—of faith.[21] In him, we learn to live our own faith commitment, by prolonging, as it were, his attitude of Son. This has been well stated by Jacques Guillet, who writes:

> This perfect intimacy of Jesus and his Father, this total transparency, this absolute certitude of not being able to be separated from the Father by anything whatsoever, this secret that constitutes the Son and belongs but to him—behold, he lives it before us, not to display it to our eyes as an inaccessible marvel, but to call us to share it. He does not call us from without, he does not invite us to change worlds and existences. In inviting us to place ourselves in our Father's hands, he is proposing to us to reproduce, in our existence, the manner that he has, which belongs to none but him, of holding everything from his Father, of feeding on him; he reveals to us that his fidelity and joy of only Son can be ours.[22]

For the Christian, this conscious participation in the very filiation of Jesus constitutes an ideal toward which one must grow. Did not Jesus himself know growth in his own filial consciousness? But what relationship is there between the religious consciousness of the Christian and the experience of *advaita*? Without any doubt, the two experiences comport differences; and syncretistic attempts to suppress or reduce these differences would be futile and vain. But equally ill-inspired is the opposite tendency, which regards the two experiences as contradictory and mutually exclusive, since the one would imply "monism" and the other (the Christian) "dualism." The truth is that—as religious experiences—neither the one nor the other can be denied; both must be welcomed and received with openness and humility. It is possible, furthermore, to show that certain alleged contradictions proceed from more or less seriously imprecise interpretations.

As for the divine filiation of the Christian, it is a faulty interpretation to reduce it to a purely adoptive filiation, a sort of juridical fiction according to which God deigns to regard us as his children although we are not. According to such a conception, the Christian's divine filiation retains no point of contact with the divine filiation of Jesus, nor our spiritual experience with that of Jesus himself. Thus, any participation in Jesus' divine filiation being lost, there remains for *advaita* no entryway into the Christian experience.

If, on the contrary, Jesus' religious experience is—as has been shown above—his human awareness of being one with the Father, and if the Christian is called to share this consciousness, then *advaita* has its place in the Christian's experience as in that of Jesus himself: The Christian participates in Jesus' experience of his *advaita* with the Father. And this is Christian *advaita*.

This experience of *advaita* doubtless differs from that of the sages of the *Upanishads*. It restores to the Absolute a communion value, and to the human self the inalienable consistency of personhood. But Christian *advaita*, for its part, learns from the religious experience of the Hindu sages—and from God's self-manifestation to them—that communion in divinity and with the divine cannot be conceived only according to a finite model. While the Christian, in Jesus, says "Thou" to the Father, contact with the *Brahman-atman* experience of the Hindu sages helps that Christian realize that the Father is also the "ground of being," the Self at the center of the created self. After all, God's self-revelation occurs not only in history, but also in the "cave of the heart." And while, in Jesus Christ, God has truly become our Parent, that God remains for us the one "who is," while we are those who "are not." Jesus Christ, Son of the Father, is the fullness of the divine revelation inasmuch as, in him, all divine revelation finds its proper accomplishment—including plenitude, for it is written: "I am come not to abolish, but to fulfill" (see Matt. 5:17).

3

Swami Abhishiktananda, or the Spiritual Experience of a Hindu-Christian Monk

In our very first chapter, we encountered a "Hindu-Christian monk" in the person of Brahmabandhab Upadhyaya, who flourished at the turn of the twentieth century. The work of this pioneer, which was compromised by political involvement that earned him a falling from grace with church authorities, was taken up and carried forward in the middle of the twentieth century by a French Benedictine monk by the name of Henri Le Saux. Both monks share an identical inspiration. In the mind of them both, in order to be presented to India, the Christian mystery must be rethought in the religious tradition of India. It must be clothed in thought patterns drawn from the Indian tradition. For both, this endeavor is feasible only in an authentically Indian monastic context. There must be Hindu-Christian monks, then.

The expression *Hindu-Christian*, however, had different meanings for Upadhyaya and Le Saux. For Upadhyaya, being a Hindu was primarily a matter of culture and social organization, rather than religious faith. To be a Hindu-Christian consisted in the "inculturation" of the Christian message, which—in theory, at least—should encounter no insurmountable obstacle. For Henri Le Saux, however, the expression took on a deeper meaning from the outset. It was not enough to assimilate Indian cultural elements in the expression and celebration of the Christian mystery. Rather, one must have an interior experience of the encounter of the religious experience of both traditions and allow them to react upon each other in one's own person, while remaining completely open to what might be produced by the shock of an encounter which surely had never before taken place at the necessary and intended depth. From the very start, then—and this will be enough to justify the study we devote to him here[1]—Henri Le

Saux appears as a model of the "intrareligious dialogue" whose theory we propose to develop later in this book.

Let us cite a second consideration that makes a study of the religious experience of Abhishiktananda—the name Le Saux adopted as an Indian monk, or *sannyasi*—particularly timely and fruitful today. The works he published during his lifetime were incomplete; nor did they entirely reveal his secret. Furthermore, numerous writings of his, unpublished during his lifetime, have become the object of important publishing projects in recent years.[2] His posthumous writings allow us to grasp his thought in depth and discover the interior combat he waged in the deepest recesses of his soul with the ebb and flow of the encounter between two seemingly irreconcilable religious traditions. Such an encounter is of singular interest for our subject, and Abhishiktananda furnishes us with a concrete instance of it that may be unique.

When Henri Le Saux (1910–1973) arrived in India in 1948, he was answering a secret call that he had felt for years. Summoned to India by Père Jules Monchanin, he decided to respond. Together the two would found an Indian monastery and welcome, in the framework of Christian monasticism, the best of what India had to offer in the way of contemplation and renunciation. The venture was based on a twin conviction: that the church would be truly present in India, that mystical land, only if its contemplative and monastic dimension were to be solidly established there; and that it would become Indian (and hence catholic) only by way of a Christian monastic assimilation of the ceaseless quest for the Absolute that characterizes the religious tradition of India. There was more to be assimilated here than a way of life adapted to circumstances and a cultural ambience: One must also allow oneself to be impregnated with the religious experience of the *sannyasi*, the Indian monks.

However, this was in 1948, fifteen years before the Second Vatican Council. It is important to realize this in order to grasp the scope of the experiment into which Henri Le Saux was about to plunge. His endeavor would be on the cutting edge of the preconciliar ecumenical movement. The Catholic climate was opening, but with great restraint. There was no liturgical movement in India; still less did the church have any thought of a liturgical adaptation to the culture of the country. To be sure, Christian theology strove to encounter the religious thought of Hinduism, but this encounter remained merely notional and was often limited to a comparative study on the conceptual level. Interreligious dialogue, if indeed it existed in those days, more often than not consisted of monologues delivered by the deaf. It had no radication in religious experience. That it might be possible, indeed necessary, to enter into our neighbor's religious experience for the sake of a fertile contact on the level of mutual experience would scarcely have seemed conceivable.

In a like climate, the concrete possibilities of an Indian-Christian monasticism threatened to be very limited. Doubtless one might adopt external forms. One could also discuss theology and undertake to switch the received Western terminology of Christian dogma into that of *advaita*. Thus one could perhaps make some contribution to the verbal transposition of the Christian message into Indian culture. But Christian monks would feel no shock waves from the mystical experience of the Hindu monks. Unconsciously, one would continue to be ruled by the stout conviction that one was already in possession of the truth and the only question was how to present that truth appropriately.

Abhishiktananda was not long in seeing things otherwise, and here he is surely a great precursor. From his first years in India, he perceived his task as that of penetrating the religious experience of India and allowing himself to be conducted by it. He shouldered none of the encumbrances of a theory of interreligious dialogue. He did not determine the aprioristic conditions to be imposed on such a dialogue in the name of his Christian faith. No, he wanted this dialogue to be true, whole, and based on personal experience. He wished to see for himself. His attitude rested on an unshakable conviction that truth is to be accepted from whatever quarter it comes; it is truth that possesses us, and not we who possess truth; and the God whose self-revelation comes to us along different paths is incapable of self-contradiction from path to path. Authentic experiences, however diverse, must be reconcilable. It is a matter of experiencing all of this interiorly and then to be able to show it to others. The church must dare this encounter and allow itself to be enriched by its contribution.

HINDU-CHRISTIAN MONK

It is in this sense that we must understand the profound experiences, often very disconcerting, to which Abhishiktananda submitted almost from the moment of his arrival in India, and in singular fashion during the early 1950s. He visited Tiruvannamalai as early as January 1949, and there made the acquaintance of that excellent sage Sri Ramana Maharshi, regarded by many as the modern saint of Hinduism. The visit was a short one, but it marked him, and Abhishiktananda gives an account of it in his *The Secret of Arunachala*.[3]

He returned to Tiruvannamalai several months later, and this time he spent a week there. The impression made on him by the Maharshi deepened, and through him, he also discovered the secret of the holy mount of Arunachala. Subsequently, the death (*mahasamadhi*) of Sri Ramana in April 1950 interrupted the visits for a time, but soon they resumed. At the close of 1951, Abhishiktananda found himself once more at Arunachala, where he explored the holy places, the grottoes where the sages meditated in silence. In 1952 he spent five months there, moving from grotto to grotto, a Christian hermit among the Hindu hermits. He was there for two more two-month stays in 1953 and for intermittent stays in 1954. His last visit to Tiruvannamalai took place in December 1955, but this end marked the beginning of a new experience: Abhishiktananda made the acquaintance of Swami Gnanananda, who soon became his *guru*. Early in 1956 he spent three weeks at Tirukoyilur, at the foot of this *guru*, whose teaching he received. He recounted this teaching in *Guru and Disciple*,[4] and saw in it an indispensable element of his initiation to Hindu mysticism which Sri Ramana, too soon gone, had no time to impart to him. Late that same year, he underwent an even more crucial experience: a thirty-two-day retreat at the Mauna Mandir of Kumbakonam.

We cannot here describe these overpowering experiences. One must read them in the words of Henri Le Saux himself. They had to be mentioned, however, or our undertaking here would be purposeless. For long months and years, then, Abhishiktananda frequented Hindu monasticism. He encountered Hinduism on the level of its rites, piercing to the heart of the temples of stone; he encountered it in the hearts of the hermits and *sadhu* (itinerant monks) in quest of the Absolute. Even more, he saw it at work in authentic Hindu mystics, whose teaching he assimilated. A deep conviction took root in him that there was a call addressed to him there, and he ceaselessly responded to it. Thus he let himself be drawn into the Hindu mystical experience of whose authenticity he had such a mighty presentiment. He owed this to his personal vocation, which he conceived as that of a Hindu-Christian monk. He owed it to the church, as well, which could accomplish its mission in India only if it encountered India at these same depths.

Consequently, the young monastic foundation of Shantivanam, as originally conceived, now seemed to correspond only very imperfectly to what Abhishiktananda felt would surely be necessary. One must read in his *Journal intime*, which he began when he arrived in India, of his sense of unreality each time he returned to the new foundation from the visits recalled above, all of them marked with such deep experiences. The holy mount, that place of the discovery of the Absolute in the "cave of the heart," never ceased to call him. There is his true abode.

In the monastery, he felt diminished. No outward adaptation, whether of manner of life, of liturgy, or even of theological discourse and dialogue on the level of concepts, provided a basis for the authentic encounter of Christianity and Hinduism. Abhishiktananda had to go further and fuse both experiences within himself, that from their shock a deeper light might gleam. This is the task of the Hindu-Christian monk.

The Hindu experience imposes radical demands on the Christian monk, especially in two distinct but inseparable dimensions. First, the most complete renunciation and genuine acosmism, having its Christian equal only in the Fathers of the desert, is a condition *sine qua non* for all authentic spiritual fulfillment here: The Hindu monk is essentially an itinerant. Second, and primarily, a total self-emptying is absolutely required for a true awakening to the Absolute. It is to this void and this awakening that Abhishiktananda was drawn by the wisdom of the Hindus.

HINDU MYSTICISM AND CHRISTIAN MYSTERY:
THE INNER ENCOUNTER

Here we touch on what will now become Abhishiktananda's unabating quest: the *advaita* experience and its relation to the Christian experience. The first is the great discovery of the 1950s. Our Hindu-Christian monk steeped himself in it, in all of its absorption and all of its crucifixion. Not that he was without fear of its ever-renewed demands and never-achieved limits. One must always go further, cross beyond, strive for the "Other Shore." But there was also joy—an immense joy, invading him to the extent that he lent himself to it and allowed himself to be drawn by it. Is this the experience of which the Christian mystics have spoken and written? It is at least akin to it: Both are in themselves ineffable, beyond words and concepts. However, is not the experience of *advaita* still more radical than its Christian counterpart, if it is really the awareness of the Absolute itself translated into a poor, reflected gleam in the ephemeral consciousness of my phenomenal self—a reflection that denies itself in the very act of self-expression, in the awakening of authentic awareness?

At all events, we shall not be surprised to find that all of Abhishiktananda's descriptions of the *advaita* experience, of its very nature indefinable, are paradoxical. The One-without-a-second (*Ekam advitiyam*) cannot be pronounced without being betrayed. The *Aham brahmasmi*—the "I am *Brahman*"—its necessary and sole valid enunciation, is only true at the level of the experience that it reports without conveying. Here and there among his writings, and particularly as the days go by, in his *Journal intime*,[5] we find various approximations of the *advaita* experience; but these are intended to suggest rather than to describe. Can even the *guru* claim to do more than set the disciple on the right path? Between the communicated teaching and the actual experience a chasm yawns, untraversed by any but whom the Beyond will lead.

We have sketched an approximative description above, relying on a quotation from Abhishiktananda (see chapter two). Another passage (an unpublished one Abhishiktananda composed during a visit to Gangotri, at the source of the Ganges, and later corrected) describes its content in powerful and graphic terms:

There is no room in me for God and myself at once. If there is God, I am not; if there is I, how might God be? Behold the dilemma of man, who either must disappear, or God must disappear.

There is but You in the depths of me, You in the depths of all. You who regard me, who summon me, who grant me being by calling me You, by making me your partner, other from You and yet inseparable, *akhanda, advaita* from you. I am only in this You that you utter to me. I am the one you eternally call throughout all the moments of time, all the movements of things, all the expansion of being. I am the one who in everything receive your call. I am the one to whom, in whom, You crown your deed of manifestation and who return it to You. I am the one to whom You utter yourself, the one in whom You utter yourself.

I am the echo of You, the return to you of all "that." I am but this return. This OM[6] in which You utter yourself to me, through all, You utter me to You, you utter me to myself—it is the very OM that wells up from me, in which I utter You. For who am I, if I am, but You? For there is but You who are. If I am, I can be but You. Not this You that I would utter to you in speaking of myself, but I am the You that You speak, to me. Until you have called me "you," I am not; You are not. For if I am not, for me You are not; and so long as, for me, You are not, how should I know You?

To call me, to regard me, to cause my regard to be born and to surge toward You, You take all forms, *sarvarupa*. You who are the Formless, *arupa, alinga*. All that is when You call me. All that is in Your call alone. It is from the bosom of all that you cry to me: "You." From the mountain, the river, the forest, from the trees that jut up from the summit of a sheer cliff, from every man I meet, from every occurrence.

On the route of the pilgrimage, every encounter is a grace, causing the OM to surge from two hearts: call and response are no longer distinguishable. Beyond me, and you, who are distinguishable, the OM of *purnam* [plenitude] that is the call to oneself, to the depths of oneself, from the depths of oneself. From the depths of You, You call me to the depths of You. From the depths of me, I answer you, in the depths of You. What are the depths of me, then, but the depths of You?

OM! All is there. All that is, has been, will be. All that is I, You, He, and all that is beyond the three times and the three persons. Here is the profoundest mystery of the "Three." Not apart from them, but in their remotest depths. Each in the deepest bosom of the other. Never a pure You. The You that delivers the Me. *Purnam*.

In his little book on prayer, characteristically entitled *Eveil à soi—éveil à Dieu*, "Awakening to Self, Awakening to God," Abhishiktananda describes the spiritual experience of the soul in terms far more simple and jejune, as through a lengthy pilgrimage to the depths of the self it discovers, ever more profoundly, the very abyss of God. Despite the frugality of expression, the purport is the same. Abhishiktananda writes, for example:

Nothing can . . . content [the soul] apart from God in himself. Yet it is incapable of attaining to this until it has become willing to pass beyond itself and to plunge and be lost in the very abyss of God. Then it is that it understands that silence is the loftiest and truest praise: *Silentium tibi laus.* [The soul] itself is now but silence, a silence to which it has been introduced by recollection in its remotest depths and the calming of its inner activity, but a silence that the Spirit now causes to ring with the echo of the eternal Word, a silence all expectancy, a simple regard toward the One who is there, simple attention, simple awakening.[7]

Thus Abhishiktananda allowed himself to sink down into this experience of the Absolute. It became more and more absorbing, imposing upon him, over and above the outer renunciations of his hermitlike life, the supreme renouncement of himself, and over and above that, the still more radical renouncement of the Divine "You" encountered in prayer. He observed in his diaries that night invades the soul that can no longer address its God in prayer as an I addresses a Thou. Now its whole previous way of living its relationship with God lies naked at its feet, and with it, the whole church tradition of liturgy and prayer. Not that he abandoned that tradition, and we must emphasize this to preclude any misunderstanding. During these years of discovery of *advaita* and throughout the years to follow, Abhishiktananda remained scrupulously faithful to the celebration of the Eucharist and to his breviary. Incidents reported in the *Journal intime* leave nothing to be desired by way of evidence; indeed, we may occasionally feel like smiling at his delicacy of conscience. And yet, over and above the rites and the psalms, beyond an interpersonal discourse with God, there is the "Other Shore," the "I am." There alone is total truth.

Abhishiktananda accustomed himself to live, as it were, on these two levels. Indeed, he was strangely at ease on both. It would be a serious mistake to think that *advaita*, with all of the renunciations and negations it implies, renders one less human. *Advaita* is not monism; neither is it acosmism. But the world of rites and discourse is not absolute. It is sheer reflection. The sage embraces both, each in its own order.

Here we touch on Abhishiktananda's authentic message, as we gather it from various parts of his writings. A lived *advaita* is the key. He did not deny his experience of it. True, he constantly questioned himself on this point. But having read of his experience above, can we possibly be surprised at this? While he nevertheless questioned its truth, in the course of the first years, as the *Journal intime* once more attests, his certitude in its regard only increased over the years, finally to be expressed altogether unambiguously when he noted, not unenthusiastically: "The experience of the *Upanishads* is true—*I know!*"[8]

While Abhishiktananda was always able to combine in his concrete life the two planes on which he would henceforth move, it is no less true that, on the level of mental synthesis, this reconciliation did not cease to be a problem for him almost to the end. It is not an exaggeration or derogatory to say that his whole life was marked by the quest for a synthesis—ever elusive, never accomplished—save in the "discovery of the Grail" that swept him off.

Only the fainthearted will be scandalized at these hesitations. We must rather admire the total self-honesty with which the drama—the word is not too strong—is lived over the course of the *Journal intime*. This is Abhishiktananda's greatness. And it still has an important message for an Indian Christianity in quest of interreligious dialogue. Abhishiktananda's spiritual adventure is his theological work.

This is not the place to go into the striking parallel, of very different context and material, of Teilhard de Chardin. He, too, knew a spiritual combat. He, too, had set out on an intense quest for a synthesis between what he called his faith in the world and his Christian faith. He, too, was able to maintain both, though their intellectual synthesis remained imperfect. Theology has not ceased to derive inspiration from Teilhard. It still has need of prophets in the new pathways of its involvement today. Abhishiktananda is one of those prophets.

ADVAITA CHALLENGES THE CHRISTIAN MYSTERY

The questions posed to Abhishiktananda by the *advaita* experience must not be underrated. One must not pretend that they are not there. Rather, one must expose them to the light in order to be able to follow Abhishiktananda in the answers he proposes.

In general terms, the question is that of the value of the traditional representations of God, the world, and the human being. Do the Christian Trinity, the Christian concept of creation, and the Christian view of the human being in dialogue with God stand up against *advaita*? Does history actually have the density that Christianity attributes to it? And what becomes of the Jesus Christ event, considered as a total engagement of God in human history? Has not Christian dogma been unduly absolutized, whereas in reality, when all is said and done, it is only relative?

I have used the word *drama*, and I have done so advisedly. It is indeed an interior drama that Abhishiktananda lived for the nearly twenty-five years that he sought to discover the relationship of his two experiences, Hindu and Christian. Few of his friends suspected it, such was his good humor and his profound conviction that he had taken the path that he must.

But the *Journal intime* reveals the drama in all its stark reality. We sense its utter keenness at the end of 1956, the time of the retreat experience at the Mauna Mandir. A fear that these two experiences may be irreconcilable is everywhere in the diary. There Abhishiktananda tells of his "ocean of anguish, wherever I turn."[9] A year later the solution still seems far off: "I cannot be a Hindu and Christian at the same time, nor can I be either simply a Hindu or simply a Christian."[10] We cannot follow all of the notations where now the exaltation of *advaita*, now the fear that it is a "mirage," now a nostalgia for the Christian mystery, now a radical questioning of the same, appear by turns. What we must say is that an inner serenity gradually established itself. This serenity was finally complete, it seems, in the last years. Abhishiktananda then resolved to accept a life of irresoluble tension transcending theoretical reconciliations. He writes: "It is still best, I think, to hold, even in extreme tension, these two forms of a single 'faith,' until the dawn appears."[11] He explains more at length to a fellow-religious in two later letters.

No wish to be a theologian. The only thing I try to do is turn souls inward, where every question is moot—to the primordial silence of the Father, or to the consuming silence of the Spirit, where the Verbum dawns, and whither it leads.[12]

Less and less do I think that the moment has come for discovering concepts calculated to facilitate an exchange of experience between East and West. . . . I think that this is the moment simply to allow ourselves to be invaded by the experience—by the two experiences, if you will—and also, with those who will share in this unsettling experience, to secure the foundations of a later, intellectual dialogue. . . . In the West, one may begin with the God/man polarity: here, the experience of the I, of the Self, is so full of mystery—this mystery in God—that it is impossible to project God before oneself, if I may put it that way, either to speak of him or to speak for him. And yet, the prophetical experience of the face-to-face is true as well. Jesus had the living experience of both. I can't explain it, but that's the way it is. And I know, in confidence, the anguish of true Christian contemplatives when the "I" has vanished by which they had up until then addressed God. I am even uneasy about introducing the *Upanishads* to those who are capable of this total experience. . . . The essential problem between East and West, it seems to me, is that of the concept-*eidos* and the existential intuition. What we so terribly need now are Christian contemplatives who are willing to go this way. They alone can help our young theologians, who are discovering, or will be discovering, this same problem more and more, but from its intellectual aspect. It is the Spirit's to breathe and blow—and ours to let ourselves be blown away.[13]

The Christian *eidos* continues to have a "visceral attachment" for him, as he still notes late in 1970.[14] And yet there remains the "fundamental anguish of no longer being able to get one's bearings in a faith that is part of one's guts!"[15] The awaited dawn is long delayed. Only at the end of the *Journal intime*, on the pages where he reports the "marvelous spiritual adventure" of the "great week"—that of the heart attack on the street in

Rishikesh (July 14, 1973) — and of the days that followed, does he finally note:

> After several days, it finally came to me, like the marvelous solution of an equation: I have found the Grail. And I say this, I write it, to anyone who can grasp the image. At bottom, the quest for the Grail is but the quest for Self. It is a unique quest, signified by all the myths and symbols. Through all, one seeks Self. And on this quest we scamper everywhere, while the Grail is right here. We need only open our eyes. And we have discovered the Grail in its ultimate truth.[16]

There seems to be no doubt that this "solution of an equation" has reference to the setting in order of the "two forms of a single 'faith'" mentioned above. Abhishiktananda does not explain himself fully on this point. But the text cited earlier authorizes us to say that the light dawned for him at the very heart of the ultimate experience that was to sweep him off. We must also keep in mind that he understands the heart attack itself in terms of a spiritual experience so intense that his body can no longer resist it.

However this may be, what is clear is that the relationship between the advaitine experience and the Christian experience, such as Abhishiktananda propounds it over the years, is always of a provisional nature. It is important to realize this in undertaking any analysis of the various ways in which he conceived this relationship.

A first way of envisaging it is the one employed by Abhishiktananda in *Sagesse hindoue, mystique chrétienne*.[17] The presiding note here seems to be that of balance. *Advaita* and Christian Trinity are harmonized. The Hindu experience and the Christian experience enrich each other profoundly. *Advaita* warns us that the Trinitarian relations infinitely transcend what we can conceive of them; the Christian Trinity, for its part, reveals the pluriform fullness of the One-without-a-second. Thus the Christian experience must pass by way of the crucible of the purifying experience of *advaita*. Abhishiktananda writes:

> As long as a man has not yet passed through the purifying realization of the non-duality of being, is he really able to say "Thou" to God? Will not his "Thou" addressed to God still correspond too closely with the "thou" that men say to each other, to be wholly the Thou of truth?[18]

One could think that here the task is accomplished. And to be sure, some will wish to stop with *Sagesse hindoue, mystique chrétienne* and venture no further. After all, it is a security-inspiring book. The Christian experience remains intact, complete with its biblical and traditional formulas. The Trinity displays *advaita*, while *advaita* purifies our too gross conceptions of the Trinity. When all is said and done, the Christian experience prevails.

Yet we must recognize that, even before this book was written (it was published in 1965), currents of thought are at work in Abhishiktananda that will forbid him to settle comfortably into this conclusion. These same currents will cause him to say later that *Sagesse* was but a step along the way. "I should no longer write the book as it is; I was still too enslaved to Greek concepts," he writes in the above-cited letter to a friend.[19] And again: "Unrepentant Greek that I was, I was too intent on intellectualizing the mystery—on conceptualizing India. *Sagesse* seems so passé to me now— with all theology and all the gnoses."[20] Other letters bear the same witness. So do numerous reflections in the *Journal intime*.

He is haunted by the question of the validity, vis-à-vis *advaita*, of concepts, biblical as well as Greek, through which the Christian experience is expressed. More broadly still, it is the entire phenomenal plane, with its concepts and dogmas, rites and liturgy, worship and Eucharistic sacrifice, that is at stake. Does not all this belong to the domain of the *nama rupa* (names and forms), surely useful and indispensable on this level, but just as surely to be transcended in the awakening to the Self? True, Hinduism itself knows its *nama rupa*; indeed, it multiplies them indefinitely. It, too, is subject to transcendence. On the phenomenal plane, which he calls the plane of myth, Abhishiktananda does not hesitate to acknowledge the superiority of Christianity. Christian myth wins out over Hindu myth. However, Hindu tradition wins over Christian tradition in its consciousness of the essential relativity of all religious myth, while Christianity tends to absolutize it into an ultimate truth. One must embrace Hindu tradition in its transcendence of myth, in the Upanishadic experience of the Self. It need not be embraced—and let us be perfectly clear about this—in the *advaita* of the theologians, of Shankara, for example, whose conceptual apparatus and the monistic interpretation of which this theology is the vehicle, themselves belong to the *nama rupa*, just as, for that matter, does Christian theology, with its essential dualism. It is to the pure experience of the *advaita* revealed in the *Upanishads* that one must awaken—beyond all theology, Vedantine as well as Judeo-Christian. Between these two theologies, we must recognize that a brutal, irreducible opposition prevails. One particularly clear note in the *Journal intime* puts it as follows:

[Between] Christianity and *advaita*, neither opposition nor incompatibility. Two different planes. *Advaita* is opposed to nothing whatsoever. It is not a philosophy, but an existential *anubhava* [experience]. The entire range of Christian formulae is valid in its own order, the order of *vyavahara* [manifestation, the provisional], not of *paramarthika* [level of the Absolute]. Surely the Christian *darsana* [philosophy] is opposed to the Vedantine *darsana*, but this is purely the doctrinal level. No formulation, not even that of *advaita* itself, can lay claim to being *paramarthika* [Absolute]. Christianity's historical transgression of its limits is another matter.[21]

But what occurs when, in order to encounter the *advaita* experience of the Upanishadic tradition, the Christian tradition dares to doff the burden of its Judeo-Hellenistic vesture—as indeed it must, if the encounter is to be fertile and contact established?

Abhishiktananda braves this fertile encounter of the mystery lived by either tradition, beyond concepts and myths. We must wonder, however, how the Christian mystery reacts to this project. At first blush, the essential Trinity seems to adapt to this stripping, and Abhishiktananda's written work will contain, after *Sagesse*, page after inspired page on the *advaita* of Father-Son-Spirit, less dependent on Greek concepts. A late note in the *Journal intime*, however, indicates the limits of this effort:

> The awakening to mystery has nothing to do with the dogmas of the Trinity, the Incarnation, the Redemption. . . . The whole Trinitarian edifice collapses. For it is still *nama rupa*. And all efforts to make *Brahma* = silence = *avyakta* = the Father coincide . . . remain on the level of *mythos-logos*. In fact, it is utterly clear that there is no way to list the Spirit in a Vedantine christology.
>
> The mystery of the Trinity is the expansion of a magnificent enunciation, *nama rupa*, of this intimate interior experience at once of oneness, of nonduality, and relation. It is the actualization of the eternity of my relationship with my brother man, etc.
>
> But trying to come up with a new Trinitarian theology only leads us down blind alleys. It is replacing *theos* with *theo-logia*, and confusing the notion of God with God.
>
> My whole *Sagesse* theme crumbles, and in this total crumbling—the awakening.[22]

However—and this is yet another problem—the Christian mystery seems indissolubly bound up to history. For the operation to be total, its conception of salvation in history, and salvation history, must itself be recognized to belong to the level of phenomenon and *nama rupa*: It is true enough, but only in its own order, that of the relative. It goes without saying that the difficulty is felt in all its trenchancy in function of the Jesus Christ event. A christology of pure experience must also doff its historical clothing. Not that the Jesus of history disappears or is inconsequential; but it is only an ephemeral, phenomenal manifestation of the real Christ of faith.

Abhishiktananda scrutinizes Jesus' religious psychology, his relationship to his Father and his divine consciousness, his *Abba* and his "I am." The former seems to him to be the expression of the latter in Jewish terms.

In Joannine terms, Jesus discovered that Yahweh's "I am" belonged to him. Or else the reverse: in the lightning-bolt of his "I am," he discovered the true, total, unimaginable sense of the name of Yahweh. To call God *Abba* is an equivalent of *advaita*, the basic experience, in Semitic terms.[23]

The experience of Jesus, then, is the fundamental experience of *advaita*. Now the question arises of just how Jesus is savior and universal Savior. An essay on "Jésus le Sauveur" attempts to work toward an answer.[24] The experience of Jesus is salvific in its paradigmatic value: It draws one to the depths, where every human being must come. In Jesus, the human being's salvation is revealed and manifested as consisting in the supreme realization of *advaita* that is the Upanishadic experience.

Thus the experience of Jesus must be part of a universal christology, which Abhishiktananda made the priority concern of his last years. We see this in the last part of the *Journal intime*. How is one to understand the unicity of Jesus Christ?

Christianity is a *symbol*—probably the most marvelous symbol there is—for the emergence into consciousness of the mystery lying in the depths of the heart of human beings and constituting them. But one must accept—from the viewpoint of the Spirit—that it is all symbol (which does not mean not true): the eternal generation, the descent in time, the resurrection, the ascension, the outpouring of the Spirit. In the symbolical system of Christianity, the elements of this symbol can be but *unique*. The unicity of the Incarnation is part of the Christian *symbol*. The reality unquestionably overflows the symbol; in its own order, however, the symbol, which is not imprisoned in its sign, represents the *whole* reality nonetheless. . . . The unicity of Christ is of a transcendental order.[25]

"The unicity of the Incarnation is a false problem."[26] Then what meaning is left to Jesus of Nazareth?

Willy-nilly, I am profoundly attached to Christ Jesus, and hence to ecclesial *koinônia*. It is in him that "mystery" has discovered itself to me since my awakening to myself and to the world. It is under his *image*, his *symbol*, that I know God, and that I know myself and the world of men. At the time of my awakening to new depths in myself (of self, of *atman*)—here this symbol found itself wonderfully broadened. Christian theology had already discovered to me the eternity of the mystery of Jesus, *in sinu Patris*. Later, India revealed to me the cosmic whole of this mystery—this total *vyakti*, revelation, in which the Judean revelation is inserted. The immense Christ, higher than the heavens, is also infinitely near. . . . For that matter, I recognize this mystery that I have always worshiped under the Christ symbol, under the myths of Narayana, Prajapati, Siva, Purusha, Krishna,

Rama, and so on: this same mystery. But for me, Jesus is my *Sadguru* [true Guru]. It is in him that God has appeared to me. It is in his *mirror* that I have recognized myself, worshiping him, loving, consecrating myself to, him. . . . Not Jesus the head and founder of a religion. That comes later. Jesus is the *guru* who proclaims the mystery.[27]

Elsewhere, the relationship of the cosmic Christ and the historical Jesus is considered once more:

The Jews reduced Jesus, the *Ben Adam*, to the Messiah of their salvation history, of their salvation. The Greeks made a divine descent of him—the descent to earth of their *Logos*. India, free of history, and especially, of historical particularity—this impossible "People of God"—and free of *logos* and *eidos*, as well, immediately seizes the universal mystery, the *Purusha* that, outside of all history and all *eidos*, appears *agre*: at the origin of all, at the origin of the cosmic all, and even at the origin of human awareness.

The notion of Messiah has diminished Jesus. Jesus is the manifestation of that original Mystery that the dualists call theandric, and the *brahmavidah* (knowers of the *Brahman*) the point of ignition between the *Brahman avyakta* (unmanifested *Brahman*) and the *Brahman* that "is attained in itself by itself."[28]

Any attempt at limitation, any reduction to Jesus of this mystery, is limitation and reduction of Jesus himself—who is so much greater— and, in this way only, so much more divine—in his *advaita* with all that is born of man and hence all that is born of God.

The problem of his uniqueness is a false problem, arising only in the context of the phenomenon, where one can add, subtract, and multiply. But Jesus came precisely to deliver man from all the knots of the heart.[29]

And again:

Christ loses nothing of his true greatness when he is delivered from the false grandeurs with which myths and theological reflection had overlaid him. Jesus is the wondrous epiphany of the mystery of Man, of the *Purusha*,[30] the mystery of every human being, as the Buddha was, and *Ramana*, and so many others. He is the mystery of the *Purusha* that seeks itself in the cosmos. His epiphany is powerfully marked by the time and place of his appearance in flesh.[31]

Finally, on the salvific act:

If we would have Christ's salvific act universal, then that salvific act cannot be sought in any *nama-rupa*: death, sacrifice, redemption, resurrection. . . . There is in truth but one act by which Jesus—every-man—passes to the Father (to use biblical language): the act of awakening. Once one awakes, by reason of the essential human connection it is with and in the name of all that one awakes.[32]

It was necessary to quote these texts at length—and we might well have cited many more—to bring out the cosmic christology toward which the *advaita* experience draws one, as well as the place the historical Jesus occupies there: the christology of the *Sat-Purusha*, according to the expression Abhishiktananda now adopts.[33] A long unfinished note, justly titled "Sat-Purusha" (February 2, 1973), takes it up again. It is a provisional, searching passage, and one should read it as such.[34]

ELEMENTS OF A CRITICAL EVALUATION

These texts, unfinished as they are in their thought and expression, nevertheless indicate the direction in which Abhishiktananda's thought seeks to articulate the relationship between the *advaita* experience and the Christian mystery. They also show that the nub of the problem is christology.

If we now wish to move, as we ought, from a rapid sketch of the development of Abhishiktananda's thought to a critical reflection on this thought, it will be very important to keep in mind its provisional character. True, our thinker has achieved certitude as to the validity of his *advaita* experience. The experience is its own verification. But he formally denies having organized it in thought or having enunciated a theology of the Hindu-Christian dialogue. For him, the *advaita* experience is inexpressible by definition.

As for theology, we have seen texts above in which he formally expresses his reservations in its regard. Doubtless he hoped that there would be a theology of the dialogue someday. But this was not his calling; and at all events, the undertaking would have been premature, as the present hour belonged to experience—all the more so in that theological discourse, theological discussion, seemed vain to him. While he lent himself to it in all good humor in circles of friends—the present writer saw this time and again—ultimately it was without any expectations. After all, he thought, you either take your position on the level of experience—and then what is there to say?—or you take your position on the level of the phenomenon, and then whatever you say about it is ultimately vain.

Nowhere has Abhishiktananda fashioned a theological synthesis of his Hindu-Christian experience. He was content with living it and reflecting on it, facing all the questions it raised in his mind and seeking for them, in a direction that becomes more and more the only direction, answers that are constantly revised, never completed. The texts available to us today vary a great deal and actually belong to different periods and genres. In perusing them, however, we notice that those that date from the first years, those marked by the great experiences we have recalled above, already bear, in germ, the theological problems that will be posed later in more explicit fashion. The theological essays of the last years, on the other hand, attempt — as the author himself assures us — to solve the problems that have been posed.[35] It is here, then, that theologians will wish to pause and formulate certain questions of their own.

Furthermore, we must formulate these questions in the new context in which the author himself seeks to resolve them — quite a different context from that in which he himself first surmised them. We have already spoken of the straitened atmosphere of his beginnings. In such an ambience, the profound experiences to which he delivered himself could not have but aroused suspicions. Even close friends were overcome with incomprehension. The climate of the last years, that of the theological essays, is quite different.

True, Abhishiktananda placed very little confidence in theology, but he was very well informed in its regard. He was invited to take part in meetings and conferences, not only monastic but theological. He was abreast of the theological discussions on the other religions in relation to Christianity, and on interreligious dialogue. He knew — and rejoiced — that theologians themselves had developed since the council, that the theory of the "fulfillment" of the religious traditions of humanity in the Christian mystery had been replaced by that of the "presence of the mystery of Jesus Christ" in the various traditions. This was a step that he appreciated, although he thought that there was a long way left to be traversed. He was abreast of the recent christological discussions in the West concerning the Jesus of history and the Christ of faith, the consciousness of Jesus and the various christologies of the New Testament, the relativity of scriptural and dogmatic expression, the unicity and divinity of Christ. He followed these debates — they were the same debates — more particularly in an Indian milieu, where, in a broader context, they became even more pressing. But he followed them in the terms and measures of his own experience, concerned as he was to preclude all apriorism and narrow-mindedness, even that of the faith in its traditional expression. He was also convinced that the experiments in adaptation, theological or liturgical, in which the church in India was currently engaged, were cheap and superficial: They failed to transpire on the level of the religious experience of India.

The climate was one of renewal, but it was a climate in which Abhishiktananda continued to feel hemmed in. The dialogue that he had to carry on, while becoming more serene, was no less intense. Among the theological questions of which it was composed, we should like to mention some of the more urgent ones. They were often raised verbally with Abhishiktananda himself, and they are the ones that he himself raised in his theological essays.

A first question refers to the religious experience itself, in its various forms, as an expression of divine revelation. Faith is a matter of experience;

of this we may be perfectly sure. The same God in whom there is no contradiction is revealed in various ways in the various religious traditions. The distinction, classic today, between mystical and prophetical religions, testifies to this. The God of a self-revelation in the deep experience of oneself is also the God who intervenes in history. Neither of these divine paths can be left out of account, leaving the other to triumph alone. Nor can the first path be reduced to the dimensions of a human search for God, to which only the second would convey a divine response.

We may be equally sure that religious experience is the starting point of theology. It remains to ask, however, whether there is not a necessary relationship between religious experience and conceptual enunciation. What does it mean for a human being to have an experience entirely beyond concepts? The question is not new, and it has often been posed in Christian tradition. It has been admitted that, in its highest degrees, the mystical experience introduces its subject into the very self-knowledge of God, and that the experience will be beyond words. The Christian mystics have perceived the *inadequatio* of the Trinitarian concepts, of creation, and of grace, to the realities they respectively represent. While taking refuge in apophaticism, however, they have not altogether emancipated themselves from concepts, of whose operative value and necessary function they remain conscious. Here they have taken their cue from the analogy of being, more as an intuition than as a theory, which remained part and parcel of their very experience. The *advaita* experience, for its part, is called ineffable in an even higher degree, and basically repudiates the analogy of being, which it calls dualistic, replacing it with the not-two. It is literally beyond words, being no longer able to express itself even to itself. The "I am" that alone enunciates it is itself only an improper expression.

The question, then, is that of the relationship between experience and enunciation. Is there a human experience that would be totally emancipated from all conceptual apparatus? Or is there not rather a necessary interaction between experience and concepts, even if the latter necessarily report and express the former only in a deficient and inadequate way? Lived in such a different context than that in which Christian mysticism is expressed, the *advaita* experience seems, by that very fact, to be distinct from the Christian mystical experience. They are not interchangeable, and Abhishiktananda is doubtless right to reject any conceptual transposition as doomed to sterility.

But has he not, along the way, in his eagerness to show the provisional character of the words in which the one is expressed, unduly delivered the other from all apparatus? At stake is the validity, with respect to God, of the concepts whose vehicle is the Trinitarian revelation, although admittedly the mode of their realization transcends human understanding. Also at stake is the ontological density of human consciousness, which awakens to this revelation as to a gift received. Are we then to say that the *advaita* experience, in its ineffability, ultimately transcends the Trinitarian experience, which depends on concepts—as it is likewise, for that matter, beyond all conceptual development in a Hindu context? Or are we rather to admit that not even the *advaita* experience is exempt from an inevitable dependency on concepts, the irreducibility of their respective conceptual paraphernalia being explained by the different contexts from which they arise?

Abhishiktananda regards the conceptual vehicle of the Christian revelation as emerging from myth and culture, first Jewish, and then Greek. Here, however, distinctions are to be made. That Jesus' consciousness—the sole vehicle of the Trinitarian revelation—is framed in the context of the consciousness of Israel, and that this consciousness finds itself partially refashioned in a Greek context even in the New Testament, is surely beyond doubt. Jesus' consciousness, as it expresses itself, bears the mark of relativity. In all events it does not exhaust, nor can it exhaust, the divine consciousness.

Should we, and can we, however—and this is the second question—identify the consciousness of Jesus with the *advaita* experience, prescinding from the Semitic conceptual apparatus in which it is imperfectly expressed? To be sure, it is akin to it, in that it is a consciousness of nonduality with God. However, it seems to be distinguished from it in that the relativity of the concepts that express it is an irreducible component of it. The "I" of Jesus' evangelical pronouncements establishes at once his oneness with the Father and his distinction, no less real, from the "Thou" of the Father. Ultimately, this "I" is not that of the Father thinking himself in Jesus, with Jesus being lost in the Father. It is that of the Son, living, in a human consciousness, his unity with and his distinction from the Father. Rather than reducing Jesus' *Abba* to his "I am" and seeing the former as a Semitic expression of the latter, to be identified with the *advaita* experience, must we not admit that, in his own particular experience, the two are inseparable components of that experience? Doubtless we might then still translate Jesus' experience in terms of *Aham brahmasmi*—but not without a difference. Perhaps we ought even to say—paradoxically—that in Jesus this proposition finds its truest application, that it becomes literally true and acquires a new sense. It enunciates Jesus' oneness with his Father, which has its foundation beyond the human condition; more precisely, it expresses Jesus' personal awareness of belonging, with his Father, to the sphere of the divinity. As we have already suggested in chapter two, this human consciousness in Jesus of his personal communion with the Father in the *advaita* of divinity would then be the crown and fulfillment of the intuition of the Upanishadic seers, and at the same time resolve the antinomy that the *advaita* experience seems to leave unsurmounted between the values of absolute unity and personal communion. To be sure, one can and should think that, if Jesus had lived and revealed his own mystery in a land of Hindu culture rather than in a Jewish land, doubtless he would have expressed himself differently, as he would not have been burdened with Semitic concepts. But the way in which he expresses himself in a Jewish context does not, it seems, authorize us to think that the *advaita* experience as such, and without a new component, would have furnished him with an adequate expression of his own experience.

And so the christological question is posed—the third question that we should like to broach here. It is, we might say, the question everywhere debated: that of the Christ of faith and the Jesus of history. Let us notice, however, that in the present context it is posed in a new way. It is not the process leading from the faith of the primitive church to the Jesus Christ event that is in question. It is the comprehensive event itself and the density attributed to it despite its particularity. The approach is not that of historical criticism; it is a critique of history itself, it is the shock that occurs between timeless interiority and the divine intervention in the time of human beings.

The *advaita* experience acknowledges a mere relative value in history. It is certainly correct in doing so, if it is simply contrasting historical time with the eternity of God. However, if God is personally involved in human history, must we not say that this event acquires a universal value in the historical order? Surely it is thus that Christian faith has understood the Jesus Christ event, attributing to it at once a unique character and a cosmic scope. It has done so by professing that the Christic mystery is inseparable from the historical Jesus. Not that it has been blind to the particularity of the event. But it has intuited that historical particularity, when it is God's personal engagement in the human, has a decisive value. Thus it has refused to dissociate the mystery of Christ from the history of Jesus. Its total content has been neither Christ nor Jesus, but Jesus-the-Christ. And in this total event it has posited human beings' universal salvation.

The *advaita* experience and the radical relativity it imposes on history seem difficult to accommodate to this decisive historical value. That experience seems incapable of altogether assimilating either the density of the event, its unique character, or its universal signification. Here, without a doubt, is the sticking point of the encounter between the *advaita* experience and the Christian mystery, the latter professing the divine manifestation in the myth of history, the former God's personal involvement in salvation history.

We have already seen with what intensity Abhishiktananda experienced this purifying, nay, crucifying, but also simplifying and unifying encounter. Perhaps we better understand the anguish that possessed him then—whose traces, indeed, had not vanished even long after. In 1969, his *Journal intime* speaks of "the anguish that has pursued me since Arunachala, these sixteen years and more."[36] But we also better understand his high resolve, which never failed him, to "maintain, even in extreme tension, these two forms of a single 'faith,' until dawn appears." He beheld the first faint glimmers of that dawn in his last years. Day was gradually breaking. His radiance evinced it, although his writings are inadequate to give a complete account of it. He saw it grow through new spiritual impulses of the years 1971–1973. A few months before his death, he wrote:

> Joy abides, grows, deepens in the ever more intimate discovery of the essential. . . . The approaches are . . . intoxicating. They cut you off from everything, but they reveal everything, like the nights of Saint John of the Cross. Overleaping limits—night for the mental only, when it seeks to understand and report its categories of the Real. Heady wine, that you fear to share. It overthrows everything. . . . Here, in solitude without and within, the solitude of the Only, in the transcendence of all uttering and all thinking, you understand *eimi*, "I am"—the name under which Yahweh revealed himself. Then Easter becomes this awakening to nothing new, but to what is—to that reality that has neither origin nor end.[37]

That dawn, that awakening, burst forth at last, carrying off everything in its incoercible light. Here, through the "discovery of the Grail," was Easter, and the ultimate encounter.

TWO DIVERGENT INTERPRETATIONS

The literature devoted to Abhishiktananda's spiritual experience is still rather limited. Here we shall only note a few articles that have appeared on the subject.[38] And we shall choose two authors, among a number,[39] whose interpretations deserve special attention, although they take different paths, not to say opposite directions.

M. M. Davy, whose authority in the area of the mystical traditions, Western as well as Eastern, is well established, has published *Henri Le Saux: Abhishiktananda. Le passeur entre deux rives.*[40] Her book favors us with a very lively account of Abhishiktananda's spiritual experience and odyssey. Its subtitle, "Between Two Shores," suggests the constant pendulum swing between the two traditions, the determination to hold them together in unity, the ceaseless effort to combine them in spite of their apparent contradictions. The author unhesitatingly credits Abhishiktananda with a mysticism of the caliber of Meister Eckhart, with this difference, however: The Hindu-Christian monk reaches the same heights as the Rhenish master by way of the mediation of the experience of *advaita*. Davy's catalog of parallel elements is excellent: the same crucifying experience of successive purifications, the same ultimate arrival at final union and illumination. In this light, the theological problems raised by the experiences of the two mystics are in some sort transcended, at least in their own eyes, even if they remain for the theologian and interpreter. Davy scarcely pauses at these problems. She prefers to listen and to quote.

On the subject of the mystery of interiority, or the experience of the "depths," which unveils the mystery of the hidden God, Davy establishes from the outset a surprising parallel between Abhishiktananda and Meister Eckhart:

> Any comparison is ephemeral. Nonetheless, were we to compare Henri Le Saux with another Christian mystic, we should have to name Meister Eckhart. . . . The shock he provokes puts one off. The unusual frightens, the use of paradoxes disquiets, the stripping provokes a vertigo. The words, as well, of Henri Le Saux, become Swami Abhishiktananda, may occasionally surprise. But those who, seduced by the mystery of the within, set off down the path of silence, will find an elder brother, a fellow-traveller, a stimulating emulation.[41]

The parallel then becomes more explicit on the precise point of total immersion and sinking to the "depths," without which, both mystics agree, total illumination cannot be attained. Davy comments:

> There comes a moment when the important thing is to overcome all fear, all anxiety, and to take the plunge. Hence the need for an antecedent rupture with the various attachments, in order to be free to be totally engulfed in the bottomless depths. According to Eckhart, the movement by which the higher part of the soul attains its original depth (*grunt*) is comparable to a "breakthrough." The latter gives access to the nameless, modeless One. Until now, one has surmised this "breakthrough" in the offing. Suddenly it appears.
>
> The engulfing demands one give all, offer all, and also lose all, and consequently be totally deprived, poor, and naked. Citing a gospel text, *perdere animam suam*, Henri Le Saux adds: "Do not think to find it again, then. Your loss must be irreparable: no thread of any tie whatever must be retained, as you let yourself slip into the abyss" (*Journal intime*, November 8, 1953). Few human beings will encounter God. For they are very rare who, capable of plunging to their depths, will make trial of this adventure. But "until one has returned to this source within oneself, from which otherness itself is sprung, one has understood nothing of God—one only adores the idol that one has fashioned for oneself."[42]

Eckhart, in his own terminology, distinguished between God (*Got*), Trinitarian and personal, and the transpersonal divinity (*Gotheit*), the supraessence, absolute oneness, in which all distinction disappears, but which is the unique principle of the Trinitarian processions. The Deity is for him the absolute divine essence, beyond all determination and relation, of which nothing can be asserted, save that it is pure oneness. The Trinitarian God, of course, is the Deity, inasmuch as the latter, as if by superabundance, makes room for multiplicity and relation. The Trinitarian persons endlessly proceed from the divine essence and everlastingly flow into it once more. B. Barzel writes:

> His notion of the divine oneness is so radical and absolute that it entails ... his relativizing the Trinitarian processions, and positing the Deity beyond the Trinity, in a relation-less and mode-less One.[43]

While employing different terminology borrowed from the Hindu mystical tradition, Abhishiktananda's spiritual experience—never actually elaborated thematically or developed into a theological synthesis—would incline, according to Davy's interpretation, in the same direction. The difference between the Rhenish Master and the Hindu-Christian *sannyasi* consists in the latter's attainment to the summit of the One, beyond all representation, through the mediation of the *advaita* experience of the One-without-a-second (*ekam advitiyam*).

But Eckhart's mysticism raises questions. Not surprisingly, Abhishiktananda's spiritual experience—whose authenticity is by no means placed in doubt—likewise raises certain questions on the part of theologians wishing to subject it to a critical theological interpretation. As we have seen above, certain questions arise concerning the meaning of history and of the salvation event in Jesus Christ.

In a recent book entitled *Dieu, le temps et l'être*,[44] Ghislain Lafont devotes an entire section to Abhishiktananda's theological essays, which we have analyzed above. The section is entitled, "L'expérience et le discours: Les orientations de H. Le Saux dans *Intériorité et révélation*."

Lafont is primarily concerned with the way in which Abhishiktananda conceives the relationship between spiritual experience and theological discourse. While rightly insisting on the primacy of experience, does he not tend to underestimate the importance of the mediation of concepts, in particular the theological discourse in which Christian tradition has conveyed spiritual experience throughout the centuries? With regard to God, Abhishiktananda seeks, through the mediation of Hindu spirituality, an experience in its pure state. Transcending all mediation of the Verbum and the Spirit, he would attain to pure Deity—to the Father-in-himself or the God-in-himself of biblical language (*ho theos*). Lafont describes Abhishiktananda's thought in these words:

> From their very origin, human beings are inhabited by a kind of spiritual intuition of self, at the deepest level, where they are at one with God and with all. Real as it is, however, this intuition is buried deep within their consciousness, and must be aroused. ... Types of language (myths, symbols, concepts, and so on), ways of purification (rituals, laws, service, and so on), stages of civilization, and forms of doctrine all receive their meaning from a point of departure in the *awakening* that brings the primitive intuition to its perfection in total

experience—an experience defying all name, except perhaps the "I am," where, as if at their common heart, the religious traditions, especially the biblical and the Hindu, meet. . . . It is in terms of this dynamic, at once spiritual and cosmic, that we must understand and interpret the words and forms (*nama rupa*) of doctrine. These find their signification in their overleaping, until the moment when GOD (the pure deity of the one we call Father, in a limited designation that cannot be directly thought but which unveils itself to the heart) will be "all in all."[45]

Lafont observes that this plenary experience, however shrouded in silence, nevertheless remains necessarily subject to interpretation with the aid of words. After all, "there is actually no total discontinuity between words and experience," even if the words seem, and are, inadequate.[46]

Thus, the terminus of a spiritual journey directed upon an unspeakable experience with the "One without a second" will not be lived in the same manner, will probably not even be the same journey, as a journey charted with the aid of a mystical tradition, . . . expressing itself in a sponsal vocabulary, focused upon the Verbum, even the Verbum incarnate.[47]

The theoretical problem of the relationship between words and experience is never really addressed by Abhishiktananda. His constantly reiterated assertion of the absolute inadequacy of words to pure and simple experience "leads him, ever and again, to return to the far side of language, as it were, to find the experience in the very act of its welling forth. . . ."[48] But such a position is not self-evident. It represents the "taking of a theoretical position" bound up with an interpretative tradition of the "apophatic" type, which is open to discussion.[49] Any apophatic tradition finds itself faced with a dilemma:

If the divine names do not *truly* utter God, then either the gospel revelation is provisional, as also that of which it speaks (thus, Trinitarian theology, and christology, in the eschaton, will be abolished), or it is not, but then it is extremely difficult to articulate the mystical nonlanguage. . . .[50]

Abhishiktananda seems to opt for the final obliteration of all distinction, for the "essential non-otherness" of God vis-à-vis the human being and the cosmos. The awakening to the "I am," of which Christ is the paradigm, returns all things to God.

The truest human words have their propaedeutic or initiatory validity. . . . Accordingly, inasmuch as it would speculatively posit a "distance" between God and the human being, analogy would constitute an obstacle in the human being's path to oneness with God. And indeed this is why there cannot be such an analogy.[51]

In the last analysis, then, Abhishiktananda rejects analogy in theological discourse inasmuch as it constitutes an obstacle on the path of unity that leads the human being to God. By way of consequence, meanwhile, the distinction between God and the world, between the Trinity and history, is beyond discourse.

We shall abstain from an attempt to settle a complex debate. Nevertheless, from our viewpoint, certain observations are evident by way of a conclusion. Abhishiktananda's spiritual experience can legitimately serve as a symbol for an existential encounter between Hindu mysticism and Christian mystery. The very sincerity of his witness is the guarantee of the authenticity of his experience. This alone would merit our attention to his witness.

We have seen that Abhishiktananda's experience poses more problems than it solves. The way in which he experienced the encounter between Hindu *advaita* and Christian doctrine seems to pose more than one dilemma: between mystical apophaticism and theological cataphaticism; between a unity that abolishes distinctions and an interpersonal communion that deepens in direct proportion to the distinctions themselves; between history conceived as an epiphenomenon of relative value and history invested with ontological density.

Abhishiktananda was unable to transcend these antinomies theologically. It was not his calling to construct their synthesis, and he left this responsibility to others. His greatness is elsewhere: It consists in having lived within himself the symbiosis of two traditions, the Hindu and the Christian, in so real a way that both became part of himself, without his ever being able to reject or disown either. His stubborn fidelity to his two faiths—or better, as he wrote one day, to the "two forms of a single 'faith' "—make of him a prophetic figure in a time when the "marriage of East and West," especially the encounter between the Christian mystery and Hindu mysticism—in full respect for their differences and without lurking ambiguity—is felt as an urgent need. His experience opens an important avenue toward a Christian theology of religious traditions that would be based on an existential encounter with these traditions in interreligious dialogue.

4

Which Christian Theology of Religions?

The foregoing chapters have sought to pose the question of a Christian theology of religions on the basis of a concrete encounter of the Christian mystery with another religious tradition. The Hindu tradition seemed especially qualified to serve as this point of departure. The elements of the encounter mentioned above are limited. But they suffice to show Hinduism as an important—indeed, redoubtable—partner in dialogue. Hinduism raises, often radically, the great christological questions posed by the context of religious pluralism and dialogue between these distinct traditions.

We must now broaden our perspectives in two directions. Henceforward we shall no longer be dealing with a single partner. Despite occasional applications to particular traditions, our sights will be set on religious traditions in general and their relationship to the Christian mystery, without losing sight of the distinct meaning of the various traditions in the divine salvation plan. Indeed, the encounter and dialogue sketched above have raised important christological questions, and these questions must be answered. We shall now undertake to construct a Christian theology of religions.

But which Christian theology? The present chapter will seek to answer this question with an overview of recent discussions on the subject and of the abundant literature to which those discussions have given rise since Vatican Council II. We shall attempt to do this in two steps. First we shall rehearse the posing of the questions from a starting point in the traditional christological schemata of Christian faith. Then we shall enter into the heart of the current debate, take account of what is at stake, and, in function of these stakes, adopt a position on the spectrum of not only divergent but opposed opinions proposed today for theologians' acceptance.

Before entering into our material in more explicit detail, let us briefly state the question in its essentials. Very broadly, we wish to know whether the traditional christocentric perspective of Christian faith—which a recent theological current applies to the theology of religions—is still defensible in a new context of religious pluralism and interreligious dialogue such as we know and live that context today. At stake is the traditional christo-centrism of Christian theology whose profound, seemingly irreducible demands are now judged by some to be passé and no longer defensible. Let us briefly recall these demands.

The uniqueness of Jesus Christ and the universal meaning of the Christ event represent more than a central belief for Christian tradition. These truths are seen as the very foundation of faith. They have always been, and still are, a stumbling block for those who do not share our faith. To be sure, uniqueness and universality are understood here in the strict sense. We traditionally affirm that Jesus is unique not only as any person whom God would choose as the vehicle of a divine self-revelation and self-manifesta-tion would necessarily be unique—so that consequently any divine revela-tion resulting from this would also be unique—but in the sense that, by and in Jesus, God effected a self-manifestation in a manner that is decisive and can be neither surpassed nor repeated.

It is the same with the universality of the meaning of Christ. Traditionally for the Christian that meaning includes not only the irresistible call rep-resented by the human Jesus for all those who draw near him, but also the scope and influence of Jesus and his work for the salvation of women and men in every time and place. Jesus is at the center of God's design for the world and of the process by which this design is deployed in history. In Jesus, God undertook an irrevocable commitment to humanity, in an irrev-ocable acceptance of that humanity. The human condition of the human Jesus—his words, his deeds, his life, his death, and his resurrection—con-stitutes God's decisive, and in this sense, final, revelation. However we may formulate this primacy of his, Christ is "the center." This is the traditional heart of the Christian faith.

However—and the christocentrism recently applied to the theology of religions forcefully underscores this—this uniqueness and universality are not exclusive, but inclusive; not closed, but open; not sectarian, but cosmic. The theologies of a Christ present but "hidden" and "unknown" in the world's religious traditions, or of an "anonymous Christianity," along with still other theologies, strive to reconcile the traditional Christian position regarding Jesus with the reality of various manifestations. Christ as mystery is God turning toward men and women in self-manifestation and self-rev-elation. The Christic mystery, therefore, is present wherever God enters into the life of human beings in an experience of the divine presence. Nevertheless, this mystery remains anonymous in a certain sense for who-ever has not been enabled, thanks to the Christian revelation, to recognize it in the human condition of Jesus of Nazareth. All have the experience of the Christic mystery, but Christians alone are in a position to give it its name. The Christ of faith is inseparable from the Jesus of history; but his presence and activity are not limited to the confines of the Christian fold.

Notwithstanding its favorable approach to other religious traditions, the theology of the cosmic Christ—or better, of the cosmic meaning of Jesus Christ—is more in danger today than before of appearing strangely esoteric for some, who scarcely appreciate being called and regarded as "anonymous Christians," as well as for others—Christians in this case—who regard it as no longer possible to maintain. True, the uniqueness and universal meaning of Jesus the Christ create inescapable theological problems. Inasmuch as and to the extent that the Christic mystery is bound up with the Jesus of history, faith in Christ as the center involves a pretention that may appear incongruous: the attribution of universal meaning to a particular historical event! The empirical fact of "Jesus of Nazareth" is essentially conditioned by time and space. How, then, can it acquire a universal scope in the realm of relations between God and the human being?

The difficulty is as old as theology itself, but it has acquired a renewed importance in recent times. The altogether new dimensions, temporal and spatial, that the world has gained under the impulse of contemporary science, call, it is said, for a "Copernican revolution" to lay to rest for good and all the "provincial" theology of the prescientific human being.

In the Indian context, as we have already seen, an even more fundamental difficulty arises. Here history itself is usually ascribed only a relative, phenomenal value. The absolute, of its very nature, is transhistorical. Thus the absolute meaning attributed by Christianity to the Jesus Christ event becomes unintelligible.

To this must be added the numerous questions raised among Christians, including theologians, on the basis of their new awareness of religious pluralism in the world.

All of these considerations conspire to pose the urgent question formulated above: Is traditional christocentrism still viable? The question deserves an answer.

CHRISTOLOGY AND CHRISTIAN FAITH

Jesus Christ at the Center of Faith

"Christianity is Christ," we have heard so often. The formulation is correct, but it is important to understand it correctly. We must make a distinction. The Christianity lived by Christians or by the church is not Christ. But Jesus Christ, his person and his work, are at the center of Christian faith. Indeed, we must say that Jesus Christ occupies in Christian faith a central, unique place such as no other religion attributes to its founder. For Islam, Muhammad is the prophet through whom God speaks, the depository of the divine message, as it were. For Buddhism, Gautama is the Enlightened One showing the way, and in this sense the great Teacher.[1] For the Christian, however, it is the mystery of Jesus Christ himself, and not just his message, that is at the very center of faith. The message and the Messenger blend into one. Christianity is not a "religion of the book," then, in the sense that Islam is. Christianity is the religion of a person, the Christ.[2]

That Jesus Christ is personally at the center of the Christian faith, the New Testament forthrightly attests. Pauline theology puts this in a most striking way when, after having considered as mystery (*musterion*), or divine plan, the common inheritance bestowed on the Jews and the nations (see Eph. 3:5–7), Paul comes to identify the mystery with the very person of Jesus Christ (see 1 Tim. 3:6; cf. Col. 1:26–27). For Paul, Jesus Christ is the sole mediator between God and men (see 1 Tim. 2:5), precisely at the point at which Paul is stressing the divine will that all men be saved (see 1 Tim. 2:4). Such is the clarity with which Jesus Christ appears to him to be the very realization of that will.[3]

Peter thought no differently in his discourse to the Sanhedrin reported in Acts: "There is no other name under heaven given to men by which we must be saved" (see Acts 4:12). We know that the name stands for the person. We could cite the great hymns of Paul and his school, the Trinitarian hymn of Ephesians 1:3–13 and the christological hymn of Colossians 1:15–20. Everywhere Christ appears at the center of the divine work. We could likewise note the New Testament texts, in and out of the gospels, in which Jesus so clearly emerges as universal Savior.[4] Perhaps such a listing would be superfluous. After all, it is abundantly clear that this is the message of the New Testament in its entirety, the assertion underlying every part of it, the deep faith without which none of the books that comprise it—gospels, letters, history, treatise—would have been written or be comprehensible.

Let us touch very briefly on the postapostolic tradition. It is arresting to observe that in the analytic table of his magisterial work on the christology of the Fathers and the councils, A. Grillmeier has thought it unnecessary to list an entry on the uniqueness of Jesus Christ.[5] I believe, as I have explained elsewhere, that this absence—surprising at first sight—can be explained by the fact that, for the patristic era, the uniqueness of Jesus Christ, the universal Savior, was outside the purview of theological discussion, being precisely at the center of faith. The problem to which we must attend is not the fact, but the why and the how. That is, what is it about the personal identity of Jesus Christ that renders the Jesus Christ event unique and unreiterable? I have written:

> One point should be clear as regards the patristic attitude to the uniqueness of Jesus Christ: it is the corner stone of the whole edifice of Christian faith, everywhere implied in the elaboration of doctrine. . . . [The Fathers] found the reason for the uniqueness of Jesus Christ in the very nature and exigencies of the incarnational economy of salvation manifested in him. If, as they believed, the Word had

become man in Jesus Christ, it was clear that this event could not but be one and have universal, cosmic implications and repercussions.[6]

But is recent Christian tradition stamped with the same christocentrism as ancient tradition was? The question has been broached of the christocentrism of Vatican II. Was the council not too strongly focused on the church, whether in itself or in its relations *ad extra* (the world, other religions, ecumenism) so that Christ does not appear as its authentic center?[7] This would not be an altogether fair statement of the case. Over the course of its sessions, the council surely moved toward a more explicit christocentrism (and pneumatology). Its great christological texts are to be found in the Pastoral Constitution *Gaudium et Spes* (nos. 22, 32, 45, etc.). Indeed, as Paul VI insisted on more than one occasion, in seeking to grasp its own mystery in greater depth, the church of Vatican II found itself compelled, as it were, to return to the mystery of Jesus Christ that is its source and raison d'être.[8]

This is the viewpoint that we ourselves must adopt if we would acquire an adequate perspective on the definition of the church selected and promulgated by the council from among so many different images: that of the church as universal sacrament of salvation (cf. *Lumen Gentium*, nos. 1, 48; *Ad Gentes*, no. 1; *Gaudium et Spes*, nos. 42, 45). The church is "in some way in Christ the sacrament, both the sign and means of intimate union with God and the unity of the whole human race" (*Lumen Gentium*, no. 1). In other words, since Christ is salvation itself, the church is defined as the sacrament of Christ. Just as Christ himself is the primordial sacrament of the encounter with God, so the church in turn is the sacrament of Jesus Christ.[9]

But this definition implies a radical "decentering" of the church, which now finds itself altogether centered on the mystery of Jesus Christ. He, we might say, is the absolute mystery; the church, by contrast, is the derived, relative mystery. (Who could fail to see how powerfully such a theological definition of the mystery of the church militates against concepts of the church as readily conducive to ecclesiological inflation as is, for example, J. Moeller's "continuous incarnation"?) Proceeding logically from the conciliar definition of the mystery of the church, we should arrive at a comprehensive christocentric perspective that goes beyond the ecclesiocentric approach.

Centrality of Christ in Ecumenical Theology and the Theology of Religions

In its Decree on Ecumenism, *Unitatis Redintegratio*, number 11, Vatican Council II introduced the important consideration of an order, or hierarchy, of truths of Catholic teaching. It explains the principle according to which this hierarchy of truths is established in terms of a different relation to the foundation of faith. What the council does not explicitly say is that the foundation of faith governing the hierarchy of truths is the mystery of Jesus Christ, but this emerges from what has been said above on the christo-centrism of Vatican II in general and the relativity of the mystery of the church in particular.

If we pursue this line of thought opened by Vatican II and apply it explicitly to ecumenical theology and the theology of religions, we can draw important conclusions, some of which (not all) were perceived by the coun-cil itself. After all, in the two areas under consideration, the real question is that of the relationship of the subordinate truths to the absolute mystery of Jesus Christ, the foundation of faith — not of their relation to the mystery of the Catholic Church, which is itself a derived truth. Let us briefly sketch the scope of these observations.

Preconciliar Catholic ecumenism traditionally posed the ecumenical problem in terms of the horizontal relation of the other "churches" (if and when these were indeed dignified with the name of church) or Christian communities to the Roman Catholic Church. The same approach was used in any consideration of their sacraments, their ministries, their authority, and so on.

We need only recall the identification in Pius XII's Encyclical *Mystici Corporis* (1943) between the Roman Catholic Church and the mystical Body of Christ, in order to realize that the question of the ecclesial meaning of the other Christian communities was posed in terms of a relativity to the Catholic Church. Catholic ecumenism was an ecumenism of return to the true Church of Christ.

But Vatican II went further, and this is due at least in part to the christological perspective that governed the council's ecclesiology. In this perspective, the real question in ecumenical theology becomes that of the respective vertical relationship of the various churches and Christian com-munities to the mystery of Jesus Christ. To what extent and in what way are they a sacrament of salvation, even if only the Catholic Church is the general means of that salvation (*Unitatis Redintegratio*, no. 33)? It is on the response to this question that that of their reciprocal relationship will inev-itably depend.

Ecumenism thus becomes an ecumenism of the reunion of the separated churches, the recomposition of the oneness (*unitatis redintegratio*) of the undivided church in the diversity of the various churches. This new per-spective bore its first fruit at the council itself. It enabled that body to accord full recognition to the ecclesiality of the Orthodox churches. It ena-bled it to admit that while the mystery of the church subsists (*subsistit*) in the Catholic Church (*Lumen Gentium*, no. 8; *Unitatis Redintegratio*, no. 4), this does not mean that the same mystery is not present in other Christian communities, although imperfectly and without the fullness of the means of salvation (*UR*, no. 3), at least through certain valuable elements com-posing the same mystery there (*UR*, no. 3). Finally, it was the key to the recognition by the council of these communities as means of salvation, that the Spirit of Christ does not refuse to use (ibid.). There is a real communion (however imperfect in various respects) between the Catholic Church and the other churches or Christian communities (ibid.). Such are the immediate fruits produced at the council itself by the decentering of the ecumenical question from the church and its recentering on the mystery of Christ.

We have the right to look for analogous fruits from an ecclesiological decentering and a christological recentering of the theology of religions. In the broader domain of the theological meaning of the other religious traditions of humanity, a correct outlook likewise enjoins an investigation of their vertical relation to the mystery of Christ present and at work in the world, not of their horizontal relationship to the church. Let us see whether we may be able to extract the immediate implications of this change in perspective.

A certain church tradition has posed the problem in terms of the horizontal relationship of the other religions to Christianity or to the mystery of the church. The adage, "Outside the church there is no salvation," has been the vehicle of this limited perspective. But it is important to observe that the adage in question, *Extra ecclesiam nulla salus*, originated in a different context from that to which it has been more recently applied.[10] It is borrowed from Fulgentius of Ruspe, who applies it not only to pagans but to Jews, and even to Christians who have separated themselves from the church, whether by schism or heresy.[11] To culpably separate oneself from the church is tantamount to separating oneself from Christ, the source of salvation.

When the adage is cited in official texts of the magisterium as in the thirteenth century by the Creed of the Fourth Council of the Lateran (1215)[12] and in the fourteenth century by the Bull *Unam Sanctam* (1302) of Boniface VIII,[13] it seems to be intended to refer to those who find themselves outside the church voluntarily and culpably. The first text of the church magisterium explicitly to extend its usage beyond heretics and schismatics, to pagans and Jews, is the Decree for the Jacobites (1442) of the Council of Florence.[14] In historical context, however, the primary intention of the council continues to be to apply the adage to those who have separated themselves from the church voluntarily and who have not reunited themselves to it before the end of their lives.[15]

These circumstances permit a reduction of the scope of the adage on which an overly narrow ecclesiocentric view of salvation has traditionally been based, even apart from the doubts that prevail as to the properly dogmatic value of the decree of the Council of Florence. However this may be, the adage implied a faulty statement of the question. The requirements for access to salvation were envisaged in a negative way and in virtue of an ecclesiocentric outlook. They should have been enunciated positively, in a christocentric perspective. Thus corrected, the adage would have read, "All salvation is through Christ," and thus would have been in perfect conformity with the New Testament proposition mentioned above.

Has Vatican Council II adopted this positive and christocentric perspective where it addresses the mystery of the salvation of the members of other religious traditions? Or has it prolonged the narrow ecclesiocentric perspective, perhaps in spite of the acknowledgment it makes of certain positive values within these same traditions? An absolute answer to this question cannot be given. On the one side, regarding the salvation of individual persons living beyond the pale of Christianity, the council adopts a decidedly christocentric perspective in the Pastoral Constitution *Gaudium et Spes*, where, having expounded the manner in which the Christian receives salvation in function of his or her association to the Paschal mystery of Jesus Christ, the document continues:

> All this holds true not only for Christians, but for all men of good will in whose hearts grace works in an unseen way. For, since Christ died for all men, and since the ultimate vocation of man is in fact one, and divine, we ought to believe that the Holy Spirit in a manner known to God offers to every man the possibility of being associated with this paschal mystery.[16]

This christological perspective is not consistently maintained, however, in the conciliar documents, particularly when it is not a matter of the individual mystery of the salvation of persons, but of the religious traditions themselves, taken in their objective, historical reality. The very title of the declaration *Nostra Aetate* — "On the Relations of the Church with the Non-Christian Religions" — demonstrates this. The question posed here is not directly that of the vertical relationship of humanity's religious traditions with the mystery of Jesus Christ. It is the question of the horizontal relationship of these same traditions with Christianity or the church. The first question could have borne on the acknowledgment of a hidden presence of the mystery of Christ in these same traditions, and of a certain mediation of this same mystery through them. The second question, of course, did not naturally lead in this direction. Is not this the reason why, despite the council's assertion of the presence of values and positive elements in these religious traditions, it does not explicitly venture in the direction of an acknowledgment of these same traditions as legitimate paths of salvation for their members, although necessarily in relation to the mystery of Christ?

Without unduly anticipating our coming discussion, we may provisionally conclude that, in the area of the theology of religions, as well as in that of ecumenical theology, the only outlook that promises appreciable positive results is the christocentric perspective, which overcomes, by transcending it, a stunted ecclesiocentric approach. The real question — the only one open to meaningful answers — is that of the vertical relation, whether of the churches and Christian communities or of the other religious traditions to the mystery of Christ. Ecumenical theology and the theology of religions must substitute this question for that of the horizontal relation between the Catholic Church and other churches, on the one hand, and between the other religions and Christianity, on the other hand. The question of the horizontal relationship can find a valid solution only from a point of departure in the more fundamental problem of the vertical relation. Thus we arrive, from another direction, at the conclusion already formulated at the end of the foregoing section: a narrow ecclesiocentric outlook must be replaced by a christocentric perspective at once more basic and broader. This is what Hans Küng observed, equivalently, when he wrote:

> Such, then, is how this problem appears when the startingpoint is not the Church but God's will and plan for salvation, as it is made known to us, and in so far as it is made known to us, in Scripture. The question of what lies outside the Church is one which can be asked but . . . can only be answered with difficulty. All men can be saved! As to what lies outside *God* and his plan of salvation, this is not a real question at all. If we look at God's plan of salvation, then there is no *extra,* only an *intra*; no outside, only an inside, for "God desires *all* men to be saved and to come to the knowledge of the truth. For there is *one* God, and there is *one* mediator between God and men, the man Christ Jesus, who gave himself as a ransom for *all*" (1 Tim. 2:4–6).[17]

The Meaning of Christ in the Divine Plan

We have just quoted one of the most explicit texts of the New Testament on the role of Jesus Christ as universal mediator between God and humanity. God has chosen to save all human beings in him. For Christian faith, this is a fact—a fact, for that matter, whose internal reason has always been a theological problem. The whole of Christian tradition, biblical and post-biblical alike, has interrogated itself on the meaning of Jesus Christ in the divine plan—or, as it has been put, on the motive of the Incarnation. If, as must be understood, not only the creation of the human being called by God to share the divine life, but also the salvation of sinful humanity in Jesus Christ are, and can only be, free and gratuitous deeds of God, the question must be asked: What intrinsic motive or reason can have fixed the choice made by God of a universal salvation effected by the death on a cross, in a determinate time and place, of a human being, Jesus of Nazareth, who called himself, and who was, the Son of God?

The particularity of the salvific event and the universal value attributed to it have always been a scandal—a scandal to which is added the seeming triviality of the event in its historical context. But the scandal takes on new proportions and appears in all its breadth in the context of the pluralism of religious traditions, and of a Christian theology of religions. It is under this aspect that the question of the meaning of Christ in the divine plan interests us here.

The question that has been more or less explicitly posed throughout the whole of Christian tradition was put more clearly in Saint Anselm's *Cur Deus Homo* and later became one of the great theological debates between the Thomists and the Scotists.[18] Here it will suffice to offer a rapid sketch of the basic positions, discuss them summarily to bring out their respective lacunae, seek a more satisfactory response, and finally, tarry on the problems that, in a context of religious pluralism, the seemingly most adequate solution itself does not fail to arouse.

Saint Anselm has been understood to say that the redemption of sinful humanity requires that God receive justice — the theory of "adequate satisfaction." The offense to God is in some way infinite (by reason of its Object). Adequate satisfaction can be offered only by Jesus Christ, the human being who was God. Thus the Incarnation seemed necessary for the redemption of humanity. This statement of the case presupposed a vengeful, vindictive image of God and a juridical conception of the mystery of salvation, as if it were a matter of appeasing an angry God, which runs counter to the message of the New Testament, where the redemption appears essentially as a mystery of love.[19]

Saint Thomas was not deceived here, and to avoid the negative consequences of a similar conception, he reduced the apparent divine intent in Jesus Christ to "reasons of suitability." Surely the Incarnation was not necessary for the salvation of humanity; still, it was appropriate that the incarnate Son satisfy, as he alone was capable of doing, the demands of justice and earn the salvation of humanity. In the divine plan, then, Jesus Christ was essentially ordered to the Redemption, to the point that it was correct to say that if humanity had not had to be saved from sin, the Incarnation would not have occurred. Thus Jesus Christ was reduced to his redemptive function, and a Christian world was purely incidental. Furthermore, Jesus Christ was an afterthought in the divine plan, which now consisted rather in two successive, superimposed plans.

The Scotist reaction ensued. Jesus could not be reduced to an afterthought in God's plan for humanity and the cosmos. Jesus Christ had been willed by God from the beginning of the mystery of creation. He was, as Saint Paul so clearly indicated, the crown and center, indeed the very principle of intelligibility, of the created world. He was not willed by God essentially as Savior. He had become Savior only incidentally, in view of humanity's sin and need for redemption. Even if humans had not sinned, the Son would have become incarnate in Jesus Christ to crown creation as the divine plan had decreed. Thus, with Jesus Christ the redeemer only incidentally, the world was essentially Christian, being thought and willed by God in Jesus Christ from the beginning.

The Scotist thesis — which is surely closer to the New Testament message, especially in Paul — has the merit of expanding Christ's function vis-à-vis humanity and the world. Its christocentrism is more accentuated and more radical. Its flaw is the same as that of the Thomist thesis: It supposes two successive plans in the mind of God. While for Saint Thomas, Jesus Christ is absent from the divine plan in a first stage and enters it as Savior only in a second stage, for Duns Scotus and his successors Jesus Christ is central to the divine plan from the beginning, but becomes Savior only in a second stage in function of humanity's sin.

It would little serve our purpose to go further into the discussion that continues to divide the two camps, or even to dwell on certain "conciliatory perspectives" that seek—perhaps in vain—to combine them. What we need is a more adequate response to the question, "Why Jesus Christ?"—a response at once deeply scriptural and theologically satisfying. It is actually a matter of overcoming, or rather transcending, the problematic of the two opposed camps, which seems too narrow. It is too narrow, particularly, in its undue distinction between two successive stages in the divine plan, as if the divine thinking could be fragmented by time. It is also too narrow in its undue reduction of the gratuity of Jesus Christ as a divine gift of salvation. We must ask ourselves what, in the divine plan for humanity (which is only one) is the meaning of the Jesus Christ event, whose entire gratuity on God's part we acknowledge a priori, both in the order of creation, in which God already calls the human being to share in the divine life itself, and then in the plan of the redemption, by which God reestablishes the human being in that life. In other words, what is the meaning of Jesus Christ in the gift of being, the gift of the divine self, and the forgiveness of sins?

It seems that we must say that God's formal intent in Jesus Christ is to inject the divine gift of self into humanity as deeply as can be, into the very stuff of the humanity that is called to share the divine life. In other words, to make the divine self-bestowal as immanent as possible. The plenary insertion of God's self-communication into the human race—the total immanence of the divine self-bestowal upon humanity—consists precisely in God's personal self-insertion into the human family and its history, that is, in the mystery of the Incarnation of the Son of God in Jesus Christ. This can be called the principle of God's creative and restorative "immanent self-communication."

If Jesus Christ is Head of created humanity, which is called and restored in him by God—without any need to distinguish successive moments in the divine plan—the explanation is this: In this personal insertion of himself as Son of God into our human condition and our history, Jesus Christ has actually placed God within our reach, along with the gift to us of the divine life itself, given on our own level. Edward Schillebeeckx says it well: While in the Old Testament itself God is already a God-of-humanity, in Jesus Christ God becomes a God-of-human-beings-in-human-fashion. Indeed, "Christ is God in a human way, and a human in a divine way."[20] This is the key to his actualization in himself of the total—and totally immanent—

gift of God to humanity. G. Martelet takes the same direction when, in an article on the motive of the Incarnation, he writes:

> The immediate premise of the Incarnation is not . . . *sin*, but *adoption*; in adoption itself, the essential is not *redemption* as such, but *deification*. . . . Adoption corresponds in us to what Incarnation is in [Christ]: "Being Son of God, he came to make himself son of man, and to grant us, who were children of human beings, to become children of God." In us, then, adoption is the counterpart of what incarnation is in Christ. . . . Incarnation is our adoption *qua* founded in Christ, and our adoption, in turn, from this viewpoint, the incarnation of Christ *qua* operative in us.[21]

But is this response to the question, "Why Jesus Christ?" anything more than one theologoumenon among others? Or does it actually present itself as being in profound harmony with the message of the New Testament? Surely the latter is the case. Suffice it to allude here to certain more characteristic passages, such as John 3:16–17, in which the coming of the Son into the world is presented as the paroxysm of the Father's love for humanity; and 1 John:1–2, where Jesus Christ, Son of the Father, figures as principle of life, deeply inserted into the very stuff of the human. The most eloquent text, however, is the passage in the Letter to the Romans in which St. Paul establishes a parallel between the two Adams that strikes us all the more by dint of its repetition: In the space of a few verses (Rom. 5:12–20), the parallel between Adam and Jesus Christ is either amplified or sketched out no less than six times. The key word throughout the passage is *anthropos*: It is by the grace of a single *human being*, Jesus Christ, that God has communicated the divine gift, just as it was by a single *human being* that sin had entered the world.

Saint Paul is not asserting merely that redemption has been wrought in Jesus Christ, but that it has been wrought *by a human being*, therefore in a manner immanent to humanity itself. The parallel between Jesus and Adam is invoked with a view to a more effective emphasis on the human causality in the free gift of God in Jesus Christ. We cannot show here that patristic tradition has often understood the mystery of Christ in the same fashion. It was to bring out the immanence of the divine gift made to humanity in Jesus Christ that the Fathers insisted not only on the integrity of Jesus' human nature but on his real identification with the concrete condition of sinful humanity. He sought us out on the level on which we found ourselves. This is the purport of the familiar axioms often repeated by the patristic tradition. "God has become a human being that we may be divinized." But to this end, God must have assumed all that is human, for "what has not been assumed has not been saved." The "wondrous interchange" between God and the human being in Jesus Christ, of which the

Fathers have spoken, required that God first descend to us in Jesus, that in him God might exalt us to divinity.

Finally we must face the problems that are surely posed by the divine plan in Jesus Christ, or the economy of incarnation, as we have felt constrained to represent it here. These problems are not new, although they become more urgent and acute in the context of religious pluralism and new dialogue. As we have seen, in Jesus Christ God seeks to be a God-of-human-beings-in-human-fashion. But is not this intrusion upon humanity on God's part terribly inhuman? Doubtless the economy of the Incarnation represents on God's part the fullest possible gift of the divine self to humanity. One may also think that it implies on God's part the most profound respect for human dignity without injury to human freedom. Still, it seems scandalous, inequitable, and unjust to make the gift of salvation dependent on a necessarily particular, allegedly unique historical event. St. Thomas appears to have admitted the possibility of multiple incarnations. Would they not have seemed desirable to avoid in part the particularity of the single event? This solution appears precluded in the New Testament; we need only think of the Pauline "once and for all" (*ephapax*), and of the Letter to the Hebrews. From the Christian viewpoint, it would actually have been superfluous, since "by his incarnation the Son of God in some sort united himself to every man" (*Gaudium et Spes*, no. 22), and the whole of humanity to himself. By the Jesus Christ event, a knot that can never more be undone has bound God to humanity. Nor, then, can that event be repeated.

However, the scandal of the temporal and spatial particularity of the event abides. It is discernible in the thinking of the Fathers themselves. In terms of the biblical chronology, according to which 4,000 years separated Christ from Adam, the Fathers wondered why Christ had come so late. They replied that humanity had to be prepared for his coming. In the gigantic perspectives that modern science has opened out upon the history of the world and humanity, that answer may well seem ridiculous. The question only becomes all the more urgent—and the particularity of the event the more scandalous—even if the opposite, too, ought to have been asked: Why so soon?

However this may be, in a context of the plurality of cultures and religious traditions that we experience today, the spatial particularity of the Jesus Christ event may be even more scandalous. That one particular culture could have received, nearly exclusively, the legacy of a solitary salvation event, an event occurring in a particular religious tradition, seems to constitute a belittling of humanity's other religious traditions and cultures—those of Asia, for example, which are actually older, and certainly no less rich. It is practically impossible to exaggerate the sense of sectarianism and parochialism, indeed of arrogance and intolerance, experienced by so many Asians, thoughtful Hindus or Buddhists, when they are confronted with what Christianity claims for such a historically obscure (even though we have better access to it today) event as that of Jesus of Nazareth.

In Eastern eyes, an economy of incarnation as Christianity understands it could never lay claim to universality. Is not the Hindu teaching of the *avataras* more human — and ultimately more divine — in virtue of the very multiplicity of the divine manifestations it posits? The question stands out in all its sharpness: Is the claim to universality that Christianity makes for the Jesus Christ event still possible to sustain? Is it enough, in order to defend it today, to call it "not exclusive, but inclusive"? And what is the actual purpose of such distinctions? In the last analysis, does the traditional christocentrism of Christian theology stand up to the shock of the current encounter of cultures and religious traditions? These questions will have to be answered. Meanwhile, let us be content with observing, with Karl Rahner, that the most urgent christological task today surely consists in demonstrating the universal signification and cosmic dimension of the Jesus Christ event, with Christ as the pinnacle of salvation history and christology as that history's sharpest formulation.

THE CURRENT DEBATE ON THE THEOLOGY OF RELIGIONS

The foregoing has afforded us a glimpse of the dangers and weaknesses of a rigidly ecclesiocentric perspective on the theology of religions. For that matter, we have cited the challenge posed by the context of religious pluralism to the traditional christocentric perspective of theology. The present section will be devoted to the debate among the various perspectives, as we find it in the abundant literature of recent years on the theology of religions. We shall begin with a presentation and critical examination of the various outlooks proposed. Then we shall attempt to answer the question: Is a christocentric perspective of universal and cosmic dimensions, such as we have sketched it above, adequate to the challenge of the context of theological reflection today, with its new historical and geographical proportions, its pluralism of cultures and religious traditions, and its interreligious encounter and dialogue?

In an article entitled "Christ and Church: A Spectrum of Views," J. Peter Schineller has arranged current theological opinions on the relationship of other religious traditions to Christ and the church in four major categories:[22]

1. Ecclesiocentric universe, exclusive christology.
2. Christocentric universe, inclusive christology.
3. Theocentric universe, normative christology.
4. Theocentric universe, nonnormative christology.

Without entering upon a detailed study of this classification, let us note the formal principles that govern it. We observe, first of all, three distinct conceptions of the universe: ecclesiocentric, christocentric, and theocentric.

Secondly, we have four christological positions: exclusive, inclusive, normative, and nonnormative. Why so many possibilities? The reason is that the so-called theocentric conception of the universe may or may not attribute to the person of Jesus Christ a "normative" function vis-à-vis relationships between God and the human being.

Let us take careful note of the introduction of a third model of the world, the theocentric model, which in turn governs two distinct categories of opinion. For many authors, the ecclesiocentric and christocentric perspectives now appear untenable, and they are accordingly replacing them with the theocentric model. This new departure is an important one. It involves nothing less than a "change of paradigm." The underlying implication, in the writings of those who propose it, is that it is no longer possible to refer universal salvation either to Jesus Christ as explicitly professed in the church instituted by him (model 1), or even to the mystery of Jesus Christ as causing salvation beyond the limits of the Christian communities (model 2). Rejected here are not only the notion of an obligatory mediation of the church in the economy of salvation, but even the universal mediation of Jesus Christ asserted by the Pauline theology, whatever be the case with the more or less important, normative or not, theological meaning still attributed to the person of Jesus Christ in the economy of the relationships between God and the human being.

Despite its apparent complexity a division of the prevailing opinions into four groups has the advantage of bringing out important distinctions in the way the movement from a christocentric perspective to a theocentric one, now judged necessary, is envisaged. Is it simply a matter of acknowledging that God's self-manifestation has taken different forms in the various religious traditions, without having to prioritize the manifestation in Jesus Christ as "normative" in any way (model 4)? Or rather, while acknowledging that it is no longer tenable to regard universal salvation as dependent on the person and work of Jesus Christ—as the christocentric outlook would have it—are we to continue to prioritize Jesus Christ in some way (even in the theocentric perspective now proposed), as the most perfect symbol, or even as the ideal model, and in this sense as "normative" in the order of divine-human relationships constituting salvation (model 3)?

Despite the admitted merits of a fourfold grouping,[23] many recent authors prefer a tripartite division of opinions. They distinguish three perspectives: ecclesiocentric, christocentric, and theocentric, and in parallel with these, three basic positions respectively designated exclusivism, inclusivism, and "pluralism."[24]

These models are readily recognizable from their names, although each may call for various distinctions. The exclusivism governing the ecclesiocentric perspective, in the minds of the authors in question, refers to the exclusivity of salvation through Jesus Christ professed in the church. If we must give it a name, we might call it the thesis of Hendrick Kraemer.[25] In order to solve the problem of the various religions, it applies the dialectical theology of Karl Barth, according to which the only valid knowledge of God is the Christian knowledge received by human beings in Jesus Christ. The God of others is an idol. It will not be superfluous to observe that the exclusivistic thesis, which postulates membership in the church as a condition of salvation, and in that church, the explicit profession of Jesus Christ, has been officially rejected by the ecclesial magisterium.[26]

We must note, however, that an ecclesiocentric perspective does not necessarily presuppose exclusivism in Kraemer's sense (and in the footsteps of Barth), which is dependent on a strict interpretation of the axiom "Outside the church there is no salvation." All Catholic theologians actually admit the possibility of salvation outside the church, however they may conceive this possibility. We shall return to this.

For the moment, let us note that the role of the church in the mystery of salvation outside the church can be, and actually is, conceived in various ways. Some theologians posit a constitutive mediation on the part of the church, in addition to the obligatory mediation—on a different level, of course—of Jesus Christ. Others are closer to the language of the New Testament, according to which Christ is the sole mediator, and conceive the role of the church not so much in terms of mediation, but rather as a presence, a sign, sacrament, and testimony.[27]

It seems difficult to conceive how the salvific mediation of the church beyond its own frontiers might be understood. As essentially sacramental, the salvific mediation of the church is exercised by the proclamation of the word and the sacraments. While reaching the church's members, and to some extent its future members, it does not reach the members of other religious traditions. Thus, although we have come by a different route, we are back at the viewpoint we have considered above. The ecclesiocentric outlook, even in its attenuated form, must be transcended. It is important to avoid, in the theology of religions, an ecclesiological inflation that would falsify perspectives. The church, as derived mystery, as utterly relative to the mystery of Christ, cannot be the yardstick by which the salvation of others is measured.

Once we have admitted this premise, however, the above-cited tripartite division poses a serious challenge to the traditional christocentric outlook. To inclusive christocentrism is opposed a theocentric view, represented in a model called (rather ambiguously) pluralism. A number of recent authors support this "paradigm change"—this shift from christocentrism to theocentrism, from inclusivism to pluralism. Their reasoning, broadly speaking, is as follows.

If Christianity sincerely seeks a dialogue with the other religious traditions—which it can only seek on a footing of equality—it must first of all renounce any claim to uniqueness for the person and work of Jesus Christ as a universal constitutive element of salvation. To be sure, this position is open to various understandings in terms of radicality. We have already observed, with J. P. Schineller, two divergent interpretations, according to which the person of Jesus Christ, understood as nonconstitutive of salvation, is nonetheless normative for some, while for others it is neither constitutive nor normative. If we must give examples, we might cite, for the normative Jesus, Ernst Troeltsch and Paul Tillich;[28] and for the nonnormative Jesus, John Hick, whose representative position deserves some attention here.

The authors who advocate a theocentric pluralism, however, differ from one another in various respects, which we need not detail here. Let us simply note that, while for some of these authors, such as Alan Race, Christianity's renunciation of its christological claims must be irrevocable,[29] others propound it as a working hypothesis, along the lines of a methodological doubt or as an at least temporary "bracketing" necessary in order for the dialogue with others to be established honestly and authentically. The very practice of dialogue may well reestablish the validity of Christian claims regarding the mystery of Christ. These claims would rest ultimately on the sole foundation that can establish them with solidity: the test of encounter.[30]

John Hick's position is so representative of a theological pluralism understood in the radical sense that it may well be worthwhile to pause a moment to consider it.[31] Hick advocates a "Copernican revolution" in christology, a revolution that must specifically consist of a shift in paradigms, a movement from the traditional christocentric perspective to a new theocentric perspective. *Copernican revolution*, an expression we frequently meet in other areas of theological discussion today, is indeed an appropriate term for what is underway here. Originally it designated the passage from one system for explaining the cosmos, now passé and overthrown, to another system that actually corresponds to reality. The Ptolemaic system was replaced by the Copernican. Having believed for centuries that the sun revolves around the earth, we finally discovered, with Galileo and Copernicus, that the earth actually revolves around the sun. Just so, having believed for centuries that the other religious traditions revolved around Christianity as their center,[32] today we must acknowledge that the center around which all religious traditions revolve (including Christianity) is actually God. Such a paradigm switch necessarily entails the abandonment of any claim to a unique meaning not only for Christianity, but for Jesus Christ himself.

To use Schineller's categories for the sake of clarity, we must say that the basic dilemma, as Hick conceives it, is between an ecclesiocentric exclusivism and a theocentric pluralism. That is, between a fundamentalist interpretation of the axiom "Outside the church there is no salvation" and a radical liberalism that regards all the various divine manifestations in various cultures, including that which takes place in Jesus Christ, as enjoying the same basic equality in their differences.

This is not to say that Hick simply ignores theological writings representing the middle position, that of inclusivism, or, in Schineller's terminology, an inclusive christology in a christocentric universe, such as that of Karl Rahner, for example.[33] Still, for Hick, all of the efforts of an impressive number of recent theologians—especially Catholic theologians—to endow the theology of religions with an inclusive, open christocentrism that would combine the "constitutive" sense of the Jesus Christ event for the salvation of humanity and the value of other religious traditions as representing interventions of God in the history of human cultures, and comprising "elements of grace" and salvation for their members—all of these efforts may be left out of account as unworthy of serious consideration. Indeed, they are comparable to the "epicycles" concocted by ancient science in its vain attempt to force certain recalcitrant phenomena into the Ptolemaic system, until the latter finally blew up in our faces, taking its epicycles with it and making room for the Copernican revolution. In analogous fashion, the Copernican revolution in theology, which Hick not only enthusiastically approves but is determined to initiate, rejects all inclusive christologies as if they were useless, abandoned epicycles. The only remaining valid theology of religions will now be that of a theocentric pluralism, which accounts for all the phenomena, transcends any Christian claim to a prioritarian, universal role for Jesus Christ, and at last establishes the interreligious dialogue on a genuinely equal footing.

Let us further observe that Hick's thinking has evolved into a veritable school of thought that vaunts a somewhat militant attitude, as its slogans attest. Besides the "paradigm change," we hear more recently of "crossing the Rubicon." "Crossing the Rubicon," of course, will designate an irrevocable acknowledgment of the equal meaning and value of the various religions and the renunciation of any claim of exclusivity or even normativity for Christianity.[34] If there is any universalism in Jesus Christ, it can only be that of the appeal his message might have in terms of the aspirations of all men and women. Of course, other salvific figures might have the same appeal.

The price to be paid by the traditional Christian faith in terms of the mystery of the person and work of Jesus Christ is, as we see, considerable. The second part of the present volume will attempt to show, from various complementary viewpoints, that an inclusive, open christocentrism remains possible and indeed represents the only way available to a Christian theology of religions truly worthy of the name.

Meanwhile, let us be content to observe that some recent authors not only reject Hick's dilemma, but show his position to be untenable.[35] A recent book by Gavin D'Costa, entitled *Theology and Religious Pluralism*, deserves special attention in this respect.[36] The author recalls two basic axioms of the Christian faith: the universal salvific will of God and the necessary mediation of Jesus Christ (and the role of the church) in every salvation mystery. He then shows that contrasting attitudes toward these two axioms account for three basic positions that he calls, using current terminology, exclusivism (represented by H. Kraemer), inclusivism (of which Karl Rahner serves as protagonist), and pluralism (illustrated by John Hick).

While exclusivism relies on the second axiom, neglecting the first, and pluralism on the first, to the detriment of the second, inclusivism alone succeeds in accounting for and holding both at once. Expounding first the pluralistic theory, the author shows that despite its seeming liberalism, Hick's either/or dilemma actually represents a rigid, self-contradictory position. Its theocentric view imposes on the encounter of religions a divine model that corresponds exclusively to the God of the so-called monotheistic religions. It is not universal.

Kraemer's exclusivism stands in the diametrically opposite corner but is equally rigid, it, too, being based on a dialectic of either/or. It, too, is untenable from a biblical and theological point of view, and actually involves internal contradictions. An exclusive emphasis on merely one of the pair of crucial axioms that ought to govern a Christian theology of religions leads to insoluble theological problems.

There remains the inclusive paradigm of which Karl Rahner is the foremost representative. Does this paradigm solve the problems left unsolved by the other two while preserving whatever measure of validity may reside in the two extreme positions? The author shows that this is indeed the case, and that the inclusivistic position alone is capable of holding together and harmonizing the two axioms of Christian faith that are obligatory for any Christian theology of religions. On the one side, Jesus Christ is clearly asserted to be God's definitive revelation and the absolute Savior. On the other side, the door is open to a sincere acknowledgment of divine manifestations in the history of humanity in various cultures and of efficacious "elements of grace" to be found in other religious traditions; elements that are salvific for their members. Revealed definitively in Jesus Christ, God (and the mystery of Christ) is nonetheless present and at work in other religious traditions. How? It is this that bears further elucidation below. For the moment, let us merely cite the author's conclusion. Referring to the stimulating, open theological and phenomenological tasks confronting the Christian in religious pluralism, he writes:

> The form of inclusivism I have argued for tries to do full justice to [the] two most important Christian axioms: that salvation comes through God in Christ alone, and that God's salvific will is truly universal. By maintaining these two axioms in fruitful tension, the inclusivist paradigm can be characterized by an openness and commitment; an openness that seeks to explore the many and various ways in which God has spoken to all his children in the non-Christian religions and an openness that will lead to the positive fruits of this exploration transforming, enriching and fulfilling Christianity, so much so that its future shape may be very different from the Church we know today.[37]

Thus, in broad strokes, we have surveyed the current debate on a Christian theology of religions and interreligious dialogue. If there is one important conclusion that is already certain, it is that the christological problem constitutes the nub of this debate. The decisive question that governs everything else is whether a theology of religions that means to be Christian has any real choice between a christocentric perspective, which acknowledges the Jesus Christ event as constitutive of universal salvation, and a theocentric perspective, which, in one fashion or another, places in doubt or explicitly rejects this central datum of traditional faith. In other words, can a theocentrism that is not at the same time christocentric be a Christian theocentrism?

Indeed, we must make no mistake on the meaning with which the christocentric outlook is invested here: To say that Christ is at the center of the divine plan for humanity is not to consider him as the goal and end toward which the religious life of human beings and the religious traditions of humanity tend. God (the Father) remains the goal and end. Jesus never replaces God. Jesus Christ is at the center of the mystery as obligatory Mediator, constituted by God and no one else, as the way leading to God. Jesus Christ is at the center because God, not human beings or Christianity, has placed him there. It follows that, in Christian theology, christocentrism and theocentrism cannot be mutually opposed as different perspectives between which a choice must be made. Christian theology is *theocentric qua christocentric, and vice versa.* Far from being passé, the christocentric *and* theocentric perspective (both adjectives at once) seems surely to be the only way open. What is at issue is not, in the last analysis, a choice between two interchangeable theologies, but the free, responsible adoption of the perspective that reveals to our gaze the very heart of faith, the mystery of Jesus Christ in its integrity and universality.

Adherence to the Christian faith is doubtless a free choice. But this choice governs all authentic Christian theology. The second part of our book will take its point of departure in this choice. It will attempt to show that faith in Jesus Christ is not closed, but open, not stingy or mean, but cosmic in its dimensions; and that the theology of the religions of humanity based on that faith establishes, on a cosmic scale, a wonderful convergence in the mystery of Christ of all that God in the divine Spirit has realized, or continues to accomplish, in the history of humanity.

PART II

Christ, One and Universal

5

Salvation History and Divine Covenants

We have now answered the question of the meaning of Jesus Christ in the divine plan for humanity and the world, placing ourselves within the faith that, in Jesus Christ, God has freely become God-for-human-beings-in-a-human-way. That is to say, the formal reason for the Incarnation is God's free and gratuitous decision to insert the divine gift of self into humanity and divine forgiveness into the very heart of human reality. In virtue of this divine will, the Incarnation of the Son of God in humanity involves concrete identification and real solidarity with humanity's historical condition.

The divine plan of salvation, however, is one thing, and its historical realization quite another. To move from the first to the second, we must now inquire into the concrete manner in which the divine plan is realized in the history of the world and humanity. We must ask ourselves what place is occupied, in virtue of the divine plan, by the Jesus Christ event in the comprehensive history of humanity, which is also the history of salvation.

We need not look far for the answer. As Jesus Christ is at the center of the plan willed by God, so also the Jesus Christ event finds itself at the center of the salvation history that gives it concrete form. How? In what sense? It will be our task to situate the decisive covenant struck by God with humanity in Jesus Christ among the manifold divine covenants of the same God with various peoples during human history. We must also make a theological determination of the meaning willed by God in these historical covenants, and of their relationship with the decisive covenant established by God in Jesus Christ. Finally—an urgent task, in the current context of religious pluralism—we must inquire into the permanent value of these covenants and the religious traditions of which they are the symbol, since the occurrence of the Jesus Christ event itself.

THE CHRISTIAN MEANING OF HISTORY

For Christianity, history has a direction, a goal set for it by God. This goal is the definitive fulfillment of the Reign of God. History is a process that, through contingent events, and often despite their fortuitous character, is directed toward a transcendent goal—the fullness of the Reign of God. The Christian concept of history is essentially positive and optimistic. It has been called linear, which does not mean that all the elements constituting human history have a positive sense and contribute positively to the achievement of the end assigned by God to the historical process. However, throughout the vicissitudes of time and the interplay of freedoms, the certitude abides that the end decreed by God will one day be accomplished in plenitude. The Reign of God, gradually inaugurated in the world, will reach its term. We know where we are going.[1]

This so-called linear Christian concept of history is readily distinguished from other concepts. We may cite two of these: the so-called circular or cyclical concept characteristic of Greek philosophy and culture; and that of the Oriental philosophies, notably Hindu philosophy, which has been called "spiral."

The circular concept is familiar enough, and it will be enough to remind ourselves of how pessimistic Greek philosophy is with regard to all that is bodily and historical. Life is doomed to death. As the body (*sōma*) is a tomb (*sēma*), salvation can consist only in escaping from it. We need only think of the contrast between the Greek belief in the immortality of the soul and Christian faith in the resurrection of the body, the contrast so effectively evoked by Oscar Cullmann.[2] Let us recall furthermore that for Socrates, as Plato reports in the *Phaedo,* the immortality of the soul was only a "good bet" (*kalos kindunos*), not a certitude. At all events, the Greek model of history is cyclical and pessimistic. There is nothing new under the sun.[3]

The Hindu model of history has likewise been styled cyclical. It would be more precise, however, to refer to it as spiral. Based on the classic cosmology of the *Samkhya,* it may be represented as follows. Time is divided into various cycles (*kalpa*), themselves composed of various periods (*yuga*). Each cycle begins with a period of creation (*krtayuga*), to terminate in a period of destruction (*kaliyuga*). As each cycle yields to the next in indefinite succession—hence the so-called spiral model—history does not seem, according to classic Hindu cosmology, to ever have a decisive term, a final end. The world has no absolute future. At most, one may speak of a personal liberation, which, whatever the way (*marga*) leading thereto, will consist in emerging from the spiral of history after an indefinite number of successive reincarnations.[4] In a model of its own, then, the Hindu concept of history falls into the same pessimism as Greek philosophy.

In other words, the vast distance separating the Hebrew and Christian conception from the Greek and the Hindu is not without theological consequences for the meaning with which a historical salvific event may be invested. As to the Hindu model, one may do one's utmost to soften the contrast, either by attempting to show that modern Hinduism is no stranger to a concept of history akin to the Western concept inherited from the Bible, or (more paradoxically) by suggesting that Christianity can adapt to a spiral model of history akin to the Hindu model, just as well as to a linear model, to which the Christian West has associated it. It has been observed, on the one hand, that modern Hindu philosophers such as S. Radhakrishnan and Sri Aurobindo develop a positive conception of history comparable to that of recent theologians such as Hans Urs von Balthasar and Wolfhart Pannenberg.[5] On the other hand, an attempt has been made to cast doubt on the compulsory association of the Christian message to the linear model of history:

> It . . . remains yet to be shown conclusively in the west or in the east, in ancient traditions or in more modern positions, that the christian faith and its (theological) interpretations are necessarily bound up with any one conception of history, which is to say with any one particular culture and experience of reality.[6]

We must recognize, however, that the historicizing concept of modern Hinduism is not exempt from the influence of Western philosophy. Furthermore, the Christian message, in particular the Christian signification of the Jesus Christ event, is, like it or not, inextricably bound up with a concept of history capable of bestowing all of its density on God's personal involvement in the history of human beings. We shall return to this below in our effort, in the context of the encounter of the religions, to account for the indissoluble link in Christianity between the Jesus of history and the Christ of faith.

However, we must draw one conclusion forthwith. True, the Christian message is in theory open to all cultures and called to express itself in each of them. This does not imply, however, the a priori capacity of that message to accommodate all that it encounters in the religious traditions of humanity. Cultures can harbor elements not assimilable by the Christian message because there is no room in these elements themselves for that message. It is scarcely evident how a cyclical or spiral concept of history might leave room for the decisive value that Christianity attributes to the historical, particular Jesus Christ event as representing God's final commitment to humanity. The linear model is inescapable here. Apart from it, history cannot take on the authentic sense of a dialogue between God and humanity through God's historical interventions or have a final destiny actually assigned to it by God. Open as the Christian message would like to be to all cultures, it cannot renounce a view of the world and reality apart from which the Jesus Christ event would find itself bereft of its true sense and genuine meaning.

The history of this dialogue between God and humanity is a history of salvation. This does not mean that it is part of universal history as a part of the whole. True, salvation history is not formally identical with "profane" history; but it is materially coextensive with it. It, too, is universal. Salvation history is universal history itself *qua* salvation dialogue between God and humanity. While distinct from profane history, it is inseparable from it.

This is tantamount to saying that salvation history extends from creation to the Parousia of the risen Lord at the end of time. Creation is part of salvation history from the outset: it, too, is mystery of salvation. As we know, Israel's religious experience is totally founded on the covenant struck by Yahweh with his people through Moses, not on some philosophical consideration of creation. It is from a point of departure in the experience of the covenant, and by retrojection, that the mystery of divine creation enters Israel's awareness. Creation is first and foremost a salvation mystery, the starting point of the salvific dialogue between Yahweh and the people of Yahweh. This progressive reflection, leading from the covenant back to creation by retrojection, is part of Israel's long journey to the discovery of the one God, culminating in absolute monotheism, as concretely expressed in the *Shema Yisra'el:* "Hear, O Israel: Yahweh our God is one Yahweh! You shall love Yahweh your God with all your heart, with all your soul, and with all your strength" (Deut. 6:4–5), and especially, as theologically established by the prophets, especially in Second Isaiah.

THE JESUS CHRIST EVENT AS CENTER OF SALVATION HISTORY

Thus salvation history extends from the beginning of history to its end, from creation to the end of the world. Christian faith places the Jesus Christ event at its center. This is to be understood not chronologically, but theologically. The Jesus Christ event is the decisive event of salvation history — the pivot, we might say, upon which the entire history of the dialogue between God and humanity turns, the principle of intelligibility of the divine plan as concretized in the history of the world. Well does Vatican II's Pastoral Constitution *Gaudium et Spes,* number 10, say that the key, the center, and the end of all human history is found in Jesus Christ.

This text rightly speaks of a center and an end. The apostolic faith distinguishes between the event of the coming of Jesus Christ into history and the Lord's eschatological return in the Parousia. The Reign of God already inaugurated in the world through the historical Jesus — in his life, his death, and his resurrection — nevertheless is still only *in via* toward its eschatological perfection. As exegesis has shown, a tension prevails between the "already" and the "not yet" of the Reign of God. A tension that is constitutive of the "time of the church," the time in which we live. In virtue of this tension, we can place the accent now on what has already occurred once and for all, now on what remains to be accomplished. As we know, a "realized" eschatology has often been associated with the name of C. H. Dodd, while a "consistent" eschatology bears that of Albert Schweitzer.

If we realize, however, that in the apostolic church there was a widespread belief at first that the Lord's return was near and imminent, we shall more readily understand why the emphasis was more on what had already occurred—the historical Jesus Christ event, which culminated in his death and resurrection. As Joachim Gnilka, in his contribution to a session of the Pontifical Biblical Commission on "Bible and Christology," said:

> A "consistent" eschatology neglects a decisive factor in Jesus' proclamation of the Reign of God, namely: that not only is the *Basileia* a *future* event, to which we look forward, but its healing, helping, saving forces are *already present and active* through Jesus' actions and preaching, and that they can be experienced by human beings. The relationship of tension thus established between a salvation already present and a salvation still to come is new, and has no parallel in Judaism. Jesus not only proclaims the *Basileia;* he also conveys it. This is why he alone could make such a proclamation.[7]

For the apostolic faith, as for Christian faith thereafter, while our whole present history is steeped in a tension between the "already" and the "not yet"—a tension that we must not seek to dissolve—the accent is nonetheless on what has already been accomplished once and for all by God in Jesus Christ.

Oscar Cullmann has excellently shown the contrast prevailing between Israel's religious psychology and that of the first Christians.[8] Israel was totally turned to the future—to the fulfillment of Yahweh's promise and the messianic expectations to be accomplished in a decisive, eschatological salvation event—without knowing when that event was to take place. The apostolic church discovered, to its astonishment and wonder, that this eschatological event had actually taken place in the immediate past, in Jesus' resurrection from the dead. Thus Jesus' resurrection, the starting point of a christological faith, wrought a 180 degree turn among the first Christians. The faith of their forebears had been orientated to an indefinite future, while the Paschal experience riveted their attention on a definite event they had experienced in the immediate past. Not that the first Christians' orientation to the future simply vanished; but their eschatological expectancy was now divided into two times: the "already" and the "not yet"—the event accomplished, and its final plenitude. Meanwhile, the role of the axis connecting these twin poles, the pivot of salvation history, fell unambiguously to the "already." Christ raised, not the Parousia, was at the center of their faith. The rest—the "not yet"—would follow as a logical consequence, as a totally reliable development of the potential of the past event. To be sure, the air is electric with the expectancy of the fullness of the Reign of God, the Parousia, but it is the Jesus Christ event that is at the center of salvation history.

DIVINE COVENANTS AND HUMANITY'S RELIGIOUS TRADITIONS IN SALVATION HISTORY

Salvation history develops throughout successive covenants. The Bible and theology list four of these covenants. First of all, we may speak of a covenant struck by God with the whole of humanity as symbolized by Adam, progenitor of the human race. The Book of Genesis records the original familiarity characterizing relationships between God the creator and the parent of humanity. A certain theology in vogue not so very long ago spoke of a "primordial revelation," whose vestiges it thereupon sought in humanity's various religions. All religions were originally monotheistic, we were told, and this original monotheism testified to a primitive revelation. However, the theological current in question regarded the religions of humanity as different expressions of a merely "natural" religion, a universal quest for God among human beings and their desire for union with God. This theory has been abandoned today.

Recent theology rightly finds in God's covenant with Noah a symbol of the divine covenant struck with the nations. Yahweh told Noah and his sons: "Behold, I have made my covenant with you and with your descendants after you" (see Gen. 9:9). The rainbow will serve as a "sign of the covenant which I [God] make between myself and you . . . for the generations to come" (see Gen. 9:12). When the rainbow appears in the sky, "I [God] shall see it and shall remember the everlasting covenant between God and all ensouled beings, in a word, all flesh upon the earth" (see Gen. 9:16).

We must make no mistake: The covenant with Noah is not to be understood as simply a cosmic theophany in the elements of nature. We are dealing with a personal, universal intervention on the part of God in the history of the nations, previous to the subsequent covenant with the chosen people. The religious traditions of humanity are the chosen testimonials of this covenant with the nations, in Noah.

Yahweh's covenant with the chosen people through Abraham and Moses calls for no special explanation here. Let us simply note that it occurs in two stages: the choice of Abraham, with the promise and the covenant sealed in circumcision (Gen. 15–17); and the revelation to Moses, with the exodus and the covenant at the foot of Mount Sinai (Exod. 3–20). The covenant thus established by God is constitutive of the chosen people: It confers on Israel a special vocation with regard to the nations. It is likewise directly ordered to the definitive covenant with humanity concluded by God in Jesus Christ. The very terms of the covenants, old and new, suggest this direct orientation of Israel and its history toward the Jesus Christ event, the culminating point of all the divine covenants.

Christian tradition has rightly valued all four of these successive divine covenants: in Adam, in Noah, in Abraham and Moses, and in Christ. We need only hear Irenaeus of Lyon, who sees in these various covenants a "fourfold manner of activity on the part of the Lord." He writes:

> Four covenants were bestowed upon humanity: the first before the Deluge, in the time of Adam; the second, after the Deluge, in the time of Noah; the third, which is the gift of the Law, in the time of Moses; finally, the fourth, which renews the human being and recapitulates all things in itself—the one which, by the Gospel, exalts human beings and sends them soaring for the heavenly Reign.[9]

The relation between the earlier covenants and the last definitive one struck by God with the whole of humanity is not one of identity. Theology distinguishes between general, universal salvation history, which embraces the first two covenants in Adam and Noah, and special salvation history comprising the latter two covenants, the Abrahamic-Mosaic covenant and the Christic. This distinction implies in turn a distinction between a universal and a special revelation.[10] Why? Because of the singular relationship that obtains between the Abrahamic-Mosaic covenant and the Christic covenant: The election of the chosen people has the value of immediate historical preparation for the decisive salvation event in Jesus Christ. True, everything before Christ belongs to the "time of preparation" and expectancy, while what follows pertains to the time of mission, the "time of the church." On the other hand, we must posit important distinctions in the time of preparation and expectancy. Not everything there is of the same value. Surely the time of preparation, in its totality, is ordered toward the Jesus Christ event. But it is not all ordered in the same manner. One must clearly distinguish between the covenant in Noah, which belongs to general salvation history, and the Abrahamic-Mosaic covenant, which pertains to the special history of salvation. The former represents the remote, indirect preparation of the nations for the Jesus Christ event; the latter represents the immediate, direct preparation for the event in the history of the chosen people. The Abrahamic-Mosaic covenant has a unique meaning, then: Jesus Christ will belong to the Jewish tradition, and the Jesus Christ event will be part of the history of Israel.

In the context of the new dialogue between Christianity and Judaism, Christian theology today has become more sensitive to the unique relationship between the Abrahamic-Mosaic covenant and the Christic covenant. Apropos of the dialogue between Judaism and Christianity, Dermot A. Lane writes:

> If progress is to be made in the Jewish-Christian encounter, then it is essential that we take a more extensive look at the relationship that

exists between Jesus and Judaism. For too long it has been said that Jesus makes sense only "over and against" Judaism. This simplistic point of view has been a source of much Antisemitism in Christian circles. However, critical studies in recent times by Jews and Christians clearly bring out the Jewishness of Jesus and his teaching (C. Vermes, D. Flusser, R. Aron, B. Z. Bokser). Not only that, but it can be argued convincingly that Christianity grew out of an "intra-Jewish critique of Israel and that the early Christian interpretation is truly a Jewish interpretation of Jesus" (E. Schillebeeckx). In other words Christianity is an extension of a particular form of Judaism. . . . This dimension of the Jewishness of Jesus and his teaching must surely figure prominently in the Jewish-Christian dialogue. The Jewishness of early Christianity and Christianness of first-century Judaism has much to contribute to the understanding of both traditions.[11]

We cannot set the preparation of Israel for the Jesus Christ event and that wrought by God among the nations on an equal footing, much less identify them for all practical purposes. Humanity's other religious traditions do not have the same signification in salvation history as the religion of Judaism. They do not all bear the same relation to the Jesus Christ event. The fact remains, however, that they are ordered to this event, and accordingly are not only pre-Christian but "pro-Christian." All are authentic "evangelical preparations," however indirect, and have been intended as such by God, who directs all human history toward its term in Jesus Christ. They are authentic personal interventions of God in the history of the nations, orientating them to the decisive divine intervention in Jesus Christ.

But now a question arises. If the covenants struck by God with the nations, as expressed in the religious traditions of humanity, are essentially ordered to the Jesus Christ event, are they not by that very fact provisional? Or may we imagine that even after the coming of Jesus Christ they retain the meaning assigned them by God in human history as "evangelical preparations"? Have the religious traditions of humanity, even today, a positive meaning in the divine salvation plan? Or, on the contrary, are they now in desuetude, transcended by the Jesus Christ event?

The Council of Florence seems to have answered with the latter alternative. On the matter of Judaism, which we may perhaps consider the prime exemplar, the Decree for the Jacobites (1442) hands down a negative judgment as to continued Jewish observance of the prescriptions and religious observances of the Old Testament:

With regard to the legal prescriptions of the Old Testament, that is, the Mosaic Law, with the ceremonies, the holy sacrifices, and the sacraments contained therein, [the Church] firmly believes, professes, and teaches as follows. Since all of these elements have been instituted with the purpose of signifying something in the future, surely in their own time they contributed to divine worship. However, with the advent of Our Lord Jesus Christ, whom they had signified [in advance], they have ceased [to be effective], and the sacraments of the New Testament have commenced. . . . [The Church] does not deny that, from the Passion of Christ to the promulgation of the Gospel (*usque ad promulgatum Evangelium*), it was permitted to abide by these prescriptions—without, however, holding that they were in any way necessary for salvation. However, it asserts that, since the promulgation of the Gospel (*post promulgatum Evangelium*), they may not be observed, under pain of the loss of eternal salvation.[12]

But how are we to understand the "promulgation of the Gospel" that is in question here? How does one decide where and when that promulgation has occurred? Must we, indeed can we, think that it has now taken place everywhere in the world, so that the old covenant no longer has currency today for Jews anywhere, or, a fortiori, for other religious traditions?

Karl Rahner rightly observes that the promulgation of the gospel should be interpreted existentially.[13] Indeed, it is impossible to pinpoint a time when the gospel can and should be regarded as having been promulgated in a particular region, still less everywhere in the world. It is a matter of the concrete situation of each human person. Each time, and for so long as, individual conscience has not imposed on an individual person, in virtue of the gift of faith, the obligation to adhere to Jesus Christ as Savior, the gospel has not been promulgated for that person. It follows that the old covenant in the case at issue, or any religious tradition whatsoever, retains its value as evangelical preparation for the individual, as willed by God in virtue of the ordering of every religious tradition in salvation history to the Jesus Christ event.

As we know, Paul himself hesitated as to the continued validity of the Mosaic covenant for the Jewish people after the coming of Jesus Christ. He never fully resolved the question. However, he clearly asserts in Romans 9–11 the irrevocability of the divine gift bestowed on the people of God. Of the people of Israel, he says, "Theirs were the adoption, the glory, the covenants, the lawgiving, the worship, and the promises" (Rom. 9:4), and they are still the chosen people, for "God's gifts and his call are irrevocable" (Rom. 11:29). While a part of Israel has become hard-hearted, then, all Israel will yet be saved at the last (Rom. 11:25–26).

In any case, the magisterium of the church has on several occasions expressed itself more favorably on this question in recent years. Even the Declaration *Nostra Aetate* (no. 4), on the relations between the church and non-Christian religions, placed the accent on the spiritual bond linking the people of the New Testament with the people of Israel and on their common spiritual patrimony. It eagerly cited the Pauline texts affirming the permanence of God's gifts to Israel. It went no further, however. Among the most explicit texts of the postconciliar years we may cite "Pastoral Orientations of the French Bishops' Commission for Relations with Judaism" (1973).[14] Referring to the "permanent call of the Jewish people," the document declares:

> While Christianity's covenant is a new one, in Jesus Christ, Judaism is to be regarded by Christians not merely as a social and historical reality, but also, and especially, as a religious one—not as a relic of a venerable and ancient past, but as a yet living reality, down through the years.[15]

The document goes on to explain:

> Notwithstanding a very ancient, but questionable, exegesis, we may not conclude from the New Testament that the Jewish People has been stripped of its election. Scripture as a whole encourages us to recognize and to acknowledge, in the concern of the Jewish people for its fidelity to the Law and the covenant, the sign of God's faithfulness to his people. . . .[16]

> The first covenant has not been invalidated by the new. It is its root and source, its foundation and promise.[17]

The Mosaic covenant abides, then. If it retains its value for Christianity, which sees its fulfillment and renewal in Jesus Christ, then a fortiori it retains its value for the Jews, who continue to receive it as God's gift to the chosen people.

Two Vatican documents also reflect a positive attitude toward the concept of the continued validity of the old covenant. First we had "Orientations and Recommendations for the Application of the Conciliar Declaration *Nostra Aetate*, no. 4," published by the Commission for Religious Relations with Judaism (January 4, 1975).[18] Then came "Notes for a Correct Presentation of Jews and Judaism in the Preaching and Catechesis of the Catholic Church," published by the same commission (June 24, 1985).[19]

"Orientations" forthrightly asserts that Christians should seek better knowledge of the religious traditions of Judaism and learn how the Jews define themselves.

Citing the bonds that link the Christian and Jewish liturgies, the document refers to the Vatican II Constitution, *Dei Verbum*, which encourages preachers and religious educators to seek a better understanding of Old Testament elements that retain their authentic value,[20] and, when commenting on biblical passages, explain the continuity of the Christian faith with that of the old covenant.

In its turn, "Notes," referring to *Nostra Aetate*, recalls the unique relationship between Christianity and Judaism, a relationship John Paul II said was founded on God's design. It was this pope who, recalling the common legacy between the church and Judaism, went on to say that considering these elements and contemporary Jewish religious life will help us understand certain elements of the church.

And "Notes" adds that the Pope presented this continued reality of the Jewish people to representatives of the Jewish community at Mainz on November 17, 1980, addressing them as "the people of God of the old covenant, which has never been revoked."

This formula speaks for itself. Going on to show the relationship between the Old and New Testament, the document explains that the word *Old* does not mean expired, or no longer in force. The document emphasizes the ongoing value of the Old Testament, which personally concerns Christians as well as Jews.

The case of the Abrahamic-Mosaic covenant is clear. It has permanent validity for Christians, as, according to their faith, it is now fulfilled and made new in Jesus Christ. A fortiori, then, it will have permanent validity for Jews, of whose faith it constitutes the very core.

The next question to be addressed is whether what is said of Israel, based on a sound interpretation of scripture, is not to be asserted theologically for other religious traditions that arise by virtue of the covenant established with Noah. Do not they, too, retain their value as evangelical preparation willed by God in the history of salvation? To give an affirmative response to this question is not to regard all religious traditions as being on the same footing, or to attribute to all of them the same meaning in salvation history. We have seen the special signification of Judaism, which, as immediate historical preparation for the Jesus Christ event, belongs to special salvation history. We must now introduce new distinctions among the religious traditions that we have said belong to general salvation history.

The place of Islam is unique from a number of viewpoints. For one thing, it belongs, with Judaism and Christianity, to the group of religions called monotheistic and prophetical. On the other hand, it follows the Jesus Christ event chronologically. May we then regard Islam as pro-Christian? Especially, may we attribute to it, even today, the value of an evangelical preparation? To ask this question is tantamount to inquiring whether the believers of the Islamic faith actually share, as they profess to do, the Abrahamic faith in response to the covenant struck by God with the patriarch.

Recent church teaching has undergone a certain development on this point. The Declaration *Nostra Aetate* (no. 3), positive as it is on the subject of the Muslims, was content to assert that Muslims seek to submit to the decrees of God, as Abraham did to whose faith they appeal. The Dogmatic Constitution on the Church, *Lumen Gentium* (no. 16), likewise states that Muslims claim to hold the faith of Abraham. Paul VI seems not to have gone beyond the council's assertion. Thus, for example, on his visit to Uganda in 1969, the Pope expressed his respect for the Muslim faith and his hope that the commonalities between Christianity and Islam would unite them in brotherhood. That is to say that Islam appeals to, and refers to the faith of Abraham, not that it actually shares this faith with Judaism and Christianity.

However, the transition from subjective reference to objective faith does occur in the magisterium of John Paul II.[21] The present Pope is not content with simply recalling that Islam appeals to the faith of Abraham as pertaining to its own origin, according to the formula of Vatican II, which thus presumes nothing as to the fact. On the contrary, he asserts that Muslims share with us the faith of Abraham. Thus, in his address to the Catholic community of Ankara, the Pope unequivocally declared that Muslims have the faith of Abraham in one almighty and merciful God. He spoke of the faith in God professed by Christians, Muslims, and Jews.[22] And in his message to the president of Pakistan, the Pope referred to Abraham's faith, with which Christians, Muslims, and Jews all link their own faiths.[23] This means a parallel among the Abrahamic references of the three monotheistic religions. It is also, it would seem, an implicit admission that Muslims are saved in their own way as heirs of the faith of Abraham, the father of all believers, who responded to God's call with faith (cf. Heb. 11:8–10). The clearest of John Paul II's statements in this area is perhaps his address on the occasion of his meeting with young Muslims at Casablanca (August 19, 1985). There the Pope established a parallel between the faith of Christians and that of Muslims, both of whom have Abraham's faith as their model.

Accordingly, just as the Mosaic covenant is still in force for the Jews, so also the faith of Abraham, which the Muslims share with us, retains its validity. In their own way, both have the value of evangelical preparation, even today, for the Jews and for the Muslims, to whom the gospel has not been promulgated in the sense defined above. Whether the other religious traditions precede or follow the Jesus Christ event chronologically, the same principle can be extended to them, beyond the purview of the monotheistic religions. We may then say that the other religious traditions, as well, still have the positive meaning assigned them by God in salvation history. Far from evanescing as transitional, or provisional, they retain the value — analogical, to be sure, but real — conferred on them by their providential ordering to the universal salvation event. They are still stepping-stones, set in place by God, in view of the Jesus Christ event. Both before and after Jesus Christ, salvation is present and effective in the religious traditions of humanity. It is found there, however, in virtue of the universal activity of the Christic mystery, to which they necessarily refer. This is what we shall attempt to show in the next chapter.

6

Salvation without the Gospel

Having considered the historical pre-Christian position of the religious traditions of humanity in salvation history, we now turn our attention to the existential question of the salvific value these traditions exercise today vis-à-vis their members. This is the difficult, disputed question of the active presence of the Christic mystery—sole source of salvation—within these various religious traditions themselves. Is this view theologically acceptable? If so, how? We must begin with a correct statement of the question.

All theologians today must agree that Christian salvation—that is, salvation by Jesus Christ, the sole Mediator, the only Way—is possible for all human beings, in virtue of the universal salvific will of God. Christians have no monopoly on the salvation bestowed by Jesus Christ. Exclusivism, in any way, shape or form, whether in the hands of Karl Barth and H. Kraemer or Leonard Feeney, is to be proscribed (see chapter four). However, we are asking another question. We are inquiring not merely into the possibility of salvation for individual persons without explicit faith in Christ, but into the role that may be played by the religious tradition to which they belong and which they sincerely practice in the mystery of their salvation in Jesus Christ.

All substitutions proposed by theology over the course of the centuries to explain how faith in Christ could reach those who know him not, for their salvation, are beside the point here. Appeal has been made to a "primordial revelation" for this purpose; the intervention of an angel sent by God (St. Thomas); fidelity to a right conscience; or even more realistically, a fundamental option in adults and its equivalent, the "act of dying," in children, in a modern theology of human death.[1] These various substitutions were supposed to convey, in one way or another, at least implicitly, a faith that would be necessary and sufficient for salvation.[2] Whatever the value of some of them, none of them can answer the question that we ask here.

What we wish to know is what role can be ascribed theologically to the various religious traditions themselves in the mystery of the salvation of their members. Are these persons saved by Jesus Christ in spite of belonging to a given tradition, notwithstanding that tradition, apart from that tradition? Or are they saved in their very adherence to that tradition—by it and through it in some way? In other words, what is at issue here is the manner in which the saving power of Christ reaches those outside the church. How does Christian salvation reach these persons? May we speak of a positive role, a salvific value in the various religious traditions and their components—sacred books, sacramental practices, moral codes—when it comes to the mystery of the salvation of their members? And if so, how are we to conceptualize the relationship between the salvific activity of Christ as universal Savior and the religious tradition within which that activity reaches the members of that tradition? In other words, are these religious traditions means or ways of salvation, and if so, in what sense? Is there salvation without the gospel?

We note that a frequently cited passage from Vatican Council II has raised the question we are asking here, without, however, giving it a clear answer. The Pastoral Constitution on the Church in the Modern World, *Gaudium et Spes* (no. 22), having explained how those who are Christians are associated to the Paschal mystery of Christ, continues as follows with reference to those who are not.

> All this [regarding Christians' association to the Paschal mystery] holds true not only for Christians, but for all men of good will in whose hearts grace works in an unseen way. For, since Christ died for all men, and since the ultimate vocation of man is in fact one, and divine, we ought to believe that the Holy Spirit in a manner known to God offers to every man the possibility of being associated with this paschal mystery.

What the council leaves unexplained is *how* the saving power of the Paschal mystery of Jesus Christ reaches the members of the other religious traditions. It is content to assert the fact. Theology, however, should ask this question, and answer it. This is what we shall attempt to do in the present chapter. First we shall present the contrasting opinions currently held. Then we shall undertake a brief analysis of the apposite data of scripture and sacred tradition. We shall examine the direction that the various texts of Vatican Council II seem to take. Finally, we shall sketch a positive solution to the problem in the light of a new theological approach based on certain fundamental principles.

TWO CONTRASTING POSITIONS

Following the lead of J. P. Schineller, we have already distinguished four major categories of opinion in the area of the theology of religions with regard to Christ and the church. The two contrasting positions that we now wish to set forth and discuss both fall within the category of "christocentric universe, inclusive Christianity." Thus Karl Barth's exclusivism, orchestrated by H. Kraemer, is beside the point here. We shall return to the two positions listed above under the heading of "theocentric universe" — equivalently, "pluralism" — when we discuss the uniqueness and universality of Jesus Christ in the order of salvation. While the two positions now under consideration fall within the same category, christocentric universe, inclusive Christianity, they are nonetheless very different — indeed, mutually exclusive.[3]

The first position has long been referred to as the theory of "fulfillment." According to this view, the various religions of humanity represent the human being's innate desire for union with the Divine, of which there are various expressions in the various cultures and geographical areas of humanity. Jesus Christ and Christianity represent God's personal response to this universal human aspiration. Thus while all other religions are varying expressions of *homo naturaliter religiosus*, and so of "natural religion," only Christianity, as the divine response to the human quest for God, is "supernatural religion."

We find this first opinion in authors who wrote during the first half of this century in an Asian context. Their titles indicate their intent. For example, we have J. N. Farquhar's *The Crown of Hinduism*, or P. Johanns' *Vers le Christ par le Vedanta*.[4] The same view was taken up again later by a number of Western theologians[5]: Jean Daniélou, Henri de Lubac, Hans Urs von Balthasar, and others. It is likewise to be found in Paul VI's 1975 Apostolic Exhortation, *Evangelii Nuntiandi* (no. 53), after the 1974 Synod of Bishops on the evangelization of the modern world.

While acknowledging that the various religions of the world contain certain positive values, the Pope limits their content to that of an echo of the human being's sincere quest for God. He continues: Even "the most estimable natural religious expressions" fail to establish "an authentic, living relationship" with God — only Christianity can do that effectively — "although they have, as it were, their arms outstretched toward heaven."[6] The other religions express only the human aspiration for God; they are natural. Christ and Christianity are the responses given by God to this human aspiration. There alone is supernatural religion. One must recognize, however, that this negative evaluation — to which we shall have to return later, in order to establish its implications for the interreligious dialogue in the mission of the church — is seriously at odds with interventions at the Synod pronounced by various Asian bishops, especially by Indians.[7] We shall return to this point.

According to the theory of fulfillment, the mystery of Christ reaches the members of other religious traditions as the divine response to the human religious aspiration, but these religious traditions themselves play no role in this salvation mystery. Henri de Lubac explains that to attribute a positive salvific value to them would be tantamount to setting them in competition with Christianity, thus obscuring the latter's uniqueness. He observes, citing Pierre Teilhard de Chardin, that the divine plan will surely be an orderly one: It must have a single axis, a single point of convergence. That point is Christianity, the sole way of salvation. To regard other traditions as playing a positive role in the mystery of the salvation of their members would be, in effect, to establish them as parallel routes to salvation, and thus to destroy the unity of the divine plan.[8]

In answer to Henri de Lubac, we may observe that while the unity of the divine plan does indeed require a single point of convergence, that point—according to Teilhard himself—is not primarily Christianity as such, or the church, but Jesus Christ. The Teilhardian outlook is unmistakably christocentric: The church represents the "Christified" portion of the world, while the eschatological fulfillment of the Reign of God is to consist in universal Christification of all things. A single citation will suffice to establish that, for Teilhard, a Christified universe represents the end point of a cosmic evolution. Teilhard writes:

> Christ . . . is the alpha and omega, the beginning and the end, the foundation stone and the keystone, Fulfillment and Fulfiller. It is he who consummates, he who gives all things their consistency. Toward him and by him, the inner Life and Light of the World, is wrought, in pangs and travail, the universal convergence of all created spirit. He is the one precious, solid Center, gleaming on the future pinnacle of the world.[9]

It is doubtful whether ascribing a positive salvific value to other religious traditions necessarily places them in competition with Christ and the religion founded by him. Will there not rather be various nonparallel modalities of the mediation of the mystery of salvation, all in relationship to the mystery of Jesus Christ?

At all events, according to the fulfillment theory, there is no salvation without the gospel or any such thing as anonymous Christianity.

The second position to be considered here can be called the theory of the presence of Christ in the religions. According to this theory, humanity's various religious traditions represent various divine interventions in salvation history. These interventions are ordered to the decisive salvific event in Jesus Christ and maintain for their members, even today, a positive value in the order of salvation by virtue of the presence of Jesus Christ and his saving mystery operative in them and through them. Admittedly, the saving mystery of Christ is unique. But all other religious traditions, in virtue of the divine plan of salvation, are set in relationship with this mystery, in whose respect they represent, each in its own way, an ordering of mediation. Thus no religion is purely natural. In every religion, historically, there is a divine intervention in the history of nations and an existential mediation of the mystery of salvation in Jesus Christ. All religions, then, for more than one reason, are supernatural.

Among the leading representatives of this theory we may mention, first of all, Raimundo Panikkar, whose first book is entitled *The Unknown Christ of Hinduism*.[10] It is from this book that our second contrasting position has received its very name. Among Western authors, the same opinion is represented, to cite only a few, by Karl Rahner, his disciples H. R. Schlette and A. Röper, and his commentator, G. D'Costa.

According to this position, the religious traditions of humanity, as social phenomena and historical institutions, have a salvific value by virtue of the presence of the mystery of Jesus Christ operative in them. The members of these traditions are saved by Christ not in spite of their religious allegiance and sincere practice of their tradition, but through that allegiance and practice. There is salvation without the gospel, then, although none without Christ or apart from him. To be sure, the operative presence of the mystery of Jesus Christ in other religious traditions is concealed, and remains unknown by their members, but it is no less real for all that.

It is this hidden, unknown operative presence of the mystery of Christ in other religious traditions that Karl Rahner has designated by the controversial term, "anonymous Christianity." He writes, for example:

> There is an implicit and anonymous Christianity. . . . There is and has to be an anonymous and yet real relationship between the individual person and the concrete history of salvation, including Jesus Christ, in someone who has not yet had the whole, concrete, historical, explicit and reflexive experience in word and sacrament of this reality of salvation history. Such a person has this real and existentiell [sic] relationship merely implicitly in obedience to his orientation in grace towards the God of absolute, historical presence and self-communication. He exercises this obedience by accepting his own existence without reservation. . . . Alongside this there is the fullness of Christianity which has become conscious of itself explicitly in faith and in hearing the word of the gospel, in the church's profession of faith, in sacrament, and in living an explicit Christian life which knows that it is related to Jesus of Nazareth.[11]

Anonymous Christianity, Rahner explains, is lived by the members of other religious traditions in the sincere practice of their own traditions. Christian salvation reaches them, anonymously, through these traditions. Thus we must acknowledge in these traditions "moments," or supernatural elements, of grace.[12] As long as the obligation to adhere to Christ as Savior is not imposed on the personal conscience of a given individual, the mediation of the salvation mystery through that individual's religious tradition, and in its sincere practice, remains effective. The anonymous Christian is a Christian unawares. The difference between such a one and the explicit

Christian is in the subjective awareness (absent in the one, present in the other) of "being a Christian." What occurs when an anonymous Christian is confronted with the message of Christ and embraces it? Rahner writes:

> The revelation which comes to him from without is not in such a case the proclamation of something as yet absolutely unknown. . . . [It is] the expression in objective concepts of something which this person has already attained or could already have attained in the depth of his rational existence. . . . In the last analysis, the proclamation of the gospel does not simply turn someone absolutely abandoned by God and Christ into a Christian, but turns an anonymous Christian into someone who now also knows about his Christian belief in the depths of his grace-endowed being by objective reflection and in the profession of faith which is given a social form in the Church.[13]

A question remains, however. Is the difference between the anonymous Christian and the explicit Christian only a matter of the reflexive awareness, absent in the one case and present in the other, of being a Christian? And if the passage from anonymous to explicit Christianity transpires, does it consist solely in coming to a formal consciousness of being what one has always been without knowing it? Is there no difference as to the manner in which the salvation mystery of Jesus Christ is mediated—no new regime of mediation of this mystery? To be sure, an awareness of being a Christian is part of the mediation of the mystery of salvation proper to Christianity. However, that mediation is not reducible to the awareness. It entails an acceptance of the word of the gospel, it involves the liturgical and sacramental life of the church, it implies a profession of faith in the communion of the church.

If the essay cited immediately above seems to allow any lingering doubts, the *Foundations of Christian Faith* erases all ambiguity. Between anonymous Christianity and explicit Christianity there are indeed, Rahner teaches, distinct regimens of salvation and distinct modalities of mediation of the mystery of Jesus Christ. Thus anonymous Christianity remains a fragmentary, incomplete, radically crippled reality. It harbors dynamics that impel it to join with explicit Christianity. Nevertheless, the same mystery of salvation in Jesus Christ is present on both sides, through distinct mediations.[14] It is to this operative presence of salvation in Jesus Christ, concealed and unconscious on the one side, reflexive and conscious on the other, and to the distinct regimes of mediation of the one mystery there conveyed, that we must now turn our attention.

THE DATA OF REVELATION AND CHRISTIAN TRADITION

Old and New Testaments

The data of the Old Testament on the subject are indecisive and ambivalent. It would be an easy matter to collate, from the historical, sapiential, and prophetic literature, a series of negative evaluations of the value of the religions of the nations and their gods, or even explicit denunciations of the same.[15] After all, what are they, compared to Yahweh, the God of the covenant?

Psalm 115:5 best expresses Israel's derision of the idols of the nations: "They have mouths but speak not, eyes but see not." The gradual development of monotheism will reduce the gods of the nations from their state of inferiority vis-à-vis Yahweh to the condition of angels (*elohim*) serving in his court, to finish in their utter nonexistence. True, the Old Testament knows holy pagans — Henoch, Melchizedek, Job, and others.[16] Nevertheless, when it contrasts the religious situation of the nations with the security that Israel draws from the covenant, it often denounces the religions of the nations (cf. 1 Kings 11:1–13; Jer. 2:26–29, 10:1–16; Bar. 6:7–72; Isa. 40:18–20, 44:9–20, 46:5–7; Song 13:1–14, 15:6–19; 1 Macc. 1:41–64; 2 Macc. 4:1–11; Dan. 14; etc.). It even foresees their abolition (cf. Isa. 2:1–5, 19:23–25, 25:6–9; Isa. 45:20–23; Zech. 8:21–23). One must wonder, however, whether these prophetic judgments have a dogmatic value or rather reflect a profound awareness of Israel's privileged condition in salvation history: Specially chosen by Yahweh as his people, Israel must never turn away to the gods of the nations. This would be serious infidelity. The prophets call it adultery.

Moreover, the Old Testament not only speaks of "saints" among the nations; it posits the foundation of their condition. God's covenant with Noah (Gen. 8:20–9:17) is doubtless the most revealing positive datum of the Old Testament on the subject that concerns us. While altogether inferior to the Mosaic covenant, the covenant with Noah is a friendship pact struck by the God of Israel with the nations. The mythic character of the personage, acknowledged by modern biblical exegesis, in no way militates against Israel's faith in God's self-revelation to the nations as well. Indeed, as we have seen (see chapter five), the covenant with Noah is not reducible to an impersonal manifestation of God through the phenomena of nature.[17] It is an actual manifestation of the divine salvific love, a personal intervention of God in the history of the nations and in the life of human beings. It is the revelation of a God who speaks.[18] This revelation and covenant constitute the oldest and most precious revealed datum on which a theology of the religious traditions of humanity may be established.

The data of the New Testament, too, are ambivalent. We must first consider the attitude of Jesus himself. On the one hand, as we know, nearly the whole of his ministry is addressed to his own people. He even explicitly declares that he has been sent only to the lost sheep of the house of Israel (Matt. 15:24) and forbids his disciples to visit pagan territory (Matt. 10:5). On the other hand, when the occasion presents itself, Jesus manifests an attitude of openness toward the gentiles, who do not belong to the chosen people. He recognizes the good to be found in them. He wonders at the Roman centurion's openness to faith and declares that he has not found the like in Israel (Matt. 8:5–13). He works miracles of healing in behalf of foreigners (Mark 7:29; Matt. 15:21–28).

The meaning of these miracles, in Jesus' thinking, is that the Reign of God being inaugurated by his activity is present and active beyond the frontiers of the chosen people of Israel. Indeed, Jesus explicitly proclaimed the entry of gentiles into the Reign of God (Matt. 8:10–11, 11:20–24, 25:31–32). This Reign of God appears from the outset as extending beyond the chosen people of Israel: It embraces the nations, whose members can likewise belong to it. Later, when the church will be the continuation of the chosen people, the Reign of God will extend beyond it, as well, just as it will overreach it at the end of time in eschatological fulfillment.[19]

We come to the attitude of the apostolic church toward the pagans. Paul's pessimism in the letter to the Romans (Rom. 1–3) is well known. Paul declares that the wrath of God will fall upon the pagans for not having recognized the divine manifestation in creation (Rom. 1:18–32). Let us note, however, that the Jews fall under the same condemnation (Rom. 2–3). Their special status as chosen people does not spare them.

Once more we must wonder whether, rather than declarations of principle, what we are dealing with in Paul here is not a reflection on the concrete situation of whoever has found Jesus Christ, and, in him, has shared in the new life of these last times (Rom. 6:4, 7:6; 2 Cor. 5:17; Gal. 6:15). In comparison with the new, the past—whether that of the nations or of Israel itself—is like a state of perdition, now a thing of the past for good and all. Faith, once offered to Christians, abolishes by virtue of a divine decree, the value of all religions (Rom. 6:6; 2 Cor. 5:17; Eph. 4:22; Col. 3:9). If such is indeed the intent of the Pauline assertion, then we may not see in it the absolute denial of any value in other religious traditions.[20]

Indeed, as we know perfectly well, Paul adopts a very different, positive attitude elsewhere. We refer to the discourse in the Areopagus (Acts 17:22–31). There Paul praises the religious spirit of the Greeks, and proclaims to them the unknown God whom they worship without knowing. Whatever the exegetical problems raised by this passage—among others, concerning the Pauline or Lucan authenticity of the discourse[21]—the message surely seems to be that the religions of the nations are not bereft of value, but find in Jesus Christ the fulfillment of their aspirations (see also Acts 14:15–17). True, in comparison with what is offered in Jesus Christ, they seem very spare. But this does not prevent them from being a preparation for Christian faith.

But we must take a larger view. We must consult the entire breadth of salvation history, as conceived by the New Testament. To this end, suffice it to sketch the purview of the Joannine prologue. All salvation history, beginning with creation itself, is wrought through the divine Logos. This history, from the beginning (John 1:1), is ordered to the incarnation of the Verbum in humanity (1:14). Long before that incarnation, the Verbum was present in the world as source of life (1:4), as "true light that enlightens every man" (see 1:9). Here we are surely dealing with the active presence of the divine Logos, not yet incarnate, throughout the whole of human history.

In conclusion, we may assert:

> Obviously we have no right to exaggerate the theological implications of the account of Noah, or of the discourse in the Areopagus. But neither may we allow ourselves to underrate such declarations. They furnish a basis for judging religions from a frankly positive standpoint, since they are seen as constituting a real relationship with God. On the other hand, neither must we forget that, for scripture, one cannot adhere to the Christian faith without a "decision" in which we take our distance from the "past."[22]

Postbiblical Tradition

Postbiblical tradition, on the whole, is undecided and ambivalent. It would be easy to assemble, from the writings of the Fathers of the church, an anthology of harsh opinions and negative judgments on the religious traditions encountered by these ecclesiastics, without even having to appeal to the adage, *Extra ecclesiam nulla salus*, whose origin and immediate intent we have examined above (see chapter four). In the second and third centuries, however, an important current of thought arose which, while concerned to safeguard the unique value of the economy of salvation established by the Incarnation, regarded other religions as more than testimonials to the highest human aspirations that find their fulfillment in Christ. These other religions are seen as already containing in themselves, however imperfectly, the very mystery of salvation and the active presence of the divine Logos. Without employing the term, of course, this theology seems to be quite akin to that of anonymous Christianity, which we have observed above. Its most outstanding representatives are Justin, Irenaeus of Lyon, and Clement of Alexandria. We can permit ourselves only a rapid survey of their thought.[23]

For Justin, the Logos sowed its seed in the pre-Christian religious traditions. While it manifested itself partially in them, for us who have known it in its incarnation, it has been revealed entirely (2 *Apol.* 6:3, 8:1, 10:1–3). All human beings share in the Logos, and thus are Christians, but in various ways (1 *Apol.* 46:1–4). Accordingly, Christianity extends beyond its visible frontiers and exists before its historical coming. Before the Incarnation, however, the manifestation of the Logos is incomplete (2 *Apol.* 13:2–3, 10:8, 13:4–6). We should note that the Logos of which Justin speaks is not Philo of Alexandria's "Reason," but the Verbum, the Word whose universal operative presence in salvation history, since before the Incarnation, is asserted by the Joannine Prologue.[24]

Irenaeus of Lyon is the great theologian of the universal revelatory function of the cosmic Christ. According to Irenaeus, the Verbum is the personal manifestation of the Father: "The invisible reality seen in the Son is the Father, and the visible reality in which the Father is seen is the Son" ("Invisibile etenim Filii Pater, visibile autem Patris Filius," *Adversus Haereses* 4, 6, 6). The Logos has revealed itself to human beings, and has been present to them, since before the Incarnation (ibid. 4, 6, 5–7; 20, 6–7), being "inhesive" in their minds ("mentibus infixus," ibid. 2, 6, 1).

Irenaeus distinguishes four covenants made by God with human beings: in Adam, in Noah, in Moses, and in Jesus Christ (ibid. 3, 11, 8). All of the divine manifestations of salvation history, all of the theophanies, are Logophanies. The Father has always been manifested through the divine Verbum, even before the Incarnation. The Incarnation, however—that supreme manifestation of God in the divine Verbum—involves something completely new. Here the Logos "has conveyed every novelty, in bringing its own person" ("Omnem novitatem attulit seipsum afferens," ibid. 4, 34, 1). For, while before the Incarnation it was perceptible only to the minds of human beings, by its coming in the flesh it has become visible to their eyes.

Here is a clear assertion of the universal operative presence in salvation history of the nonincarnate Verbum, and at the same time of the absolutely unprecedented novelty of its personal insertion into human history by the Incarnation. According to Irenaeus, through its first manifestations the Verbum was, as it were, readying itself for the Incarnation. It is Irenaeus again who asserts, on the subject of the peoples who have not received Christian preaching fecundated by the activity of the Spirit, that they "believe in Christ," and that they "possess salvation, written, without paper or ink, by the Spirit in their heart" (ibid. 3, 4, 2).

According to Clement of Alexandria, Greek "philosophy" (which we must not distinguish too crisply from theology, which would be anachronistic) comes from God. It has been willed by God as a propaedeutic to the philosophy of Christ, to which it was intended to lead human minds (*Stromata* 7:2). The parallel shows quite clearly that it is not only their philosophy, but the religiousness of the Greek people, that is under consideration. This Greek piety has actually been (and still is) a providential means of salvation for this people, "until the Lord should will to call them" (*Strom.* 1:5). It served as a schoolteacher (*paidagogos*), to lead Hellenistic minds to Christ—not only because it naturally disposed them to receive his message, but because it served as a first "covenant" established by God with them through the divine Word. Greek philosophy, then, was a stepping-stone to the "philosophy of Christ" (*Strom.* 6:8).

Its function was transitory, however. Once it had prepared human beings for the coming of Christ, it would at last make way for him. Like a lamp that is useless after sunrise, Greek philosophy must pale and flicker to extinction after the coming of Christ (*Strom.* 5:5).

It is worthy of note, however, that according to Clement, it is not the

Greek philosophers who, enlightened by God, best directed the nations toward Christ. The most authentic guides of humanity were actually the "ancient philosophers" who, profoundly inspired by God and impelled by the Logos, have taught the nations the profoundest divine verities. He explicitly mentions, among others, "the Indian philosophers, and other non-Greek philosophers," including the Brahmans and the disciples of the Buddha (*Strom.* 1:5).

This is tantamount to asserting the presence of fragments of Christian truth in the Hindu and Buddhist traditions and assigning them a positive role in the order of salvation. Besides the *Stromata*, we have the *Protreptikos*, where Clement emphasizes the identity of the not-yet-incarnate Logos with the Word incarnate in Jesus. Here he develops a Logocentrism, asserting that the Logos was at work in Judaism, in the best of what the Greek philosophers and poets have to offer, as well as in Hinduism and Buddhism (*Protrep.* 1:7–8, 5:66, 6:67–72, 7:73–76, 8:77–81, 9:82, 11:112, etc.).

By way of conclusion of this cursory overview, let us say that the second and third Christian centuries testify to a theology of a salvation history consisting of successive stages and manifestations of God. All of these theophanies are Logophanies. The manifestations of the Verbum before the Incarnation represent the cosmic dispensation of salvation. The Incarnation is the historical climax of these manifestations. And there is more: What we have here is an anticipation of the theology of anonymous Christianity. Whatever their historical situation or tradition, men and women who have encountered the preincarnate Word are already in some way Christians. Their religious traditions are authentic means of salvation for them, then, in virtue of the objective ordering of these traditions to the event of Jesus Christ. The Verbum is present and active in these traditions. The Christic mystery is at work in the world, albeit imperfectly, even before the manifestation of the Word in flesh by the Incarnation.

This same perspective was later adopted and further developed more than two centuries later by St. Augustine. Augustine is harsh enough in his rebukes of Plotinian philosophers whose minds are closed to the gospel. Further, he cannot be suspected of having minimized the absolute novelty of the Incarnation (cf., for instance, *Contra Academicos*, 3, 19; *Sermo* 141, 1; etc.). However, in his *De Civitate Dei*, and in other works of the late period of his literary production, this same Augustine argues for the universal presence and influence of Christ before the Incarnation. He goes on to assert that the church itself existed before the coming of Christ in the flesh. Indeed, the church has always existed, for he speaks of an *ecclesia a justo Abel*. Abel represents the first just human being, and every just human being after him; all, in their pre-Christian historical situation, belong to Christ and the church (*Ennarrationes in Psalmos* 142, 3; 118; *Sermo* 29, 9).[25] Augustine knew that, in God's plan, the universal influence of the preincarnate Word was ordered to the historical event of the Incarnation. The encounter of the human being with God could never have been as real, as authentic, or ultimately as human as in the flesh of the Word incarnate. And yet, in virtue of the divine economy, God has encountered human beings in the Son since the very creation of the universe. According to an oft-cited passage in his *Retractationes* (1,13,3), Christianity has somehow existed since the inception of the human race. Augustine writes:

> The raw reality of what is called the Christian religion existed among the ancients. Nor was it absent from the inception of the human race to the coming of Christ in the flesh at the moment when the true religion, which had preexisted, began to be called Christian. If, then, I have written: "Behold the religion that exists in our days, it is the Christian religion," this means not that it had never existed before, but that it only later acquired the name "Christian."

In the light of these hasty data,[26] Karl Rahner surely seems justified in writing:

> When the early fathers kept a lookout for such an activity of the Logos, the beginnings of his Incarnation as it were, in saving history before Christ . . . they were better advised than we are, for whom God rules there simply from heaven. . . . The history of religions as a whole . . . [must be] integrated (as Yes or No) in the single history of the dialogue between God and the world, a dialogue which flows into the Word become flesh. . . . If this is true, it holds good also of the history of religions in so far as they were an unconscious Yes or No to the Word of God who was to come in human flesh.[27]

ORIENTATIONS OF VATICAN COUNCIL II

The Second Vatican Council adopted the patristic doctrine of an "evangelical preparation" and "seeds of the Word" in other religious traditions. True, it does not favor us with an authoritative interpretation of this teaching. Does this text lend its support to the opinion that Christian salvation is not only available to all human beings (cf. *Gaudium et Spes*, no. 22), but reaches them in and through the sincere practice of their religion, which somehow serves as a mediation of the mystery of Christian salvation? Does the council regard other religious traditions as legitimate ways of salvation today?[28]

Vatican II, let us recall, was the first ecumenical council to speak of other religions in a positive tone. This is one of its claims to greatness, and not the least of them. Still, we must be careful to understand the scope of its assertions. A rather more attentive study of the documents of the council seems to show that, without explicitly asserting that the various religious traditions are actually ways of salvation for their members, it nonetheless lays the foundation for the theological opinion according to which Christian salvation reaches the members of other religions in, and in some way by, their mediation. Indeed, the council acknowledges the activity of the Word and its Spirit not only in the human heart, but also in certain objective elements comprised in humanity's religious traditions. This is what we must now establish by analyzing the principal texts of the conciliar documents, especially the Dogmatic Constitution on the Church, *Lumen Gentium* (nos. 16–17), the Decree on the Missionary Activity of the Church, *Ad Gentes* (nos. 3, 7–9, 11), and the Declaration on the Relationship of the Church to Non-Christian Religions, *Nostra Aetate* (no. 2).

Divine providence, the Constitution *Lumen Gentium* (no. 16) explains, denies to no one of good will—of whom all have been the object of grace— the aids necessary to their salvation. Everything they have that is good and true is regarded as evangelical preparation and a gift of God, who enlightens every person so he or she may ultimately have life.

While it proclaims the gospel, the text continues, the missionary activity of the church seeks to heal and elevate every bit of good in the hearts and thoughts of men, as well as in their rites and culture, for the glory of God and the happiness of man (no. 17).

In the thinking of the council, "good" is found not only in the subjective dispositions of the devotees of other religions, but in certain objective elements in those religions, such as their rites and their culture.

The Decree *Ad Gentes* (no. 3) expresses itself in a similar way. It speaks of God's universal design for salvation, which is executed not only in the souls of human beings, but (once more, in a hidden way) by "initiatives, even religious," (*etiam religiosa*), through which they seek God. These ways need guidance and correction, but can be regarded as an orientation toward God or preparation for the gospel. The same decree, in number 7, declares that God, in ways known to him, can lead peoples to faith who, through no fault of their own, do not know the gospel. But it also emphasizes, in partial reliance on *Lumen Gentium* (no. 17), that the missionary activity of the church liberates and restores to Christ the truth and grace that is present in the nations, the good found in the hearts and souls of men, or in their rites and civilizations (*Ad Gentes*, no. 9).

Once again the good to be found in others is not reducible to subjective dispositions of persons, but extends to objective elements of the traditions to which they belong. The decree goes on to identify the source of these germs. Adopting the patristic expression, it speaks of seeds of the Word found hidden in national and religious traditions which are to be uncovered with joy and reverence; or again, of riches that God has given to the nations, which are to be discovered through a sincere, patient dialogue (*Ad Gentes*, no. 11). Thus the Word of God has sown seeds not only in the human heart, but in the religious traditions of humanity.

This is the same teaching that we find in the Declaration *Nostra Aetate*. In certain objective elements of the religious traditions—which are set forth here in more detail—the council discovers a ray of that Truth that enlightens all men. Although the direct reference is not to light but to Truth, so that the intent to refer to the Joannine Prologue (John 1:9) is not clear, the emphasis placed on that Truth (*radium illius Veritatis*) clearly indicates that the document is speaking of the divine Word, the source of all Truth, present and active in the other religious traditions. The council speaks as follows in *Nostra Aetate* (no. 2):

> The Catholic Church rejects nothing which is true and holy in these religions. She looks with sincere respect upon those ways of conduct and of life, those rules and teachings which, though differing in many particulars from what she holds and sets forth, nevertheless often reflect a ray of that Truth which enlightens all men. Indeed, she proclaims and must ever proclaim Christ, "the way, the truth, and the life" (John 14:6), in whom men find the fullness of religious life, and in whom God has reconciled all things to Himself (cf. 2 Cor. 5:18–19).

These are the principal texts that bear directly on our subject. Clearly they sketch a response to the question left open by *Gaudium et Spes* (no. 22), cited above. Not only does the Spirit offer to every woman and man the opportunity to be associated to the Paschal mystery of Jesus Christ, and therefore to be saved, but the divine Word has sown its seeds in the religious traditions themselves, which thus comport elements of grace and salvation for their members. Such, it seems, is the teaching that can and must be attributed to the council. While the council does not explicitly say that the religious traditions are means of salvation or ways of salvation for their adherents, in dependence on the active presence of the Christic mystery in them, it nevertheless moves in that direction.[29]

It is instructive to compare Vatican II's reservations vis-à-vis other religious traditions with the more decisive assertion of the council on the subject of the non-Catholic Christian churches and communities. Addressing itself to a consideration of the separated churches and communities, the Decree on Ecumenism, *Unitatis Redintegratio* (no. 3), unambiguously asserts not only that these communities are not deprived of validity in terms of the salvation mystery, but that the Spirit of Christ makes use of them as a means of salvation. The council does not explicitly say this with regard to other religious traditions, and rightly so. Still, does not the doctrine according to which the Catholic Church is the "general means" of salvation, permit us to think that, beyond the church—and the Catholic Church itself—there may be particular means, or particular sacraments of salvation—to be sure, not without a relationship and orientation to the general means and the universal sacrament? Is this not what is implied by the acknowledgment, in the "religious initiatives" (*incepta religiosa, Ad Gentes*, no. 3) and various objective elements characterizing other religious traditions, of a genuine evangelical preparation and authentic seeds of the Word? Once again, without explicitly asserting that other religious traditions constitute ways of salvation for their members, the council certainly takes this direction.

Of course, as we see very clearly, this teaching is unequivocally founded on the basis of a relationship to the Christic mystery and the active presence of the Word. It would seem legitimate, then, to say that the other religions may be providential ways to salvation in the sense that God, in Jesus Christ, saves—in their own religion with their own doctrines and practices—men and women who have not been personally summoned by the gospel message.

In our consideration of salvation history, we have distinguished a "general" and a "special" salvation history (see chapter five). The language that we are presently employing, of course, following the council's lead, reverses the terms. Still, *particular* means of salvation correspond to the *general* salvation history spoken of above, and, conversely, the *general* means of salvation corresponds to *special* salvation history.

Hans Küng, for his part, has proposed the following terminological reversal: The various religions would represent the "ordinary" means of salvation, and Christianity the "extraordinary" means.[30] This terminology has raised some eyebrows, and objections have been lodged against it. It has been observed that according to the divine plan, salvation by explicit faith in Jesus Christ in the church is the norm. However, even apart from the fact that the vast majority of humanity reaches salvation outside the church, Küng's distinction has the advantage of connoting the eminence of membership in the church as means of salvation and the essential orientation toward that membership of all those whose salvation goes another route. Let us further notice, however, that Pope Paul VI, in his Apostolic Exhortation *Evangelii Nuntiandi* (no. 80), forthrightly asserts that the "ordinary paths of salvation" are those revealed by the Word and the life of Jesus Christ, even though God can work salvation by extraordinary ways known to him alone.[31]

Considerations of terminology aside, a document published by the Secretariate for Non-Christians, entitled "The Attitude of the Church towards the Followers of Other Religions: Reflections and Orientations on Dialogue and Mission" (no. 26), sums up the council's thought well:

> This vision induced the Fathers of the Second Vatican Council to affirm that in the religious traditions of non-Christians there exist "elements which are true and good" (LG 16), "precious things, both religious and human" (GS 92), "seeds of contemplation" (AG 18), "elements of truth and grace" (AG 9), "seeds of the Word" (AG 11, 15), and "rays of the truth which illumines all mankind" (NA 2). According to explicit conciliar indications, these values are found preserved in the great religious traditions of humanity. Therefore, they merit the attention and the esteem of Christians, and their spiritual

patrimony is a genuine invitation to dialogue (cf. NA 2, 3; AG 11), not only in those things which unite us, but also in our differences.[32]

RELIGIOUS TRADITIONS: WAYS OF SALVATION?

Theological Perspective

In order to sketch a solution to this problem, let us first place in evidence two recent theological currents calculated to afford us the appropriate perspective. One is the theology of salvation history. The other, for want of a more adequate term, we shall call the existential approach to theology.

It was Oscar Cullmann who, while Vatican Council II was in session, suggested to Pope Paul VI that theology be recentered on *salvation history*, and we are familiar with the efforts made in this direction after the council.[33] A consideration of the problematic of salvation history—of the relationship between God and humanity through which God, on the divine initiative, becomes more and more deeply involved in the history of human beings—is essential if we hope to be able to sketch a solution to the question of the salvific value of humanity's religious traditions. Here, however, a brief summary of our presentation in chapter five will suffice.

Salvation history developed in various stages, all of them integral to the process of God's self-manifestation to humanity. The various covenants established by God represent the successive stages of this process. Each covenant inaugurates a particular regimen of salvation, although all of the divine manifestations preceding the event of Jesus Christ are essentially ordered toward him and find in him, as Cullmann has shown so well,[34] their meaning and fulfillment.

It does not follow, however, that a new stage in salvation history automatically abolishes the regime of salvation that God has established in a previous era of the same history. The regime of salvation established by God through the covenant in Noah, which symbolizes humanity's religious traditions, remains in effect during the time of the church, wherever the gospel of Jesus Christ has not been effectively promulgated. In other words, the members of other religious traditions who have not been personally and existentially summoned by the gospel in their conscience continue to live under the regime of the cosmic covenant to which other religions belong. For these persons, these religious traditions maintain the role assigned to them by God as means of salvation, real although essentially incomplete; but they perform this role in relationship to the mystery of Jesus Christ and under the influence of its power.

As H. R. Schlette shows,[35] the theology of salvation history compels us to think of other religions dynamically, not statically. If we take the process of salvation history seriously, we must acknowledge that other religious traditions are still authentic means of salvation, imperfect though they be, even after the decisive epiphany of God in Jesus Christ has taken place in history. The coming in time of "special" salvation history does not abolish the validity of "general" salvation history.

The second current of thought bearing on a sketch of a solution to the problem of the value of the other religions is the *existential approach to theology*. By this we mean the effort incumbent upon every honest, sincere scholar to transcend the level of the imperfect ideas of God conveyed by the religions which, as they are outside the Jewish and Christian traditions, live in the dispensation of the "cosmic covenant" — as well as to transcend the level of the concepts that they themselves enunciate on the subject of God — in order to attain, insofar as possible, to the living experience of God underlying all these ideas and concepts.

We must acknowledge the certainty that many women and men living under the dispensation of the cosmic covenant have encountered the true God in an authentic religious experience. For example, prayer, of its very nature, entails a personal relationship between an "I" and an infinite "Thou." One does not pray to an impersonal God.[36] Authentic prayer is always a sign that God, in whatever secret, hidden way, has undertaken the initiative of a personal approach to human beings and has been welcomed by these human beings in faith. Whoever entrust themselves to God in faith and charity are saved, however imperfect their conception of God. After all, salvation depends on the response made by sinful human beings, in faith, to a personal communication initiated by God.

There is a gap, however, between religious experience and its formulation. This is true even of the Christian experience; a fortiori, it will be true of the others. We never have access to the religious experience of another in its pure state, without the garment in which it is clothed by its enunciation in a discourse. True, language, our sole access to this experience, communicates this experience; but it does so inadequately. Indeed, in transmitting it, it betrays it, inasmuch as religious experience, of its very nature, is beyond all expression.

If we wish to reach the religious experience of others and discover the hidden elements of grace there, we shall be obliged to go beyond the concepts that enunciate that experience. Insofar as possible, we shall have to gather the very experience through the faulty concepts in which it is expressed. As we know, in other religious traditions, religious experience is not always expressed in terms of a personal relationship with God. As we have recalled above, Hindu mysticism conceives it as an awakening to identity with the *Brahman*.

Although Buddhism, despite its atheistic appearance, does proclaim an (impersonal) Absolute, no personal relationship with God is expressed here, either. Buddhists speak of contemplation and meditation, not of prayer. By contrast, in Christianity and the other monotheistic or prophetical religions, religious experience takes the form of an interpersonal dialogue between God — who takes the initiative — and the human being — who responds to that initiative. Thus while the "mystical" Asian religions cultivate instasy (the quest for the Absolute "in the cave of the heart"), ecstasy, or the encounter with the utterly other God, predominates with their pro- phetical counterparts; the former emphasize apophaticism (*nirvana, suny- ata*), the latter place the emphasis on cataphaticism. It is easy to grasp the reasons for the deficiencies entailed in the concept of God in other religious traditions: They lack the benefit of the "special" revelation of God in the history of Israel and, a fortiori, the decisive, definitive self-revelation of God in Jesus Christ.

However, despite the limitations and shortcomings marking the enun- ciation of the experience of God in other religious traditions, still, wherever there is genuine religious experience it is surely the God revealed in Jesus Christ who thus enters into the life of men and women, in hidden, secret fashion. While the concept of God remains incomplete, the interpersonal encounter between God and the human being is authentic, and God takes the initiative, awaiting the response of faith on the part of the human being.

This is not the place to ask whether there is such a thing as a "purely natural" mysticism or whether, instead, all mysticism is de facto, if not of its very nature, "supernatural."[37] However the case may be, theologically we must hold that wherever and whenever human beings turn toward an Absolute that addresses and bestows itself upon them, an attitude of super- natural faith is thereby on the scene. While its expression is deficient, ontologically it is an attitude of faith and prayer that is at work.

This attitude is directed toward, as well as originally aroused by, the God of Jesus Christ. Wherever there is a personal communication of God, it is always necessarily the God of Jesus Christ who engages in a self- bestowal there: that is, the triune God, Father, Son, and Spirit. The Father is bestowed through the Son in the Spirit. Indeed, in any personal com- munication, God is given as God is. Only one order of salvific grace is concretely conceivable, then—the one in which God communicates the divine Spirit to human beings, and by that Spirit grants those human beings to share in the filiation of the divine Son himself.[38] In other words, every human being who is saved is a child of the living God in the Spirit of God. And of course he or she is such by Jesus Christ. This is the unprecedented novelty inaugurated in the order of grace and salvation by the incarnation of the Son of God. By his glorification, the incarnate Son, who died and was raised, has been constituted Lord and Christ (Acts 2:36), head and Savior (Acts 5:31).

Consequently, the life in the Spirit of God, which is the very essence of the grace of salvation, reaches each human being through the glorified humanity of Jesus Christ, inasmuch as the Spirit of God has become the Spirit of Christ and is communicated by him. The immanent presence of the Spirit thus no longer only makes human beings children of God in the divine Son himself; it incorporates them into Christ, organically joining them to the resurrected humanity of the Lord of glory. Every saved human being is a child of God by Christ in the Spirit.

This incorporation into Christ is given to the Christian through the visible sign of incorporation into the church, the body of Jesus Christ. How are others incorporated into Christ? How does Christian salvation reach those who are outside the economy of the visible sign of the church and its sacramental actions? Is it only through an invisible activity of the Lord of glory, whose power attains human beings individually, secretly, and in hidden fashion? Or do other religions actually themselves lend a certain vicarious visibility and social character to the saving power of Christ? Are they signs, however incomplete and imperfect, of his saving activity? This is the question that we must now attempt to answer.

Three Fundamental Principles

In order to answer it, we must appeal to three fundamental principles. We may call them the anthropological principle, the christological principle, and the ecclesiological principle. Let us briefly set them forth, in order.

THE ANTHROPOLOGICAL PRINCIPLE

Human existence is essentially historical. This means two things. First, the human person, as incarnate spirit, is a becoming, which expresses itself in time and space, in the history of the world. It exists only in thus expressing itself. What we call our body is, very precisely, this expression. This is the deep meaning of St. Thomas' theory of a substantial union between soul and body. That the soul is the substantial form of the body means that soul and body do not compose two distinct, essentially independent elements in a merely accidental union, and are therefore readily separable. Quite to the contrary; human beings are persons only to the extent that they, as spirit, are incarnate. Modern existential philosophy has seen this and stated it better than Thomism. However, what is true of the life of a human being in general is also true of his or her religious life. The latter does not and cannot consist in purely spiritual states of soul. In order to exist, the religious life must express itself in religious symbols, rites, and practices. In view of the human being's essentially composite nature, such symbols, rites, and practices are necessary for the very existence of the religious life, as they serve both as expression and support of the aspirations of the human spirit. There is no religious life without religious practice. In this sense, neither is there faith without religion.

Second, the anthropological principle, as thus propounded, also implies that the human being is not an isolated monad, but a person living in human society. Every human being becomes a person in virtue of his or her interpersonal relationships with other human beings. While it is true that one must first exist as a person in order to be able to maintain an interpersonal relationship with others, it is also true that the human being becomes and grows as a person only through that relationship. One becomes what one is. This is what the recent philosophy of personalism has emphasized. It applies also to the human being's religious life. Religious human beings subsist not as separated individuals but as members of determinate religious communities with particular traditions. They grow and become by sharing the religious life of their respective communities, by entering personally into the respective historical religious tradition in which they are placed, and by taking up its social manifestations, ideas and teaching, moral code and ritual practices.

If this principle is true, and if many members of the other religious traditions have an authentic experience of God, the inescapable conclusion is that these traditions contain, in their institutions and social practices, traces of the encounter of human beings with grace, "supernatural grace-filled elements."[39] A dichotomy has often been erected between human beings' subjective religious life and the religion they profess, between their personal religious experience and the historico-social religious phenomenon, or religious tradition composed of sacred books and practices of worship, to which they adhere. Then it is said that while the persons belonging to these traditions can obtain salvation thanks to the sincerity of their subjective religious lives, their religion itself has no salvific value for them.

In the light of the principle just expounded, however, it clearly appears that the dichotomy upon which such a pejorative judgment rests is gravely inadequate. Subjective and objective religion can and should be distinguished; however, they cannot be separated. The religious traditions of humanity are actually sprung from the religious experience of the persons or groups that have founded them. Their sacred books contain the memory of concrete religious experiences with Truth. Their practices, in turn, result from the codification of these experiences. Thus it seems both impracticable and theologically unrealistic to maintain that, while the members of the various religious traditions can obtain salvation, their religion plays no role in the process. As there is no purely natural concrete religious life, so neither is there any such thing as a purely human historical religion.

THE CHRISTOLOGICAL PRINCIPLE

Our second axiom is christological. All salvation is Christian: It transpires through Christ. But who is Christ? Christ—the historical Jesus, constituted by God Christ and Lord in his resurrection—is, in the current order, God turning to human beings in self-manifestation and self-giving. He is God-with-human-beings. In other words, Christ is the primordial sacrament (*Ursakrament*), unique and necessary, of human beings' encounter with God.

Once the mystery of Christ has been revealed, it is given to us Christians to recognize him in the human face of Jesus. Others are incapable of this discernment; however, they can encounter the mystery of Christ unconsciously and can attain salvation in this encounter. Indeed, in order to be saved, they must have this encounter, as there is no other way by which God turns to human beings in self-communication. Since Christ is God in a personal relationship with human beings, or personally present to them, salvation always involves an encounter with the mystery of Christ. The members of the other religious traditions who are saved have been and are personally confronted with his mystery. Their Christic experience, however, is an implicit one. As long as the human Jesus has not been revealed to them, they cannot recognize the mystery of Christ in his humanity. An implicit experience of the Christic mystery is one thing; its explicit discovery in Jesus of Nazareth is something else again. The former is a necessary condition of salvation; the latter is the privilege of Christians.

That Christ is personally God—very God turned toward human beings in self-bestowal—is exactly what the traditional doctrine of Christ's unique, universal mediation expresses. In the Word Incarnate, who died and was raised, God and humanity have in some sort been joined by an unbreakable bond. Jesus Christ, identically and personally, is the mystery of salvation whose active presence is universal. From the theological viewpoint, it is important to refer the salvation of the members of other religions first of all to the mystery of Christ, not to the church. We have shown above that the ecumenical problem of the union of the Christian churches ought to be broached from a christocentric, not an ecclesiocentric, perspective. As we have shown, this is valid a fortiori when the question is that of the theological meaning of the religions.[40] The question of their salvific value can have a valid solution only if we attempt to explain how they are related to the mystery of Christ, to his person and his work, to his revelation and his saving power.

The question, then, is the following: How do other religious traditions contain, however imperfectly, the Christic mystery of which the church is the eminent manifestation? Notwithstanding the unique value of the church as eschatological sign of the mystery of Christ in the world, incomplete signs of the same mystery are possible. Christ is the primordial sacrament (*Ursakrament*). The church, in turn, is related to him as sign to signified. He is the fundamental mystery; the church, the derived mystery. The church finds in him its *raison d'être* and meaning: Its life is centered on him. The church is a mystery "because it is wholly related to Christ, having existence, validity, and efficacity only by him."[41] It remains to be determined, however, how—apart from the ecclesial sign of salvation that reaches Christians— religious traditions can represent, vis-à-vis others, true signs, albeit incomplete, of the mystery of salvation in Jesus Christ.

THE ECCLESIOLOGICAL PRINCIPLE

The ecclesiological axiom is determined by the christological. The church is the eschatological community that proclaims and sacramentally represents the mystery of Christ. It incorporates—eminently, visibly, and socially—Christian salvation. It is the historical epiphany of the glory of God revealed in this mystery. In a word, the church is the efficacious sign in which the Christic mystery is contained, the sign in which it subsists (*Lumen Gentium*, no. 8) and is fully operative.

In the order of the signification of the mystery of salvation, then, the church is perfect and complete. That is, it represents the preeminent manner in which the mystery of salvation is subject to visible signification in the world. The reason for this is that, as the Second Vatican Council explicitly states with regard to the Catholic Church, in it is contained the entire fullness of the means of salvation (*Unitatis Redintegratio*, no. 3), which compose the visibility, throughout time and space, of the mystery of Christ.[42] Therefore the church is the universal sacrament of salvation (*Lumen Gentium*, no. 48), the general means of salvation (*UR*, no. 3), the organism that dispenses, throughout space and time, the mystery of Christ in the complete visibility of the signs instituted by him. This mediation of the Christic mystery through the church consists principally in the proclamation of the word of God contained in the New Testament and in the celebration of the sacraments instituted by Jesus Christ, principally the Eucharist.

The unique position of the church as preeminent sign and perfect mediation of the Christic mystery for Christians does not, however, mean that other signs, doubtless imperfect, do not exist for others, or that for others an incomplete mediation of the same mystery is not operative through their own religious traditions. While the church, the eschatological community, is the perfect means of Christian salvation, other religious communities, as essentially ordered to the church (*LG*, no. 17), can, in virtue of this very orientation, constitute imperfect means of the same salvation. The universal sacrament does not exclude particular sacraments. In the church, the perfect, complete mediation of the mystery is found; outside the church, in other religious traditions, this mediation remains imperfect and incomplete, and by that very fact essentially ordered to the ecclesial mediation. Accordingly, while the mystery of Christ attains to its total visibility only in the life of the church, it can nevertheless find a lesser expression in the life of the other religious communities.

Despite the various orders of mediation of the mystery of Christ—perfect and complete in the ecclesial community, imperfect and incomplete outside the same—we must observe that the differences do not place Christians in an advantageous situation with respect to salvation. Their situation in the church does not of itself make them more perfect, more holy, or actually closer to Christ and his mystery than others are. It would even be false to say that their salvation is easier or less laborious. Salvation depends on the manner, on the intensity with which each person responds in his or her concrete situation, to the Christic mystery of salvation present and active in each one, whether consciously or unconsciously. In the last analysis, rather than conferring an advantageous situation in the order of salvation, membership in the church imposes on Christians a tremendous responsibility to render credible testimony to the salvation mystery that they have explicitly recognized in Jesus Christ.

Sketching a Solution

In order to show how the various religious traditions can serve their members as a mediation of the mystery of salvation, we must begin with the mystery of Christ himself and then proceed to a consideration of the presence of Christ among human beings. Christ, we have said, is God in a personal relationship with human beings—God becoming present to them. Every authentic experience of God, among Christians as among others, is an encounter of God in Jesus Christ with the human being. God's presence to the human being, *qua* a "being with" of the intentional order like any personal presence, sets God in relationship with the human being in an interpersonal exchange of a "Thou" and an "I." The order of faith or salvation consists precisely in this personal communication of God to the human being, a communication whose concrete realization is in Jesus Christ and whose efficacious sign is the humanity of Jesus.

God, however, is infinite Person, beyond all finitude, and the transcendence of God profoundly stamps the nature of the personal divine presence to human beings. Inasmuch as an infinite distance separates the Infinite from the finite, the personal presence of God to the human being—and, a fortiori, to the sinful human being—can only be gratuitous. The initiative of God's relationship to the human being comes necessarily from the side of the Divine. God's condescension to human beings is at the center of the mystery of Christ.

In Christianity, God's personal presence to human beings in Christ reaches its highest and most complete sacramental visibility. Christ raised, as Vatican Council II recalls in its Constitution on the Liturgy (*SC*, no. 7), is dynamically present in the proclamation of the gospel by the church. It is Christ himself who proposes his message of salvation through the sacrament of the ecclesial proclamation. Again, Christ is dynamically present in the sacraments celebrated by the church, which culminate in the Eucharist. Through them he exercises his sanctifying power. However, this perfect mediation of the mystery of Christ attains only Christians, members of the sacrament-church who receive its word and take part in its liturgical and sacramental life.

Can other religions contain and signify, in some way, the presence of God to the human being in Jesus Christ? Does God become present to their members in the very practice of their religion? It seems necessary to admit this. Indeed, their own religious practice is the reality that gives expression to their experience of God and of the mystery of Christ. It is the visible element, the sign, the sacrament of that experience. This practice expresses, supports, bears, and contains, as it were, their encounter with God in Jesus Christ.

Accordingly—and in this particular sense—the religious conclusion of others is indeed for them a way and means of salvation. To refuse that conclusion would be to commit the error of an undue separation of the personal, subjective religious life and objective religious tradition—made up of word, rites, and sacraments—in which the former is expressed. Such a separation is, as we have said, theologically inviable.

It is difficult, however, to determine in what precise sense the historical religions serve as a mediation for their members to the presence of the Christic mystery. Obviously it will be an inferior manner of mediation by comparison with the one at work in Christianity and the church. We must not place the two on the same footing, nor may we say that it is merely a matter of degree. It is a matter of mediations of distinct natures, which thus institute distinct regimes of Christian salvation.

Thus we must distinguish distinct modalities of the sacramental presence of the Christic mystery. The mystery of Christ, that mysterious reality of God's presence to human beings, employs the mediation of Christianity and other religions, but in distinct modalities. The grace of God, while surely one, is visibly mediated in different modes, whose necessary distinctions are preserved by a difference among them not only in degree but in kind. This means that the religious practices and sacramental rites of the other religions cannot be placed on the same footing as the Christian sacraments instituted by Jesus Christ; but it also means that they must be ascribed a certain mediation of grace.[43] Thus the mystery of salvation remains one: It is the mystery of Christ. But this mystery is present to men and women beyond the boundaries of Christianity. In the church, the eschatological community, it is present to them overtly and explicitly, in the full visibility of its perfect mediation. In other religious traditions it is present in an implicit, concealed manner, in virtue of the imperfect mode of mediation constituted by these traditions.

The distinction and the unity between cosmic religions and Christianity eludes a perfect analysis. One thing, however, is certain, and must be insisted upon. Inasmuch as the mystery of Christ is contained and signified differently on the two sides, the novelty of Christianity cannot be reduced to the simple awareness of a salvation mystery that would itself be present elsewhere in the same manner.

Christian revelation not only "unveils" or "discovers" something that is hidden or veiled in other religions. The scope and meaning of Christianity cannot be limited—perilous nostalgia for some Christian gnosticism!—to a communication of knowledge. To be sure, the novelty of Christianity, in the order of the divine grace, involves a new revelation. But it is not reduced to that revelation. Taken in its totality, the Christian novelty comports at once the plenary revelation of the mystery of Christ and the highest form of its visible mediation and presence to the world. Revelation and visible mediation are the two components of the mystery of Christ, and they employ distinct modalities. While in other religious traditions the mystery of Christ is imperfectly revealed and Christ's grace is imperfectly mediated, Christianity is the whole "revelation" of the mystery and the perfect mediation of grace. The novelty of Christianity is more than that of the mere unveiling of a mystery already completely experienced, although unconsciously: It comports the plenary sacramental realization of the presence of God to human beings.

In this respect, the expression *anonymous Christianity* must be applied cautiously to the cosmic religions. It could seem to imply an undue reduction of the novelty of Christianity to a process of gnosis. It could suggest that non-Christians are simply Christians unawares—that they are Christians already and merely unconscious of their true identity. The fact of the matter, however, is that, in becoming explicitly Christian, the religious life of others must undergo an intrinsic transformation consisting of entering into a new order of the mediation of the grace of Christ. Perhaps *latent Christianity* would be a less-inadequate term, since it suggests a reality not merely hidden and veiled, but needing to be fully developed, and to become manifest. *Implicit Christianity*, or even *subjectively implicit Christianity*, is not altogether satisfactory, either. It does not say what it is precisely that differentiates other religions from Christianity. The transition from the former to the latter is more than a process of explicitation. It is entry into a new order. The novelty of the transition must not be glossed over. The term *non-Christian*, furthermore, traditionally employed with reference to the world religions, is equally inadequate. Besides defining other religions by what they are not, it seems to deny them all relationship with Christ, which would be erroneous.

But the difficulty is a semantic one, and disputes over words will avail us naught. Rather let us seek to understand the essential difference between other religions and Christianity. The way in which the mystery of Christ is mediated is eminently different. It is one thing to receive the word spoken by God to human beings by the mediation of sages who have heard it in the depths of their hearts and conveyed their experience to others. It is another to hear the decisive Word that God speaks to human beings in the incarnate Son who is the fullness of revelation. Other sacred scriptures may contain profound intuitions on the mystery of God's personal gift to women and men; yet they remain incomplete and ambiguous. That God's personal communication remains imperfectly enunciated and conceptualized in these scriptures is amply explained by the fact that they have not had the advantage of explicit, public revelation as their guide. Indeed, incomplete truths—even errors—may be found in them, which are less apt to lead human beings to an experience of the true God. After all, sin is always at work, everywhere in the world, distorting the reception of the word spoken by God to human beings. Only the words which Christ speaks directly to the world contain God's decisive revelation to human beings, and nothing can be added to them.

Again, it is one thing to enter into contact with the mystery of Christ through the symbols and ritual practices that have sustained and given visible form throughout the centuries to the faith response of women and men and to their commitment to God; it is another thing to encounter that mystery as represented in the full sacramentality of the symbolic acts instituted by Jesus Christ and entrusted by him to the church.

Not all the ritual practices of other religions are capable of giving expression to an authentic religious commitment. They contain distorted elements. While capable of bearing the response that the human being gives to God in faith, they as yet lack the guarantee that they are currently assumed by Christ as ways by which the mystery reaches human beings. Only the church's sacraments, instituted by Christ, carry the guarantee that they are paths by which the mystery of Christ is directly and infallibly encountered in their signs. Christian grace is infallibly offered in them, although its real efficacy continues to depend entirely on the human being's response in faith to God's gratuitous approach.

Finally, it is one thing to have the experience of the mystery of Christ and live by it unconsciously, in a hidden way, without a clear awareness of the infinite condescension shown to us by God in the divine Son, without full knowledge of the earnestness and authenticity of God's descent to us in that Son; and it is another thing to recognize the mystery in the humble condition of the human Jesus, in his human life, his death, and his resurrection, with full awareness that, in this human being, who is a member of our race, God has personally come to meet us on our own level. Apart from Christianity, God encounters human beings in Christ, but the human face of God remains unknown. In Christianity, God encounters women and men in the human face of the human Jesus, who reflects for us the very image of the Father. While every religion contains an approach to the human being on the part of God, in Christianity God's advance toward the human being becomes fully human.

There is an anonymous, or implicit Christianity, then, as there is an explicit Christianity. Both are Christian, despite the breadth of the gap between them. We have already alluded to what would seem to be the most serious criticism of the expression, and have dissipated any possible ambiguity. Other objections are less solid.[44] To the objection that the term is offensive to non-Christians, we may answer, with Karl Rahner, that it is intended for use in a context of Christian theological discourse, where it has the merit of evincing the relationship of other religions to the mystery of Christ, not in interreligious dialogue.[45] To the objection that the expression defines others in negative terms, rather than positively through their own identity and proper specificity, we may answer that to show in others and in their religious traditions the active presence of the mystery of Christ is to give them an eminently positive definition. Finally, to the objection that the theory of anonymous Christianity is a subtle form of Christian religious and cultural imperialism, the answer is that the universality of Christ, who is the obligatory Savior of all men and women, is—as we shall see once more, below—the very center of Christian faith. The theory of the "presence of the Christic mystery," and that theory alone, has the capacity to link both fundamental (seemingly contradictory) axioms of Christian faith: the universal salvific will of God, and the central place of the mystery of Christ in the concrete realization of the divine salvific plan.[46]

However authentic the hidden presence of the mystery of Christ in others and in their religious traditions, we must acknowledge the distinctive note of the Christian experience of God, which is summed up in the explicit experience of the mystery of Jesus Christ in the church. The Christian alone, with "the eyes of faith," is capable of an adequate, though never exhaustive, articulation of the mystery of Christ. The transition from another religion to Christianity entails a genuine novelty. It consists in insertion into the new order of the Christian economy of salvation. It implies a breach with the past with a view to embracing the new. It is an authentic *metanoia*, or conversion. The passage from the pre-Christian regime of salvation to the Christian regime comports a process of death and resurrection and is an actual conformation to the Paschal mystery of Christ. Death is not an end in itself, but without it, there is no resurrection.

The fact remains that the hidden presence of the mystery of Christ in other religions has profound implications for the Christian. He or she should approach others in a spirit of openness and receptiveness. A choice is necessary, of course, which must be guided by an alert discernment of spirits. Not everything in other religions is a presentiment of Christ. Not everything there is true and good.

Nevertheless, since others have an experience of God in Jesus Christ, their religious traditions have something to offer to Christians. They can help them to discover new facets of the mystery of Christ. Certain aspects of the mystery of Christ may be felt more profoundly by others than by many Christians. A sharing in the religious experience of others in the interreligious dialogue can help Christians deepen their own perception of the Christian mystery, even though they have already received its authentic revelation. After all, Truth is not an object to be possessed, but a person by whom to allow oneself to be possessed. The others are possessed by the same Truth. Thus, while it may seem somewhat paradoxical, it is theologically correct to say that they can teach us something of the mystery of Christ.

In this sense, Christianity and other religions converge. Not that they are all equal or interchangeable; Christianity belongs to a different order of sacramental realism. Christianity represents the decisive presence of eschatological grace in the world. Other religions are mediators of divine grace, if not in the same manner: In them, too, Christ is present. True, the divine grace is less visible there than in Christianity. Still, Christ can be just as personally present—or even more so—to some of their deeply committed members than to less committed Christians. In the last analysis, the presence of Christ to each person depends on that person's response to God's intervention in his or her life. The presence of God in Christ is a spiritual reality open to various orders of mediation. In itself, it transcends them all.

7

Economy of the Spirit, Word of God, and Holy Scriptures

The christological approach to the problem of the salvific value of the religious traditions of humanity, the problem that we have outlined in the foregoing chapter, has the advantage of posing the central question: How do other religions relate to the mystery of Jesus Christ? Inasmuch as the Christic mystery is at the center of Christian faith, a theological evaluation of the salvific values contained in these traditions must be based on their relationship to this mystery.

Another avenue, however, is possible, founded more directly on the experience of God of the members of other religions. It consists of discovering, in their religious life, the active presence and life-giving influence of the Holy Spirit. This approach is based on the fact, attested by Christian faith, that the present world is a saved world: It is saved because the historical mystery of Jesus Christ, which culminates in Pentecost, has brought into being a new creation. The eschatological outpouring of the Spirit that results from the glorification of Christ is not limited to the boundaries of the church: It extends to the whole universe. The Holy Spirit gives life to the cosmos, transforming all within it. What meaning does this universal life-giving activity of the Spirit have for the members of other religious traditions? Can we say that it comes to them by the mediation of their own faith, by the holy scriptures and religious practices of their tradition? More specifically, the problem that arises here is the problem of a possible divine revelation contained in the sacred books of these traditions, a word uttered by God through them. May we acknowledge such a word in the holy scriptures of other religions? And if the answer is yes, then what is the difference between other revelations and Christian revelation? In what sense does Christian revelation represent the fullness of revelation? Just where is this fullness to be found?

Let us note from the outset that the pneumatological outlook we are adopting here, while distinct from the christological perspective developed earlier, differs from it only partially. Above, it was a matter of discovering the hidden presence of the mystery of Christ in the religious traditions; here, it is a matter of finding the cosmic influence of the Spirit operative in those traditions. But these two perspectives, the christological and the pneumatological, are inseparable in the Christian mystery, the cosmic influence of the Spirit being essentially bound up with the universal activity of the risen Lord. In virtue of the necessary correspondence between the immanent Trinity and the economic Trinity, the Spirit is the obligatory point of entry of God's self-communication to the human being,[1] but this Spirit in whom God makes this self-bestowal is at the same time the Spirit of Christ, conferred by the risen Lord. The proper function of the Spirit is to center, by its immanent presence, the human being—and the church—on Christ, whom God has personally established as mediator and as the way leading to God. The Spirit is not at the center.[2]

It would be erroneous, then, to set christocentrism and pneumatology in mutual opposition, as if they functioned as two distinct economies. They are actually two inseparable aspects of one economy of salvation. To be sure, the great currents of Christian tradition, Eastern and Western, place the accent differently. The West emphasizes the salvific activity of the risen Savior. The East insists more on the influence of the Spirit. In all authentic Christian tradition, however, it is merely a matter of emphasis on complementary elements.[3] The Fathers knew that the sanctifying activity of the risen Lord consists essentially in the conferral of his Spirit upon us. This is true even in the Eucharist, where, through the sacramental presence of his body and blood, Christ bestows upon us his Spirit.[4]

Inseparable as the activity of the risen Christ and that of the Spirit may be, it nevertheless remains true that the point of immediate contact between God and the human being, from the side of God in the divine self-bestowal, is indeed the immanent presence of the Spirit in that human being. This is true both for the Christian and for the church. It is also true for the members of other religious traditions. For all, the Spirit is the bond of the interpersonal relationship with God. One must expect, then, that the hidden presence of Christ in the life of other religious communities will be manifested by the "touches," the personal imprint, of the Holy Spirit in their members. The influence of the Spirit reveals and manifests the activity of Christ, and not the other way around. Thus the pneumatological perspective has the advantage over the christological approach of directly evidencing the more immediate elements in the religious experience of others.

What we are about, then, is the discovery of the various ways in which the Spirit is at work in the personal and social religious lives of the members of other religious traditions. Once more, it must be a matter not merely of the subjective religious life of individuals, but of the religious traditions to which these individuals belong. Do these traditions serve them as a mediation of the activity of the Spirit? How? Concretely, we shall proceed as follows. First we shall study the universal activity of the Spirit in the New Testament. Then we shall examine the teaching of Vatican Council II and the postconciliar magisterium on the subject of the activity of the Holy Spirit in others and their religious traditions. Third, we shall sketch a theology of the nonbiblical holy scriptures as revelation and word of God, and examine their relationship to Christian revelation in Jesus Christ.

THE SPIRIT IN THE NEW TESTAMENT

The Old Testament had conceived the fulfillment of the Messianic times as an eschatological outpouring of the Spirit of God. According to the message of the prophets, this outpouring of the Spirit would be a source of inner renewal (Ezek. 11:19). God would place the divine Spirit within human beings (Ezek. 36:37); God would place within them a new spirit (Ezek. 36:26). In the thinking of Israel, however, the divine blessings of the new age extended to the chosen people alone. These blessings would mark God's new and everlasting covenant with that people (cf. Jer. 3:31–34). It is this eschatological outpouring of the Spirit of God that the apostolic church sees realized at Pentecost in fulfillment of the ancient promises. The description of the Pentecost event in the Acts of the Apostles characteristically evokes the Old Testament roots of the *ru'ach Yahweh*. The Pentecost event verified the prophecy, and the group of first Christians gathered around the apostles received the gift of the Spirit that Jesus had promised them (John 14:26, 16:7–15). The baptism of the apostolic community in the Spirit marks the birth of the church.

But can we show that, in the thinking of the apostolic church, the outpouring of the Spirit at Pentecost extends beyond the community of Christian faith and consists in the re-creation by the Spirit of the whole of humanity and the entire cosmos? In other words, does the New Testament testify to a life-giving influence and transforming activity of the Spirit actually extending to the entire world in virtue of the salvation event accomplished by God in Jesus Christ? The Lucan account of Pentecost supposes at least an intentional universality of the gift of the Spirit (Acts 2:4, 5–6), transcending the narrow bounds of the people of the covenant. The message entrusted to the apostles is destined for all; the universality of tongues symbolizes universal mission. Those who believe in Jesus will receive the Spirit of Pentecost (Acts 2:38) bestowed by Christ (Acts 2:33).

Can we go further and assert that the life-giving influence of the Spirit poured out at Pentecost reaches human beings before the time of the apostolic message, and independently of it? Here one might be tempted to refer to Peter's discourse on the occasion of the Jerusalem controversy (Acts 15): "God, who knows hearts, has borne witness in favor of [the pagans], by giving the Holy Spirit to them just as to us" (see Acts 15:8). Here Peter asserts a Pentecost of the Gentiles resembling the initial Pentecost. They, too, have received the Spirit, he says, just as the Spirit was conferred upon the apostles in the Upper Room.

We must take equal cognizance, however, of the event reported earlier in Acts 10:44–11:18, to which Peter alludes here. From this latter text, it clearly appears that the Pentecost of the Gentiles with which we are confronted is tied to the hearing of the apostolic message. While Peter was still speaking, proclaiming the message of Christ to the Gentiles of Caesarea, "the Holy Spirit fell upon those who were hearing the word" (see Acts 10:44), incidentally occasioning stupefaction among the Christian Jews who accompanied Peter (Acts 10:45–46). As for Peter himself, the fact that in hearing his message the Gentiles had received the Spirit was a clear sign that they, too, were suitable candidates for baptism (Acts 10:47, 11:15–17).

We must bear in mind that all of the writings of the New Testament were addressed to Christian communities. It was natural for these writings to forge a strong bond between the re-creation of the human being in the Holy Spirit and the obedience of faith, and in particular, to link that re-creation with Christian baptism (cf. John 3:5; Tit. 3:5). However, texts are not lacking concerning the new life of the human being in the Spirit of God which it would be erroneous to refer only to the members of the Christian communities. Jesus Christ, raised from the dead, has become a life-giving spirit (see 1 Cor. 15:45). The Spirit of God has become the Spirit of Christ (cf. Rom. 8:9), and is dispensed to human beings by him, because the Lord is the Spirit (2 Cor. 3:17). To whom is that Spirit given, and how is one to recognize its presence?

According to St. Paul, "where the Spirit of the Lord is, there is freedom" (see 2 Cor. 3:17). The spiritual freedom that delivers from the slavery of sin and the servitude of selfishness is the unequivocal sign of the presence of the Spirit of Christ in men and women. That freedom presupposes the gift of faith and the love of God that has been "poured forth in our hearts by the Holy Spirit that has been given to us" (cf. Rom. 5:5). Christians have no monopoly on these gifts.[5] The Letter to the Hebrews testifies to the gift of faith made by God to the holy pagans of the cosmic covenant (Heb. 11:4–7). In order to be salvific, this faith must furthermore be expressed in deeds, by love (James 2:14–23).

The Spirit, then, is present in every human being who is saved. Its presence is recognized by the influence it exercises in their lives. After all, it is true of the Spirit, too, that it is recognized by its fruits (cf. Matt. 7:16). St. Paul lists the fruits of the Spirit in the person under its guidance: "The fruit of the Spirit is charity, joy, peace, longsuffering, availability, goodness, trust in others, gentleness, self-mastery" (see Gal. 5:22–23). And he concludes, "Since the Spirit is our life, may the Spirit have us act, as well" (Gal. 5:25).

While it is true that St. Paul is directly envisaging the activity of the Spirit upon the members of the Christian community, it is no less certain that the re-creation of the human being by the event of Jesus Christ, which issues in new life in the Spirit, is understood by him as extending to all men and women.

For Paul, God "was reconciling the world to himself" in Christ (see 2 Cor. 5:19). The Jesus Christ event is a cosmic event in that, in the person and mystery of Christ, God has wrought a new creation (cf. 2 Cor. 5:17). The "sole new human being" created of the two ancient ones—Jews and Gentiles—is the prototype of this new humanity (Eph. 2:15–16). Their reconciliation with God and with one another due to their union with the resurrected body of the Lord is the tangible sign of what God has accomplished in Jesus Christ for all of humanity (Col. 3:10–11). By Christ, who has opened a new way to all, "both [Jews and gentiles], in one Spirit, [have] access to the Father" (see Eph. 2:18). Christ's reconciliation of all things (cf. Col. 1:20), their convergence on him who is the head (cf. Eph. 1:10), are central themes of the Pauline vision of the work accomplished in Jesus.

Thus Paul professes that the mystery of the Lord's cross and resurrection has repercussions of cosmic dimensions. The action of the mystery of Christ reaches the whole universe. Surely the church constitutes a privileged sphere of this influence; but the latter far outstrips the former, to attain the limits of the cosmos itself. The church and the world represent two concentric circles around their Christ-center, whose universal activity embraces both. The church is the inner circle, the immediate sphere of the activity of Christ through his Spirit. The cosmos is the outer circle. Therefore Christ is head of both the church (Col. 1:18, 2:19), and the universe (Col. 1:15–18; Eph. 1:22), while the church alone is his body (Col. 1:18; Eph. 1:22–23). "The inner surface stands in closer relation to Christ than does the outer one; and yet, Christ is the common center."[6] For the same reason, while the Holy Spirit is in a special way the soul of the church, it is also the soul of the universe, for Christ pours forth his fullness upon the whole of creation, and the universe is filled with his presence (cf. Col. 1:19).

Summarizing, we may say:[7] The Spirit poured forth on Pentecost causes the action of the Paschal event to be an action of today, as well. It is by the Spirit that the mystery of salvation, accomplished once for all in Jesus Christ, becomes concrete reality for human beings. As principle of the new creation, the Spirit makes the sovereignty of Christ actually present in history. The activity of the Spirit gives birth to the community of the church, but transcends the boundaries of the Christian fold to give life to men and women and transform the cosmos.

The signs by which the activity of the Spirit can be discovered are the union and peace of human beings with God and among themselves. For "all whom the Spirit ensouls are children of God" (see Rom. 8:14). Those who live according to the Spirit seek what is of the Spirit (cf. Rom. 8:5), and "the desire of the Spirit is life and peace" (see Rom. 8:6). The calling of all human beings to the divine filiation and to the sharing of a universal siblingship are inseparable. Both are in course of a progressive actualization in the world. Called to freedom, the whole of creation, from the commencement down to our own day, has "groaned in the pangs of birth" (see Rom. 8:22; cf. 8:12–22); and while the firstfruits of the Spirit have already appeared, creation still awaits the plenitude of its salvation (cf. Rom. 8:23–25), when the ultimate restoration will at last appear (cf. Acts 3:21).

A recent author is correct in saying:

In the New Testament as in the Old, the Holy Spirit everywhere appears as the bearer of the creative and motive deed of God: the Spirit is very God, setting in motion and fulfilling the great cosmic renewal toward which the divine salvation plan tends. The Spirit extends to human beings, and seeks to extend to the world, the living bond of love that it constitutes from all eternity between the Father and the Son. The Spirit is divine fullness, aspiring to penetrate and fill creation altogether, as it has penetrated and filled Jesus, the Son of God eternally blessed.[8]

Bringing out the role of the Holy Spirit in its relationship with the salvation event in Jesus Christ, Ignace Hazim, Metropolitan of Latakia, has written:

The Paschal event becomes ours by him who is its artisan, from the beginning and in the fullness of time: the Holy Spirit. ... Without him, God is far, Christ remains in the past, the Gospel is a dead letter, the Church is a simple organization, authority is domination, mission is propaganda, worship is evocation, and Christian action is a slave morality. But in him, and in an indissociable synergy, the cosmos is exalted, and groans in the childbirth of the Reign ... the risen Christ is here, the Gospel is the power of life, the Church signifies the Trinitarian communion, authority is a liberating service, mission is a Pentecost, the liturgy is memorial and anticipation, human activity is deified. ...[9]

THE ECONOMY OF THE SPIRIT

Has Vatican Council II openly acknowledged the activity of the Holy Spirit in the religious life of persons belonging to religious communities other than the Christian community? Has the council said that the Spirit is at work in the religious traditions of the world?

We have already recalled in the foregoing chapter the principal texts of the council that deal with the members of other religions. They are the Constitution *Lumen Gentium*, the Declaration *Nostra Aetate*, the Decree *Ad Gentes*, and, we should have to add, the Pastoral Constitution *Gaudium et Spes*. We have shown that the first three of these documents cite positive elements not only in the personal religious life of the members of other traditions, but in these traditions themselves, which contain seeds of the

Word and can serve as evangelical preparation. If the council does not explicitly say that they can be ways of salvation for their members, it surely seems to incline in that direction and does set the positive elements of other traditions in relationship with the mystery of Christ.

On the specific question of the activity of the Spirit in the members of other religions, however, we observe a certain evolution in the documents of the council. While the Constitution *Lumen Gentium* and the Declaration *Nostra Aetate* are silent on this subject, the Decree *Ad Gentes* and the Constitution *Gaudium et Spes* make explicit reference to it. *Ad Gentes* (no. 4) formally acknowledges the work of the Spirit in the world before the glorification of Christ as well as, after Christ, outside the church:

> In order fully to realize [the work of salvation], Christ sent the Holy Spirit from the bosom of the Father, to accomplish his salvation-bearing deed in the inner depths of souls, and impel the church to expand. Beyond the shadow of a doubt, the Holy Spirit was already at work before the glorification of Christ. However, on the day of Pentecost he descended upon the disciples to remain with them forever (cf. John 14:16).

In support of its affirmation of the activity of the Spirit in the world before the glorification of Christ, *Ad Gentes* (no. 5) specifically cites St. Leo the Great:

> When, on the day of Pentecost, the Holy Spirit filled the Lord's disciples, it was not the inception of a gift, but a largess superadded to others: the patriarchs, the prophets, the priests, the saints who lived in ancient times were nourished with the same sanctifying Spirit . . . although the measure of the gifts was different.

According to *Ad Gentes* (no. 15), it is once more the Holy Spirit who "summons all men to Christ by the seeds of the Word and the preaching of the Gospel." While, as we have observed above in our study of council documents, the Word has sown its seeds in the religious traditions of humanity, it belongs to the Spirit to see that these seeds fructify by addressing a call to human beings for faith in Jesus Christ.

Gaudium et Spes is more explicit. We have already quoted the central text, in which the constitution states that it is possible for any human being, in virtue of the activity of the Holy Spirit, to be associated, for his or her salvation, to the Paschal mystery of Jesus Christ (*GS*, no. 22). Clear as it is on the subject of the activity of the Spirit on persons outside of Christianity and the church, this text has nothing to say on the active presence of that Spirit in the religious traditions themselves.

This text is not the only one, however. The Constitution *Gaudium et Spes* makes constant reference to the activity of the Spirit in the world outside of the church. It sees that activity present not only in the religious initiatives of humanity, but also in the cultures, the universal aspirations, even secular, that characterize the present world. Here we touch on a characteristic note of the Pastoral Constitution. A consideration of the universal possibility of salvation now gives way to the joyous recognition of the current, actual presence of the Holy Spirit among human beings throughout the whole of humanity. The Spirit is currently at work among the members of the other religious traditions. Its influence extends to them, mysteriously and secretly, in the concrete situation of their religious lives.

This new emphasis and more concrete approach of the Constitution *Gaudium et Spes* are due to a methodological shift in the work of the council. With the Pastoral Constitution we might say that the methodology of the council is reversed: The deductive method is now replaced by the inductive. The premises on which the constitution is constructed consist not in dogmatic and theological principles, but in a lucid, sincere analysis of the concrete situation of the modern world. The church seeks to situate itself in this context and discover its role there. Such a method naturally leads the constitution to an honest encounter with the human realities that the Christian message should animate. The fruit of all this is an open attitude toward the cultures, currents of thought, human successes, and aspirations that give today's world its physiognomy. In particular, the council was able to recognize the influence exerted by the Holy Spirit on various domains of human activity in the world as a whole.[10]

The new insistence on the action of the Spirit in the world, as we have it in the Constitution *Gaudium et Spes*, is actually in keeping with a more general characteristic of the same document. If we set the various documents side by side, we perceive that the council gradually rediscovered the economy of the Holy Spirit. The Constitution *Gaudium et Spes* is the fruit of this gradual rediscovery. Treating of the life and activity of the church, the Constitution *Lumen Gentium* has time and again referred to the role of the Spirit. Still, as we know, this document did not fully satisfy the Eastern bishops at the council, or the Orthodox observers, as to the function of the Spirit as principle of the very existence of the church.[11] Nor was their reproach without foundation,[12] and Yves M. J. Congar is justified, in an effort to supply for this shortcoming, in speaking of Jesus Christ and the Spirit as "co-instituting" the church.[13] At all events, while the viewpoint is not directly doctrinal, the deed of the Spirit emerges more clearly in the Constitution *Gaudium et Spes* than in any other council document. Here the Spirit is seen to be at work not only in the church, but outside it. The influence of the Spirit is discovered not merely in human beings' religious initiatives, but in the various fields of human activity, as well.

Gaudium et Spes (no. 11) states:

The People of God believes that it is led by the Spirit of the Lord, who fills the earth. Motivated by this faith, it labors to decipher authentic signs of God's presence and purpose in the happenings, needs, and desires in which this people has a part along with other men of our age.

Furthermore, "the Church believes that Christ, who died and was raised up for all, can through His Spirit offer man the light and the strength to measure up to his supreme destiny" (*GS*, no. 10). Impelled by this faith, the church acknowledges that "it is . . . through the gift of the Holy Spirit that man comes by faith to the contemplation and appreciation of the divine plan" (*GS*, no. 15). "The Church truly knows that only God . . . meets the deepest longings of the human heart, which is never fully satisfied by what this world has to offer. She also knows that man is constantly worked upon by God's Spirit, and hence can never be altogether indifferent to the problems of religion" (*GS*, no. 41). The church likewise professes that, "redeemed by Christ and made a new creature in the Holy Spirit, man is able to love the things created by God, and ought to do so" (*GS*, no. 37).

Among the realities rightly cultivated by the women and men of our times, the constitution draws special attention to the aspiration to a universal siblingship. In his priestly prayer (cf. John 17:21–22), Christ himself "implied a certain likeness between the union of the divine Persons, and the union of God's sons in truth and charity" (*GS*, no. 24). In this light, the church recognizes that "God's Spirit, who with a marvelous providence directs the unfolding of time and renews the face of the earth, is not absent from this development" (*GS*, no. 26), which characterizes the social order of the modern world.

Gaudium et Spes (nos. 38, 39) states:

God's Word . . . was Himself made flesh and dwelt on the earth of men. Thus He entered the world's history as a perfect man, taking that history up into Himself and summarizing it. He Himself revealed to us that "God is love" (1 John 4:8). At the same time He taught us that the new command of love was the basic law of human perfection and hence of the world's transformation.

To those, therefore, who believe in divine love, He gives assurance that the way of love lies open to all men and that the effort to establish a universal brotherhood is not a hopeless one. . . .

. . . Appointed [i.e., constituted] Lord by His resurrection and given plenary power in heaven and on earth, Christ is now at work in the hearts of men through the energy of His Spirit. He arouses not only a desire for the age to come, but, by that very fact, He animates, purifies, and strengthens those noble longings too by which the human family strives to make its life more human and to render the whole earth submissive to this goal.

After we have obeyed the Lord, and in His Spirit nurtured on earth the values of human dignity, brotherhood and freedom, and indeed all the good fruits of our nature and enterprise, we will find them again, but freed of stain, burnished and transfigured. This will be so when Christ hands over to the Father a kingdom eternal and universal. ... On this earth that kingdom is already present in mystery. When the Lord returns, it will be brought into full flower.

It was necessary to transcribe lengthy passages here in order to show that many human values, religious or other, which only the message of the gospel can explain completely, are, according to the council, nevertheless grasped and cultivated by all human beings. These texts should be read in the broad, universal perspective from which they were written. The cosmic effects of the Jesus Christ event and the universal activity of the Holy Spirit that derives from that event are everywhere present.

Never had an official document of the church so openly acknowledged the active presence of the Spirit in the hearts of women and men, irrespective of their religious persuasion. The Spirit is perceived as raising up the whole of humanity through human beings' religious aspirations and human enterprises. This faith on the part of the church is based on the fact that, "by His incarnation the Son of God has united Himself in some fashion with every man. ... By suffering for us He not only provided us with an example for our imitation. He blazed a trail . . ." (*GS*, no. 22). Become flesh in order that, as perfect man, he may save all men and women and recapitulate all things in himself, he is "the goal of human history, the focal point of the longings of history and of civilization, the center of the human race, the joy of every heart, and the answer to all its yearnings" (*GS*, no. 45). As a result of his glorification, "enlivened and united in His Spirit, we journey toward the consummation of human history, one which fully accords with the counsel of God's love: 'To re-establish all things in Christ, both those in the heavens and those on the earth' (Eph. 1:10)" (*GS*, no. 45).

The prophetic sign throughout the world of this universal activity on the part of Christ's Spirit is the church, the "new fraternal community" constituted by the resurrected Christ by the gift of his Spirit (*GS*, no. 32). It has the mission of "illumining the whole universe by the message of the Gospel, and of uniting in one Spirit all men, to whatever nation, race or culture they belong." In order to promote the human siblingship of which it is the sign, the church desires to enter into a sincere dialogue with "all who acknowledge God, and whose traditions contain precious religious and human elements," confident that such a dialogue "can lead all of us together frankly to accept the appeals of the Spirit and to follow them with ardor." Indeed, the desire for such a dialogue "excludes no one" (*GS*, no. 92).

Gaudium et Spes (no. 93) continues:

Now, the Father wills that in all men we recognize Christ our brother and love him effectively in word and in deed. By thus giving witness to the truth, we will share with others the mystery of the heavenly Father's love. As a consequence, men throughout the world will be aroused to a lively hope—the gift of the Holy Spirit—that they will finally be caught up in peace and utter happiness in that fatherland radiant with the splendor of the Lord.

The Pastoral Constitution *Gaudium et Spes* ends with what we might call the Magna Carta of the dialogue between Christians and all humankind, believers and others. This dialogue is based on the acknowledgment of the active presence of the Holy Spirit in others. It consists in a common discernment of the suggestions of the Spirit experienced by all. It leads to action in common with a view to the establishment on earth, in hope and through the Spirit, of a universal communion of sisters and brothers in God, one that will presage, however imperfectly, the perfect communion of the family of God in the everlasting Reign.

Such is the teaching of the council. We cannot doubt that, in the Constitution *Gaudium et Spes*, it has brought out the active presence of the Holy Spirit in the members of other religious traditions.

Does the postconciliar magisterium reflect this vision? Here we must content ourselves with a rapid survey of the papal magisterium. As for the Apostolic Exhortation *Evangelii Nuntiandi* (1975), which Paul VI wrote following the Synod of Bishops on Evangelization in the Modern World (1974), we have already observed that its attitude on the subject of the world religions is, on the whole, negative.[14] It views other religions as various expressions of the human being's natural aspiration to union with God (*EN*, no. 53). We should not expect, then, that this exhortation should take cognizance of the active presence of the Holy Spirit among the members of other religions—apart from the hearing of the gospel message—or, still less, in their religious traditions themselves. Indeed, the document speaks of the Holy Spirit only in connection with the church's mission of evangelization: The Spirit is the "principal agent of evangelization," in that it impels the church and each of its members to proclaim the gospel, and furthermore, "in the depths of consciences, causes the word of salvation to be accepted and understood" (*EN*, no. 75).[15]

Pope John Paul II, for his part, ever more clearly, refers explicitly to the active presence of the Holy Spirit in the religious life of the members of other religious traditions. This can be shown quickly, as we skim through certain major documents that testify to this gradual insistence. As early as the Encyclical *Redemptor Hominis* (1979), he acknowledged the activity of the Holy Spirit beyond the confines of the church in more than one way. The Pope regarded the belief of the members of other religions as "one more effect of the Spirit of truth working beyond the visible boundaries of the mystical Body" (*RH*, no. 6). He exhorted the mission of the church to respect "all that the Spirit who 'blows where it wills" (see John 3:8) has wrought" in the members of other religious faiths (*RH*, no. 12).[16]

In like manner, in the message delivered over Radio Veritas in Manila to all the peoples of Asia (February 21, 1981), the Pope expressed the hope that the practice of the interreligious dialogue might grow, especially in the Asian context, that cradle of ancient religious traditions. He made explicit reference to the need for prayer, as the "expression of the spirituality of the human being, directed toward an Absolute," which seems to gather and unite, in a special way, Christians and the believers of other religions (no. 4). And he added:

Even when, for certain persons, [the Absolute] is the great Unknown, it ever remains in reality no less the same living God. We can be sure that, every time the human spirit opens in prayer to this unknown God, an echo will be heard of that Spirit who, knowing the limits and weaknesses of the human person, himself prays within us and for us "in inexpressible groanings" (Rom. 8:26). The intercession of the Spirit of God who prays in us and for us is the fruit of the mystery of Christ's redemption, in which the plenary love of the Father has been shown to the world.[17]

A few days later (February 24, 1981), speaking in Tokyo to representatives of other religions, the Pope stated that he finds "in the virtues of graciousness, goodness, discretion, sweetness, and courage, inculcated by your religious traditions, the fruits of that divine Spirit who, according to our faith, is a 'friend of man,' 'fills the entire universe,' and 'holds all things together' (Wis. 1:6–7)" (no. 1).[18] Once more, meeting with members of other religions in Madras (February 5, 1986), the Pope spoke of the interreligious dialogue that the church seeks to maintain with them. He stated:

The Church's approach to other religions is one of genuine respect; with them she seeks mutual collaboration. This respect is twofold: respect for man in his quest for answers to the deepest questions of his life, and respect for the action of the Spirit in man [no. 2].

The fruit of dialogue is union between people and union of people with God, who is the source and revealer of all truth and whose Spirit guides men in freedom only when they meet one another in all honesty and love [no. 4].[19]

Throughout all these texts, we see the first, widening dawn of the same teaching: The Holy Spirit is present and active in the world, in the members of other religions, and in the religious traditions themselves. Authentic prayer (even to an as-yet unknown God), human values and virtues, the treasures of wisdom secreted in the religious traditions, true dialogue and authentic encounter among their members, are so many fruits of the active presence of the Spirit.

We must not omit a reference to the important discourse pronounced by Pope John Paul II to the members of the Roman Curia on December 22, 1986. This allocution was entirely devoted to the event of the World Day of Prayer for Peace, which had been held at Assisi two months before (October 27, 1986).[20] The Pope explained the meaning of this event, showed that it is a prolongation and concrete application of the teachings of Vatican II, and indicated its theological foundation.[21] The overall fabric of the discourse—the oneness of the human race in creation and redemption and the consequent unity of its origin and divine destination—was taken from the documents of Vatican II, although the address developed these elements further. Likewise directly based on the documents of the council is the role of the church as sacrament of the union of humanity with God and of human beings with one another, as well as the orientation of other religious groups toward the oneness of God's people.

On one point, however, just as in the documents recalled above, the Pope spoke more clearly than any of the council documents: on the active presence of the Holy Spirit in the religious life of the members of other religious traditions. Having observed that at Assisi all of the participants had prayed for peace in their own respective religious identities, and in the quest for truth, the Pope remarked that, nevertheless, there had been an "admirable manifestation of that oneness that binds us over and above differences and divisions of all kinds." He gave the reason for this as follows:

> All authentic prayer is uttered under the influence of the Spirit, "who intercedes with insistence for us, for we can only ask to pray as we ought"; but he prays in us "with inexpressible groanings, and he who searches hearts knows what the desires of the Spirit are" (Rom. 8:26–27). We may conclude that all authentic prayer is aroused by the Holy Spirit, who is mysteriously present in the heart of every person [no. 11].[22]

This text recalls—but states more clearly—what the Pope had already said in his message to the peoples of Asia (February 21, 1981). The most explicit text, as we might expect, is to be found in the Encyclical on the Holy Spirit, *Dominum et Vivificantem* (May 18, 1986). There the Pope explicitly mentioned the universal activity of the Holy Spirit before the time of the Christian dispensation and today outside the visible body of the church. Before the time of the Christian dispensation, the activity of the Spirit, in virtue of the divine plan of salvation, was ordered to Christ. Outside the church today, it results from the saving event accomplished in him. Thus the Pope explains the christological content and pneumatological dimension of the salvation event (no. 53):

> We cannot limit ourselves to the two thousand years that have elapsed since the birth of Christ. We must go back further, to embrace as well

all the activity of the Holy Spirit before Christ—from the beginning—
throughout the world, and in a special way in the economy of the Old
Covenant. This activity, in every place and at all times, indeed in every
human being, was wrought in virtue of the eternal design of salvation,
in which it is strictly bound up with the mystery of the Incarnation
and Redemption. This mystery had itself exerted its influence on those
who believed in the Christ to come. . . . Thus, grace comports at once
a christological and a pneumatological character, which are found
especially in those who adhere explicitly to Christ. . . .

But . . . we must also raise our eyes and advance "toward the deep,"
knowing that "the Spirit breathes where it will" (cf. John 3:8). . . .
The Second Vatican Council . . . reminds us that the Holy Spirit also
acts outside the visible body of the Church. It rightly speaks of "all
men of good will in whose hearts grace works in an unseen way. For,
since Christ died for all men, and since the ultimate vocation of man
is in fact one, and divine, we ought to believe that the Holy Spirit in
a manner known to God offers to every man the possibility of being
associated with this paschal mystery" (*Gaudium et Spes*, no. 22).[23]

TOWARD A THEOLOGY OF NONBIBLICAL SCRIPTURES

The active presence of the Spirit is universal, then. It anticipates the
event of Jesus Christ, and after that event, extends beyond the confines of
the church. The Jesus Christ event, as we have said, has cosmic repercussions. It establishes the new creation. The Spirit spreads throughout the
world, vivifying all things. The cosmic revelation itself is caught up in this
transformation. These premises bring up new questions, which now call for
a response.

Is it true that the activity of the Spirit reaches the members of other
religious traditions precisely by the intervention of their traditions? If so,
then what specific role might their sacred books play with respect to this
activity? Do the nonbiblical scriptures mediate the activity of the Spirit in
the religious life of others? How do these writings nourish and sustain their
religious experience? How do they invite the members of these religions to
the obedience of the faith that saves?

Can theology discover in the holy scriptures of other religious traditions
the harvest of an authentic divine revelation—a genuine word addressed
by God to human beings? Can theology apply to these sacred books the
Christian concept of "inspiration"?[24]

The Bible, especially the New Testament, possesses a unique value in
Christianity. It is the authentic collection of God's self-revelation to Israel,
which has been accomplished in Jesus Christ. This does not exclude a priori
the possibility that other scriptures might also refer to an authentic manifestation of God in history deserving to be called "divine revelation," even
if certain precisions will have to be made on the manner in which this is

to be understood. The Spirit of God may have been at work in the extra-biblical holy books, as well. If this is the case, we shall have to try to determine the nature of that activity.

Fundamental Principles

By way of presuppositions, we must first establish two fundamental principles that will enable us to recognize in humanity's religious traditions a divine intervention, inscribed in salvation history and attributable to the influence of the divine Spirit.

ANY PERSONAL EXPERIENCE OF GOD IS THE VEHICLE OF THE PRESENCE AND ACTIVITY OF THE HOLY SPIRIT.

This assertion rests on the axiom, fundamental in the theology of the Trinity, according to which the order of God's personal manifestations to the human being corresponds to the origin of the divine persons in the trinitarian life itself. Whenever God personally enters the life of a human being, the gift given by God is the gift of God as God is—Father, Son, and Spirit.

God's self-bestowal is the communication of the Father through the Son in the Holy Spirit. The Spirit, who, in the cycle of trinitarian processions, draws its origin from the Father through the Son, is, so to speak, the culminating locus, the crowning instance of God's personal manifestation to the human being, where God opens the divine substance to this human being to grant a participation in the divine life itself.

Viewing this divine call from the side of the human being to whom it is addressed, we must say that the Spirit, as we have seen above, is the human being's only possible "point of entry" into the divine life, in virtue of the same necessity that, from the side of God, makes the Spirit the bond of God's personal relationship with us. This means that any personal encounter of God with the human being and the human being with God occurs in the Holy Spirit. God becomes God-for-the-human-being in the Spirit, and it is in the Spirit that we can respond to the divine advances. All "being together" of God and the human being is made fast in the Spirit, or—and this is the heart of the matter—all religious experience becomes truly personal in the Spirit. In the order of divino-human relationships, the Spirit, in the last analysis, is God rendered personally present to the human being—God felt by the human being in the depths of the human heart.

As this is an axiomatic truth in trinitarian theology, we must say that all authentic experience of God is an experience in the Spirit. Thus in all authentic experience of God, the Spirit is present and active, whatever be the manner in which human beings are situated in salvation history or the particular stage of this history to which they belong.

A distinction is doubtless necessary between pre-Christian grace and Christian grace. But it will not consist in the presence of the Spirit in the one and its absence from the other. What would divine grace be without the gift of the Spirit? The difference will rather be that, under the Old Testament dispensation, God's self-bestowal occurred through the Verbum not yet incarnate (but already destined to be) in the Spirit, while under the new dispensation this self-bestowal reaches us through Christ glorified in the Spirit. This is the content of the theological proposition according to which Jesus' humanity, transformed in glory by the Resurrection, becomes the source of all grace. Under both dispensations, and in every state of affairs, God's self-gift to us entails the active presence of the Spirit. In virtue of the glorification of the humanity of the incarnate Word, the Spirit of God has become the "Spirit of Christ," as well, and accordingly is bestowed on human beings by the resurrected Lord.

We can go back one step further in the development of salvation history and ask ourselves what is implied by the reality of divine grace under the dispensation that historically precedes the covenant with Israel. We must give the same answer and say that there, as well, grace signifies the gift God makes to human beings in the divine Spirit and the active presence of this same Spirit in their hearts. No other theology of grace can be conceived that would accord with the basic datum of trinitarian theology.

The "holy pagans" of which the Old Testament speaks lived under the pre-Jewish economy of salvation. The New Testament itself extols the faith of persons who have known neither the Jewish covenant nor the Christian covenant (Heb. 11). All of these persons lived by God's Spirit and responded in faith to the call of that Spirit. Hans Urs von Balthasar has correctly written of the pre-Christian economy of salvation: "Cognition by grace of the *mysterium* of God can never be produced but by the assumption of the creature into the process of trinitarian love"[25] — a process of which the Holy Spirit must be the agent.

THE HOLY SPIRIT IS AT WORK THROUGHOUT THE ECONOMY OF SALVATION.

The first principle has considered God's self-gift to the human being as an individual person. Despite differences between the pre-Christian economy of salvation and the Christian dispensation, this gift always involves that of the Spirit. We may now broaden our perspective and consider the economy of salvation in its social dimension throughout the history of humanity. We have already distinguished four successive periods in the history of salvation, corresponding respectively to four divine covenants: the covenant in Adam with humanity, that in Noah with the nations, the Mosaic with Israel, and finally, the covenant established by God in Jesus Christ with the new people of God.

The whole economy of salvation is dynamically ordered by the providence of God toward its plenary manifestation in Jesus Christ. At each stage of this development, in various ways, God is personally committed to humanity. All salvation history is summed up in the history of God's love for the human family. From stage to stage, love draws God to undertake a more profound self-involvement in human history. God proffers an ever more urgent invitation to the human being to a personal encounter in a dialogue of love. Thus the entire economy of salvation is the deed of trinitarian love overflowing upon humanity in the course of the stages of its religious history, from our creation in the image and likeness of God to our re-creation in the image of the incarnate Son in view of the fullness of Christ.

In this continuous overflow of trinitarian love upon humanity, we must say that the Spirit of God plays a special role. That role corresponds to the proper character of the person of the Spirit, the bond of love between the Father and the Son, in the trinitarian relations. Thus the Holy Spirit is at work at every stage of salvation history. In each of the progressive covenants struck by God with the human family, the Spirit is the immediate agent of the divine advance, and of the immersion of God in human history. Thus we might say the Holy Spirit presides over the divine destiny of humanity, in the sense that each divine covenant reaches humanity in this Person.

Accordingly, in the various stages of the public history of salvation, just as in the personal story of human beings' salvation, the same Spirit is revealed and manifested. But the Christian alone is capable of recognizing and identifying its activity. When, from the moment of Jesus Christ's entry into glory and the outpouring of the Holy Spirit wrought in the world by that entry, Christians cast a backward glance to contemplate all this salvation history, they discover, in its gradual unfolding, a movement testifying to a well-ordered plan.

Through this plan, the Christian also discovers the manifestation and revelation in human history of a trinitarian love that, ever more intensively, flashes forth in self-communication to men and women in the Spirit. The Christian knows that the mystery of salvation in every woman and man is the mystery of that individual's obedience through faith to the breathings of the Spirit, and of the openness of his or her personal freedom to the gift of God in the same Spirit. When, in virtue of their contacts and dialogue, it is given to them to discover this mystery at work in the lives of persons belonging to other religious faiths, it seems to Christians to testify to the presence—hidden, mysterious, and yet evident and undeniable—of the Spirit in others. Then they are in a position to weigh the secret manner in which the active presence of the Spirit attains human beings whose faith differs from theirs. More specifically, they are in a position to discover how the holy scriptures of their religious traditions become for them a mediation of the divine activity.

The Holy Spirit and the Nonbiblical Scriptures

The Second Vatican Council, as we have seen, adopted the expression, "seeds of the Word," which certain of the Fathers of the early church had used with reference to the religious traditions of the peoples to which they sought to carry the Christian message. Here the expression is directly applied to the sacred books of the various religious traditions of humanity, more especially to the writings that they regard as holy scripture.

As we know, in certain of these traditions — in Hinduism, among others — the concept of holy scripture is more fluid than in Christianity. A given sacred book, the *Bhagavad Gita*, for example, may be recognized as holy scripture (*sruti*) by some branches of religious Hinduism, without the same value necessarily being attributed to it by other currents of Hindu religious thought, according to which it will be merely part of tradition (*smrti*), rather than of sacred scripture.

Let us recall, however, that there is no complete agreement among the various branches of Christianity, either, on the "canonicity" of the holy books. Even Catholic tradition distinguishes between canonical and "deuterocanonical" books. The problem of canonicity is that of the identification made by a religious community of the sacred writings to which it ascribes the value of holy scripture. But the particular question concerning us is different, and more basic. What makes a sacred book holy scripture? The questions may easily be confused, which scarcely militates in favor of theological lucidity. In any case, our first question should be formulated as follows: On the basis of the theological criteria for the constitution of holy scripture, can the "holy scriptures" of other religions be acknowledged as such by the theologian? And if so, to what extent, and in what way?[26]

Here we must recall the distinctions between divine revelation, propheticism, and holy scripture, although the realities respectively denoted by these various terms are bound together by manifold relations. God has wrought a personal self-manifestation in the history of nations in such wise that theology can speak of a divine revelation,[27] even if this revelation is still only a preliminary stage in salvation history, ordered to the Jewish and Christian revelation. To this effect we need only recall the pagan saints of the Old Testament and the divine covenants with humanity and the nations. At the same time, it is becoming more and more widely admitted today that the prophetical charism had antecedents outside of Israel,[28] both before Christ and after. Thus we must broaden what the Prologue of the Letter to the Hebrews has to say of the prophets of Israel: Outside of Israel, too, God has spoken "on manifold occasions and under many forms," speaking "by the prophets" (Heb. 1:1).

Indeed, the prophetical charism itself must be correctly understood. It primarily consists not in a prediction of the future, but rather in the interpretation, for a people, of the sacred history currently being lived by that people: an interpretation of the divine interventions in its history. Nor is it legitimate to erect an artificial opposition between "prophetical" religion and "mystical" religion. After all, the source of the prophetical charism is a mystical experience. This has been excellently formulated for the case of the prophets of Israel:

[The prophet] has no doubt that the word of God has come to him and that he must pass it on to others. The source of this conviction is a mysterious, we may call it mystical, experience of a direct contact with God. . . . The divine seizure often provokes "abnormal" manifestations but, as with the great mystics, these are incidental. It is important to notice that the prophet, like the mystic, is raised to a "supranormal" psychological state by this divine intervention. To deny this would be to reduce the prophet to the rank of poet or to credit him with the illusions of misguided visionaries.[29]

The prophetical charism is not the exclusive privilege of Israel. Even the Old Testament acknowledged as genuine prophecy, having its origin in God, four Oracles of Balaam (Num. 22–24). As for Christian antiquity, it has sometimes regarded the Sibylline Oracles as prophetic.

The case of the prophet Muhammad is instructive here. On the basis of the description of the prophetical charism just cited, R. C. Zaehner observed that Muhammad (as Zoroaster) is a genuine prophet. And comparing the Old Testament with the Qur'an, he added: "It is impossible to read the two books together without concluding that it is the same God who speaks in both: the prophetical accents are unmistakable."[30] The acknowledgment of Muhammad as a genuine prophet of God is no longer unusual in Christian theology.[31]

Christian theologians who admit this, let us observe, are altogether aware that the Qur'an in its entirety cannot be regarded as the authentic word of God. Error is not absent from it. But this does not prevent the divine truth it contains from being the word of God uttered through the prophet. Seen in its historical context, Muhammad's monotheistic message indeed appears as divine revelation mediated by the prophet. No, this revelation is not perfect or complete. But it is no less real for all that.[32]

Actually, the problem is not that of revelation, or even that of propheticism, but of the sacred scriptures as containing the word of God uttered to human beings over the course of salvation history. From the Christian standpoint, holy scripture contains the collation, the memorial, of a divine revelation in such a way that God is the very author of this writing. Not that the human authors of the sacred books, or the compilers who gathered the oral or written traditions contained therein, are bereft of the full exercise of their human faculties and cease to be the authors of their works. Rather, both God and the human being at once are to be ascribed, albeit on different levels, the status of author. Holy scripture is "the word of God in the words of human beings." Because God is its author, it is not reducible to a human pronouncement concerning God; rather it is the actual word of God.

But because the human being is the author as well, this word addressed by God to human beings is authentically a human word—the only word, after all, that would be intelligible to them. To elucidate the mystery of

God and the human being as coauthors, as realized in unique fashion in holy scripture, Christian theology has recourse to the concept of inspiration. Traditionally, by divine inspiration we mean that God, while respecting the human author's activity, guides and assumes this activity in such wise that what is written is, in its entirety, the word of God to the human being.

It is doubtless a shortcoming of the traditional theology of holy scripture that the proper role of the Holy Spirit therein is largely passed over in silence. That it constantly uses the term "in*spir*ation" changes nothing: The origin and deeper significance of the word seem most often to have fallen into oblivion, or retain little attention. Despite the church's Profession of Faith,[33] despite the title of the Encyclical *Divino Afflante Spiritu*, despite even Vatican II's Constitution *Dei Verbum* (no. 11), the current theology of holy scripture continues to assert that God is its author only in rather indeterminate terms that fail to do justice to the personal influence of the Spirit. Divine inspiration is understood as the activity of God *ad extra*, common to the three Persons, by which God is the genuine author of scripture. It does not seem to refer to an active presence of the Spirit of God who, in inspiring the sacred authors, imprints its personal seal on what is written.

To remedy this state of affairs, we might propose an analogy between the incarnation of the Son of God in Jesus Christ and the inspiration of the holy scriptures by the Holy Spirit. To be sure, this analogy cannot be pushed too far. Evidently there is a difference between the assumption of human nature by the Son of God and the inspiration of the written word by the Holy Spirit. Nevertheless, the theology of the holy scriptures should once more, and more earnestly than in the past, make an effort to show the personal influence of the Spirit in the inspiration of these scriptures. Only then shall we be in possession of a theology of holy scripture that will permit a more open attitude toward the holy scriptures of other religious traditions.

Karl Rahner has emphasized the communitarian character of the holy scriptures. "The Bible is the church's book": it contains the word of God addressed to the ecclesial communion.[34] In other words, in the books that compose it, especially in those of the New Testament, the church has recognized the authentic expression of its own faith and the word of God that founds that faith. Holy scripture is thus a constitutive element of the mystery of the church, the community assembled and called into being by the word of God. But this does not require that the sacred author be aware of being moved by the Holy Spirit to write. As we know, the charism of scriptural inspiration extends well beyond the group of authors to whom various books are attributed. These authors often performed the function of the redactors, or editors, of oral or written traditions that they had received. The apocryphal gospels may likewise have preserved authentic words of Jesus.

This being the case, the question is whether Christian theology may acknowledge, in other sacred scriptures, a word of God inspired by the Holy Spirit and addressed by God to other religious communities; and if so, how this word is the word of God. To put it another way: Are the writings recognized as holy scriptures by other religious traditions, in which Christian theology is today accustomed to see "seeds of the Word," holy scripture in the theological sense of the word? When Christian theologians speak of "seeds of the Word" here, what do they mean by *seeds*? Do they mean that the Word is actually contained here, in an initial way, or are they referring only to a human expectancy of the Word? Are we to acknowledge an initial word of God to the human being, inspired by the Holy Spirit—or are we to see only a human word concerning God—or again, a human word addressed to God in the expectation of a divine response? If indeed it is a matter of an initial word of God, then we must further ask: What is the connection between this initial word, uttered by God to human beings, as contained in the holy scriptures of various religious traditions, and the decisive word spoken by God to human beings in Jesus Christ, of which the New Testament constitutes the official record? To answer these questions, we shall appeal to the notion of a progressive, differentiated revelation, and to an analogical concept of scriptural inspiration.[35]

We must maintain that the religious experience of the sages and *rsi* of the nations is guided and directed by the Spirit. Their experience of God is an experience of God's Spirit. To be sure, we must simultaneously admit that this experience is not the good fortune of the *rsi* alone. In the divine providence, God, to whom alone belongs the initiative of any divino-human encounter, has willed to speak to the nations themselves, through the religious experience of their prophets. In addressing the prophets personally in the secret recesses of their hearts, God has willed to be manifested and revealed to the nations in the divine Spirit. Thus God has secretly entered the history of peoples, guiding them toward the accomplishment of the divine design. The social character of the holy scriptures of the nations can thus be said to have been willed by God. These scriptures represent the sacred legacy of a tradition-in-becoming, not without the intervention of divine providence. They contain words of God to human beings in the words of the *rsi*, inasmuch as they report secret words uttered by the Spirit in hearts that are human, but words destined by divine providence to lead other human beings to the experience of the same Spirit. To say anything less, surely, would be to cheapen the realism of God's self-manifestation to the nations.

What is suggested here is not tantamount to saying that the *whole* content of the holy scriptures of the nations is the word of God in the words of human beings. In the compilation of the sacred books of other traditions, many elements may have been introduced that represent only human words concerning God. Still less are we suggesting that the words of God contained in the holy scriptures of the nations represent God's decisive word to them, as if God no longer had anything to say to them that he has not already told them by the intermediary of their prophets.

Our proposition comes down to this, that the personal experience of the Spirit by the *rsi*, inasmuch as, by divine providence, it is a first personal overture on the part of God to the nations, and inasmuch as it has been authentically recorded in their holy scriptures, is a personal word addressed by God to them through intermediaries of divine choosing. In a true sense, but a sense that would doubtless be difficult to submit to further specification, this word may be called a "word inspired by God," provided we do not impose too strict an acceptation of the concepts and that we take sufficient account of the cosmic influence of the Holy Spirit.

Fullness of Revelation in Jesus Christ

The Letter to the Hebrews clearly states (Heb. 1:1) that the word uttered by God in Jesus Christ—in the Son—is God's decisive, and in this sense, definitive word. However, in what sense, and how, is Jesus Christ the fullness of revelation? Where precisely is this plenitude? To avoid any confusion, let us note that the fullness of revelation is not, properly speaking, the written word of the New Testament. The latter constitutes the official record, the authentic memorial of that revelation. Traditionally, from the chronological point of view, it has been said that this record comes to its conclusion with the death of the last apostle. It is more meaningful, however, to observe, from the textual viewpoint, that it ends with the composition of the last book of the New Testament. In any case, this authentic memoir—which is part of constitutive tradition—is to be distinguished from the Jesus Christ event itself, to which the accredited witnesses give testimony. It is the very person of Jesus Christ, his deeds and his words, his life, his death, and his resurrection—in a word, the Jesus Christ event itself—that constitute the fullness of revelation. In him, God has uttered to the world his decisive word, to which nothing can be added by way of divine revelation.

This is the understanding of Vatican II's Constitution *Dei Verbum*, when it distinguishes the fullness of revelation in the Jesus Christ event (no. 4) from its "transmission" in the New Testament, which belongs to apostolic tradition (no. 7). The authentic memorial transmitted by the New Testament is of course normative (as *norma normans*) for the faith of the church of all times. But this does not mean that it constitutes the fullness of the word of God to human beings. The New Testament itself bears witness that this memorial reports the event of Jesus Christ only incompletely (cf. John 21:25).

Thus Jesus Christ is personally the fullness of revelation. Furthermore, let us note, this fullness is a matter not of quantity, but of quality. It is owing to his personal identity as Son of God that Jesus Christ is, properly speaking, the pinnacle and culmination of the revealed word. In order to understand this, we must begin with the human awareness that Jesus had of being the Son of God. Jesus lived his personal relationship to the Father and to the Spirit in his human awareness. His human consciousness of being the Son entailed the immediate vision of his Father, whom he called *Abba*. Thus he revealed God from a point of departure in a unique, unsurpassable experience. This experience was actually none other than the transposition to the key of human awareness and cognition of the mystery of the very life of God and of the trinitarian relations among the persons. Thus Jesus prayed to the Father in whom he had his origin, while he promised to send the Spirit that came from him.

If divine revelation attains its qualitative plenitude in Jesus, it is because no revelation of the mystery of God can match the depths of what occurred when very God, in the divine Son incarnate, lived, in a human key, in a human consciousness, his own divine mystery. This is what took place in Jesus Christ, and it is this that is at the origin of the divine revelation that he delivers to us.

Nevertheless, this revelation is not absolute. It remains relative. Jesus' human consciousness, while it is that of the Son, is still a human consciousness, and therefore a limited one. It could not have been otherwise. Now no human consciousness, even the human consciousness of God, can exhaust the divine mystery. On the other hand, it is precisely this human experience that Jesus had of being the Son, in relation to the Father and the Spirit, that enabled him to translate into human words the mystery of God that he reveals to us. We must go further, and say that the trinitarian mystery could be revealed to human beings only by the incarnate Son living as a human being his own mystery of Son and uttering that mystery to his sisters and brothers.

The qualitative fullness—let us say, the intensity—of the revelation in Jesus Christ is no obstacle, even after the moment of the historical event, to a continuing divine self-revelation through the prophets and sages of other religious traditions, as, for example, through the prophet Muhammad. That self-revelation has transpired, and continues to transpire, in history. No revelation, however, either before or after Christ, can either surpass or equal the one vouchsafed in Jesus Christ, the divine Son incarnate.

The church, meanwhile, must continue to grow in a more profound intelligence of the words uttered by God "once for all" in the divine Word incarnate. To this end, the church is assured of the constant assistance of the Spirit that guides it "toward the whole Truth" (see John 16:13) that is Jesus Christ in person.[36] The church does this, furthermore, in reference to the authentic record of the event contained in the New Testament, which remains for all time the norm (*norma normans*) of an ecclesial comprehension of the mystery of Christ.

A Progressive, Differentiated Revelation

Thus the reason we must attribute to the New Testament a special, unique charism of scriptural inspiration is that it contains the official record of the definitive revelation addressed in Jesus Christ by God to all men and women. As incomplete as the record is, it bears, by virtue of the inspiration of the Holy Spirit, a seal of authenticity that enables the church community to recognize in it the official expression of its faith—the true sense of what God has done for human beings in Jesus Christ. In order to be correctly understood, the special influence exerted by the Holy Spirit on the composition of the New Testament must be regarded as an integral part of the activity by which that Spirit creates the church.

The church was born, on the day of Pentecost, of the outpouring of the Spirit of the resurrected Christ. The presence of the Spirit among the first believers, and its continuous *paraklesis*, make the church the eschatological community whose task it is to bear witness to the revelatory event of God that has occurred in these latter days. The composition of the New Testament is an essential part of this creation of the church: Without it, the church community would be unable to offer its authentic witness. Under the special influence of the Holy Spirit, the primitive church has recorded, for itself and for all generations to come, the sense of the Jesus Christ event. The record that it makes of this event is not only a word addressed by God to human beings through the personal experience of the Spirit by individual seers; it is the definitive word of God to human beings, written under the special guidance of the Holy Spirit by members of the eschatological community that it fills with its presence. It is in this sense that the New Testament is a constitutive element of the mystery of the church.

But even given the unique character of the Jesus Christ event and the unequivocally unique place of the official record of this event by the eschatological community of the church in the mystery of God's revelation to the world, there is yet room for an open theology of revelation and holy scriptures. Such a theology will posit that, before uttering the ultimate divine word in Jesus Christ, even before speaking through the prophets of the Old Testament, God had already uttered an initial word to human beings through the prophets of the nations—a word whose traces can be found in the holy scriptures of the world's religious traditions. The last word does not preclude a first; on the contrary, it supposes it. Nor may we say that God's initial word is the one reported in the Old Testament. No, the Old Testament itself bears witness that God spoke to the nations before ever addressing Israel. Thus the holy scriptures of the nations, along with the Old and New Testaments, represent the various manners and forms in which God addresses human beings throughout the continuous process of the divine self-revelation to them.

In the first stage, God grants to the hearts of seers the hearing of a secret word, of which the holy scriptures of the religious traditions of the world are able to contain, at the least, traces. In the second stage, God speaks officially to Israel by the mouth of its prophets, and the entire Old Testament is the record of this word. In both of these stages, the word of God is ordered, however differently in each, to the plenary revelation that will take place in Jesus Christ. In this third and last stage, God utters the decisive divine word in the divine Son, and it is to this word that the whole New Testament bears official witness.

The holy scriptures of the nations can contain only initial, hidden words of God. These words do not have the official character that we must ascribe to the Old Testament, to say nothing of the definitive value of the New. We may call them divine words, however, inasmuch as God utters them by the divine Spirit. From the theological point of view, the sacred books containing them deserve, in a certain sense, the term "holy scriptures." In the last analysis, the problem is a terminological one — a question of what we are to understand by *word of God, holy scripture*, and *inspiration*.

We can give these terms a strict theological definition, in keeping with the traditional way of speaking. In that case we are compelled to limit their application to the scriptures of the Jewish and Christian traditions alone. But we can also assign them a broader definition, not without valid theological foundation, according to which they will be applicable to the scriptures of other religious traditions. *Word of God, holy scripture*, and *inspiration* will then not express precisely the same reality in different stages of the history of revelation and salvation; but at each stage these terms will designate an authentic reality and will thus be applicable to each stage, saving the necessary distinctions. Important as it is to preserve intact the unique signification of the word of God reported by the Jewish and Christian revelation, it is no less important to recognize the full value and meaning of the words of God contained in the cosmic revelation. *Word of God, holy scripture*, and *inspiration*, then, are analogical concepts, applied differently to the different stages of a progressive, differentiated revelation. Claude Geffré puts it well. Having acknowledged in the Qur'an "an authentic word of God, although in part formally different from the Word revealed in Jesus Christ," he goes on:

> A like acknowledgment leads us to a deeper theological appreciation of revelation as differentiated revelation. While the theology of the non-Christian religions has not yet emerged from the stumbling, searching stage, we must try to think how a single revelation can include different Words of God.[37]

The history of salvation and revelation is one. In its various stages — cosmic, Israelite, and Christian — it bears, in different ways, the seal of the influence of the Holy Spirit. By this we mean that throughout the stages of the divine revelation itself, God, in the dispositions of divine providence, personally guides humanity toward the goal divinely set. The positive divine disposition of the cosmic revelation, as a personal revelation of God to the nations, includes the divine disposition of the holy scriptures of those nations as evangelical preparation. The seeds of the Word contained in their scriptures are seminal words of God, from which the influence of the

Spirit is not absent. The influence of the Spirit is universal. It extends to the words uttered by God to humanity in all of the stages of the self-revelation lavished by that God upon that humanity.

An important question remains. Has this incomplete word of God to be acknowledged in other religious traditions the value of word of God only for the members of these traditions? Or may we say, on the contrary, that it has an analogous value for Christians themselves? May we think that God speaks to us Christians through the prophets and sages whose religious experience is the source of the sacred books of these traditions?

The fullness of revelation contained in Jesus Christ and transmitted by the church does not gainsay this possibility.[38] Nor is it opposed to the use in Christian prayer, even in the Liturgy of the Word, of the words of God contained in the sacred books of other traditions.[39] Indeed, this ought to be done, with prudence and with respect for the different stages of revelation history.[40] Also required will be the discernment necessary to avoid any ambiguities by a responsible selection of texts, in harmony with the mystery of Jesus Christ in which the Liturgy of the Word culminates.[41] Under these conditions, we shall discover, with joy and surprise, astonishing convergences between the words of God and the divine Word in Jesus Christ. Certain aspects of the divine mystery may actually be given more emphasis in other sacred scriptures than in the New Testament. We need only think of the deep sense of the divine majesty and the holiness of the divine decrees on every page of the Qur'an, or the sense of the immanent presence of God and the interiority in which religious experience is steeped in the sacred books of Hinduism. Paradoxical as it may appear, a prolonged contact with the nonbiblical scriptures — practiced within their own faith — can help Christians to a more in-depth discovery of certain aspects of the divine mystery that they behold fully revealed in Jesus Christ.[42]

8

The Christ of Faith
and the Historical Jesus
in the Encounter of Religions

In Christian faith, the Jesus Christ event is at the center of the divine plan for humanity, as it is at the center of the salvation history in which that divine plan is executed. Accordingly, the religious traditions of humanity are ordered to it throughout the course of history. It is in their relationship with the Christic mystery that even today these traditions have salvific value for their members. Thus these religious traditions represent a true, if incomplete, modality of mediation of the Christic mystery to their adherents. In particular, the sacred books of these traditions may contain words of God addressed to them and awaiting fulfillment in the decisive Word uttered by God in Jesus Christ.

In all that we have said thus far, we have been dealing with the event of Jesus Christ: with the historical person of Jesus of Nazareth, constituted by God as Christ in his resurrection. Christian faith does not permit the separation of Jesus from Christ. That faith professes both the personal identity of Jesus with the Christ, and the real transformation of his human existence in virtue of the resurrection by which he is established as the Christ. The object of the apostolic faith is not simply Jesus or simply Christ, but Jesus the Christ (cf. Acts 2:36).

Here, however, Christian faith finds itself confronted with questions too crucial to be ignored. We shall address the two that seem most decisive. The first bears on the relationship, apparently indissociable for faith, between Jesus and the Christ. The second bears on the seemingly contradictory assertion of the absolute value that Christian faith appears to attribute to the Jesus Christ event, despite its historical particularity. The first is the problem—by no means a new one—of the historical Jesus and the Christ of faith. The second—again not a new one, but recently formulated in novel terms—is that of the uniqueness and the universality of the Jesus

Christ event. We shall devote each of the following two chapters to one of these problems. The present chapter, then, will study the question of the Jesus of history and the Christ of faith. It will do so in the context of the encounter of religions.

STATE OF THE QUESTION

Let us state from the outset that, old as it is, the problem of the historical Jesus and the Christ of faith is posed in a context of the encounter of the religions not only in partly different terms, but in a more radical way. It may seem paradoxical that, in this precise context, what should cause a problem is not primarily the Christ of faith but the Jesus of history. And yet this is the case. We have already seen the problem. We saw it posed in chapter one, by certain Hindu interpretations of Jesus, such as those of S. Radhakrishnan and Akhilananda. We met it again when we set the Christian mystery in confrontation with Hindu *advaita* mysticism. We followed it once more in the spiritual experience of a Hindu-Christian monk and his ceaseless quest to join what he believed to be the "two forms of a single faith." The problem, as it arises in a context of religious pluralism in general and the encounter between Christianity and Hinduism in particular, is not new.

In order to grasp how radically it is posed in the context in which we are working here, it will be useful to draw up a brief sketch of its roots in exegetical and theological discussion in the West. We shall limit ourselves to what is strictly necessary for an understanding of the problem.

The exegetical discussion begins with the obvious fact that all the writings of the New Testament, being composed after, and in light of, the Paschal experience, reflect that experience as they report the historical event of Jesus and the facts of his life. These writings transmit to us not a history of Jesus, but a faith interpretation of Jesus. What they convey directly is not the historical Jesus, but the Christ of faith. The problem is whether (and how) from a point of departure in this faith datum concerning the person of Jesus, one can retrieve or rediscover the actual pre-Paschal Jesus.

Is the Jesus of history accessible to historical criticism? If so, how? Rudolf Bultmann can serve as our reference point here, in view of his key place in modern exegesis and the development of the historico-critical method. There is surely no need to elucidate here the methods set in motion by Bultmann. Suffice it to recall the general conclusions which he thought necessary to draw. According to Bultmann nothing certain can be said of the historical Jesus other than that someone by that name lived in a certain place in a certain time and died on a cross. The reasons for his too-pessimistic position are of little importance for our purposes here: a Lutheran conception of faith; the influence of existential philosophy, especially that of Heidegger; a rationalism that scouts the supernatural and the preternatural.

The important thing is that, for Bultmann, our all-but-complete igno-rance of this historical Jesus has no implications whatever for Christian faith. Christian faith is not dependent on history, Bultmann held. Christian faith, essentially, is God's appeal, God's challenge, through the word. God can challenge us, can call us to account, and in fact does so, through the word of the New Testament, independently of any historical foundation. We must rid the faith of its pretended historicity. Such is Bultmann's pro-gram of demythologization. For this thinker, Christian faith is indifferent to the historical Jesus. It can dispense with any historical certitude in his regard. Being an existential experience, it need not take on the unnecessary burden of attempting to lay a solid historical foundation.

Bultmann drove a dangerous wedge between the Christ of faith and the Jesus of history. The separation is highly prejudicial to the content of faith. Rudolf Bultmann's followers saw this very well. While employing the meth-ods established by their teacher, they refused to adopt his conclusions, which they regarded as neither proven nor acceptable. A celebrated address by Ernst Käsemann at Marburg on October 20, 1953, marked the turning point.[1] Contradicting Bultmann's insistence on demythologization, Käse-mann declared that, if the bond between the Christ of faith and the Jesus of history is severed, Christ himself becomes a myth. Faith requires certi-tude of the identity between the pre-Paschal Jesus and the glorified Christ. Faith cannot dispense itself from a solid foundation in the Jesus of history. Why would the gospels have been written in the first place, even in the light of Easter, unless the primitive church had thought that the history of Jesus was of interest and ultimately of importance for its own faith? Indeed, as the post-Bultmannians have shown, the method known as historical crit-icism, provided we employ it in unprejudiced fashion, permits us, if not to retrace the history of Jesus, at least to discover the essential traits of his person and the principal moments of his career. Thus modern exegesis can hold its head up again, confident once more that it can reach the historical Jesus through the gospel accounts: Witness the many books about Jesus written by eminent exegetes over the last decades.[2]

This is of major importance for christology. Christology—if it would follow an inductive, nondeductive, genetic, nondogmatic method—must commence with the historical Jesus. It must consist in following the route traversed by the disciples themselves in their gradual discovery of who Jesus was, the meaning of his life, his death, and his resurrection—in a word, his mystery—and the meaning of the salvation event accomplished in him.

The Paschal experience was the decisive step in this gradual discovery. The road must be traversed once more, as in the beginning, "from below." It will rest on the self-consciousness of the historical Jesus as manifested in his actions and his words, his options and his claims, his demands and his promises. From Jesus' own implicit christology, and from the pre-Pas-chal experience of the disciples, it will move on to the explicit christology of the New Testament: the interpretation of the person and event of Jesus

Christ in the light of the Paschal experience, such as the faith of the apostolic church delivers it to us. Here it will take up the task of showing the long maturation of the intelligence of the faith, leading from the christology "from below" of the first apostolic kerygma to the christology "from above" of the later writings of the New Testament.[3]

In all of this, its essential task will be to demonstrate the continuity between the pre-Paschal Jesus and the Christ of Easter — to show that there is no breach between the historical Jesus and the Christ of faith, but on the contrary, clear continuity and personal identity. The identity will be a differentiated one, of course: The post-Paschal Christ, while personally identical with the pre-Paschal Jesus, was genuinely transformed in his human existence by his resurrection. Between the two, then, there is at once the continuity of personal identity and the discontinuity of a human condition first brought low, then glorified. Jesus *is* the Christ, having become that Christ by his resurrection from the dead. This is the faith of the apostolic church (cf. Acts 2:36).[4] It is the task of christology to show that this is the case.

Thus christology today is characterized by a return to the historical Jesus as its starting point. This is true of "Northern" christology, which directly assimilates the new contributions of recent exegesis,[5] and it is true, in another context, and with different accents and another method, of liberation theology, first in Latin America,[6] then on the other continents of the third world.[7] One of the tests of all of these various christologies is the way in which they succeed in establishing the continuity — in difference — between the Jesus of history and the Christ of faith. To this purpose, it is important above all that the historical Jesus be rediscovered and recognized in the integrity of his mystery, without minimalist reductions and without an a priori rejection of the faith interpretation of the apostolic church as an "alienation" or "corruption" of the pre-Paschal Jesus.

There are two extreme positions, mutually opposed, both failing to manifest and account for the continuity, necessary for a valid christology, between the pre-Paschal Jesus and the Christ of Easter. One is the Bultmannian position, which retains only the Christ of faith. Faith is the human being's existential calling-to-account by the word of God. It is said to have no need of the encumbrance of a mythical, or at least uncertain, historical datum. But in thrusting the demythologization program to its ultimate conclusions, such a position paradoxically ends by reducing the mystery of Christ to a myth. At the other extreme we find the position which, in its efforts to base itself primarily on the historical Jesus, so reduces the latter's scope and content that the Christ of faith is regarded as an "alienation" or "corruption" of the historical Jesus by the faith interpretation of the apostolic church. The result is a reconstruction of the historical Jesus that robs him of his authentic personal identity and his mystery. On the one side, then, we end up with a Christ without Jesus, but this Christ is a myth. On the other side, we have a Jesus without Christ, but this Jesus is empty.

In either case, the fault lies with the methodology. We have lost the real continuity in real discontinuity between Jesus and the Christ—the personal identity of both and the genuine transformation of the pre-Paschal Jesus into the Easter Christ.

Of these two inviable extremes, it is the former that sometimes presents a danger for theological reflection in the encounter of the religions, especially that between Hinduism and Christianity. But in this new context, there is a difference. The question is put more radically. Now the question is not only what New Testament material can be relied upon as representing the Jesus of history; now it is the historical Jesus Christ event itself, across the board, that is called in question.

We are no longer dealing merely with historical criticism. With the Hindu-Christian dialogue, we have a criticism of history. What is being challenged is the absolute, transhistorical meaning ascribed to the Jesus Christ event by Christian faith. After all, like any other particular historical occurrence, this event is circumscribed in time and space. It could not have been otherwise. How can a particular occurrence have an absolute meaning in the order of relationships between God and humanity, in the order of salvation? We have recalled above that in Hindu philosophy, history by definition can belong only to the relative order of phenomena (*vyavaharika*), never to the order of absolute reality (*paramarthika*). We have also observed that Hinduism's genuine challenge to Christianity is its challenge to the density of history as professed by Christianity—without which Christianity would be without its object. We are asked, then, whether the Western concept of history, and the value attributed to it by Christianity, is not itself a myth[8]—or at all events, whether the salvation-history model is viable in the encounter between Hinduism and Christianity.[9]

The question, then, is whether the Christic mystery is so intimately bound up with its manifestation in Jesus of Nazareth that the two are simply inseparable: whether the Jesus of history is necessarily involved wherever the Christic mystery is present and operative. When, in the foregoing chapters, we have spoken of the active presence of the mystery of Jesus Christ— and of his Spirit—among the members of other religious traditions, and in these traditions themselves, we were presupposing this necessary relationship to be valid everywhere. We must now examine this relationship more closely, through an analysis of certain theological positions that tend in one way or another to loosen these ties. In so doing, we are pursuing the dialogue on the fundamental positions on the theology of religions mentioned above. We have observed the categories employed by J. P. Schineller to take account of these fundamental positions. What we have written up to this point falls under the heading of a "christocentric universe" and an "inclusive christology." The present subject opens a discussion—to be pursued in chapter nine—on the two succeeding models: "theocentric universe, normative christology" and "theocentric universe, nonnormative christology."

CHRIST WITH OR WITHOUT JESUS?

There are various possible ways of loosening the ties between the mystery of Jesus Christ and the mystery of salvation. One consists in undoing the knot between the Christic mystery and the Jesus of history. Then the pluralistic model is applied to the manifestations of the Christic mystery. The centrality and obligatory presence of this mystery in any experience of salvation is maintained, as constituting that salvation; but instead of claiming salvation to be inseparable from Jesus of Nazareth, it is suggested that Jesus is only one particular historical manifestation of it among others. "Christ" is still the "sacrament of the encounter with God"—God turning to the human being in self-revelation and personal communication. But Jesus is no longer essentially linked to this mystery. He is one symbol of it among others, a manifestation or expression—perhaps special, perhaps eminent somehow, but surely not unique. Krishna, for example, or Gautama, the Buddha, are also historical manifestations of the mystery of Christ. While the Christic mystery is obligatory for salvation, Jesus is optional. This position is akin to the model of "normative christology," in that it professes—perhaps gratuitously, since it denies a Jesus Christ "constitutive" of salvation—a relative superiority, indeed even the normative character, of the manifestation of the Christic mystery in Jesus of Nazareth.[10]

There is another way, however. One can also, while maintaining the bond between the Christic mystery and the historical Jesus, question the obligatory mediation of this mystery for the salvation of the members of other religions. The mystery of the undivided Jesus Christ, being particular and subject to historical conditioning, is necessarily contingent. As such, it can have no transhistorical value. On the contrary, it is ineluctably contingent, so that we must forthrightly admit the existence of other mediations of salvation having no relationship with the mystery of the undivided Jesus Christ.

We shall then speak of an ineffable mystery of salvation, which reaches human beings through various mediations, of which Jesus Christ is only one. Jesus Christ, we shall be told, is the sacrament of the encounter with God for us, for Christians, but for us alone. True, the mystery of salvation in all circumstances must reach women and men through some mediation. But the Christic mediation is not the only effective one. There are other equally effective mediations not bound up with Jesus Christ. The christocentrism that asserts that the mystery of Jesus Christ is the sole way of salvation—even though this mystery can reach the members of the other religious traditions by the mediation of those traditions themselves—is replaced by a theocentric perspective, according to which God has provided for human beings belonging to other geographical and cultural climes other mediations of salvation adapted to their respective situations. Among them is neither priority nor rivalry. None will have privilege or eminence, even relative. In Schineller's categories, we recognize the position described above as that of a "theocentric universe, nonnormative christology."[11]

It is the former of the two possible ways that is directly in question here. Furthermore, it is important to have a clear grasp of what is at stake. We must appreciate what separates the theological perspective of a christocentric universe with its inclusive christology from that of a theocentric universe with a normative christology. The distance between them can be measured with the help of positive data. However, this distance does not always readily appear, a priori, in the texts.

The declaration of the theological conference held at Nagpur, India, in 1971 devotes a section to a "theological understanding of the religious traditions of humankind."[12] This section declares:

> An ineffable mystery, the centre and ground of reality and human life, is in different forms and manners active among all peoples of the world and gives ultimate meaning to human existence and aspirations. This mystery, which is called by different names, but which no name can adequately represent, is definitively disclosed and communicated in Jesus of Nazareth [no. 13].[13]

The professed intent of the declaration, in its own terms, is to recognize "the positive relation of the religious traditions of mankind to Christ" (no. 17). The salvation of human beings—as the Christian knows by faith—consists in "union with Christ, his liberator and saviour" (no. 15). While "men who are saved attain their salvation in the context of their religious tradition," nevertheless "this in no way undermines the uniqueness of the Christian economy, to which has been entrusted the decisive word spoken by Christ to the world and the means of salvation instituted by Him" (no. 16).[14]

In other words, salvation, in all circumstances, involves contact with the Christic mystery; but this mystery, which the Christian encounters in and through the Christian economy, in the case of other persons is conveyed by a different mediation—one available through their own respective religious traditions. This viewpoint coincides with the outlook referred to above as that of the presence of Christ in the religious traditions. There is nothing in this theory that could provide a pretext for any loosening of the bond between the Christic mystery and the Jesus of history.

Raimundo Panikkar has been one of the protagonists of the theory of the "presence of Christ." We have noted the influence exerted by his first book, *The Unknown Christ of Hinduism* (1964)[15]—in French, *Le Christ et l'hindouisme: Une présence cachée* (1972).[16] There is no reason to suspect here, in Panikkar's view either, any loosening of the bond between Christ and Jesus of Nazareth. Clearly, it is the mystery of Jesus Christ that is present in a hidden way, perceptible to Christian faith alone, in the religious traditions, and Hinduism in particular. But Panikkar's thinking has evolved on this point, as we may observe from an analysis of his more recent publications.

True, even in Panikkar's first book we discern a lack of clarity regarding the difference between the modes of active presence of the mystery of Jesus Christ in Christianity and elsewhere. Thus, we wrote, in a review of that first work:

> I am not sure that Fr Panikkar distinguishes as clearly as is desirable the two different levels. For he writes: "We are not self-sufficient monads, but fragments of the same, unique religion, though the level of the waters may be, and is, different" (p. 22); we must "dis-cover" our unity, and, "because we are all the same", "discard (the) veil of maya" that separates us (p. 21). The "anonymous Christianity" (K. Rahner) of non-Christian religions does not warrant such conclusions. However active Christ may be — and is — in Hinduism, what distinguishes us can never be reduced to a veil of maya.[17]

The reader will recognize the question addressed earlier to Karl Rahner, which was then clarified in the light of Rahner's own writings (see chapter six). The difference between the mediation of the Christic mystery in the Christian regime and that of the other religious traditions is not one of simple awareness. At any rate, our review of Panikkar's first volume uncovered nothing that might suggest the loosening of the ties between the Christ of faith and the Jesus of history.

The situation changes, however, with some of Panikkar's more recent writings.[18] *The Unknown Christ of Hinduism* appeared in a new English edition in 1981, revised and enlarged. Even the title of the work was expanded, to become: *The Unknown Christ of Hinduism: Towards an Ecumenical Christophany*.[19] In a lengthy Introduction,[20] the author explains that while he still regards the basic intuition of the first book as valid, he now sees it in a new light. He now describes his general theme as follows: "I speak neither of a principle unknown to Hinduism, nor of a dimension of the divine unknown to Christianity, but of that unknown *reality*, which Christians call Christ, discovered in the heart of Hinduism, not as a stranger to it, but as its very *principle of life*. . . ."[21]

He goes on to explain that the thesis of his book is mystical. Then he continues: "The Christ of whom this book speaks is the living and loving reality of the truly believing Christian in whatever form the person may formulate or conceptualize this reality."[22]

What, then, does Christ represent? Panikkar explains that, for him, Christ is the most powerful living symbol — but not one limited to the historical Jesus — of the fully human, divine, and cosmic reality that he calls the Mystery.[23] This symbol can have other names: for example, *Rama, Krishna, Ishvara,* or *Purusha*.[24] Christians call him "Christ," because it is in and through Jesus that they themselves have arrived at faith in the decisive reality. Each name, however, expresses the indivisible Mystery,[25] each being an unknown dimension of Christ.[26]

We need these citations in order to appreciate the new light under which Raimundo Panikkar now approaches his own subject. It would take a new book, he admits, rather than a corrected edition, to take advantage of this new light. What we have observed in Panikkar's Introduction now suffices to force a question. How are we to conceive the relation of the "reality" or "Mystery," the Christ symbol, to the historical Jesus? It is on this point that Panikkar's thinking seems to have evolved, not without consequences: A distinction is now introduced between the Christ of faith and the Jesus of history that no longer seems to give adequate account of the Christian assertion that Jesus *is* the Christ.

In the Introduction to the new edition of the book in question, Panikkar remarks that in order to do justice to his current thinking, many more changes would have to be introduced than would be possible in a new edition. It seems, indeed, that his actual thought on the subject appears more clearly in *The Intra-religious Dialogue* (1978), published shortly before the new edition of *The Unknown Christ of Hinduism*.[27] From the viewpoint with which we are here concerned, we are constrained to call attention to the distinction Panikkar introduces here between faith and belief. As we know, the distinction is not new: It has been made often enough since Barth. Still, we must observe what is meant by faith, as contradistinguished from belief. Faith, Panikkar explains, is one's basic religious attitude; belief is the expression adopted by this fundamental human attitude in any given tradition.[28] The content of faith, which he calls "the Mystery," is the lived relationship to a transcendence which seizes the human being. It is common to all religions. Panikkar calls this "Mystery" cosmotheandric, to denote a transcendence experienced by the human being in the cosmos. The content of beliefs, on the other hand, consists in the various religious myths in which faith takes concrete expression. In Christianity, we have the Jesus myth. All of these myths have equal value. Christianity gives the Mystery the name of Christ, but it can assume other names. While the various religious traditions differ on the level of belief, they are all seen to coincide on that of faith. The intrareligious dialogue cannot require a bracketing (*epoche*) of faith; but it can demand a bracketing of beliefs—indeed, their transcending. Panikkar hopes for a cross-fertilization of the beliefs of the various traditions—a syncretism that he is careful to distinguish from eclecticism.

If this too-rapid description gives a faithful account of Panikkar's thought, which is complex, it is easy to see that the place held in Christian faith by the Jesus of history is again a problem. For the first Christians, as the apostolic kerygma testifies (Acts 2:36), the Jesus of history was the Christ of faith. He had become that Christ in his raising by the Father. He was also the very Mystery (Rom. 16:25; Eph. 3:4; Col. 4:3, 2:2; 1 Tim. 3:16) preached by Paul. Thus Jesus is part of the actual object of faith. He is inseparable from Christ, on whom he bestows historical concretion.

But Panikkar makes a dangerous distinction between the Mystery and the Jesus myth—that is, the Christ of faith and the Jesus of history. He surely seems to separate them as objects of faith and belief, respectively. Is a reduction of the Jesus myth to an object of belief as distinct from faith compatible with the Christian profession of faith in the person from Nazareth? And as if by backlash, is not the content of faith reduced to a vague, neutral relationship to a transcendence, empty in its own turn, and as without an object? Is it not itself reduced to a myth, an abstraction?

In response to these questions, which he had actually been asked, Panikkar responded as follows:[29]

"Jesus is the Christ" is the Christian *mahavakya* [great axiom]. . . . The Christian is he who discovers . . . the Christ *in* and *through* Jesus, the Son of Mary. . . . Without Jesus there is no Christ for the Christian. . . . It is through Jesus that the Christian is able (or capable) to discover the Christ present in other religions or other places.

The relationship you ask about is of total identity in the one direction: Jesus is the Christ. And [it is] open in the other direction: the Christ is Jesus. As nobody [can] exhaust the Mystery (in Pauline terms), the Christ is "more" (*aliud* or *aliquid*, but not *alius*) than Jesus. This is true, even in the normal Christian economy. . . . The risen Jesus is the Christ. In this sense not only Jesus but also Christ belongs to history. But Christ is transhistorical (which does not mean less than historical but more).[30]

Christ is transhistorical; nothing could be more true. But it is Jesus who became the transhistorical Christ, in virtue of the real transformation of his raised human existence. While Jesus is the Christ, there is, conversely, no Christ who is not Jesus himself, raised, transformed, transfigured, and as such, transhistorical. His real transformation has not altered the personal identity. The discontinuity is no impediment to continuity. One may not conceive of Jesus as an imperfect manifestation in time of a Christ who transcends him. On the contrary, we must say that the historical Jesus is the transhistorical Christ: He is because he became so. And it is the indissoluble mystery of Jesus the Christ that is present both in Christianity and in the other religions. It is in and through this mystery that not only Christians, but others, too, encounter and receive the mystery of salvation. With all his explanations, Raimundo Panikkar's thought does not appear to preserve the indissoluble link between the Christ of faith and the Jesus of history. It betrays this link, weakening it and threatening, in spite of itself, to reduce the Christian message to a kind of gnosis. Were we to follow it, we should arrive, willy-nilly, at both a Christ-myth and a Jesus-myth.

R. Smet may well not have fully measured what is at stake in this problem in his "Essay on the Thought of Raimundo Panikkar."[31] In the conclusion of his work, he correctly observes that Panikkar's Hindu-Christian theology is an attempt to respond to the challenge to Christianity of an-historical Hinduism. But in seeking to ease the shock of a historical event of transcendent value, has not Panikkar himself relativized the historical? Smet hesitates to draw this conclusion. He writes:

> Conscious of what unites human beings, R. Panikkar proposes a "Hindu-Christian" theology. If the latter means to remain Christian, of course, it will still have to proclaim that the Christ, the *Logos* or Lord, became incarnate in Jesus. Here Panikkar recognizes that India is not prepared to believe in a spatiotemporally situated Divine; as for himself, however, while he finds an already existing *in-esse*, and existential convergences, as well as a unity in the single source, he remains attached to the inalienable specificity of Christianity. Jesus is the Christ, who died and was raised for the salvation of all, the historical redeemer, the only Son of God. He is the *Pantocrator* and the *Logos*, assuming the totality of creation, gathering up the scattered parts of the human race along their pilgrimage. He is the *Alpha* and the *Omega*.[32]

However, the same author can be critical, as well. For example, he writes:

> The Panikkarian outlook ... has both the advantage of not limiting the manifestation of the *Logos* ... to a limited moment of history, and the disadvantage of failing to deploy a logic that would center on the identification, especially the Joannine identification, of the *Logos* with Jesus—the logic of the Incarnation. The Christian can perfectly well admit a presence of the *Logos* outside of the Christian and Jewish traditions, but is not disposed to believe that the *Logos* acts elsewhere in identical fashion.[33]

Panikkar's intentions are not on trial. Still, clarifications are in order. We can, of course—and we must—following the Joannine Prologue, speak of an activity of the Word (*Logos*) in the world and in salvation history before its incarnation in Jesus Christ. We can even call this preexisting and "preacting" person "Christ," following St. Paul. But in either case, it is important to place this anticipated activity of the Word of God in relationship with the mystery of Jesus Christ, to which it is ordered as to its end, and in which the mystery of salvation is wrought. P. Lamarche puts it in excellent fashion, summing up the thought of both sacred authors. On John, he writes:

> The *Logos* denotes Christ the Savior as foreseen at the beginning of time in the Son by God the Father, and as realizing the divine plan.

The first expression of the Prologue (*en arche*, "in the beginning") denotes the commencement, not of the Trinity, which has no beginning, but of the history of the world; and we must return to this beginning to ensure the unity of the divine plan. In the first verses, the propositions linked by agraphics and framed by the *en arche* describe a divine person ("and the *Logos* was God"), distinct from the Father ("and the *Logos* was toward God"), in whom God the Father, from the commencement of the world, formed a salvific design, a design which, before being realized, was face to face with the Father, as is any reflection ("and the *Logos* was toward God"). Beginning with verse 3, the divine plan is realized: everything — creation, the history of peoples, human awareness, the provisional Mosaic law, the incarnation, the universality of the church — all is accomplished by him who is the design of God. All that has occurred "by his intermediary" (*dia*) has contributed to the realization of the divine plan, but it is only by the events that have occurred directly through him and in him (*en auto*), that is, in Jesus Christ, that the divine salvific design is accomplished. These events were, and are for us, the source of eternal life, and Life itself is Jesus Christ as he lived among human beings in order to enlighten them. . . .[34]

And on the christological hymn of the Letter to the Colossians (1:15–20):

When we say with St. Paul that the world has been created by Christ, we understand that it has been created precisely by this person *qua* destined to become Christ. . . . To say that the world has been created by Christ is to place all creation, from the beginning, under the sign of the Incarnation. . . .

Thus we may say, with St. Paul, that the world is created not only for Christ, but by Christ personally present from the beginning of creation *qua* second Person of the Trinity destined to become incarnate. While eternal God, and not as yet, properly speaking, incarnate, nevertheless from this moment he is the firstborn of every creature. . . .[35]

. . . This primacy, which is one at once of excellence and of interiority, is attributed to the second person of the Trinity, destined to become incarnate — that is, to Christ, *qua* foreseen by the Father "from before the creation of the world" (cf. Eph. 1:4).[36]

One may not separate, then, in the divine plan, the anticipated activity of the *Logos* from the Jesus Christ event in which this plan is accomplished. The *Logos* destined to become incarnate and the *Logos* incarnate are one and indivisible. Jesus Christ, Word incarnate, remains, at the center of the divine plan, the mystery of salvation.

There remains, however, as Smet reminds us, the scandal of a God who becomes human history. "India is not prepared to believe in a spatiotemporally situated Divine." Still, this scandal must not be softened by loosening the bond between the Christic mystery and Jesus of Nazareth. Between the "myth of history" and the "myth of Jesus," Christian faith has no choice to make. It must rather be seen that God, in the divine personal insertion into the history of human beings, gives that history a new meaning and an unprecedented concretion. This is what confers on the Jesus Christ event an absolute, irreducible sense. This is likewise what places Jesus Christ, one and indivisible, beyond all myth. Since God is incarnate once and for all in Jesus of Nazareth, the human existence of Jesus is, for all times and for all places, the sacrament of the encounter between God and human beings.

This is also that which, in Christianity, enables us to surmount the false dilemma between two perspectives, one theocentric, the other christocentric. If it is true that Jesus Christ is God turned toward human beings in self-revelation and self-giving, then the encounter between God and the human being can transpire only in Jesus Christ. He is the center—not as God's replacement, but because God has set him there as mediator and the path to God. To be sure, the humanity of Jesus is of the order of "signs" and "symbols," since it is in him that God works the divine self-communication. But at the same time, that humanity outstrips the order of signs and symbols, for it is part of the divine mystery itself. In that humanity the human being encounters God because it is there that God has become a human being and human history. There is no Christian theocentrism that is not at the same time a christocentrism. Nor is there a Christic mystery dissociable from Jesus of Nazareth—a Christ of faith without the Jesus of history.

9

Unicity and Universality of Jesus Christ

We could not have dealt with the problem of the Christ of faith and the Jesus of history, as it arises in the context of the encounter of the religions, without thereby addressing at least indirectly the implied problem of the unicity, or uniqueness, of Jesus Christ in the order of relationships between God and human beings. We have distinguished, in the foregoing chapter, two possible ways of dissolving the ties between the mystery of Jesus Christ and that of salvation. One consists in undoing the bond between the Christic mystery and the Jesus of history, and we have shown that way to be inviable. The other, while it maintains that bond, calls in question the obligatory mediation of the mystery of Jesus Christ for the salvation of the members of other religious traditions. This is the question of the uniqueness and universality of Jesus Christ the Savior, and it is this question that we must now address explicitly.

The uniqueness and universality of Jesus Christ in the order of salvation represent the cardinal, key question of every Christian theology of religions. As old as christology itself, and reappearing in recent times, it is becoming more urgent and more radical in the current context of religious pluralism and the blending of the various traditions. The current literature testifies to the renewed importance of this question.

The first thing we must do is clarify our terms. The uniqueness in question here is not the "relative" uniqueness that the science of comparative religion may very well assert apropos of every religious tradition simply in virtue of its specificity, its singularity, and its resulting differences from the others. Such a relative uniqueness is accessible to scientific observation. Faith, however, and the theology that rests on faith, goes beyond this. The uniqueness of Jesus Christ in the order of salvation, as traditionally understood by Christian faith, is an absolute uniqueness: Ineluctably, Jesus Christ is constitutive of the salvation of all human beings. He is the universal Savior.

Let us recall, however, that the uniqueness in question is an ontological one, not an epistemological one — as if it had to impinge on the awareness in order to exist. Furthermore, so-called relational uniqueness (akin to "relative" uniqueness) fails to account for traditional Christian faith. It is not enough to acknowledge that the mystery of Jesus Christ is capable, even today, perhaps more than any other symbol, of inspiring and nourishing an authentic religious life. The Christian must profess that, by virtue of God's plan, the mystery of Jesus Christ is universally constitutive of salvation. Let us also note that some authors prefer to replace the term *uniqueness* with "finality," or "centrality." These terms would have the advantage of indicating that, while the divine revelation in Jesus Christ is decisive, and in this sense final and central, it nevertheless does not represent, as we have shown, God's "unique" manifestation to humanity.

Oneness and universality: We must find a way of combining both and holding them together if we hope to give an account of the open theology of religions that we intend to propose. Without universality, uniqueness is exclusivism. Without uniqueness, universality would lead us down the pluralistic path. In combination, however, the notes of uniqueness and universality accord with the inclusive christology presented above.

Let us also recall the two dimensions, christological and pneumatological, of this inclusive christology. We have developed them in two chapters in our study: the active presence of the mystery of Christ (chapter six), and the influence of the Holy Spirit (chapter seven) in the religious traditions of humanity. We have likewise explained the organic bond linking these two aspects as integral parts and complementary elements of one mystery (see chapter seven). A "pneumatological christology," it has been observed, seems best calculated to demonstrate how the mystery of Jesus Christ is at once unique and universal. Walter Kasper writes:

> A Christology in a pneumatological perspective is ... what best enables us to combine both the uniqueness and the universality of Jesus Christ. It can show how the Spirit who is operative in Christ in his fulness, is at work in varying degrees everywhere in the history of mankind....[1]

STATE OF THE QUESTION

The uniqueness and universality of Jesus Christ still raise difficult questions, especially in the current context of religious pluralism. In what does this uniqueness consist, and how is it to be understood? Further, what is its theological foundation? Is it enough, in order to establish it theologically, to appeal to certain human values proposed by Jesus — for example, to the values of the Reign of God proclaimed by him? Or again, to refer to a human project for society that his activity would imply? Or to the particularly profound sense of the human person and its destiny, as these flow from his teaching? Or even to the relationship with God of intimate filiation that he recommends to his disciples? Or instead—without excluding any of the above, but going more to the heart of the matter—must the uniqueness of Jesus Christ and his universality finally and necessarily rest on the mystery of his person and his personal identity as Son of God?

In this last case, as we see at once, only a "high" christology will manage to establish that uniqueness securely. Any christology that sticks on the functional level and fails to enter into an ontological perspective will condemn itself—perhaps despite its intentions—to rest the uniqueness of Christ upon a fragile foundation. In all events, the various theological opinions concerning the uniqueness and universality of Jesus Christ as the Savior will reflect (as we should expect) their respective authors' fundamental options and basic positions in christology itself.[2]

To take up once more the categories we have used so far to define these positions, the same two models are in question here as in the preceding chapter: a "theocentric universe and a normative christology," on the one hand, and a "theocentric universe and a nonnormative christology" on the other. On either side, the adoption of a theocentric perspective is based on a rejection of christocentrism. This refusal is itself based on a christological option. Here, whether we continue to regard christology as empirically "normative," or refuse it even this character, we adopt a "low" christology, or at least we confine ourselves to a functional christology. In either case, we fail to raise christology to the level of the ontology of God's only Son, which remains the only adequate foundation of the uniqueness and universality of Jesus Christ. Let us quickly illustrate this by means of some carefully selected examples.

If we leave out of account, for the moment (to return to them later), works directly devoted to the theology of religions, rare are the christologies, even recent ones, that are concerned to situate the mystery of Jesus Christ in the context of the pluralism of the religious traditions.[3] Hans Küng constitutes an exception here, in his *On Being a Christian.*[4] Let us note from the outset that, open as Küng means to be, his evaluation of the other religions remains unsatisfying and is quite negative. In the section of the volume entitled, "The Challenge of the World Religions," he summarizes as follows the concrete questions that Christianity has the right to pose to these religions.

> Unhistoricity, circular thinking, fatalism, unworldliness, pessimism, passivity, caste spirit, social disinterestedness: the concrete questions to be put to the world religions in order to provide a diagnosis, so far as this is possible here, may be summed up under these headings.[5]

To suppose on all these points a negative balance would be to make it too easy a task to establish, as the author purports to do, the credibility and superiority of Christianity.[6] Küng recommends to Christians, with regard to the other religions, an attitude of openness to a mutual critique and an honest confrontation from a point of departure in faith. He rejects an "exclusivistic particularism" and a "syncretistic indifferentism."

Be this as it may, it is upon the person of Jesus Christ that Küng intends, altogether correctly, to establish the specificity and originality of Christianity. To this end he examines, from the historical viewpoint and according to the method of historical criticism, Jesus' project or "program." Jesus appears different in every way. He fits into none of the established categories of his time. He is a nonconformist: He does not identify with the power and established order. However, he does not share the revolutionary aspirations of the Zealots. Nor is he an escapist, who, like the members of the Qumran community, would lock himself up in a retreat to await better days. On the contrary, he is, in his own way, a radical. His gospel admits of no compromise. His difference is that he commits himself uncompromisingly to, and makes his own, both the cause of God and the cause of human beings.

From a point of departure in Jesus' program and values, Küng attempts to establish his difference and thereby justify the Christian assertion of his "uniqueness," which he enunciates as follows: "The special feature, the most fundamental characteristic of Christianity is that it considers this Jesus as ultimately decisive, definitive, *archetypal*"[7] for human beings in their relations with God, with their fellows, and with society.

For the Christian, Jesus is "ultimately decisive" (*letztlich entscheidend*).[8] In him are opened to human beings "completely new possibilities, the possibility of a new life and a new freedom, of a new meaning in life: a life according to God's will for [their] well-being, in the freedom of love...."[9]

Thus, under the pen of Hans Küng, we find the terms that have served to designate the "normative christology" according to which Jesus Christ is the eminent model, the most perfect symbol, of humano-divine relationships. The human and divine values that he proposes, however, the sublime morality that he proclaims, the perspectives on a new life that he presents—are these enough to establish, beyond all doubt, this normativity? Might we not wonder whether other figures have defended analogous, or even the same, values? Did not Mohandas K. Gandhi, for example, promote the same values as Jesus did in his proclamation of the Reign of God: justice, freedom, and a communion of brothers and sisters? And did he not also give his life for the defense of human beings and in fidelity to his message? Does the cross, then, really distinguish Jesus from other religious founders, it being there that he gives his life for the cause of God and that of human beings, the causes that he made his own, as Hans Küng believes?[10] Gautama, the Buddha, also preached a complete renouncement of self to the death, in view of a new existence.

Doubtless there are differences between Jesus and these others, and Küng is right to insist on them, finally resting his case on Jesus' resurrection. The ultimate distinction, the one that establishes Jesus' "determining, normative" character in the area of divino-human relationships, is his resurrection from the dead: Easter-after-Good-Friday. Jesus' resurrection stamps his entire life with the absolute seal of divine approval. In spite of his ignominious death on the cross, Jesus' cause is revealed to be the very cause of God. To take a decision in his regard, then, is to decide for or against God. Jesus crucified and raised personifies God's final commitment to the world. He offers the last response to the ultimate questions of human life, including those of suffering and death.[11]

All this is true. Yet the way Küng establishes the "difference" of Jesus Christ is ultimately incomplete, and thereby inconclusive. The reason for this is that only the personal identity of Jesus Christ as only Son of God can establish that difference in a decisive manner. Thereby it is not only his normative character vis-à-vis the other religious founders that acquires its theological foundation; it is also his obligatory mediation, as "constitutive" of salvation for all human beings, as Christian tradition understands it.

But Küng's christology falls short of this ultimate foundation. Once posited on the functional level, it remains there, never deliberately elevated to the ontological plane. For Küng, the fact that Jesus is "the *real revelation* of the one *true* God,"[12] the fact that Jesus is Son of God, is tantamount only to the notion of Jesus as *"God's representative"* vis-à-vis human beings—the mandatory, plenipotentiary, advocate, spokesman, representative, deputy, delegate[13]—all functional terms that fall short of the decisive assertion of his unique divine filiation. Even apart from the fact that the representative character of Jesus Christ in the order of relationships between God and human beings, if not ultimately founded on his personal identity as Son of God, may seem to obtain in virtue of an arbitrary decree on the part of God, surely only that personal identity can serve as adequate theological foundation for the uniqueness of Jesus Christ the universal Savior. For faith, nothing else can account for it. Apart from faith, all the rest may seem to assume an arbitrary, gratuitous character.[14]

Has Küng's position evolved on the point concerning us? In *On Being a Christian*, as we have seen, Küng asserts (although he does not satisfactorily establish it) the uniqueness of Jesus Christ and his normative character in the salvific order. Queried more recently about his position and pressed by his interlocutors to "cross the Rubicon" and deliberately adopt a pluralistic model,[15] Küng responded with a list of criteria for the truth of the various religions. These criteria are: the *humanum*, as a general ethical criterion; authenticity and canonicity, as a general religious criterion; and finally, a specifically Christian criterion, according to which a religion is true and good insofar as, in theory and in practice, it radiates the Spirit of Jesus Christ. Küng ends on a personal note:

> I am a Christian because I ... with confidence and in practice trust that the God of Abraham, Isaac ... and Jacob ... has ... bestowed

self-revelation in an incomparable, and for me a decisive manner in
the life and work, suffering and death, of the Jew Jesus of Nazareth.
... He is ... for us, *the* way, *the* truth, and *the* life! ... Jesus Christ
is for Christians the *decisively regulative* norm.[16]

While Küng can serve as an example of the theological model of a "theocentric universe" and "normative christology," John Hick, as we have
observed above, is the recent champion of the model of a "theocentric
universe" accompanied by a "nonnormative christology." We have already
set forth, in its broad lines, Hick's thought on the matter. Surely there is
no need to return to it.[17] Under the common heading of "pluralism," we
must, however, take note of the various nuances of opinion. They bear not
only on the conditions imposed on Christians by a sincere interreligious
dialogue, but also on the sense in which we may still speak of a "relational
uniqueness" of Jesus Christ, as well as on the demands of a "universal"
theology of religions.

Thus, while for Alan Race the dialogue poses the absolutely basic
demand that Christianity renounce all claims to uniqueness for Jesus
Christ,[18] Paul F. Knitter reduces this requirement to one of a provisional
bracketing, a kind of methodological doubt, without which an authentic
dialogue cannot be initiated on a footing of equality, as of course it must
be. The dialogue must serve as its own genuine criterion. Perhaps it will
lead to the rediscovery, this time by way of verification, of what indeed is
unique about Jesus Christ.[19] Furthermore, while for Race one can only
acknowledge the basic equality of all manifestations of God in history,[20]
Hick and others insist that this does not militate against a relational uniqueness of Jesus Christ — neither a greater nor a lesser uniqueness, for that
matter, than that of other salvific figures whose message has the capacity
to respond to the religious aspirations of all persons.[21] Others, such as W.
C. Smith, postulate the basic equality — in their respective specific differences — of all of humanity's religious traditions, as the obligatory presup-
position of the "universal theology of religions" that they so earnestly
desire.[22]

Now we see what is at stake in the question. The constitutive uniqueness
of Jesus Christ is most assuredly the focal point of the current debate on
the theology of religions. It is the stumbling block, we might say, the line
of demarcation between contradictory positions. Its theological foundation
is no less that. The preceding analysis of positions brings out one thing
perfectly clearly: Only the personal identity of Jesus Christ as only Son of
God constitutes a theological foundation sufficient to establish the constitutive uniqueness of Jesus Christ as universal Savior. From that point
onward, the opposed theological positions fall in with the logic of things.

The two assertions dovetail: Either Jesus Christ is the only Son of God,
and then his universal mediation follows; or he is not, and the Christian
claim of his constitutive uniqueness is without theological foundation. To

assert the divine filiation of Jesus Christ is a matter of faith, however. One does not arrive at it as the conclusion of a process of ratiocination, nor of a comparative study of the religions of humanity. Of course this assertion, which is at the heart of Christian faith, encounters serious objections in the current context of religious pluralism and interreligious dialogue. These objections regard either the New Testament itself, Christian tradition, or theology. We cannot dispense with the responsibility of a brief response.

TO BELIEVE IN JESUS CHRIST, THE SON OF GOD

The New Testament

The New Testament clearly asserts the universal mediation of Jesus Christ in the salvific order. This is evinced by more than just a few formal texts (such as 1 Tim. 2:5–6, Acts 4:12), or by texts that make the assertion only equivalently, but no less clearly (such as John 3:17; Acts 5:31, 10:44–48, 17:24–31), or again, by the christological hymns in which Christ appears at the center of the divine plan (as Eph. 1:3–13; Col. 1:15–20). As we have observed above (see chapter four), this is the message of the New Testament in its entirety, the deep faith that underlies the whole, which gives the New Testament its very raison d'être, and without which it would not have been written.

The case is the same with the divine filiation of Jesus Christ in the New Testament. Doubtless it is unveiled there at varying depths, from the first apostolic kerygma (Acts 13:32–33) to the Pauline reflections (Rom. 1:1–4; Heb. 1:1–5), and through the synoptic presentation (Mark 1:1, 15:39; Luke 1:32) down to the Joannine theology (John 5:18, 8:18–19, 10:30, 21:30, etc.). But once again we see the whole New Testament to be shaped in the silhouette of Jesus Christ the Son of God, its leitmotiv.

None of this is generally challenged. The New Testament's massive assertion of the uniqueness of Jesus Christ the Savior is readily acknowledged. The question is asked, however, whether this assertion still can and ought to be held today in the current context of religious pluralism. It is suggested, in various ways and for various reasons, that that statement ought to be relativized. Recent hermeneutic investigations show that the claims to an absolute uniqueness for Jesus Christ—which surely appears as the interpretative key of the whole New Testament—actually result from a historically conditioned worldview and language modes dependent on a particular cultural context. We can no longer regard that uniqueness precisely as the "referent" of the gospel message, then—the intangible kernel of the Christian message.[23]

It is then pointed out that, in the context of the Jewish apocalyptical mentality, impregnated as it was with such an eschatological expectancy, it was natural for the primitive church to interpret the experience of God in Jesus Christ as final and unsurpassable. But this apocalyptical mentality is culturally limited. The finality it implies for the Jesus Christ event therefore cannot be regarded as pertaining to the essence of Christianity; it belongs rather to the fortuitous cultural context in which it was first experienced and presented. If Jesus had been encountered and interpreted in some other cultural context, involving some other philosophy of history, he would have been considered neither final nor unique.[24]

As St. Paul is often held to bear the responsibility for the explicit assertion of the uniqueness of Jesus Christ, it is suggested that if he had entered into contact with the rich mystical traditions of the Oriental religions, he would have softened his absolute, unnuanced assertion. Or again, this time with regard to St. John, it is observed that the uniqueness of Jesus Christ is articulated in terms of "incarnation," but this is a mythical modality of thought, like the concept of preexistence with which it is bound up. But mythical language ought to be taken for what it is, and thus understood not literally, but metaphorically. The Incarnation must therefore be demythologized. The result would be the demythologization of Jesus Christ as absolute Savior, a concept now recognized as belonging to a mythic mode of thought and hence not comporting literal meaning.[25]

Finally, it is remarked that, in the historical context in which Christianity arose, and in the face of the opposition it encountered, it was natural for the disciples to present Jesus' "way" as unique. This absolute language is historically conditioned. It is a survival language.[26]

What are we to answer? It is true that the mystery of Jesus Christ, as conceived by the New Testament, is set forth in terms of a concept of history inherited from Jewish culture and the religious history of Israel. But it is equally true that this mystery, in turn, furnishes history with a new, astonishing density. As for Jewish eschatology and the apocalyptical mentality, we must observe that the Jesus Christ event bursts through the Israelite sense of history in which it is inscribed. While it fulfills the messianic expectancy of the latter days, it does so in transcendent fashion, outstripping it.

As Oscar Cullmann has so well shown, the difference between the religious psychology of the first Christians and that of the Judaism that preceded them was a profound one. Israel was wholly directed toward a decisive intervention of God in history in some indefinite future. The first Christians, to their own astonishment, seemed to grasp that this decisive intervention had taken place under their very eyes in the recent event of the death and resurrection of Jesus. History's driving force was different now. The eschatological expectancy was now divided in two, into an "already" and a "not yet."[27] One cannot make the Christian interpretation of the Jesus Christ event depend purely and simply on Jewish eschatology. This is where it occurs, surely, but it transforms it in depth.

In St. Paul's case, while it is true that he had no experience of a religious pluralism like that of our times, still he had to measure his faith in Jesus Christ not only against the Jewish religion from which he had come, but also against the Hellenistic culture that he had encountered along his way.

The christological hymns, while they adopt current Jewish cosmology, nevertheless assert the absolute primacy of Jesus Christ and the cosmic dimension of his event: He is beyond the "Thrones, Dominions, Principalities, and Powers" (see Col. 1:16). Pierre Benoit writes:

> Having to range under the primacy of Christ not only redeemed humanity, which becomes his body, but also the cosmic framework of that humanity, and in particular the heavenly Powers, which he has restored to their proper place, [Paul] declares that Christ has taken charge of the whole universe, and must now restore it to oneness: the divinity, which he possesses by nature, and the created world, which he takes in charge in becoming incarnate.[28]

To label the Pauline claims to an absolute primacy for Jesus Christ frivolous would be a gratuitous assertion. As for St. John, it is true that he is the first to employ the concept of incarnation to account for the mystery of Jesus Christ (John 1:14). That of "preexistence," however, was already implied before John (cf. e.g. Phil. 2:6–11). It is true as well that both concepts are open to misunderstanding: Preexistence is not existence in a fictitious time-before-time; and incarnation does not mean that the divine being becomes human existence. However, the fact remains that the incarnation of the Son of God involves, in a very real way, the becoming-human, in history, of the Word, who, independently of this becoming, exists eternally in the mystery of God.[29] Such is the literal sense of a term which simply cannot be reduced to a "mythical" language.[30] St. John's Prologue, which formulates the mystery of the personal identity of Jesus Christ in terms of an incarnation of the Word of God, is surely the culmination of a long reflection of apostolic faith; nevertheless, it is a legitimate finale, borne by the very dynamism of that faith. The functional christology of the first apostolic kerygma called for the ontological christology of God's-Son-become-a-human-being.[31]

The notion that it was the opposition encountered by the Christian message that incited the apostolic church to assert the uniqueness of the "way" established by Jesus calls for no extensive rebuttal. In those circumstances, would not the natural thing for those entrusted with the message have been to soften their claims concerning their Master? For that matter, far from being a "language of survival," the proclamation of Jesus Christ the Savior is presented in the New Testament as "good news" for all men and women—good news that was worth the trouble to witness to with strength and courage, and even the ultimate witness of martyrdom.

Christian Tradition

While the universality of salvation in Jesus Christ is clearly asserted in the great professions of faith,[32] patristic tradition is more reticent concerning his uniqueness. We have already shown why this should be the case.[33] For the Fathers, the uniqueness of Jesus Christ was the very core of faith, and thus beyond all theological suspicion. This doctrine was not discussed because it was not open to discussion. What is open to discussion is not the fact, but the "how" of the uniqueness of Christ: his personal identity as Son of God.

The key question today, in the context of religious pluralism, is not Christian tradition's claim as to the uniqueness of Jesus Christ the Savior. It is its "why." One explanation suggests that the declaration of faith in Jesus the Savior is of a doxological nature: Its scope must then be attenuated, as all doxological language proceeds from an impulse of loving, blind faith. However, it is important to make some distinctions here. First of all, there is a difference between doxological texts and professions of faith or dogmatic decisions. Second, a doxological note does not exclude a doctrinal content: The doxological texts are not bereft of dogmatic value, any more than the professions of faith and even conciliar decisions are without a doxological accent. To acknowledge the doxological nature of certain documents in no way means denying their doctrinal value.[34] Let us further observe that, while faith is loving impetus, this does not make it blind. Quite the contrary; faith gives new "eyes," to see the truth.[35] In this sense, it is its own verification: Christians know that what they believe is true.

More serious, and more persistent, is the objection that the Christian doctrine of the uniqueness and divinity of Jesus Christ proceeds from a process of undue Hellenization of the Christian message, with its first beginnings in the New Testament itself and later developed by postbiblical tradition.[36] This objection has long since been refuted.[37] Let us summarize the refutation as follows.

If by Hellenization you mean that Hellenic and Hellenistic culture was the vehicle of faith in Christian tradition, then yes, the Christian message was surely Hellenized. In that case tradition was only responding to the imperative of inculturation of the message, an imperative of which we have become more conscious today. On the other hand, if by *Hellenization* you mean that biblical and postbiblical Christian tradition falsified the message, confusing it with some Hellenistic philosophical speculation or other, nothing could be further from the truth. It was precisely in order to preserve the Christian message and the mystery of Jesus Christ from all adulteration with surrounding philosophies that tradition sought to plot the contours of that message in precise terms. It had to make use of known concepts. But in utilizing these concepts to express mystery, it stamped them with a new signification and unprecedented, superadded meaning: The *homoousios* of the Council of Nicaea (A.D. 325) is an eminent example, but not the only one.[38] In this sense, we actually see not a Hellenization, but a de-Hellenization of Christian dogma.

Theology

In the current context of religious pluralism, a growing number of theologians regard the Christian claim to an absolute uniqueness for Jesus

Christ as untenable. It must be either softened or abandoned, if there is to be any dialogue. To soften it is to reduce it to a relative uniqueness. Jesus Christ would then no longer be constitutive of universal salvation. However, we should continue to see in him the ideal, most inspiring symbol—the one that best responds to human aspirations—the perfect type or paradigm of human relations with God. So here is normative christology in a theocentric universe, which we have seen. It is in this sense that E. Troeltsch sees in Jesus Christ the purest revelation of the religious world. Troeltsch writes:

> Accordingly, [one] will be a Christian because he discerns in Christianity the purest and most forceful revelation of the highest world. He will see in the Christian faith not the absolute but the normative religion, the religion that is normative not only for him personally but also for all history up to the present time.[39]

Schubert Ogden echoes this view when he speaks of Jesus Christ as revealing in a decisive and normative manner the universal love of God.[40] Eugene TeSelle does the same when he sees in Jesus Christ the touchstone of the value of the other revelations, the center of gravity about which they revolve.[41] Or again, for Paul Tillich, without being constitutive of salvation, Jesus Christ is nonetheless the "ultimate criterion of every healing and saving process."[42] These are mere examples.

Or else, going further, one abandons, as a thing of the past, any Christian pretension to the uniqueness of Jesus Christ, constitutive or even merely normative. This, we hear, is the price of dialogue. This is the thesis of a "theocentric universe" accompanied by a "nonnormative christology." All religious traditions enjoy a fundamental equality, since they represent divine manifestations—different manifestations, all relative—in humanity's various cultures. We have remarked that the Copernican revolution proposed by John Hick is now the symbol of this theory, to which a number of recent authors have rallied.[43] The theory is not new, however. Arnold Toynbee had already argued that nothing in the history of religions indicates that Jesus Christ (or Christianity) is unique or even normative. All religions have their particular characteristics and their different viewpoints. In this situation, no value judgment bearing upon any uniqueness is possible.[44]

Among the above-cited authors, some adopt a phenomenological viewpoint, that of the comparative history of religions. It would not be to our purpose to investigate their reflections here, since a Christian theology of religions begins with Christian faith and develops each successive step in the same faith. Faith, however, does not dispense its subject from all comparisons. We shall retain certain elements of comparison, then, and proceed to discuss more in detail the properly theological difficulties raised against the uniqueness of Jesus Christ as universal Savior in his quality of Son of God, upon which Christian faith founds that uniqueness.

Do not the other religious traditions, on the subject of various salvific figures, make claims analogous to the claim of Christian faith on the subject of Jesus Christ?[45] For example, in Hindu *bhakti*: the *Bhagavad-Gita* surely seems to present Krishna as a universal savior. He saves not only those who have recourse to him (*Bhagavad-Gita* 9:22, 25), but even those who, with faith, "adore other gods": "Even those who worship other gods, with love (*bhakti*), and offer sacrifices to them, full of faith, really worship me, even though the rite departs from the norm" (*Bhagavad-Gita* 9:23).[46]

Must we not see here the Hindu counterpart of anonymous Christianity—Krishna appearing as the savior even of those who, by ignorance, but in the sincerity of their hearts, adore other gods and offer sacrifices to them? Let us observe, however, that the breadth of the outlook of the *Bhagavad-Gita* does not extend beyond that of the Hindu tradition or *bhakti* itself. Furthermore, while Krishna is presented as savior, his power does not rest on an incarnation of a god among human beings. As all Hindu commentators agree, the Hindu *avatara* teaching, whose main text we have recalled above (*Bhagavad-Gita* 4:6–8), while implying an earthly manifestation of the Absolute in human form, is never conceived as a personal insertion of God into human history, as Christian faith understands the Incarnation of the Son of God.

Coming to Buddhism, specifically *Mahayana* Buddhism, it has been observed that this religious current underwent a development similar to that of primitive Christianity. Just as the first Christians gradually recognized a divine presence in Jesus, so the Mahayanist Buddhist tradition registered deification of the Buddha. Both employ the same model of a divine descent to humanity.[47] In the case of Gautama, the Buddha, however, a process of deification is precisely what we have. By contrast, Jesus is not a deified human being, but God humanized. The former is an act of human beings; the latter is an act of God. Surely the Buddha preaches a message of liberation (*dharma*), as Jesus preaches the gospel, and he does so with the authority that comes to him from an extraordinary religious experience (*nirvana*), as that of Jesus comes to him from his experience of God as Abba. However, if the Buddha is a "savior," it is in virtue of the fact that, as "enlightened," he shows human beings the way of salvation. Jesus is himself the way. From the apostolic age, Christian faith has recognized Jesus as the universal Savior of all human beings. While the church of the apostles progressed in the intelligence of his mystery as Son of God and Savior, it was only a matter of recognizing its profound meaning as God had revealed it through his life and finally manifested it in his resurrection.[48]

Let us move on to the properly theological objections. We have already seen the position of John Hick, which has been embraced by various recent authors. The Copernican revolution and theocentric perspective that he inserts into a theology of religions are intimately connected with, and logically based on, the christology he champions: that of the Myth of the Incarnate God.

According to Hick, the Christian belief in the incarnation of the Son of

God emerges from the transposition of Jesus' message into a "mythic" language employed by the Joannine and postbiblical tradition under the influence of Hellenism. Not that this language is necessarily false: The error of Christian tradition consists in taking literally what ought to be understood metaphorically. The result has been the ontological christology of the Son of God made man. We must demythologize Jesus Christ, release him from the myth of incarnation. Then the christocentric outlook in the theology of religions will logically give place to the theocentric perspective. Jesus Christ is neither constitutive of salvation nor normative for relationships between God and the human being. With this demythologization in place, what remains is a global theology, that accords an equal place to all divine manifestations and interventions in the history of humanity.

We cannot enter into this complex and familiar debate in detail here. Hick's thesis on the theology of religions,[49] and his christology of the Myth of the Incarnate God have both been dealt with adequately by others. Here it will be enough to refer to what we have said above, apropos of Christian tradition, concerning the problem of the Hellenization or de-Hellenization of christological dogma, and to recall that Christian faith in no wise permits a reduction of the divine filiation of Jesus Christ to a metaphorical filiation. We are dealing with an ontological filiation: It is to be taken in its literal sense, although the concept of generation is an analogical concept realized in God supereminently.

Among the theological difficulties is the problem of historical consciousness and the inevitable relativity of all truth—even (and especially) revealed truth, while it is admitted that such a truth suffices to justify an absolute commitment of persons to the partial truth of their tradition.[50] Here we may refer to what has been said above regarding the unique character of the revelation occurring in Jesus Christ (see chapter seven). That revelation is characterized by both fullness and relativity. Its fullness is one of intensity: The Son of God lived his interpersonal divine relations in human terms and his human consciousness. Its relativity, of course, is just as real: No human consciousness, not even one personally assumed by God, can exhaust the divine mystery that only the divine consciousness can adequately comprehend and embrace. The fact remains, however, that the transposition of the personal consciousness of Jesus as Son of God into communicable human concepts bestows upon the revelation that he lavishes of himself and of God a transcendent, unmatchable, and unsurpassable objective value.

Another problem: Should not Christians practice, vis-à-vis religious traditions—especially their own—what contemporary psychology calls a hermeneutic of suspicion?[51] A tree is known by its fruits. Just so, a religion is "true" in the measure that it renders human beings really human within themselves and in their relationships with others. But can we say that Christianity produces fruits of humanity, humaneness, to match its exorbitant claims? If Jesus Christ is really unique, should not that uniqueness be reflected in the life of Christian communities of faith? Is it? Here we must call attention to a fallacy in the principle on which this objection is based. Christianity advances no claims concerning Christians. Its claims regard Jesus Christ. It is he who is unique, not they. Surely the Christian community has received the mission to bear a worthy faith-witness to his mystery. Often enough it betrays this mission, consciously or unconsciously. The fact remains, however, that the mystery of Jesus Christ and his uniqueness does not depend on the quality of the testimony of his disciples. From the side of God, Jesus Christ is an irrevocable gift to humanity. God's fidelity does not depend on our Christian infidelities. It is incorrect, then, to suggest that the truth of Jesus Christ depends on Christians' praxis. Nor is it true that there is no truth that is not verified by praxis: Praxis itself has need of criteria of truth to direct it.

The objection based on the principle of the verification of truth reappears under another form. This time we hear that the praxis of the interreligious dialogue must serve as a criterion by which to judge the truth of any religious tradition, including the Christian tradition. Christianity must leave aside, then, at least provisionally, any claim of uniqueness for Christ, with a view to entering into an authentic, equal-to-equal dialogue with others. If Jesus Christ is indeed unique, it will be the task of the dialogue to show it. Nothing else can.[52] From the practice of dialogue, we are told, "perhaps Jesus the Nazarene will stand forth (without being imposed) as the unifying symbol, the universally fulfilling and normative expression, of what God intends for all history."[53]

We must ask, however, how a dialogue practiced with the uniqueness of Jesus Christ in brackets can lead to the faith rediscovery of this uniqueness. Does faith come at the conclusion of the dialogue, and can it be conceived as resulting from it? Indeed, does sincerity in the dialogue require, as claimed (does it even permit), the bracketing, even the temporary bracketing, of one's personal faith? We shall return to this point later, apropos of the theology of the interreligious dialogue, and attempt to show that the reverse is true. Let us note, furthermore, that the rediscovery of the uniqueness of Jesus Christ, envisaged as a potential conclusion of the dialogue, is not that of the uniqueness professed by Christian faith. A normative christology falls short of an adequate account of the constitutive nature of the mystery of Jesus Christ in the order of salvation.

Another suggestion is that the traditional christocentric perspective be replaced with an eschatological perspective. This paradigm change would consist in centering the theology of religions not on the Jesus Christ event, but on the Reign of God, which is built all through history, finally to arrive at its eschatological plenitude. Thus, the theology of religions would be centered no longer on the past, but on the future. In other words, christocentrism would now stand in the shadow of a theocentric outlook. God and the Reign of God constitute the end of history toward which all religions journey, Christianity included.[54]

But we must make a distinction here.[55] That the Reign of God has irrupted into history and is to grow throughout that history in order to attain its eschatological plenitude does coincide with the theocentric outlook of the New Testament—but only in part. In centering all on the Reign of God, should we really be introducing a new paradigm of the relationship between the religious traditions of humanity and the mystery of Jesus Christ? To be sure, the perspective would enable us to transcend an inappropriate ecclesiocentric outlook. The Reign of God is a broader reality in history than are Christianity and the church: The other religious communities and traditions of humanity belong to it. It is also true that, in the accomplishment of the Reign of God beyond history, Christianity and the other religious traditions are called to meet in God.

Must we therefore say that the perspective of the Reign of God effects a paradigmatic change vis-à-vis the christocentric perspective? This would be to forget that the Reign of God has already made its irruption into history in Jesus Christ and through the event of Jesus Christ; that it is by the combined activity of Jesus Christ raised and of his Spirit that the members of the other religious traditions share in the Reign of God already historically present; and that the eschatological Reign to which all members of all religious traditions are invited is at one and the same time the Reign of God and that of the Lord Jesus Christ. Once more in Christian theology, christocentrism and theocentrism are inseparable. This is also true in the perspective of the Reign of God, whether we regard the Reign already inaugurated in history or destined for its plenitude beyond history.

We may speak, then—following Pierre Teilhard de Chardin—of a marvelous convergence of all things and all religious traditions in the Reign of God and in Christ-*Omega*—a mystique of unification toward which the Western and Eastern spiritualities both tend.[56] But such a convergence in no way overshadows the Jesus Christ event: Christ is the end (*Omega*) because he is the beginning (*Alpha*), the sole center and unique axis. The finality, centrality, and uniqueness of the Jesus Christ event are all the same thing.

However, may we speak of a "complementary uniqueness" of the mystery of Jesus Christ vis-à-vis other salvific figures and the founding experiences of other religious traditions?[57] Yes, in the sense that these experiences represent genuine divine interventions and authentic manifestations of God in the history of peoples, that the mystery of Jesus Christ completes and carries to their perfection (although, for that matter, they can demonstrate certain aspects of the mystery even better than Christianity itself) without reducing the uniqueness of Jesus Christ to a relative or relational uniqueness that fails to account for Christian faith in its character as constitutive of the salvation of all women and men. While it is true that Christianity has nothing to gain from absolute independence and it must accept a position among various religious expressions, this does not mean that a "unicity of position" or the "modesty of a logical unicity"[58] must replace the theological form of a "unicity of excellence." It is a matter not of Christian excellence, but of the excellence of Jesus Christ, God's gift to the whole of humanity.

Of course, the originality and difference of the Christian experience of God, as based on the mystery of Jesus Christ—God become a human being among human beings—will have to be shown.[59] As we have seen so clearly (see chapter two), to know God in Jesus Christ is to meet God in the human face of Jesus, the only Son of the Father, and to follow him into the experience of being a child of God. In the last analysis, the sole valid theological foundation of the uniqueness of Jesus Christ is his personal identity as Son of God. But to confess him as such is, ineluctably, to make an act of faith. As St. Paul says: "None can say 'Jesus is Lord' but under the impulse of the Holy Spirit" (see 1 Cor. 12:3).

10

Interreligious Dialogue in the Evangelizing Mission of the Church

Words, like persons, have a history. They are not accidents. Their development testifies to a gradual conscientization of the realities that they are intended to convey.[1] This observation, which is verified in many a sphere of theology, is applicable in a singular manner to the concepts used by the church, in the past as today, to define its mission. The evolution of the concepts corresponds to the evolution of the theology of mission. For example, mission itself (in the singular), or the missionary activity of the church, is a broad concept today, embracing the missions (in the plural). The priority of mission over the missions indicates that the calling of the church is fundamentally the same in all regions, while the level of its development may vary.[2] We see an evolution, akin to the first but even more profound, in missionary semantics consisting of a gradual emergence, in recent years, of a broad concept of evangelization as understood in the sense of the overall mission of the church. Having surveyed this semantic development during and since Vatican II, D. Grasso rightly concludes:

> The postconciliar church continues to expand its use of the term "evangelization," to the point where the latter is gradually coming to express the totality of its mission. Thus, we may say that everything in the church is "evangelization," since the church performs its mission in all that it does.[3]

Obviously a change in the theology of mission must underlie this new terminology. As we know, the main current in pre-Vatican II missiology defined the goal of the missions as "planting the church." Characteristically, Vatican II, without repudiating this traditional view, adds another concept, which at that time was beginning to win favor among scholars. Thus, for example, we read in *Ad Gentes,* no. 6, that "the proper end of this missionary activity [on the missions] is evangelization and the implanting of the church among the peoples and human groups in which it has not yet taken root."[4] The association of these two terms, while legitimate, is an indication that at the moment of Vatican II, the concept of evangelization had not yet uniformly taken on the vast, comprehensive signification by which it would subsequently be identified with the overall mission of the church. This was to be a postconciliar development.

The present chapter is directly concerned with the interreligious dialogue and more specifically with the role and meaning that the church can or should assign it in mission. In order to answer this question, however, we must attend to the semantic evolution of the terminology of mission in recent years. Is interreligious dialogue in its own right a part of the mission of the church, or is it still in some way extrinsic, simply useful as a first approach to others? Are we dealing here with evangelization in the proper sense, or merely with pre-evangelization? May we regard it as an end in itself, or must it be seen as a means ordered to the proclamation of the gospel? Is it, as the members of other religious traditions often maintain, the last stratagem of a missionary church for gaining new members? Can it eliminate all attitude of proselytism while claiming to be an expression of the evangelizing mission of the church?

The response to these questions has not been uniform, either in the council or in postconciliar theology. Still, we can discern over the past two decades a certain evolution in the direction of a positive appreciation of the interreligious dialogue as a full-fledged, authentic expression of the comprehensive evangelizing mission of the church. We propose to trace that evolution as it appears in certain important documents of this period, belonging in various degrees to the teaching authority of the church, or even outside of the same. Our investigation does not pretend to be exhaustive; however, the documents we present may surely be regarded as representative points of reference. We shall not attend explicitly to the opinions, discernible in the texts, of the individual theologians who have evidently contributed to the development of these documents.

One last observation before we proceed. The place assigned to the interreligious dialogue in the mission of the church depends first of all on a theological evaluation of the religious traditions of the world and their meaning in the comprehensive salvation plan as willed by God for humanity and as realized in history. These two elements are necessarily interdependent. A minimalizing evaluation of the religions themselves naturally leads to a negative view of the relationship between interreligious dialogue and mission. On the other hand, a positive outlook on the former normally evokes an attitude of openness toward the latter. In analyzing the documents, we must always look for their theological evaluation of other religious traditions, if we wish to determine the role and place these documents assign to the interreligious dialogue in the mission of the church.

ANALYSIS OF THE DOCUMENTS

The Encyclical **Ecclesiam Suam** *and Vatican II*

On August 6, 1964, between the second and third sessions of Vatican II, Pope Paul VI published his programmatic encyclical, *Ecclesiam Suam.* The date is not without importance for our considerations, since the documents of Vatican II which were to deal with interreligious dialogue (*Nostra Aetate, Ad Gentes, Gaudium et Spes*) were still in the preparatory stage. The Secretariat for Non-Christians had been created by the Pope less than three months before the appearance of the encyclical (May 17, 1964). We may say, then, that *Ecclesiam Suam* marks the appearance of the interreligious dialogue in the new perspective inherent in the program of church renewal: It constitutes an important dimension of the openness to the world urged by the council. The term *dialogue* itself appears here for the first time in an official document of the church.[5]

As the Pope declares, the encyclical is concerned with "the problem of the dialogue" (*colloquium*) between the church and the modern world (*AAS* 56 [1964]:613). "The church must enter into dialogue with the world in which it lives and works. It has something to say, a message to deliver, a communication to offer" (p. 639). The dialogue, in the Pope's thinking, is conceived as "a method for carrying out the apostolic mission, a means of spiritual communication" (p. 644). Distinguishing the various forms that can be taken by the "dialogue of salvation," he insists on "the prime importance of the proclamation of the word of God ... for the Catholic apostolate. ... Preaching is the primary form of the apostolate" (p. 648). The church, the Pope observes, must be in readiness to "enter into dialogue with any person of good will, within and without its own sphere" (p. 649).

The encyclical goes on to trace a series of concentric circles "around the central point at which God has placed us [the church]" (p. 650). In this way, it hopes to show how the dialogue of salvation implied in the church's mission reaches different categories of persons in different ways. The Pope distinguishes four concentric circles, beginning with the furthest (the whole of humanity and the universe), then moving to a second (the faithful of other religions), a third (other Christians), finally coming to the inner circle (the dialogue within the church itself).

The second circle is "composed essentially of those who worship the one sovereign God, whom we, too, adore," and includes not only Jews and Muslims, but the faithful of the great Afro-Asian religions (pp. 654–55). The Pope writes (p. 655): "Out of our duty of loyalty, we ought to manifest our conviction that the true religion is one, and that it is the Christian religion, while fostering the hope to see it recognized as such by all who seek and worship God."

Nevertheless, "we do not wish to refuse to acknowledge, and revere, the spiritual and moral values of the various non-Christian religious confessions" (p. 655), and we are prepared to enter into dialogue, indeed to take the initiative in doing so—a dialogue bearing upon the ideals that we have in common in the domain of the promotion and defense of religious freedom, human fellowship, culture, social welfare, and the civil order.

This part of the encyclical ends on a note of genuine, but prudent, openness. The theological evaluation it makes of the other religions, like its overtures in respect of an interreligious dialogue, remain limited. The role and place of this dialogue in the mission of the church are developed or specified no further.

Nevertheless, a breach was made, and the Second Vatican Council was soon to widen it. Where the conciliar documents are concerned, we have already developed an analysis of their theology of the religions of the world.[6] Let us recall that an objective evaluation should neither exaggerate nor minimize what the council actually asserted. Here we shall only repeat certain observations of a general character. On the one hand, the documents of the council evince a desire to acknowledge whatever is already present in these religions by way of truth and grace (*Ad Gentes,* no. 9), not only in the religious lives of the faithful of other religions, but also in the objective elements composing these religious traditions themselves, whether in their own rites and culture (*Lumen Gentium,* no. 17), certain religious initiatives (*incepta, AG,* no. 3), or other riches that God has given to the nations (*AG,* no. 11). These elements are viewed as "a ray of that Truth (*illius Veritatis*) that enlightens all men" (*NA,* no. 2).

On the other hand, an attentive consideration of the text reveals, on the part of the council, an increasing awareness of the influence of the Holy Spirit, which extends well beyond the confines of Christianity, to the ends of the universe. The Spirit of God—who is the Spirit of Christ, as well— fills the universe (*GS,* no. 11). *Ad Gentes* and *Gaudium et Spes*—both being fruits of the last session of the council—make explicit reference to this universal presence of the Spirit in space and time. "Beyond the shadow of a doubt, the Holy Spirit was already at work before Christ's glorification" (*AG,* no. 4). That Spirit is also at work in the world today, in the aspirations of the men and women of our times for a better quality of life (*GS,* no. 38), a social order more worthy of the human being (*GS,* no. 26), and a universal communion of sisters and brothers (*GS,* no. 39). The constant influence of that Spirit keeps the question of human beings' religious destiny alive in human hearts (*GS,* no. 41), and offers them the light and strength to confront it (*GS,* no. 10). The human being has been redeemed by Christ and has become a new creation in the Holy Spirit (*GS,* no. 37). Indeed, the Spirit now calls all women and men to Christ, not only by the preaching of the gospel, but by anticipatory seeds of the Word (*AG,* no. 15). The Spirit offers to all, "in a way known to God, the possibility of being associated with the Paschal mystery" (*GS,* no. 22). In this way, animated and gathered into one in the Spirit of Christ raised, humanity walks toward the consummation of human history (*GS,* no. 45), with a living hope that is the gift of the Spirit (*GS,* no. 93).

Such is the deep foundation of the interreligious dialogue in the documents of the council. It is not surprising to see these same documents inviting the members of the church to enter into the practice of interreligious dialogue. Such an exhortation is already found in *Nostra Aetate:* the church exhorts its children, "with prudence and charity, by dialogue and cooperation (*per colloquia et collaborationem*) with those who follow other religions, and witnessing to the Christian faith and life, to recognize, preserve, and foster the spiritual, moral, and sociocultural values found in them" (*NA,* no. 2). Similar appeals reappear in *Ad Gentes* and *Gaudium et Spes.* Following the example of Christ himself, his disciples exhibit a special comportment (*AG,* no. 11):

> Profoundly steeped in the Spirit of Christ, they must know the people in whose midst they live, and strike up a conversation with them, in order that they, too, may learn, in sincere and patient dialogue (*dialogo*), what riches God in his munificence has dispensed to the nations. They should at the same time make an effort to illuminate these riches with the light of the Gospel, set them free, and bring them once more under the authority of the Saving God.

Vatican II's Magna Carta of the dialogue is found in *Gaudium et Spes,* no. 92, where the council reviews, in reverse order, the four concentric circles already presented in the encyclical *Ecclesiam Suam.* Where believers of other religious traditions are concerned, the text desires that a "frank conversation [*colloquium*] . . . compel us all to receive the inspirations of the Spirit faithfully and to measure up to them energetically" (*GS,* no. 92).

These are generous words, never before pronounced by an ecumenical council. They do not indicate, however, the place assigned by the council to interreligious dialogue in the mission of the church. After all, the terms *mission* and *evangelization* underwent an evolution during the council, an evolution that did not come to an end with the council. These terms will remain somewhat ambiguous during the council itself, referring sometimes simply to the missionary proclamation of the church and sometimes embracing more broadly the overall missionary activity of the church.[7] However, even in the conciliar documents in which mission and evangelization take on this broader signification, no explicit mention is ever made of interreligious dialogue as constituting, in and of itself, one of the intrinsic elements of this mission, this evangelization. The same silence is observed in the key texts concerning the dialogue, recalled above. In *Ad Gentes,* no. 11, the dialogue is directly connected to the witness of the Christian life. As for *Gaudium et Spes,* no. 92, after declaring that, "in virtue of the mission that is hers of enlightening the whole universe by the gospel message . . . the church appears as the sign of this fellowship that makes possible and reinforces a loyal dialogue," the text goes no further. In virtue of its mission, it is asserted, the church holds a privileged position for dialogue. However, the meaning of the interreligious dialogue itself in its evangelizing mission remains unexpressed.

Theological Congresses and Conferences

It is not surprising that the question left unanswered by Vatican Council II should frequently recur in postconciliar discussion, especially on the occasion of theological congresses and conferences. This question was invested with an altogether special theological importance for the renewal of pastoral methods, especially in countries in which Christians represent only a minuscule minority amid a pluralistic religious society. Is entering into interreligious dialogue evangelization, or is it not? If not, then what is the role of such a dialogue in the mission of the church? It would be impossible, in these pages, to take account of all the theological meetings in which these questions have been posed in the years since the council. We shall confine ourselves to two of them, which seem sufficiently representative.

In 1969, SEDOS, in Rome, held a Symposium on Mission Theology for Our Times. We need only examine its theological conclusions on three precise points: the theology of religions, the concepts of mission and evangelization, and the place assigned to the interreligious dialogue in mission.[8]

On the theology of religions, the symposium's conclusions acknowledge the active universal presence of the Spirit. Yet "the one and only pathway of salvation" is Christ, while, being "creations of man's religious genius in search of his destiny," the other religions "cannot be pathways of salvation" (I, 1, 1). Nevertheless, the authentic religious values that they contain, "purified and elevated by grace . . . can be a means of arriving at the act of faith and charity that is necessary for salvation." In their rites and their beliefs, "supernatural elements—wherever they may come from"—can also be found (I, 1, 2). In these religions, then, we find "an ordering to Christ which can only be fulfilled by the proclamation of the Gospel" that leads back to their source any supernatural elements that may be contained in these religions (I, 1, 3).

On mission and evangelization: It is the work of mission that permits human beings already orientated to Christ "to reach full knowledge of his mystery" (I, 2, 1), revealing to them their true nature, their destiny, and the ultimate meaning of their lives (I, 2, 2). The proclamation of the gospel, by mandate of Christ, is ordered to this end: that "everything might gradually be subjected to his Lordship" (I, 2, 3).

On the dialogue:

Missionaries never start from zero. Through dialogue, they must discover the authentic values present in non-Christian religions, in order to purify and elevate them by inserting Christ's Gospel in them. In this way, Christ will be manifested to non-Christians, not as a stranger but as the one they have been looking for (I, 3, 1).

The success of the dialogue presupposes, as necessary conditions, identification with others and a genuine encounter with them (I, 3, 2).

In sum, the attitude of the SEDOS meeting toward the religious traditions of the world, while positive, does not seem fully consistent. Mission and evangelization are still mainly identified with the proclamation of the gospel. The interreligious dialogue seems reduced to a means to evangelization, a method offering a useful point of departure.

This unsatisfactory evaluation of the dialogue is all the more surprising when compared with the very positive evaluation, in the same conference, of the relationship between evangelization and the task of development. The latter, provided it be pursued as Christian witness, "should be recognized as evangelization in the strict sense. . . . It is one of the pathways of evangelization," even though it calls proclamation (II, 2) the "second pathway of evangelization" (II, 2) with which it is necessarily tied up (II, 3). The contrast is arresting: While development is a *way* of evangelization, however bound up with proclamation, interreligious dialogue is but a *means for* proclaiming the gospel.

Shortly after the SEDOS Symposium, in 1971, an important International Theological Conference on Evangelization and the Dialogue in India was held at Nagpur, India. We shall examine the final declaration of this congress, more specifically, its theology of religions and its understanding of the mission of the church, in order to be able to evaluate the role and meaning it assigns to the interreligious dialogue and its relationship to mission.[9]

The Nagpur Conference's theological understanding of humankind's religious traditions is remarkably positive. The declaration sees Christ and his grace at work in them (no. 12). An ineffable mystery, "which is called by different names, but which no name can adequately represent," is at work among the peoples of the world—the same mystery that is "definitively disclosed and communicated in Jesus of Nazareth" (no. 13).[10] God's self-revelation "extends to the whole of humankind in different ways and degrees within the one divine economy" (no. 14). The fulfillment of human beings' destiny "can only be reached by [their] positive response to the mystery [they] discover in [their] personal experience." The Christian knows this destiny to be "union with Christ, the liberator and savior" (no. 15).

Since [men and women] are social beings, concrete religious traditions provide the usual context in which they strive for their ultimate goal. Therefore the religious traditions of the world can be regarded as helping them toward the attainment of their salvation. . . . The different sacred scriptures and rites of the religious traditions of the world can be, in various degrees, expressions of a divine manifestation, and can be conducive to salvation ... (no. 16).

Lest there be any ambiguity, the declaration clearly asserts that its positive evaluation of the religious traditions of the world in no way undermines the "uniqueness of the Christian economy" (no. 16), or "lessen[s] the urgency of the Christian mission" (no. 17). This mission is treated under the heading of "evangelization."

Evangelization, however, is conceived strictly in terms of witness borne to Christ and of the preaching of Christ (no. 18). The declaration continues (no. 19):

> The mission of the church has to be realized through evangelization. By evangelization we mean the imparting of the good news of salvation in Jesus Christ ... not only through proclamation ... but also through a life of Christian witness.

In the context of religious pluralism, such an evangelization is necessary and meaningful, "because it communicates the explicit knowledge of Christ" (no. 22).

Since evangelization is identified with the proclamation of the good news, it is clear that, whatever value be ascribed to interreligious dialogue, the latter cannot be regarded as belonging to evangelization proper. The next section of the document, however, offers a very positive evaluation of this dialogue. Through it, Christians and others offer each other mutual enrichment (no. 25). It aims at "mutual understanding, communion, and collaboration." "By its very nature, [it] ... tends toward the ultimate vision of a perfect unification of all human beings, which can be discerned in the convergent aspirations of the various religious traditions" (no. 26). It is "good in itself, because it fosters mutual communion and edification" (no. 26). From a brotherly and sisterly sharing of spiritual experiences results, especially, a "mutual spiritual enrichment."

> This enrichment comes from the fact that in dialogue each partner listens to God speaking in the self-communication and questioning of his fellow-believers. It leads to a spiritual growth, and therefore to a kind of deeper *metanoia,* or conversion to God (no. 27).

If the term *evangelization* had not been reduced a priori to the proclamation of the gospel, the positive, rich description of the interreligious dialogue contained in the Nagpur declaration could have been expressed in terms of mutual evangelization between Christians and others. However, this was not asserted here.[11]

Preliminaries to the Celebration of the 1974 Synod on Evangelization

Before each synod of bishops to be held at Rome, the various bishops' conferences of the world are invited to send a communication to Rome. In the preparatory process for the 1974 synod on evangelization, the main concerns of the bishops' conferences of Asia, as might have been expected, were the great religious traditions of Asia and interreligious dialogue. It would be repetitious to show the positive approach adopted by the various communications from Asia to this pastoral reality that had become, in a few years, a subject of growing currency.[12] Nor will it be necessary to do so, since we have a more extensive basic document we can regard as generally representative of the approach adopted by the Asian bishops' conferences on this subject. The First Plenary Assembly of the Federation of Asian Bishops' Conferences (FABC), held at Taipei, Taiwan, April 22 – 27, 1974, in preparation for the synod, published a Final Declaration and some Recommendations. What do these documents have to say about our problem?[13]

In sum: The preaching of Jesus Christ and his gospel are invested today with "an urgency, a necessity, and a magnitude unmatched in the history of our faith in this part of the world" (no. 8). The prioritarian outlook in this work of evangelization is the upbuilding of a genuinely local church (no. 9). "In Asia, especially, this includes a dialogue with the great religious traditions of our peoples" (no. 13).

A very positive evaluation of these religious traditions follows. They are "significant and positive elements in God's design of salvation" (no. 14). "How can we not acknowledge that God has drawn our peoples to himself through them?" (no. 15). The dialogue with them "will reveal to us also many riches of our own faith which we perhaps would not have perceived" (no. 16), and will teach us to receive from them (no. 17), while "on our part, we can offer what we believe the church alone has the duty and the joy to offer to . . . all human beings" (no. 18).

Among the recommendations then made by the plenary assembly was Recommendation 3, which is to "evolve a working concept of evangelization that embraces, as integral to that concept, genuine dialogue with the great living religions of Asia and other deeply rooted forms of belief, such as animism" (p. 35; FAPA, p. 39). Apropos of the promotion of justice, the declaration had noted that "evangelization and the promotion of true human development and liberation, are not only not opposed, but make up today the integral preaching of the gospel, especially in Asia" (no. 23). Despite a still hesitant terminology, what is asked for is a broad concept of evangelization that would include as integral parts both the promotion of justice and interreligious dialogue.

To move on to the celebration of the Synod on Evangelization in the Modern World (1974): it is noteworthy that the Asian representatives, while they shared the concern of Latin Americans for justice and liberation and that of the Africans for inculturation, became, in the spirit of the Assembly of Taipei, the champions of a theology open to the great religious traditions of the world and a positive approach to the interreligious dialogue, as belonging intrinsically to the mission of the church.

We cannot stop to examine the individual interventions here.[14] We shall confine ourselves to the reports of the special secretaries and the final documents of the synod. These various documents testify to the fluctuations in the treatment of our theme at the hands of the synodal debates. In his report on the first part, D. S. Amalorpavadass, the secretary, writes (p. 16):[15]

> The dialogue is good in itself, and an end in itself, as it encourages mutual assistance and communion. It may not, however, be detached from evangelization, nor does it dispense us from our duty of evangelizing. While evangelization and the dialogue are theologically distinct, they are nevertheless joined together in a single life, in the case of many Christians. . . .

Earlier the same secretary had defined evangelization in terms of proclamation: "By evangelization we may understand the proclamation, by word, works, and the testimony of one's life, of the good news of the salvation of all human beings in Jesus Christ" (p. 15).

The report of the secretary for the second part, which followed,[16] speaks differently. D. Grasso recalled the recent evolution of the term *evangelization* toward a comprehensive notion encompassing "the entire mission of the church" (p. 16). This evolution, he thought, could be observed over the course of the synod itself. However, he made no allusion to a possible relationship between interreligious dialogue and the mission of evangelization.

It will not be necessary here to rehearse the history of the synod.[17] It is widely known that the hope of publishing a detailed final document had to be abandoned at the last moment. But it is interesting to note what the schema of this final document proposed to the assembly had to say concerning our subject.[18] It reads (no. 34):

> The interreligious dialogue ought not to be regarded as extrinsic to the church's mission of evangelization. . . . In itself, it is already a concrete expression of the mission of the church. . . . [In the dialogue] the members of the church, impelled by love, and a great reverence for the action of the Spirit among others, share with these others their Christian experience. The interreligious dialogue is salutary, then, and ought to be encouraged as pertaining to the mission of the church.

As it had failed to win preliminary approval, the entire schema of the final document had to be abandoned, and with it the proposition cited above. With the hope of producing a detailed document shattered, the synod chose to publish a short declaration.[19] Despite its intention to represent the major orientations of the synod, however, this text scarcely succeeds in doing so, and the thrust of the work of the synod is not faithfully reflected. Of the interreligious dialogue, the text asserts (no. 11):

> Trusting in the action of the Holy Spirit, which overflows the boundaries of the Christian communities, we wish to extend the dialogue to the non-Christian religions, in such wise as to reach a more profound understanding of the novelty of the gospel and the fullness of revelation, and to be able to give [the members of these religions] a broader view of the salvific truth of the love of God accomplished in Christ.

Here interreligious dialogue seems reduced to a convenient means for the proclamation of the gospel. It is not in itself an expression of the evangelizing mission of the church.

The Apostolic Exhortation Evangelii Nuntiandi

One year after the synod, Pope Paul VI published his Apostolic Exhortation, *Evangelii Nuntiandi,* dated December 8, 1975, by which he intended to prolong the reflection of the synod and present its conclusions to the entire church. Our analysis of this important document must be limited to its direct bearing on our subject.[20]

The notion of evangelization employed by the exhortation is, in many respects, a broad one. Evangelization, which is the church's mission and very raison d'être, involves the evangelizer's whole person: his or her words, works, and life witness. As for its object, evangelization spans the whole gamut of the human, as its aim is the renewal of humanity and the transformation, by the power of the gospel, of human culture and cultures. Despite this broad, inspiring outlook, however, when the Pope comes to define evangelization, he still has primarily in view the explicit proclamation of the gospel and all the ecclesial activities directly flowing from this proclamation (no. 14):

> [The Church] exists in order to evangelize, that is to say, in order to preach and teach, to be the channel of the gift of grace, to reconcile sinners with God, and to perpetuate Christ's sacrifice in the Mass, which is the memorial of his death and glorious Resurrection.

The proclamation of the gospel is so much at the heart of evangelization that it is often simply identified with it: evangelization is proclamation — kerygma, preaching, and catechesis. In any case, "there is no true evangelization if the name, the teaching, the life, the promises, the Kingdom and the mystery of Jesus of Nazareth, the Son of God are not proclaimed" (no. 22). At the same time, evangelization acquires its integral extension only if the adherence of the heart of the hearer is concretely expressed by entry, by means of the sacraments, into the community of believers that is the church (no. 23).

The Pope is concerned to emphasize "the reality of evangelization in all its richness, complexity and dynamism" (no. 17), and his concern "to evangelize human culture and cultures" enters into this prospect. However, one must wonder what role the apostolic exhortation assigns, in the mission of evangelization, to the promotion of justice, human liberation, and interreligious dialogue.

With respect to the former, the Pope notes that evangelization comports "an explicit message, adapted to the different situations constantly being realized" (no. 29). In today's world, this means (no. 30):

> The Church . . . has the duty to proclaim the liberation of millions of human beings, many of whom are her own children—the duty of assisting the birth of this liberation, of giving witness to it, of ensuring that it is complete. This is not foreign to evangelization.

Warnings follow—necessary and important ones—against possible deviations in the work of human liberation (nos. 31–37), with a reassertion of the "specific religious finality of evangelization" (no. 32). This rather restrictive outlook on the task of liberation as merely not foreign to evangelization stands in contrast with the much more positive assertion of the 1971 synod of bishops which, in its document, *De Justicia in Mundo,* had declared it "a constitutive dimension of the preaching of the Gospel."[21]

Where are we with the other question? What place does the apostolic exhortation leave to the interreligious dialogue in the church's mission of evangelization? It places in evidence the role of the Holy Spirit as the primary agent of evangelization, in virtue of the Spirit's animation of the church (no. 75); but nowhere is it stated that the Spirit is at work in the world beyond the frontiers of the church. And yet this had been a fundamental assertion of Vatican II, and had reappeared in the debates of the synod.

By contrast, *Evangelii Nuntiandi's* evaluation of other religions seems unduly negative. Positive values are acknowledged, along the lines of the council; despite these, however, the religions only bear the echo of the human being's sincere quest and search for God. Even their "natural religious expressions most worthy of esteem" fail to establish "an authentic, living relationship" with God, "although they have, as it were, their arms outstretched to heaven" (no. 53).

There is no need to pursue this discussion on the evaluation of other religions—a subject which, in the opinion of the Pope himself, raises many questions that bear further study by theologians.[22] Let us only observe that the exhortation leaves little room for interreligious dialogue and no room for it in the evangelizing mission of the church. In *Evangelii Nuntiandi,* the faithful of other religions are regarded only as beneficiaries of evangelization: It is to them that the church's proclamation of the gospel should be primarily addressed. Evangelization is a one-way street. The dialogue — of which the exhortation does not speak—cannot be regarded as evangelization, still less as mutual evangelization between Christians and others.

John Paul II and the Secretariat for Non-Christians on Dialogue and Mission

We cannot present the entire magisterium of the present Pope on the subjects of other religions, evangelization, and interreligious dialogue. Let us simply observe some precise reference points and some representative texts.[23]

As might have been expected, John Paul II broaches the subject of other religions in his first encyclical letter, *Redemptor Hominis* (1979).[24] He does so with an attitude of great openness. He wonders (no. 9):

Does it not sometimes happen that the firm belief of the followers of the non-Christian religions—a belief that is also an effect of the Spirit of truth operating outside the visible confines of the Mystical Body— can make Christians ashamed . . . ?

He recommends all "activity for coming closer together" with them, "activity expressed through dialogue, contacts, prayer in common, investigation of the treasures of human spirituality, in which, as we know well, the members of these religions also are not lacking" (no. 9). And he adds (nos. 11, 12):

The Fathers of the Church rightly saw in the various religions as it were so many reflections of the one truth, "seeds of the Word," attesting that, though the routes taken may be different, there is but a single goal to which is directed the deepest aspiration of the human spirit as expressed in its quest for God and also in its quest . . . for the full dimension of its humanity. . . .

The *missionary* attitude always begins with a feeling of deep esteem for "what is in man" (cf. John 2:26). . . . It is a question of respecting everything that has been brought about in him by the Spirit, which "blows where it wills" (John 3:8).

We have noted above the Pope's insistence on the importance of recognizing the active presence of the Spirit of God in the faithful of other religions (see chapter seven). We must add that he regards this activity as the theological basis of the significance of the interreligious dialogue in the mission of the church.

Addressing the peoples of Asia in 1981, over *Radio Veritas,* Manila, the Pope once more emphasized this theme.[25] The church today, he asserted, "feels a deep need to enter into contact and dialogue with all of these religions." What seems to gather and unite Christians and the believers of other religions in a special way is the recognition of a need for prayer (no. 4):

> We are sure that, whenever the human spirit opens in prayer to this Unknown God, an echo will be heard of this Spirit who, knowing the limits and frailties of the human person, himself prays in us and for us ... (Rom. 8:26). The intercession of the Spirit of God who prays in us and for us is the fruit of the mystery of the Redemption of Christ. ...

The Pope concludes (no. 5):

> All Christians, then, should engage in the dialogue with the believers of all religions, in such wise that their mutual understanding and cooperation may increase; in such wise that moral values be strengthened; in such wise that God be glorified in all creation. Means must be developed to bring it about that this dialogue become reality everywhere, but very especially in Asia, the continent that is the cradle of ancient cultures and ancient religions. ...

While the call becomes more urgent here, the doctrine remains that of the encyclical. An acknowledgment of the active presence of the Spirit among others transforms the interreligious dialogue into an important task and a need felt by the church. But this doctrine is not yet explicitly propounded in terms of mission and evangelization.

Interrupting our review of the declarations of the present Pope,[26] let us move on to the recent document issued by the Secretariat for Non-Christians. This text, the result of years of reflection, places the interreligious dialogue explicitly within the evangelizing mission of the church.[27] Published on Pentecost Sunday, 1984, the twentieth anniversary of the foundation of the Secretariat, the document is entitled "The Attitude of the Catholic Church towards the Followers of Other Religions: Reflections and Orientations on Dialogue and Mission." This document was approved by the Pope, who, in his allocution to the plenary assembly of the Secretariat, during which the document was finalized, confirmed by his authority certain important assertions of the document itself.[28]

The Pope observes that dialogue is fundamental for the church (no. 2), founded as it is on the life of God, one and triune. God is the Father of the entire human family; Christ has joined every person to himself (*Redemptor Hominis,* no. 13); the Spirit works in each individual; therefore dialogue is also based on love for the human person and on the bond existing between cultures and the religions which people profess (no. 2).

Experience, the Pope goes on, shows that dialogue takes various forms, which he lists (no. 4). He concludes that dialogue finds its place within the church's salvific mission and is therefore a dialogue of salvation (no. 5). No local church is exempt from this duty (no. 3). In order to grasp the place of the dialogue in the overall mission of the church, it is necessary, the Pope asserts, to avoid exclusivism and dichotomies (no. 5)—meaning by "dichotomies" anything that might be seen to sunder the bond between interreligious dialogue and evangelization and by "exclusivism" whatever would reduce evangelization to proclamation. The Pope explains that "authentic dialogue is witness, and genuine evangelization is realized in respect and attentiveness toward others" (*Redemptor Hominis,* no. 12 [no. 5]).

The Secretariat's document insists even more explicitly on these same aspects. There we find a broad definition of interreligious dialogue (no. 3): "It means not only discussion, but also includes all positive and constructive interreligious relations with individuals and communities of other faiths which are directed at mutual understanding and enrichment."

The document is especially interested in the relationship between dialogue and mission (no. 5). It is to be noted—and regretted—that in the introduction to the document, this relationship is still conceived in terms of the dichotomy between evangelization and dialogue. Mention is made "of the simultaneous presence, in mission, of the demands of evangelization and dialogue," and of the difficulties that can arise from this (no. 7). However, this impression of a dichotomy is quickly dissipated. In the first part, bearing on mission, the document explains that the church's mission "is one, but comes to be exercised in different ways, according to the conditions in which mission unfolds" (no. 11). It recalls that *Redemptor Hominis,* no. 15, echoing the 1971 synod of bishops, regards "the commitment to the human being, to social justice, to freedom and to human rights, as well as the reform of unjust social structures," as an "essential element in the mission [of the church], indissolubly bound to that mission" (no. 12). However, the promotion of justice is only an aspect, whereas the document intends to catalog "the different aspects and manners of mission" (no. 12). It does so in a passage which, while not claiming to be exhaustive, lists five principle elements of the "single, but complex and articulated, reality" of the evangelizing mission of the church. The importance of this text calls for its extensive citation (no. 13):

Mission is already constituted by the simple presence and living witness of the Christian life (cf. *EN* 21), although it must be recognized that "we bear this treasure in earthen vessels" (2 Cor. 4:7). Thus the difference between the way the Christian appears existentially and that which he declares himself to be is never fully overcome. There is also the concrete commitment to the service of mankind and all forms of activity for social development and for the struggle against poverty and the structures which produce it. Also, there is liturgical life and that of prayer and contemplation, eloquent testimonies to a living and liberating relationship with the active and true God who calls us to His kingdom and to His glory (cf. Acts 2:42). There is, as well, the dialogue in which Christians meet the followers of other religious traditions in order to walk together towards truth and to work together in projects of common concern. Finally, there is the announcement and catechesis in which the good news of the Gospel is proclaimed and its consequences for life and culture are analyzed. The totality of Christian mission embraces all these elements.

"The totality of Christian mission embraces all these elements," but the list is not complete.[29] Let us make some observations. The proclamation of the gospel by announcing and catechesis comes last, and rightly so, since mission or evangelization should be seen as a dynamic reality, or process.[30] This process indeed culminates in the proclamation of Jesus Christ by *kērugma* (announcing) and *didachē* (catechesis). On the same principle, however, the phrase "liturgical life and that of prayer and contemplation" ought to have been inserted following the proclamation of Jesus Christ, to which they are directly bound—just as in Acts 2:42, to which the text refers—and of which they are the natural issue. Then the order would have been: presence, service, dialogue, proclamation, and sacramentalization—the last two corresponding to the ecclesial activities which in the narrower, but traditional, view constitute evangelization.

In the broader perspective adopted by the document, the "single reality" of evangelization is presented as "complex and articulated" at the same time: It is a process. This means that while all of the elements of the process are forms of evangelization, not all have the same place or meaning in the church's mission. For example, interreligious dialogue normally precedes proclamation. The former may or may not be followed by the latter, but the evangelization process is not brought to its term unless proclamation follows dialogue: Proclamation and sacramentalization represent the culmination of the evangelizing mission of the church.

At the end of the first part, the document insists once more on "the important place (*l'importance*) of the dialogue in mission" (no. 19). Our analysis could end on this note. However, let us make some rapid observations on the second part, where the dialogue is studied more closely. According to our document, dialogue is not only in itself a distinct aspect of evangelization; it is also "an attitude and a spirit," and thus "the norm and the indispensable style (*le style indispensable*) of every form of Christian mission, as well as of every aspect of it, whether it be a matter of simple presence and witness, service, or direct proclamation" (no. 29). All of the forms of mission listed previously must be "permeated by . . . a dialogical spirit" (no. 29).

The interreligious dialogue itself, as a specific task of evangelization — "which finds its place in the great dynamism of the church's mission" (no. 30) — can take several forms. There is the dialogue of life, open and accessible to all (nos. 29–30). There is the dialogue of a common commitment to the works of justice and human liberation (nos. 31–32). There is the intellectual dialogue in which scholars engage in an exchange at the level of their respective religious legacies, with the goal of promoting communion and fellowship (nos. 33–34). Finally, on the most profound level, there is the sharing of religious experiences of prayer and contemplation, in a common search for the Absolute (no. 35). All these forms of dialogue[31] are, for the Christian partner, so many ways of working on the "evangelical transformation of cultures" (no. 34), so many opportunities of sharing with others the values of the gospel in an existential way (no. 35). It will be unnecessary here to examine the third part of the document, which further develops the theology of dialogue and mission.

More Recent Papal Documents

We must, however, without pretending to be complete, also mention certain more recent documents of Pope John Paul II. We have already cited them in order to show the Pope's growing insistence on the acknowledgment of the presence of the Holy Spirit among the members of other religious traditions, which is the ultimate foundation of the interreligious dialogue (see chapter seven). We need not review this teaching here. We need only show what follows from it with respect to the dialogue itself, and the place of that dialogue in the church's mission. In his Discourse to the Indian Bishops' Conference, pronounced at Delhi during his visit to India in February 1986, the Pope declared, on the subject of the interreligious dialogue:

> As ministers of the Gospel here in India, you have the task of expressing the Church's respect and esteem for all your brethren and for the spiritual, moral and cultural values enshrined in their different religious traditions. In doing so you have to bear witness to your own convictions of faith. . . . In this interreligious dialogue, which of its nature involves collaboration, *the supreme criterion is charity and truth*.[32]

We have already referred to the discourse pronounced by John Paul II to the members of the Roman Curia (December 22, 1986), in which he explains the meaning of the World Day of Prayer for Peace held at Assisi (October 27, 1986).[33] The Pope sees, in this World Peace Day, a concrete application, a "visible illustration, a lesson in things" of the meaning of the church's engagement in the interreligious dialogue recommended by Vatican Council II (no. 7).[34] He cites, as theological foundation of the dialogue, the "mystery of unity" already prevailing between Christians and those who remain only ordered to the people of God (no. 8): This "universal oneness" is based on the common origin and destiny of all humanity in creation, on the oneness of the mystery of the redemption in Jesus Christ (nos. 5–7), and on the active presence of the Spirit of Christ in the sincere prayer of members of the other religious traditions (no. 11).

First, then, there is a "radical unity" proceeding from creation: "There is but one divine design for every human being coming into this world (cf. John 1:9)" (no. 3). "Differences are a less important element when confronted with the unity, which is radical, fundamental, and decisive" (no. 3). Next there is the fundamental unity based on the mystery of universal redemption in Christ (no. 4). In the light of this twofold mystery of unity, "differences of any kind, and first of all religious differences, to the extent that they are reductive of God's design, are actually seen to belong to another order. . . . [They] must be overcome, in progress toward the realization of the mighty plan of unity that presides over creation" (no. 5). Despite these differences, sometimes felt as insurmountable divisions, all men and women "are included in God's great, single design in Jesus Christ" (no. 5). "The universal unity founded on the event of creation and redemption cannot fail to leave a trace in the concrete life of human beings, even of those who belong to different religions" (no. 7). These "seeds of the Word" sown among others constitute the concrete foundation of the interreligious dialogue encouraged by the council (no. 7). Likewise belonging to that foundation is the influence of the Spirit on all authentic prayer, since "the Holy Spirit . . . is mysteriously present in the heart of every person" (no. 11).

The church, for its part, is "summoned to toil with all its might (in evangelization, prayer, and dialogue), that the breaches and divisions that remove people from their Origin and Goal, and render them hostile toward one another, may be healed" (no. 6). Let us note that, in this last citation, evangelization and dialogue once more seem distinguished as two different tasks in the mission of the church. This impression is strengthened when the document says that the church exercises its essential ministry of reconciliation "by evangelization, the administration of the sacraments," and that, at Assisi, this same ministry was exercised "in unprecedented fashion, but no less efficacious or less engaging for all that" (no. 10), in the prayer of Christians and others, the practice of ecumenism, and the interreligious dialogue. It is regrettable that the document thus seems to slip back into a narrow notion of evangelization, from which the interreligious dialogue would remain distinct.[35]

Two More Recent Bishops' Synods at Rome: 1985 and 1987

The Extraordinary Synod of bishops convoked in 1985 to celebrate the twentieth anniversary of Vatican Council II offered an opportunity to reassert the teaching and once more promote the church's commitment regarding the members of other religious traditions and the interreligious dialogue. Was the opportunity turned to account? Certain interventions on the part of Asian bishops did not fail once again to insist on the role of the interreligious dialogue in the mission of the church. One intervention was especially noteworthy: that of Bishop F. M. Fernando of Chilaw, Sri Lanka. Bishop Fernando spoke, in part, as follows:[36]

> The interreligious dialogue should be regarded as an integral element of the Church's evangelizing mission. It deserves to be considered an apostolic priority. We must take an open, positive attitude toward other religious traditions, situating them in the overall salvation plan willed by the merciful love of God for all humanity in Christ.

Recalling the position taken by the General Assembly of the Federation of Asian Bishops' Conferences (FABC) held at Taipei, Taiwan (1974), the interventions of the Asian bishops at the 1974 Synod on Evangelization, and the confirmation of these opinions in the document of the Secretariat for Non-Christians on "The Attitude of the Church toward the Followers of Other Religions" (1984), Bishop Fernando briefly expounded the theological foundation of an open attitude toward other religions:

> The hidden but active presence of the mystery of Jesus Christ in the other religious traditions is the theological foundation of the practice of interreligious dialogue. This explains how the exchange of religious experience between Christians and others, at the level of the Spirit, is actually, although unconsciously on the part of the non-Christian, an exchange in the mystery of Christ, who is, for Christians and non-Christians alike, the very reality of salvation. This also explains why the interreligious dialogue can and ought to be regarded as an expression of evangelization in its own right.

Here we find, once more—without having to cite the entire text of the intervention—what we have observed above concerning the interreligious dialogue in the evangelizing mission of the church, and its theological foundation. Despite this intervention, among others, the second report (unpublished) issued by Cardinal Danneels during the synod made no reference to the interreligious dialogue. The theme reappeared, however, in the final, synthetic report voted by the assembly (December 7, 1985) and published with the consent of the Pope under the title, "The Church under the Word of God, Celebrating the Mysteries of Christ for the Salvation of the World."[37] Once more we must say that it appears there in rather unsatisfactory, even ambiguous, terms, which depart from what had been asserted by the Secretariat for Non-Christians in 1984. We read (II, D, 5):

> Dialogue must not be regarded as opposed to mission. True dialogue leads the human person to open himself, and to communicate his

interiority to his interlocutor. Further, all Christians have received from Christ the mission to call all men to become disciples of Christ (cf. Matt. 28:18). In this sense, God can make use of the dialogue between Christians and non-Christians, and even nonbelievers, as a channel for the communication of the fullness of his grace.[38]

Even apart from the negative form in which the relationship between dialogue and mission is expressed here, dialogue seems once more to be regarded as a means to the proclamation of the gospel, not as an actual expression of the evangelizing mission of the church.

The 1987 synod on "The Vocation and Mission of the Laity in the Church and the World" offered another opportunity to restate the role of the interreligious dialogue in mission, in which mission the laity are called, today more than ever before, to take part—mostly, perhaps, in a context of religious pluralism. However, the first redaction of the "List of Propositions" to be proposed by the synod had had nothing on the subject of dialogue.[39] Once more the lack had to be supplied for later.[40] In the final list of propositions,[41] a distinct proposition ("Witness before the Members of the Other Religions," no. 30-bis) is devoted to it, sandwiched between "Power of the Missionary Witness" (no. 30) and "Concrete Practice of Ecumenism" (no. 31). What is said about the interreligious dialogue is disappointing. We read:

> The dialogue between religions has a preeminent importance (*partem habet praeeminentem*), for it leads to mutual love and respect; suppresses, or at least reduces, the prejudices among the adepts of the various religions; and promotes unity and friendship among peoples.[42]

Despite the preeminent importance assigned to the dialogue, we hear nothing about either its foundation or its value as evangelization in the proper sense. The latter seems once more to be identified with the proclamation of the gospel, although (not very logically) it is acknowledged that a commitment to justice and peace is indeed an integral part of evangelization. The document seems to wish to avoid this kind of statement apropos of the interreligious dialogue.[43] The Apostolic Exhortation, *Christifideles Laici* (1988), published after the synod, is content, for its part, to refer to the above-cited synodal proposition (no. 35) regarding the interreligious dialogue.

SOME THEOLOGICAL CONCLUSIONS

The more than twenty-year evolution of the concept of the interreligious dialogue, and of the place and meaning to be ascribed to it in the overall mission of the church, is eventful, if rather fluctuating. However, our survey of this evolution allows us to draw certain theological conclusions.

A Broad and Comprehensive Concept of Evangelization Is Necessary

By a broad and comprehensive concept of evangelization, we mean not only a concept that will reflect the fact that the whole personhood of the evangelizer is involved—words, works, and life witness—nor only that evangelization extends to the whole of the human, seeking the transformation of culture and cultures by evangelical values. We also mean a concept that will include the various forms of ecclesial activity that are part of evangelization. The concept must embrace such activities as the promotion of justice and interreligious dialogue, which do not belong to the proclamation of Jesus Christ and the subsequent sacramentalization of life. Both of these activities must be regarded as authentic forms of evangelization in their own right. This means that we shall have to overcome our inveterate habit of reducing evangelization to explicit proclamation and its sacramentalization in the church community, with the consequent relegation of the promotion of justice and the task of human liberation to secondary status, and the interreligious dialogue to an area foreign to evangelization altogether.[44]

The Interreligious Dialogue Is an Intrinsic Dimension of Evangelization

The 1971 Synod of Bishops forthrightly asserted that the promotion of justice and participation in the transformation of the world are a constitutive dimension of the evangelizing mission of the church. We can and must say the same thing of the interreligious dialogue.[45] Rather than distinct parts, they are different elements or dimensions, or better still, different forms, modalities, or expressions of mission, which is a single, complex and articulated reality. The concrete forms adopted by the evangelizing mission in practice will depend largely on circumstances of time and place and on the human context—social, economic, political, and religious—in which it is at work. In the context of such a rich variety of religious traditions, which continue even today to be a source of inspiration and values for millions of faithful, the interreligious dialogue will naturally be a prominent form of evangelization. There may even be circumstances in which, at the very least temporarily, dialogue will be the only way open to the exercise of mission.

Evangelization Represents the Overall Mission of the Church

"Evangelization," wrote Paul VI in *Evangelii Nuntiandi,* "is the church's proper grace and vocation—its deepest identity" (no. 14). Once evangelization, whatever the variety of forms in which it is expressed, is understood as identical with mission, certain distinctions, long traditional, are seen to be passé. Among these will be the distinctions between pre-evangelization and evangelization, or between direct and indirect evangelization, which

were founded on the identification of evangelization with the explicit proclamation of Jesus Christ.[46] The disadvantage of such distinctions was that
whatever pertained to pre-evangelization or indirect evangelization seemed
to pertain to the order of means, tending more or less, and leading more
or less directly, to the explicit proclamation of Jesus Christ in evangelization
as such. On the contrary, the interreligious dialogue ought to be conceived
as a good in itself, and not as a means to attain an end distinct from it. It
is a form of evangelization in its own right.

Evangelization Reaches Its Fullness in the Proclamation of Jesus Christ

What has just been said on the subject of the interreligious dialogue
being a form of evangelization in its own right does not militate against the
fact that the proclamation of Jesus Christ represents the summit or apogee
of the evangelizing mission of the church. Evangelization remains incomplete unless Jesus Christ is explicitly announced. The mission process culminates, then, in proclamation and sacramentalization. Nevertheless, in
concrete reality the moment to move from interreligious dialogue to proclamation, if it arrives, should be left in each case to divine providence.
When and where this passage takes place, the Christian partner in the
dialogue commences to exercise a prophetical function. It now devolves
upon that partner to interpret the mystery of salvation that has been shared
and experienced together by the partners in the dialogue, to identify Jesus
who is the Christ as the source of this mystery, and to name and announce
him to others as the Savior of all men and women. Let us observe, however,
lest there be any ambiguity, that circumstances may be such that proclamation may be possible from the outset of the evangelization process. This
is the case with groups often rather inelegantly referred to as constituting
"responsive areas."

The Interreligious Dialogue Constitutes a Mutual Evangelization, under the Impulse of the Spirit

Whether or not the interreligious dialogue culminates in proclamation,
the dialogue is itself evangelization. In fact it is mutual evangelization in
the sense that, through the dialogue, the Christian partner and the other
evangelize each other, under the impulse and movement of the Spirit of
God.[47] This is because the partners, together, live—consciously on the one
side, unconsciously on the other—the same mystery of Jesus Christ, which
becomes active in them by the action of the Spirit. The council says (*Gaudium et Spes,* no. 22):

Since Christ died for all men, and since the ultimate vocation of man
is in fact one, and divine, we ought to believe that the Holy Spirit in

a manner known to God offers to every man the possibility of being associated with this paschal mystery.

The practice of the interreligious dialogue is the actualization, in concrete reality, of what the council thus asserts as a theological principle. Under the influence of the Spirit of Jesus Christ, the partners in the interreligious dialogue are called—together and by each other—to a more profound conversion to God. This constitutes mutual evangelization.

11

Toward a Theology of Dialogue

The foregoing chapter has been an effort to show the place of the inter-religious dialogue in the evangelizing mission of the church. We have seen that it is not a means for the proclamation of the gospel, but, in and of itself, a form of evangelization. More precisely, the dialogue is an integral part (or shall we say, "constitutive dimension"?) of evangelization—one of the distinct modalities in which the evangelizing mission is expressed. We have shown its threefold theological foundation—anthropological, christo-logical, and pneumatological: the basic unity of all humanity by the mystery of creation; communion and redemption in Jesus Christ and the active presence of the Christic mystery in human beings and their religious traditions; finally, the universal economy of the Spirit of Christ, who oper-ates beyond the confines of the church and is at work in the other religious communities. It is through dialogue that the Christian can and should dis-cover this twofold presence among others of Jesus Christ and his Spirit.[1]

However, this does not solve (far from it) all the theological questions posed by the dialogue. Is the interreligious dialogue really possible? How, and in what conditions, is it an authentic expression of the evangelizing mission of the church? Must we and may we make concessions in the area of faith in order for the dialogue to become practicable? Can Christians, as it has been recommended, even "bracket" their faith as a precondition for a dialogue of equals? Or at least may they be allowed to smooth the way for dialogue by honing down any sharp corners in their own beliefs, with a view to finding a least common denominator and thereby securing some basic point of accord and communion?

If, on the contrary, we must maintain our own faith intact, where will the partners find common ground to serve as point of departure for the dialogue? Another question: If the goal of the dialogue is not to proclaim Jesus Christ explicitly and to invite others to become his disciples in the church, then to what goal does that dialogue tend? What fruits does it produce, and in whom? Does the Christian partner gain anything at all from the dialogue? Does he or she receive something through the mediation of the partner who does not share the Christian faith? Or is the dialogue only a one-way "conversation," like it or not — even though the word itself seems to denote a reciprocal process?

All of these questions and others that they imply call for a response. We must deal with them in an orderly fashion, however. First, then, we shall ask what preconditions the dialogue imposes on the partners if it is to be authentic — what demands it imposes on them. Then we shall study the various forms under which the dialogue can be practiced. Finally, we shall come to the question of the starting point of the dialogue. Where does the dialogue begin? Certain reflections on the fruits of the dialogue (where it leads) and on the challenges it raises for the Christian partner will conclude our inquiry.

DEMANDS OF THE DIALOGUE

There is no need to delay on the indispensable psychological conditions for anyone wishing to enter upon the practice of the interreligious dialogue. A positive attitude is required toward others and their religious traditions. One must be able to rise above one's prejudices. There must be an openness to the discovery and recognition of the mystery present and active in other religious traditions. There must be the modesty necessary to "walk together toward the truth;"[2] the sympathy without which true comprehension is impossible; and many other conditions as indispensable as they are demanding.[3]

However, the conditions posed by the dialogue go beyond psychological dispositions. They include demands that are intrinsic to authentic dialogue. Each partner in the dialogue must enter into the experience of the other, in an effort to grasp that experience from within. In order to do this, he or she must rise above the level of the concepts in which this experience is imperfectly expressed, to attain, insofar as possible, through and beyond the concepts, the experience itself. It is this effort of "com-prehension" and interior "sym-pathy" that Raimundo Panikkar terms the "intrareligious" dialogue, an indispensable condition for true interreligious dialogue.[4] A recent author describes it as a spiritual technique consisting of "passing over and returning." Here is how he describes what is involved in the "passing over," by which one encounters both the other and the religious experience which that other bears within, together with his or her worldview or *Weltanschauung*:

To know the religion of another is more than being cognisant of the facts of the other's religious tradition. It involves getting inside the skin of the other, it involves walking in the other's shoes, it involves seeing the world in some sense as the other sees it, it involves asking the other's questions, it involves getting inside the other's sense of "being a Hindu, Muslim, Jew, Buddhist, or whatever."[5]

Here, however, we encounter serious difficulties, and numerous questions arise. To what extent is it possible and legitimate for the partners in the dialogue to enter into each other's experience and share a faith different from their own? Let us set our questions in order here.

First of all, one may not, on the pretext of honesty in the dialogue, bracket one's faith (employ an *epoche*), even temporarily, against the expectation, as has been suggested,[6] of rediscovering the truth of that faith through the dialogue itself. On the contrary, honesty and sincerity in the dialogue specifically require the various partners to enter upon it and commit themselves to it in the integrity of their faith. Any methodological doubt, any mental reservation, is out of place here. Were it otherwise, one could no longer speak of interreligious, or interconfessional, dialogue. After all, at the basis of any authentic religious life is a faith that endows that life with its specific character and proper identity. This religious faith is no more negotiable in the interreligious dialogue than it is in one's personal life. It is not a commodity to be parceled out or exchanged; it is a gift received from God, of which one may not lightly dispose.

By the same token, just as sincerity in the dialogue authorizes no bracketing of faith, even a provisional one, so its integrity in turn forbids any compromise or reduction of the same. Authentic dialogue does not accommodate such expedients. It admits of neither the syncretism that, in the quest for a common ground, attempts to surmount oppositions and contradictions among the religious faiths of the various traditions nor the eclecticism that, in the search for a common denominator among the various traditions, chooses scattered elements among them and combines these into a shapeless, inconsistent amalgam. If it is to be true, the dialogue may not seek facility, which is illusory in any case. Rather, without wishing to dissimulate any contradictions among religious faiths, it must admit that they are there, when they are, and face them with patience.

Differences and possible contradictions must not be hidden or ignored. They must be mutually respected by the partners in the dialogue and admitted in a responsible manner. Indeed, sincere dialogue presupposes on both sides an engagement in the integrity of one's own faith. To dissimulate differences and possible contradictions would amount to cheating and would actually end by depriving the dialogue of its object. After all, dialogue seeks understanding in difference, in a sincere esteem for convictions other than one's own. Thus it leads each of the partners to question themselves on the implications for their own faith of the personal convictions of the others.[7]

It is self-evident that in the practice of the interreligious dialogue, Christians may not dissimulate their own faith in Jesus Christ, the universal Savior, and in his finality in the order of salvation. In turn, they acknowledge in their partners who do not share their faith the inalienable right and duty to engage in dialogue while maintaining their own personal convictions — even claims to universality that may be part of their faith. Such convictions cannot be "relativized." It is in this fidelity to personal, nonnegotiable convictions, honestly accepted on both sides, that the interreligious dialogue takes place "between equals"—in their difference. In the area of Christian ecumenism, the Second Vatican Council recommends meetings in which, on an equal footing, representatives of the various churches would deal with the theological questions dividing them (*Unitatis Redintegratio*, no. 9). This does not prevent them from maintaining the faith convictions of their respective churches. In fact, just the opposite is the case. Neither does an interreligious dialogue on an equal footing require that we abolish our differences.

As the seriousness of the dialogue forbids the relativization of deep convictions on either side, so its openness demands that what is relative not be absolutized, whether by incomprehension or intransigence. An awareness of the relative has nothing in common with relativism, which consists in relativizing the absolute. The former is a matter of discernment and intelligence. But in every religious faith and conviction there is the danger, and a real one, of absolutizing the relative. We have seen a concrete example apropos of the fullness of revelation in Christ. This plenitude is not quantitative, but qualitative: one not of extension, but of intensity. It is in no way opposed to the limited nature of Jesus' human awareness, nor therefore to that of the Christian revelation expressed in a particular, relative culture—nor again, a fortiori, to the limited character of Christian dogma, which is always historically conditioned.[8] We shall have to take account of these relative aspects of Christian revelation if we wish to approach in dialogue the question of the word of God as contained in the various sacred scriptures.[9]

Under these premises, we must ask ourselves whether it is possible, and up to what point, to share two different religious faiths, making each of them one's own and living both at once in one's own religious life. From an absolute viewpoint, this seems impossible. Even apart from any interior conflicts that might arise in an individual, every religious faith constitutes an indivisible whole, and calls for a total commitment. It seems a priori impossible that such an absolute engagement might be divided, as it were, between two objects.

Does this mean, however, that the concept of the hyphenated Christian is self-contradictory—that one cannot be Hindu-Christian or Buddhist-Christian, or even Muslim-Christian, or the like? To assert this would contradict experience, as such cases are not rare or unknown. We have seen two famous Hindu-Christians above: Brahmabandhab Upadhyaya (see chapter one) and Swami Abhishiktananda (see chapter three). We have no intention of suggesting that the experiences of these two were identical; on the contrary, the point is that there are various possible acceptations of a concept that it would be a mistake to label "hybrid."[10]

To be a Hindu-Christian, Brahmabandhab Upadhyaya seemed to think, can mean joining in oneself the Hindu culture and the Christian faith.

Hinduism would then not be a religious faith, strictly speaking, but a philosophy and a culture, which, with the necessary corrections, could serve as a vehicle for Christian faith. Then the problem of the Hindu-Christian would be that of the inculturation of Christian faith and doctrine. Here, obviously, the concept of the Hindu-Christian will offer no difficulty in principle.[11] But does this explanation fully correspond to reality? Hinduism, while it is neither doctrinaire nor primarily and uniformly doctrinal, nevertheless involves, in the concrete lives of men and women, a genuine religious faith.

For that matter, the distinction between religion and culture is difficult to manage. Representing as it does the transcendent element in culture, religion is scarcely separable from culture. Can one nevertheless hold in conjunction, and make one's own, Hindu faith and Christian faith? We must exercise discernment here. Surely there are elements of other faiths that are in harmony with Christian faith and can be assimilated by the latter and integrated into it. They may even serve to enrich it.[12] No less surely, elements that formally and explicitly contradict it are not assimilable. Between these two groups, however, is a field, sometimes a broad one, of elements of faith that, for all their apparent contradiction and the difficulty in analyzing their synthesis, nevertheless coincide in an individual's concrete spiritual experience. We have cited the eminent example of a Hindu-Christian monk who conjoined, albeit in extreme tension, his two faiths — the Christian and the Hindu. He preferred to call them "two forms of a single faith" (see chapter three).

In all events, with the cautions that we have indicated, we can be sure that, in order to be true, the interreligious dialogue requires that both partners make a positive effort to enter into each other's religious experience and overall vision insofar as possible. We are dealing with the encounter, in one and the same person, of two ways of being, seeing, and thinking. That this "intrareligious" dialogue is an indispensable preparation for an exchange between persons in the interreligious dialogue was well formulated by Abhishiktananda:

> Each partner in dialogue must try to make his own, as far as possible, the intuition and experience of the other, to personalise it in his own depth, beyond his own ideas and even beyond those through which the other attempts to express and communicate them with the help of the signs available in his tradition. For a fruitful dialogue it is necessary that I reach, as it were, in the very depth of myself to the experience of my brother, freeing my own experience from all accretions, so that my brother can recognise in me his own experience of his own depth.[13]

FORMS OF DIALOGUE

The interreligious dialogue must not be understood in a narrow sense, as if it consisted solely in an exchange of religious experiences on the level of the spirit. Were that to be the case, instead of being—especially in a context of religious pluralism—an expression of the evangelizing mission of the church incumbent upon all of its members, the interreligious dialogue would be the preserve of certain researchers with special qualifications. Nothing could be further from the truth. The document published by the Secretariat for Non-Christians, "The Attitude of the Church towards the Followers of Other Religions" (1984), distinguishes four forms of interreligious dialogue. We have already briefly noted them (see chapter ten): the dialogue of life, accessible to all (nos. 29–30); the dialogue of a common commitment to the works of justice and human liberation (nos. 31–32); the intellectual dialogue of the scholars (nos. 33–34); and the dialogue of the sharing of religious experiences in a common quest for the Absolute (no. 35).[14]

The content, and even the order, of these principal model forms of dialogue calls for certain reflections.[15] First of all, we must insist on the primary role of the dialogue of life, accessible to all, which the Secretariat's document rightly places at the head of the list. This form of dialogue requires "concern, respect, and hospitality towards the other. It leaves room for the other person's identity, his modes of expression, and his values" (no. 29). "Every follower of Christ, in virtue of his human and Christian vocation, is called to live [this form of] dialogue in his daily life" (no. 30).

Furthermore, that the interreligious dialogue cannot be regarded as the monopoly of theologians and scholars, or of persons specially endowed with the gifts of the Spirit, the theological conference of Nagpur, India (1971), had already explicitly declared. Indeed, it was in reaction to an elitist conception of the interreligious dialogue that the Nagpur conference asserted, in its declaration (no. 24):

> In our personal relations with men of other beliefs, dialogue will be truly religious when, however different its object, its partners share a religious concern and an attitude of complete respect for one another's convictions and a fraternal openness of mind and heart. Religious dialogue, therefore, does not necessarily mean that two persons speak about their religious experiences, but rather that they speak as religiously committed persons, with their ultimate commitments and religious outlook, on subjects of common interest.[16]

The conference was saying, still rather hesitatingly, that the interreligious dialogue extends beyond the actual sphere of religious experience, to that of a common, religiously inspired engagement in behalf of human beings and society. The Secretariat's document is correct, then, in assigning priority to a common commitment to justice and human liberation over theological discourse. It is correct in insisting that this form of dialogue should consist more in common action than in shared discourse (no. 31): "A further level of dialogue is that of deeds and collaboration with others for goals of a humanitarian, social, economic, or political nature which are directed towards the liberation and advancement of mankind."

This dimension of the dialogue assumes extreme importance in the present context of a society of cultural and religious pluralism, and a society beset by universal problems of justice and human rights, human promotion and liberation in addition. The members of the various religious traditions can and should make a common commitment, from a point of departure in their respective religious convictions, to the promotion of a more humane world. The dialogue of life should issue in that of deeds. Both together form the common human substrate without which theological discourse among scholars and an exchange of religious experiences would have no foundation.

But we may question the basis of the order in which the Secretariat document lists the two remaining forms of dialogue. Should that order not be reversed? Does not religious experience precede theological discourse? Should not the exchange on the level of experience serve in its turn as foundation for a common discourse? To be sure, a theological discourse on the respective worldviews and religious doctrines of the partners in the dialogue is theoretically possible without being based on a mutual exchange at the level of religious experience. However, concrete experience shows that a mutual understanding on the level of theological discourse remains precarious—supposing it to be possible—unless preceded by a profound communion in spirit, which can be established only by a mutual exchange of religious experience. Without the latter, discourse may become abstract discussion or even degenerate into confrontation. It is on the level of spiritual exchange that dialogue is both most demanding and most promising. We have already considered the personal asceticism demanded by the mutual effort to enter into the experience and vision of the other. As for the profound communion established between those who consent to make this mutual effort:

> If all are living in their own depth, as intimately aware as they can of the Spirit present in them—no matter under which name or form he makes himself known—there takes place between them, beyond words, a wonderful communication at the level of the Spirit—through the *milieu* that is the Spirit. . . . It is from such a communion of life and discovery of the Spirit in each other that the ecumenical movement derives its power, and those pioneering it the boldness to forge ahead with prophetic initiatives.[17]

It is upon this spiritual exchange in depth that the theological dialogue will best be established, if it is to bear fruits of mutual understanding; for that matter, exchange and communion will normally call forth discourse.

POINT OF DEPARTURE FOR THE DIALOGUE

Where will the dialogue begin? What will its agenda be? We cannot, of course, fix its program in advance, since the Spirit blows where it will. One question, however, can be asked: What will be its point of departure? Where will a common ground be found on which Christians and others can carry on a theological conversation?

It has been suggested that the point of encounter is the Christic mystery, universally present and active, even though its activity reaches Christians and others in different ways. The starting point for the theological dialogue must not be sought in any doctrine. Doctrines, while they may partially coincide in their profound intent—such as the Christian doctrine of the Incarnation and that of the *avatara* in Hindu *bhakti*—nonetheless profoundly differ, as well. The Christic mystery, however, is common to all. Raimundo Panikkar puts it this way: "Christianity and Hinduism encounter one another in Christ. Christ is their point of encounter, and the real union of the two can take place only in Christ; for they meet only in him."[18]

Let us notice, however, that the universal, active presence of the mystery of Jesus Christ represents the theological foundation of the interreligious encounter and dialogue, rather than being the concrete point of departure of the dialogue itself in its theological aspect. It is clear that, as Panikkar agrees, the mystery of Jesus Christ as Christian faith understands it cannot serve as a point of departure upon which to agree in advance of the dialogue. We must therefore look elsewhere.

One possible starting point is the experience of the divine mystery in the Spirit. As we have remarked above, a spiritual exchange and a communion in the Spirit are necessary conditions for a fruitful theological dialogue. They can also serve as its immediate object. However, this raises a difficult question: Is the experience of God basically identical in the various religious traditions, so that divergencies in expression are due solely to cultural differences? Or rather does the experience itself differ in content, although, as we must say, the same God is present, consciously or unconsciously, in any authentic religious experience?

We have already furnished elements of a response to this question in comparing the Christian experience of God in Jesus Christ and the *advaita* experience of Hindu mysticism (see chapter two). The Christian mystery of communion and the Hindu mysticism of identity are not mutually reducible. Despite profound differences, however, which are based on the specificity of diverse experiences, the fact remains that the religious, mystical experience of both partners can furnish excellent grounds for theological dialogue. As W. Johnston says so well on the subject of the encounter between Christianity and Buddhism:

Obviously, a mystical theology based on the Bible will be specifically Christian. As such, it will be the basis for dialogue with the mysticism of non-Christian religions. For . . . Buddhism has its mystical theology based on the experience of the Buddha and on the Buddhist scriptures—based on the experience of becoming a Buddha. When Jesus and the Buddha meet in their disciples, real mystical dialogue will have begun.[19]

A more humble but no less valid, and more accessible point of departure consists in the fundamental questions asked by every religious human being, of whatever tradition, in the depths of the heart: Where do we come from, and where are we headed? What is the meaning of human existence, of suffering and death? What is the source of this movement within us— experienced and shared by both partners in the dialogue—which urges us to emerge from ourselves in friendship, fellowship, and communion with others, thrusts us beyond ourselves to respond to a divine Absolute that ever precedes us? Vatican Council II thought that these most basic questions are asked today by a growing number of persons, and felt by them with a new urgency (*Gaudium et Spes*, no. 10). The Declaration *Nostra Aetate* expresses as follows "those profound riddles of the human condition which, today even as in olden times, deeply stir the human heart," for an answer to which human beings "look to the various religions" (*NA*, no. 1):

What is man? What is the meaning and the purpose of our life? What is goodness and what is sin? What gives rise to our sorrows and to what intent? Where lies the path to true happiness? What is the truth about death, judgment, and retribution beyond the grave? What, finally, is that ultimate and unutterable mystery which engulfs our being, and whence we take our rise, and whither our journey leads us?

The Constitution *Gaudium et Spes* places an analogous series of questions on the lips of the women and men of our times.[20] Indeed, it is no accident that the same conciliar document calls attention both to the questions asked today by all human beings and to the universal presence of the Spirit in them, as manifested in the hopes and aspirations, the projects and strivings of contemporary humanity. After all, the same Spirit both inspires the projects and raises the questions. It is once more the same document that, more than any other, attempts to stir Christians to the dialogue with all human beings, and especially with "all who acknowledge God, and who preserve in their traditions precious elements of religion and humanity. We want frank conversation to compel us all to receive the inspirations of the Spirit faithfully and to measure up to them energetically" (*Gaudium et Spes*, no. 92).[21]

The question of the human being leads to the question on God. Thus it will serve as a secure point of departure for the theological dialogue. For the rest, the agenda of this dialogue should be left to the Spirit who animates the partners. Its principal agent is the Spirit, who has already been the source of the spiritual communion on which all common theological discourse must necessarily be based.

CHALLENGES AND FRUITS OF THE DIALOGUE

We have just recalled that the Spirit is at work on both sides in the interreligious dialogue; thus the dialogue cannot be a monologue. The Christian partners will not only give, but will receive, as well. Their receipt of the fullness of revelation in Jesus Christ does not dispense them from listening. They do not possess a monopoly on truth. They must rather allow themselves to be possessed by it. Indeed, their interlocutors in the dialogue, even without having heard God's self-revelation in Jesus Christ, may be more deeply submitted to this Truth that they yet seek, and to the Spirit of Christ that spreads its rays in them (cf. *NA*, no. 2). One can certainly say that, by the dialogue, Christians and others walk together toward the truth.[22]

Christians have something to gain from the dialogue. They will derive a twofold, combined advantage. On the one hand, they will win an enrichment of their own faith. Through the experience and testimony of the other, they will be able to discover at greater depth certain aspects, certain dimensions of the divine mystery that they had perceived less clearly, and which had perhaps been communicated less clearly by Christian tradition. At the same time, they will gain a purification of their faith. The shock of the encounter will often raise questions, force Christians to revise certain gratuitous assumptions and destroy certain deep-rooted prejudices, or overthrow certain overly narrow conceptions or outlooks. Thus the benefits of the dialogue constitute a challenge to the Christian partner at the same time. Let us point up certain aspects of this in the precise context of the encounter between the Christian mystery and Hindu mysticism (see chapter two).

In the light of the mysticism of the *advaita*, does not a tripersonal communion with God seem a propaedeutic to be transcended, that one may be lost at last, beyond all distinctions, in the divine mystery? The question is a plausible one, even in the context of Christian tradition. The concept of person—an analogical one—is a fragile thing, as applied to God. If, furthermore, the Father is the unfathomable trinitarian Source beyond the Spirit and the Word, have we not the right to ask whether there is in turn a Beyond-the-Father? Is not the insurmountable Abyss beyond all personhood? Certain Christian mystics have thought so and have spoken of the "Superessence" of the Deity, beyond the three Persons (see chapter three).

Hinduism, for its part, regards all personal determination as imperfection: God is impersonal, then, because it is superpersonal, or beyond personhood. For Hindu mysticism, all that the Christian mystery asserts of the "unknowable" Father is to be transcended, like any other propaedeutic— useful, surely, at its own level, but ultimately an encumbrance. One must not stop still at the threshold of the mystery: One must enter there, crossing to the other shore: *neti, neti — nada, nada*.

The challenge is all the greater for the exaltation of its perspective. True, we have shown above that the Christian mystery of communion surpasses, by completing it, the Hindu mysticism of identification. Nonetheless, the challenge presented by the latter forces Christians to cast off all simplistic conceptualizations, to rid themselves of certain gross anthropomorphisms; in sum, to purify their own faith. Indeed, the temptation is a real one to reduce interpersonal and pluripersonal relationships with God to the level of relations among human persons. The intimacy characterizing the divine relations in Jesus Christ only renders the danger more real. But to reduce God to our own dimensions is to recreate God to our image and likeness — to make an idol of God, through forgetfulness of the inalienable transcendence of the Deity.

It is here that the values of interiority cultivated by Hindu tradition can come to the Christian's aid. God is the Utterly Other, but the divine Otherness is not to be located outside ourselves, as on a horizontal plane. The relationship between the human being and God must be interiorized as it grows. This interiorization is the deed of the Spirit of God in the spirit of the human being. The Hindu tradition of the *atman* can aid the Christian to interiorize the Christian experience of the God of history. Therefore a certain visionary theologian saw the church of India as providentially destined to write a new page of the theology of the Holy Spirit.[23]

In this theology, the Holy Spirit will appear more as the mystery of the divine intimacy and interiority, of the being-together or nonduality (*advaita*) of the Father and the Son, and consequently, of the nonduality of God and the human being. The experience of oneness of being may be necessary in order for the human being's invocation of the Absolute as the "Thou" of interpersonal communion not to risk being surreptitiously reduced to the dimensions of an I-Thou relationship among human beings. God's "being-together" with human beings presupposes a radical mutual otherness; but the irruption of the Spirit of God into history, be it the personal history of the human being or the history of the world, surmounts all distances without suppressing distinctions:

> The Spirit is, as it were, the fruit of the unity and non-duality of Being, present at the heart of the Father and of the Son. He is the mystery of their inseparable and indivisible oneness. He is the infinite Love which opens up Being to communion, so that love may come to expression, and seals it in non-duality, so that love may come to perfection.[24]

The mystery of God is communion in "nonduality." The mystery of the human being is that of our insertion, through Jesus Christ, into this divine communion. While the communion is the specific, inalienable contribution of God's revelation in Jesus Christ, the unity which necessarily underlies it can be strengthened by the experience of the nonduality (*advaita*) of Hindu mysticism.

The fruits and challenges of the dialogue go hand in hand, then. However, above and beyond these sure benefits, we must say that the encounter and exchange have value in themselves. They are an end in themselves. While at the beginning they have supposed openness to the other and to God, they effect the openness to God of each through the other.

Thus the dialogue does not serve as a means to an ulterior end. Neither on one side nor the other does it tend to the "conversion" of one partner to the religious tradition of the other. Rather it tends to a more profound conversion of each to God. The same God speaks in the heart of both partners; the same Spirit is at work in all. By way of their reciprocal witness, it is this same God who calls and challenges the partners through each other. Thus they become, as it were, for each other and reciprocally, a sign leading to God. The proper end of the interreligious dialogue is, in the last analysis, the common conversion of Christians and the members of other religious traditions to the same God—the God of Jesus Christ—who calls them together by challenging the ones through the others. This reciprocal call, a sign of the call of God, is surely mutual evangelization.

Conclusion

At the end of a long journey, it is useful to cast a backward glance and measure the distance covered. There is no intent to repeat the journey, even swiftly; rather one seeks to evaluate the method followed and assess the results.

From the outset, we adopted a specific method: We defined our research in terms of a Christian theology of religions. To call it *theology* meant that, rather than observing the phenomena of the history of religions from the outside, we would seek their meaning from a standpoint within a religious faith. For this theology to be Christian meant that the faith that guided our reflection would be the Christian faith: We left it to others to do a Hindu, Buddhist, or other theology of religions. At this point it became evident that a Christian theology of religions would necessarily be a christology of religions. How could it have been otherwise? The mystery of Jesus Christ, the center of Christian faith, could only be the principle of understanding, the yardstick by which the data of other religious traditions would be measured. This assessment would call for a combined method, at once deductive and inductive, based simultaneously on a living faith and on the practice of a dialogue. We now return to our method, to establish its legitimate basis and assess its results.

A CHRISTIAN THEOLOGY

A Christian theology of religions is consciously distinguished from the universal theology of religion proposed by certain recent authors.[1] W. C. Smith conceives such a theology as one that "emerges out of all the religions of the world," and as constituting a "theology of the religious history of humankind." Transcending, as it will, the various faiths, while integrating them as well, it "should be acceptable to, and even cogent for, all humankind." Smith hopes to create "a theology of the faith of man . . . a statement of God and of his diverse involvements with humankind."[2] In a word, he is working toward a world theology to which all religious traditions will contribute and which they will all share.

We cannot adopt such an outlook, for many reasons. In the first place, in its attempt to transcend the differences in faith among the various religions, it reduces them to a lowest common denominator, and thereby ignores their specificity. Second, it seems utopian in the present context of a religious pluralism in which the identity of each tradition seems to be reasserting itself with renewed vigor. Third, not being developed within a specific faith, a "supraconfessional" theology is no longer a theology.[3]

A confessional theology, on the other hand, is not necessarily parochial. On the contrary, the theologian's task is to show that a Christian theology of religions can and should be truly universal. Let us note, however, the element of truth in the above perspective, even if, taken as a whole, it seems unacceptable. That the various religious traditions can agree on many things is certain. That they ought to do so, wherever it is possible, while maintaining their proper identity, is just as certain. That, besides all of this, they can work together is most certain of all. It is part of interreligious dialogue in its various forms to discover whatever Christians and others can say and do in common, despite their irreducible differences, and it is part of ecumenical goodwill to provide the thrust for this. A Christian theology of religions must necessarily adopt a global perspective. Sharing, as it does, with the other religions certain basic intuitions, it can itself be enriched by contact with specific elements of other religious and theological traditions. This principle needs to be recalled.

A COMPREHENSIVE THEOLOGY

That a Christian theology should adopt a global, all-embracing perspective is certainly true in general terms. In order to be adapted to the present moment, it must open itself to the problems of today's world, especially those that concern society and peoples, oppression and the crying need for integral liberation. "A church-centered theology is inadequate for Christians to relate meaningfully to the planetary reality of our times."[4] This is equally true of a theology of religions. It, too, must get beyond an ecclesiocentric perspective: The church is at the service of the salvation mystery present in this world and of the Reign of God being built up throughout history. But this does not imply that a christocentric universe is a thing of the past. Christ is universal. He belongs to all religions. More precisely, they all belong to him, since he is present and active in them all, just as in all human beings. What must be shown, then, is that a christocentric view fosters a comprehensive, universal perspective, one capable of embracing the self-manifestation and personal communication of God "in so many times and in so many forms" (see Heb. 1:1) to the various peoples of the earth throughout the history of humanity.

In order to see this, we need to recall that the divine Word is the universal agent of all historical divine self-manifestation, even before his incarnation in Jesus Christ; that his historical incarnation transpires in view of its metahistorical and universal operative presence as the resurrected Lord; finally, that his salvific activity extends to the ends of the universe, in virtue of the universal economy of his Spirit. God's self-communication through the divine Word, the metahistorical condition and universal presence of the resurrected Christ, and the economy and universal activity of the Spirit of Christ—these are the three elements that furnish a Christian theology of religions with a global perspective capable of integrating all divine revelations contained in the other religious traditions of humanity. Thus the Jesus Christ event, the center of history, acquires cosmic dimensions.

Since the Word, the Christ, and the Spirit are one, a Christian theology of religions, without any wish to grasp everything for itself, finds its advantage everywhere. Not only will it account for all the data furnished by the religious history of humanity, but it will be able to enrich itself with the intuitions of other religious traditions, since these other traditions contain an authentic manifestation of God through the mediation of the divine Word, the Christ of God, and the divine Spirit. It will also be able to recognize in the holy scriptures of other traditions not only a word addressed by God to their members, but a word through which God speaks to Christians themselves, even though in Jesus Christ God has spoken the decisive divine Word to the world.

Let us add, furthermore, that a Christian theology of religions will find a source of enrichment in the theologies of the other religious traditions. There was a time when, in Christian circles, *theology* meant "Christian theology," as if Christianity could monopolize reflection on an attitude of faith. We must recognize the full right to existence of other theologies: Hindu, Buddhist, Muslim, and others.[5] We must also acknowledge that the respective theologies of other religious traditions have developed in a distinct and creative way. Not only have they provided different answers to the same questions; they have also asked different questions, because they have seen the world through other lenses. They have used another reading key. Christian theology, while maintaining its own perception of the world and history, can nevertheless broaden and expand it through contact with different theologies. It will not manage to do so without genuine empathy. After all, "to understand others, it is necessary in some degree to see the world through *their* eyes, in the light of *their* questions as they emerged in their history."[6] On this condition, Christian theology, in dialogue with other religious traditions, can experience a renewal today, as it did in ages past through contact with Greek philosophy:

> Just as the dialogue with the rediscovered Aristotle enabled Aquinas to deepen his theological understanding and to recast Christian theology in the medieval situation, so too can the dialogue with Hindus, Buddhists, Muslims, Jews, and so on, in different parts of the world enable us to deepen our theological understanding and to recast some of our theological ideas in the modern situation.[7]

True enough, up to a certain point, but there are limits to be observed if Christian theology is to maintain its own identity intact. Thomas Aquinas did not accept everything Aristotle had to say, and what he did borrow, he recast in-depth before employing it as a vehicle of his own thought. What basic elements and religious intuitions can Christian theology borrow from other religious traditions to enrich its own perception of truth? Where are the theoretical limits? We must keep account of the fact that each religious tradition constitutes a whole, whose distinct elements cannot easily be isolated. We are dealing with all-embracing, distinct *Weltanschauungen,* within which—as with living organisms—each part plays so specific a role that a dynamic equivalence between the seemingly corresponding parts of different religious systems is not easily available.[8]

True, there are universal archetypes among the symbols. It is less certain, however, that among different religious traditions a strict equivalence is verifiable with certain basic theological concepts such as God, creation, the world, grace, freedom, salvation/liberation, and the like. While all authentic religious experience places its subject in contact with the same God, the actual experience of the ultimate reality—as of the Christian God the Father, the Jewish Yahweh, Islam's Allah, the Hindu Brahman, the Buddhist nirvana, the Taoist Tao, and so on—is different. Is it not the case, then, that each religious faith, and therefore each theology, is so closely bound up with a particular worldview that it can scarcely express itself in, or be transposed into, another? At least we must become aware of the profound mutations that concepts undergo with such a transposition and of the consequent limits of that transposition.

We have already seen a precise example of transposition that seems inviable. The Christian faith experience presupposes a certain density in history, a legacy from the Jewish tradition, but a legacy into which it has infused an even fuller meaning. Christianity is all but incomprehensible apart from this historical density, and finds it difficult to accommodate a transposition to an an-historical cultural model. This does not mean, however, that all cultural transposition between Christianity and the Eastern mysticisms is impracticable. History and interiority are two equally valid pathways for an authentic experience of God. The One who, according to Jewish and Christian tradition, acts in history is the very One whom Hindu tradition, for example, experiences "in the cave of the heart." The God of history is also the "ground of being."

A CONTEXTUAL THEOLOGY

While founded on a global perspective, a Christian theology of religions will also be contextual. What do we mean by this? First, beginning with the experience of an encounter with a particular religious tradition—whichever is offered by the context—it will address specific problems raised by this situation of bilateral dialogue, and not be content with general considerations—however valuable these may be for all religions—since they remain abstract in virtue of their very generality. Much of what has been said in this book consists only in basic principles, which will have to be applied differently to specific situations and different religious traditions. While all religions enter into the divine plan for humanity and have their place in salvation history, not all have the same place or the same signification. Judaism and Islam—merely to cite two evident examples—enjoy a special status vis-à-vis Christianity and Jesus Christ, as we have briefly suggested in these pages. In this sense, it is not of *a* Christian theology of religions that we should have to speak, but of various theologies, each in function of a concrete encounter with some specific religious tradition.

This gives us one more reason to repudiate a universal theology of religions that would transcend the various religious faiths. Entirely apart from the fact that it is impossible to theologize in neutrality, without a specific faith attachment,[9] it is equally vain to seek to embrace all religions at once as an object of inquiry. A theology of religions developed for all religious traditions and integrating them all is not only utopian; it is an atheological act. "Plural" theologies, each emerging from the concrete, localized encounter of the Christian message with a specific religious tradition, must replace it. There is no such thing as a pluralistic view of the world; there is only a variety of specific views of the real. There is no such thing, then, as a universal theology of religions; there is only a plurality of theologies, each founded on a dialogic situation among particular religious traditions.[10]

To speak of a contextual theology of religions bears on method, as well. We shall be dealing with a hermeneutical theology.[11] A hermeneutic-type theology has been recently defined as a "new act of interpretation of the Jesus Christ event on the basis of a critical correlation between the fundamental Christian experience testified to by tradition, and the human experience of today."[12] A new interpretation of the Christian message springs from the "circularity that obtains between a believing reading of the foundational texts that witness to the original Christian experience, and Christian existence today."[13]

But Christian experience today is everywhere conditioned by the historical context in which it transpires, with its cultural, social, political, and religious components. Hermeneutical theology will consist in a gradual, continuous oscillation between current contextual experience and the witness of the foundational experience of which tradition is the memorial. This continuous back-and-forth movement between context and text, present and past, is what is meant by the "hermeneutic circle." In reality it is not an alternation between two members, but a triangularity with reciprocal interaction among its three angles: the text or faith datum, the historical context, and today's interpreter; or again: Christian memory, history in genesis, and the ecclesial community or local church.

The concept of a hermeneutical theology is astonishingly applicable to a Christian theology of religions built on an encounter with a particular religious tradition that furnishes its context. It even provides a basis for singling out the major characteristics that ought to distinguish such a theology. First of all, it is a question, here, of a Christian interpretation. Thus we are far from a neutral discourse uncommitted to a specific faith. On the contrary, we find ourselves in a Christian "locus," where Jesus Christ is the center. Next, the context refers us, not in theoretical fashion to the objective data of the history of religions, but concretely to the experience of an encounter between Christians and the members of another religious tradition, all personally committed to their faith. There is no such thing as a dialogue between two religions; there is only a dialogue between persons who practice those religions and live by them.

Finally, the "hermeneutic circle" indicates the continuous rotation, the progressive interaction, between the datum of faith, the key of interpretation, and the experience of the dialogic encounter. The method becomes at once inductive and deductive. The praxis of the interreligious encounter (as, in another context, all liberating praxis) serves as the starting point for theological reflection—in the present instance, for a contextual theology of the religious traditions of humanity, and within this plural context of religions, for a hermeneutic of the plan of salvation revealed and realized by God in Jesus Christ.

In order to stress both the priority of dialogic praxis and the continuous interaction between text and context, in the precise framework of the encounter between Christianity and Hinduism, Raimundo Panikkar speaks of a Hindu-Christian theology and a diatopical hermeneutics.[14] He distinguishes a Hindu-Christian theology from an Indian-Christian theology. The latter seeks to adapt Western Christian thought to the context of India. It deals with the inculturation of the Christian message in the modality of transculturation into another idiom.

Hindu-Christian theology, on the other hand, begins with Hinduism and discovers Christ there, refusing to allow him to be monopolized by Western Christian thought.[15] It evinces the presence in Hinduism of the Christic mystery whose activity has no limits. In doing so, however, Panikkar's Hindu-Christian theology employs a "diatopical hermeneutics" that is "more a hermeneutics of Christ than a hermeneutics of Jesus-the-Christ."[16] We need not return to our earlier discussion of Christ, Jesus, and Jesus Christ (see chapter eight). Let us simply cite Panikkar once more, who notes, in another context: "My point of departure is not, perhaps, Christian theology as it is traditionally understood, but rather a faith, a naked faith, I should say, in Christ—in a Christ who is not *absolutely* identified with Jesus of Nazareth."[17]

With all due allowance for the priority of the praxis of dialogue, the hermeneutic key of a Christian theology of religions is not a Christ without Jesus, but Jesus-the-Christ. It is he whose active, universal presence must be shown. It is of the mystery and the event of Jesus Christ that the cosmic meaning must be demonstrated. A Christian theology of religions will be a christology. Far from fostering exclusivism, Christian christocentrism is capable of integrating, in their difference, all religious experiences into a truly catholic—inclusive and universal—theology.[18]

Notes

INTRODUCTION

1. Walbert Bühlmann, *The Coming of the Third Church* (Maryknoll, N.Y.: Orbis Books, 1976); idem, *The Church of the Future* (Maryknoll, N.Y.: Orbis Books, 1986); Virginia Fabella and Sergio Torres, eds., *Irruption of the Third World: Challenge to Theology* (Maryknoll, N.Y.: Orbis Books, 1983).

2. See Gustavo Gutiérrez, *Theology of Liberation* (Maryknoll, N.Y.: Orbis Books, 1973).

3. Paul F. Knitter, *No Other Name? A Critical Survey of Christian Attitudes toward the World Religions* (Maryknoll, N.Y.: Orbis Books, 1985), pp. 91–92.

4. See Wilfred Cantwell Smith, *Toward a World Theology: Faith and the Comparative History of Religion* (Philadelphia: Westminster Press, 1981; Maryknoll, N.Y.: Orbis Books, 1989).

5. Frank Whaling, *Christian Theology and World Religions: A Global Approach* (London: Marshall Pickering, 1986), p. 108.

6. See "The Inaugural Discourse at the Second Session of the Council (29 September 1963)," *Documentation Catholique* 60 (1963):1345–61, and the public audience of November 23, 1966, *Documentation Catholique* 63 (1966):2121–22.

7. We may refer to two recent works that treat separately of the relationship of the various religions to the mystery of Christ. See Hans Küng, *Christianity and World Religions* (London: Collins, 1987), for dialogue with Islam, Hinduism, and Buddhism; and Kenneth Cragg, *The Christ and the Faiths: Theology in Cross-Reference* (London: SPCK, 1986), for dialogue between Christianity and Islam, Judaism, Hinduism, and Buddhism.

8. An allusion to the title of the work by Stanley J. Samartha, *The Hindu Response to the Unbound Christ* (Madras: Christian Literature Society, 1974).

9. See M. M. Thomas, *The Acknowledged Christ of the Indian Renaissance* (London: SCM Press, 1969). The title is intentionally reminiscent of Raymond Panikkar's *The Unknown Christ of Hinduism: Towards an Ecumenical Christophany* (London: Darton, Longman and Todd, 1964. See also rev. ed., Maryknoll, N.Y.: Orbis Books, 1981), whose theological position we shall analyze later.

10. Here we may recall that the collection, "Jésus et Jésus-Christ," has already published a work by A.-M. Cocagnac, *Ces pierres qui attendent: Pour un dialogue entre l'hindouisme et le christianisme* (Paris: Desclée, 1979). The expression "stepping-stones," however, is older. It was commonly used, precisely with regard to Hinduism, by Pierre Johanns, *Vers le Christ par le Vedanta*, 2 vols. (Louvain: Museum Lessianum, 1932–1933), and more recently, *La pensée religieuse de l'Inde* (Namur: Facultés Universitaires, 1952).

11. See Yves M.-J. Congar, *The Word and the Spirit* (London: Chapman, 1986),

which, however, does not apply this principle to the theology of religions.

12. See, for example, Claude Geffré, *The Risk of Interpretation* (Mahwah, N.J.: Paulist, 1987).

1. THE "UNBOUND" CHRIST ACKNOWLEDGED IN HINDUISM

1. Thomas, *Acknowledged Christ.*

2. Samartha, *Hindu Response.*

3. Besides the books by M. M. Thomas and S. J. Samartha, the reader may consult: Hans Staffner, *The Significance of Jesus Christ in Asia* (Anand: Gujarat Sahitya Prakash, 1985); Robin H. S. Boyd, *An Introduction to Indian Christian Theology*, 2d ed. (Madras: Christian Literature Society, 1975); idem, *India and the Latin Captivity of the Church* (Cambridge: Cambridge University Press, 1974); Maurice Maupilier, *Les mystiques hindous-chrétiens (1830–1967)* (Paris: Oeil, 1985).

4. Samartha, *Hindu Response,* p. 117.

5. Ibid.

6. Staffner, *Significance of Jesus Christ.*

7. Ibid., pp. 3–168.

8. Maupilier, *Les mystiques hindous-chrétiens.*

9. Ibid., p. 10.

10. On the Christ of Gandhi, the reader may consult, among the works already mentioned, Thomas, *Acknowledged Christ,* pp. 193–238; Samartha, *Hindu Response,* pp. 73–97; Staffner, *Significance of Jesus Christ,* pp. 17–26.

11. Mohandas K. Gandhi, *The Message of Jesus Christ* (Bombay: Bharatiya Vidya Bhavan, 1963), cover page, cited by Thomas, *Acknowledged Christ,* p. 198.

12. Gandhi, *Message of Jesus Christ,* p. 79, cited by Thomas, *Acknowledged Christ,* p. 199.

13. Gandhi, *Message of Jesus Christ,* p. 37, cited by Thomas, *Acknowledged Christ,* p. 199.

14. Gandhi, *Message of Jesus Christ,* p. 21, cited by Thomas, *Acknowledged Christ,* p. 200.

15. Thomas, *Acknowledged Christ,* p. 201.

16. Gandhi, *Message of Jesus Christ,* pp. 6–7, cited by Thomas, *Acknowledged Christ,* p. 201.

17. Mohandas K. Gandhi, *Christian Missions* (Ahmedabad: Navajivan Publishing House, 1941), pp. 33–34; cited by Thomas, *Acknowledged Christ,* p. 203.

18. Gandhi, *Christian Missions,* p. 13, cited by Thomas, *Acknowledged Christ,* p. 203.

19. Thomas, *Acknowledged Christ,* p. 208.

20. Gandhi, *Message of Jesus Christ,* pp. 10–11, cited by Thomas, *Acknowledged Christ,* p. 209.

21. E. Stanley Jones, *Mahatma Gandhi: An Interpretation* (London: Hodder and Stoughton, 1948), pp. 76, 79, cited by Thomas, *Acknowledged Christ,* pp. 225–26.

22. Jones, *Mahatma Gandhi,* pp. 80, 105, cited by Thomas, *Acknowledged Christ,* p. 226.

23. Jones, *Mahatma Gandhi,* pp. 80–81, cited by Thomas, *Acknowledged Christ,* p. 226.

24. Thomas, *Acknowledged Christ,* pp. 235–36.

25. David C. Scott, *Keshub Chunder Sen* (Madras: Christian Literature Society, 1979), p. 64.

26. Ibid., p. 65.

27. Ibid., p. 217; Manilal C. Parekh, *Brahmarshi Keshub Chunder Sen* (Rajkot: 1931), p. 104.

28. Scott, *Keshub Chunder Sen*, p. 199; Parekh, *Bramarshi Keshub Chunder Sen*, p. 94.

29. Keshub Chunder Sen, *Lectures in India*, 2 vols. (London: Cassell, 1901–1904).

30. Scott, *Keshub Chunder Sen*, pp. 202–203, cited by Staffner, *Significance of Jesus Christ*, p. 41.

31. Scott, *Keshub Chunder Sen*, p. 203.

32. Parekh, *Bramarshi Keshub Chunder Sen*, pp. 98–99, cited by Thomas, *Acknowledged Christ*, p. 59.

33. Parekh, *Bramarshi Keshub Chunder Sen*, pp. 99–100, cited by Thomas, *Acknowledged Christ*, p. 60.

34. Parekh, *Bramarshi Keshub Chunder Sen*, pp. 101–102, cited by Thomas, *Acknowledged Christ*, p. 61.

35. Parekh, *Bramarshi Keshub Chunder Sen*, pp. 149–50, cited by Thomas, *Acknowledged Christ*, p. 64.

36. Parekh, *Bramarshi Keshub Chunder Sen*, pp. 149–50, cited by Thomas, *Acknowledged Christ*, p. 64.

37. Parekh, *Bramarshi Keshub Chunder Sen*, pp. 102–103, cited by Thomas, *Acknowledged Christ*, p. 70.

38. Parekh, *Bramarshi Keshub Chunder Sen*, p. 160, cited by Thomas, *Acknowledged Christ*, p. 70. The expression is reminiscent of Teilhard de Chardin's "ever greater Christ."

39. See Parekh, *Bramarshi Keshub Chunder Sen*, cited by Thomas, *Acknowledged Christ*, pp. 72–73.

40. Cited by Staffner, *Significance of Jesus Christ*, p. 71.

41. Sarvepalli Radhakrishnan, *Indian Philosophy*, vol. 1 (London: Allen and Unwin, 1929), pp. 545–46.

42. Sarvepalli Radhakrishnan, *The Philosophy of Rabindranath Tagore* (London: Allen and Unwin), p. 15.

43. Sarvepalli Radhakrishnan, *Eastern Religions and Western Thought* (London: Allen and Unwin, 1939). Idem, *An Idealist View of Life* (London: Allen and Unwin, 1937), and *The Hindu View of Life* (London: Allen and Unwin, 1926), will also be found useful.

44. Paul Arthur Schilpp, ed., *The Philosophy of Sarvepalli Radhakrishnan* (New York: Tudor, 1952), p. 807, cited by Thomas, *Acknowledged Christ*, p. 153.

45. Radhakrishnan, *Eastern Religions and Western Thought*, p. 97, cited by Thomas, *Acknowledged Christ*, p. 153.

46. Radhakrishnan, *Eastern Religions and Western Thought*, p. 47, cited by Thomas, *Acknowledged Christ*, p. 153.

47. Schilpp, *Philosophy of Sarvepalli Radhakrishnan*, p. 79, cited by Thomas, *Acknowledged Christ*, p. 154.

48. Radhakrishnan, *Eastern Religions and Western Thought*, pp. 220–21, cited by Thomas, *Acknowledged Christ*, p. 157.

49. Radhakrishnan, *Eastern Religions and Western Thought*, pp. 304–305, cited by Thomas, *Acknowledged Christ*, p. 158.

50. Schilpp, *Philosophy of Sarvepalli Radhakrishnan*, p. 371, cited by Thomas, *Acknowledged Christ*, p. 159.

51. Radhakrishnan, *Eastern Religions and Western Thought,* p. 371, cited by Thomas, *Acknowledged Christ,* p. 159.

52. Radhakrishnan, *Eastern Religions and Western Thought,* p. 327, cited by Thomas, *Acknowledged Christ,* p. 161.

53. Schilpp, *Philosophy of Sarvepalli Radhakrishnan,* pp. 75–76, cited by Thomas, *Acknowledged Christ,* p. 161.

54. Schilpp, *Philosophy of Sarvepalli Radhakrishnan,* pp. 80–81, cited by Thomas, *Acknowledged Christ,* p. 161.

55. See Thomas, *Acknowledged Christ,* pp. 161–86.

56. See, for example, P. D. Devanandan's reaction, in Thomas, *Acknowledged Christ,* pp. 164–70, esp. 167–69.

57. Thomas, *Acknowledged Christ,* p. 187.

58. Ibid., p. 190.

59. Swami Akhilananda, *The Hindu View of Christ* (New York: Philosophical Library, 1949).

60. Ibid., p. 22.

61. Ibid., p. 19.

62. Ibid., p. 72. See also Stanley J. Samartha, *Hindu Response,* p. 64.

63. Akhilananda, *Hindu View of Christ,* p. 261.

64. Akhilananda, *Hindu View of Christ,* p. 180, cited by Samartha, *Hindu Response,* p. 65.

65. Jacques Albert Cuttat, *La rencontre des religions* (Paris: Aubier-Montaigne, 1957), p. 62.

66. *The Light of the East,* July 1930, p. 6.

67. See Samartha, *Hindu Response,* p. 67.

68. Manilal C. Parekh, *A Hindu's Portrait of Jesus* (Rajkot: 1953).

69. Cited by Staffner, *Significance of Jesus Christ,* p. 120.

70. Cited ibid., p. 122.

71. Robin H. S. Boyd, *Manilal C. Parekh, Dhanjibhai Fakirbhai* (Madras: Christian Literature Society, 1974), pp. 145–46, cited by Staffner, *Significance of Jesus Christ,* p. 111.

72. Boyd, *Manilal C. Parekh,* p. 27, cited by Staffner, *Significance of Jesus Christ,* p. 114.

73. Staffner, *Significance of Jesus Christ,* p. 117.

74. Boyd, *Manilal C. Parekh,* p. 56, cited by Staffner, *Significance of Jesus Christ,* p. 117.

75. Boyd, *Manilal C. Parekh,* p. 53, cited by Staffner, *Significance of Jesus Christ,* p. 118.

76. Staffner, *Significance of Jesus Christ,* p. 123.

77. See Thomas, *Acknowledged Christ,* p. 100.

78. Cited by B. Animananda, *The Blade* (Calcutta: Roy and Son, 1947), p. 40.

79. The hymn to the Trinity is cited in English translation by Thomas, *Acknowledged Christ,* pp. 101–102. For a commentary on the hymns, see George Gispert-Sauch, "The Sanskrit Hymns of Brahmabandhab Upadhyaya," *Religion and Society* 19 (1972):61ff.

80. Animananda, *The Blade,* pp. 70–71, cited by Staffner, *Significance of Jesus Christ,* p. 94.

81. *Sophia* (March 1896): 7, cited by Thomas, *Acknowledged Christ,* p. 102.

82. *Sophia* (January 1895): 6–7, cited by Thomas, *Acknowledged Christ,* p. 103.

83. *Sophia* (August 1898): 122, cited by Thomas, *Acknowledged Christ,* p. 103.

84. *The Twentieth Century* 1: 2 (February 1901): 32–33, cited by Thomas, *Acknowledged Christ,* pp. 104–105.

85. *The Twentieth Century* 1: 1 (January 1901): 6–8, cited by Thomas, *Acknowledged Christ,* p. 105.

86. *The Twentieth Century* 1: 1 (January 1901): 6–8, cited by Thomas, *Acknowledged Christ,* pp. 105–106.

87. See Thomas, *Acknowledged Christ,* p. 108; and, for the patristic *Logos-Anthropos* christology, Aloys Grillmeier, *Christ in Christian Tradition,* vol. 1, *From the Apostolic Age to Chalcedon* (London: Mowbrays, 1975), pp. 345–439.

88. Animananda, *The Blade,* pp. 71–73, cited by Staffner, *Significance of Jesus Christ,* pp. 99–101.

89. Animananda, *The Blade,* pp. 71–73, cited by Staffner, *Significance of Jesus Christ,* p. 100.

90. Ibid.

2. HINDU AND CHRISTIAN CHRISTOLOGIES

1. See, for example, Josef Neuner, "Das Christus-Mysterium und die indische Lehre von den Avatars," in Aloys Grillmeier and Heinrich Bacht, eds., *Das Konzil von Chalkedon: Geschichte und Gegenwart,* vol. 3 (Würzburg: Echter-Verlog, 1954), pp. 785–824.

2. (Henri Le Saux) Abhishiktananda, *Saccidananda: A Christian Approach to Advaitic Experience,* rev. ed. (Delhi: ISPCK, 1984) p. 33.

3. Thomas Matus, *Yoga and the Jesus Prayer Tradition: An Experiment in Faith* (Ramsey, N.J.: Paulist Press, 1984), p. 26.

4. Ibid., pp. 154–55.

5. The present section appeared as part of an article published under the same title in *Revue théologique de Louvain* 8 (1977/4):448–60.

6. See Swami Akhilananda, *Hindu View of Christ,* p. 95; Radhakrishnan, *An Idealist View of Life* p. 104.

7. See Abhishiktananda *The Further Shore* (Delhi: ISPCK, 1984), p. 52: "This 'Son'/'Father' is the nearest equivalent in a semitic context to the 'tattvamasi'/'aham brahmasmi'. . . ."

8. Raymond E. Brown, *The Gospel According to John,* vol. 1 (New York: Doubleday, 1966), pp. 407–408.

9. Robert C. Zaehner, *Hindu Scriptures* (London: Dent, 1966), p. 37. Similar texts: *Brhad Up.* 1, 4, 17; 4, 3, 20; also *Chand. Up.* 7, 25, 1.

10. Zaehner, *Hindu Scriptures,* p. 109. See also *Chand. Up.* 6, 9, 4; 6, 10, 3; 6, 11, 3; 6, 12, 3; 6, 13, 3; 6, 14, 3; 6, 15, 3; 6, 16, 3.

11. The advaitine mysticism described here, I realize, does not necessarily entirely correspond to the interpretation of *advaita Vedanta* given by certain theologians, for example, by Shankara.

12. Henri Le Saux, *Saccidananda,* p. 39.

13. Martin Buber, *I and Thou* (New York: Charles Scribner's Sons, 1970), p. 116.

14. Ibid., p. 133.

15. Le Saux, *La rencontre de l'hindouisme et du christianisme* (Paris: Seuil, 1965), pp. 151–77 (English translation: *Hindu-Christian Meeting Point* [Delhi: ISPCK, 1983], pp. 77–93).

16. Le Saux, *Saccidananda,* p. 82.

17. Ibid., pp. 85–86.

18. Henri Le Saux, *Hindu-Christian Meeting-Point,* p. 77.

19. I have already developed this outlook in an article entitled "Knowing Christ through the Christian Experience," *Indian Journal of Theology* 18 (1969):54–64.

20. See James D. G. Dunn, *Jesus and the Spirit* (London: SCM, 1975); also Jean Mouroux, *L'expérience chrétienne: Introduction à une théologie,* Théologie, no. 26 (Paris: Aubier, 1952).

21. Cf. Hans Urs von Balthasar, *La foi du Christ* (Paris: Aubier, 1968); Jacques Guillet, *La foi de Jésus-Christ* (Paris: Desclée, 1980).

22. Jacques Guillet, *Jésus-Christ dans notre monde* (Paris: Desclée de Brouwer, 1974), p. 156.

3. SWAMI ABHISHIKTANANDA, OR THE SPIRITUAL EXPERIENCE OF A HINDU-CHRISTIAN MONK

1. Some of the following paragraphs are taken from the introduction to Henri Le Saux (Swami Abhishiktananda), *Intériorité et révélation: Essais théologiques* (Sisteron: Editions Présence, 1982), pp. 11–34.

2. Especially: *The Secret of Arunachala:* (Delhi: ISPCK, 1979); *The Eyes of Light* (Denville, N.J.: Dimension Books 1983); *The Further Shore* (Delhi: ISPCK, 2nd ed., 1984); *Intériorité et révélation: Essais théologiques* (Sisteron: Présence, 1982); *La montée au fond du coeur: Le journal intime du moine chrétien-sannyasi hindou (1948–1973)* (Paris: Oeil, 1986). We may also mention Abhishiktananda's abundant correspondence by James D. M. Stuart, *Swami Abhishiktananda: His Life Told Through His Letters* (Delhi: ISPCK, 1989).

3. Delhi: ISPCK, 1979.

4. London: SPCK, 1974.

5. Le Saux, *La montée au fond du coeur.*

6. "OM" is the sacred syllable symbolizing *Brahman.*

7. Henri Le Saux, *Eveil à soi — éveil à Dieu: Essai sur la prière* (Paris: Centurion, 1971), p. 96. The original English edition was published as *Prayer* (Delhi: ISPCK, 1967).

8. Le Saux, *La montée au fond du coeur,* May 11, 1972, p. 425.

9. Ibid., November 27, 1956, p. 222.

10. Ibid., December 4, 1957, p. 390.

11. Letter to O. B., December 5, 1970.

12. Letter, February 4, 1972.

13. Letter, September 2, 1972.

14. Le Saux, *La montée au fond du coeur,* September 9, 1970, p. 390.

15. Ibid., September 10, 1970.

16. Ibid., September 11, 1973, p. 469.

17. Paris: Centurion, 1965. English translation *Saccidananda: A Christian Approach to Advaitic Experience* (Delhi: ISPCK, 1984, revised edition).

18. Le Saux, *Saccidananda,* p. 85.

19. Letter, September 2, 1972.

20. Letter, April 21, 1973.

21. Le Saux, *La montée au fond du coeur,* October 23, 1970, p. 393.

22. Ibid., February 30, 1973, pp. 449–50.

23. Letter, January 16, 1973.

24. Le Saux, *Intériorité et révélation,* pp. 275–93.

25. Le Saux, *La montée au fond du coeur,* July 3, 1970, p. 385.

26. Ibid., July 9, 1970.

27. Ibid., July 24, 1971, p. 406.

28. "Sambabhuva atmani atmana atmanam" (cf. *Mahanar Up.,* no. 64).

29. Le Saux, *La montée au fond du coeur,* December 25, 1972, p. 442.

30. *Purusha:* the archetypal human being, the total human being in the fullness of that being.

31. Le Saux, *La montée au fond du coeur,* January 2, 1973, p. 447.

32. Ibid., February 30, 1973, p. 450.

33. *Sat-Purusha:* the real, authentic human being.

34. See Le Saux, *Intériorité et révélation,* pp. 295–301.

35. See ibid., where this distinction clearly appears in the two parts of the volume: the first contains texts from the initial period, 1953–1956; the second, essays from the last years, written between 1970 and 1973.

36. Le Saux, *La montée au fond du coeur,* January 11, 1969, p. 372.

37. Letter, April 21, 1973.

38. See especially James D. M. Stuart, "Swami Abhishiktananda," *Vidyajyoti* 38 (1974):80–83; Sara Grant, "Swamiji—the Man," ibid., pp. 487–95; Vandana, "A Messenger of Light," ibid., pp. 496–500; Xavier Irudyaraj, "Sannyasa—Swami Abhishiktananda," ibid., pp. 501–508; James D. M. Stuart, "Abhishiktananda on Inner Awakening," *Vidyajyoti* 46 (1982):470–84; Vandana, ed., *Swami Abhishiktananda: The Man and His Teachings* (Delhi: ISPCK, 1986) (contains various contributions to a workshop held in 1985).

39. The reader may consult Emmanuel Vattakuzhy, *Indian Christian Sannyasa and Swami Abhishiktananda* (Bangalore: Theological Publications in India, 1981).

40. Marie-Madeleine Davy, *Henri Le Saux: Swami Abhishiktananda. Le passeur entre deux rives* (Paris: Cerf, 1981).

41. Ibid., p. 11.

42. Ibid., p. 124.

43. Bernard Barzel, *Mystique de l'ineffable dans l'hindouisme et le christianisme: Çankara et Eckhart* (Paris: Cerf, 1982), pp. 74–75.

44. Ghislain Lafont, *Dieu, le temps et l'être* (Paris: Cerf, 1986), pp. 295–307.

45. Ibid., pp. 302–303.

46. Ibid., p. 303.

47. Ibid., p. 304.

48. Ibid.

49. Ibid., p. 305.

50. Ibid.

51. Ibid., p. 307.

4. WHICH CHRISTIAN THEOLOGY OF RELIGIONS?

1. On the myth in *Mahayana* Buddhism according to which the "deified" Buddha is said henceforth to possess a "glorious body" (*sambhogakaya*) by which he is held to be really present to those who believe in him, see Edward Conze, *Buddhism: Its Essence and Development* (New York: Harper and Row, 1959), pp. 34–38, 171–73.

2. These distinctions have often been noted. See, for example, Hans Küng, *On Being a Christian* (New York: Doubleday, 1976), pp. 150, 212, 278, 283, 334, 436–37; idem, *Christianity and World Religions* (New York: Doubleday, 1986); Gerald O'Collins, "The Founder of Christianity," in Mariasusai Dhavamony, ed., *Founders of Religions,* Studia Missionalia, no. 33 (Rome: Gregorian University Press, 1984), pp. 385–402; Clifford G. Hospital, *Breakthrough: Insights of the Great Religious Discoverers* (Maryknoll, N.Y.: Orbis Books, 1985).

3. See Jerome D. Quinn, "Jesus as Savior and Only Mediator," in *Foi et culture à la lumière de la Bible: Actes de la session plénière 1979 de la Commission Biblique Pontificale* (Turin: Elle Di Ci, 1981), pp. 249–60; Jean Galot, "Le Christ, Médiateur unique et universel," in M. Dhavamony, ed., *Mediation in Christianity and Other Religions,* Studia Missionalia, no. 21 (Rome: Gregorian University Press, 1972), pp. 303–20.

4. For example, John 3:17; Acts 10:44–48, 17:24–31, etc.

5. See Grillmeier, *Christ in Christian Tradition.*

6. Jacques Dupuis, "The Uniqueness of Jesus Christ in the Early Christian Tradition," *Jeevadhara* 47 (September–October 1978: *Religious Pluralism*): 393–408; here, pp. 406–407.

7. See Jacques Dupuis, *Jesus Christ and His Spirit: Theological Approaches* (Bangalore: Theological Publications in India, 1977), pp. 33–58.

8. See the Inaugural Discourse of Pope Paul VI at the Second Session of the Council (29 September 1963), *Documentation Catholique* 60 (1963):1345–61; see also the public audience of November 23, 1966, ibid., 63 (1966):2121–22.

9. See Edward Schillebeeckx, *Christ: Sacrament of the Encounter With God* (London: Sheed & Ward, 1963); Otto Semmelroth, *Die Kirche als Ursakrament* (Frankfurt am Main: Josef Knecht, 1953); International Theological Commission *L'unique Eglise du Christ* (Paris: Centurion, 1985), pp. 53–58.

10. The reader may consult, for example, W. Kern, *Ausserhalb der Kirche kein Heil* (Freiburg: Herder, 1979); Hans Küng, "The World Religions in God's Plan of Salvation," in J. Neuner, ed., *Christian Revelation and World Religions* (London: Burns and Oates, 1967), pp. 25–66.

11. Fulgentius of Ruspe, *De fide liber ad Petrum* 38:79, 39:80 — *PL* 65:704AB. Likewise, Cyprian of Carthage, *Epist. (73) ad Iubaianum,* chap. 21 (*PL* 3:1123AB), where "Salus extra Ecclesiam non est" is applied to the heretics.

12. *DS* 802; see Josef Neuner and Jacques Dupuis, eds., *The Christian Faith in the Doctrinal Documents of the Catholic Church* (London: Collins, 1983), no. 21.

13. *DS* 870; see Neuner-Dupuis, op. cit., no. 804.

14. *DS* 1352; see Neuner-Dupuis, op. cit., no. 810.

15. See Josef Ratzinger, *Das neue Volk Gottes* (Düsseldorf: Patmos, 1970), pp. 339–61; Paul F. Knitter, *No Other Name?* pp. 121–23.

16. *Gaudium et Spes,* no. 22. Please note that the official Latin text does not contain the word "only," to make the key phrase "known *only* to God," which one often finds as a mistranslation of GS 22.

17. Hans Küng, "World Religions in God's Plan," pp. 25–66; here, p. 46.

18. For an extended treatment of the question, see, for example, the recent book by Joseph B. Carol, *Why Jesus Christ? Thomistic, Scotistic and Conciliatory Perspectives* (Manassas: Trinity Communications, 1986).

19. Saint Anselm's position is actually more nuanced. See Michel Corbin's Introduction, "La nouveauté de l'incarnation," in *L'oeuvre de S. Anselme de Cantorbéry,*

vol. 3 (Paris: Cerf, 1988), pp. 11–163; see also Paul Gilbert, "Justice et miséricorde dans le 'Proslogion' de Saint Anselme," *Nouvelle Revue Théologique* 108 (1986):218–38.

20. See Schillebeeckx, *Christ the Sacrament,* pp. 32–38; see also his *Jesus: An Experiment in Christology* (New York: Crossroad, 1979), pp. 626–69.

21. Gustave Martelet, "Sur le problème du motif de l'Incarnation," in H. Bouëssé and J. J. Latour, eds., *Problèmes actuels de christologie* (Paris: Desclée de Brouwer, 1965), pp. 35–80; here, p. 51.

22. J. Peter Schineller, "Christ and Church: A Spectrum of Views," *Theological Studies* 37 (1976):545–66; reprinted in *Why the Church?,* Walter J. Burghardt and William G. Thompson, eds. (New York: Paulist Press, 1977), pp. 1–22.

23. Knitter, *No Other Name?* also adopts a fourfold division: the conservative evangelical model (one true religion); the most widespread Protestant model today (all salvation comes from Christ); the open Catholic model (various paths, Christ the sole norm); and the theocentric model (various paths, with God as center). In an article entitled, "Catholic Theology of Religions at the Crossroads," *Concilium* 183 (1986/1, *Christianity among World Religions),* pp. 99–107, Knitter partly adopts the categories proposed by H. Richard Niehbuhr *(Christ and Culture* [New York: Harper & Row, 1951]) for the relationship between Christ and "Culture," and distinguishes a Christ against the religions, in the religions, above the religions, and together with the religions. Previously, in his "Roman Catholic Approaches to Other Religions: Development and Tensions," *International Bulletin of Missionary Research* 8 (1984):50–54, he had distinguished: exclusive ecclesiocentrism; inclusive ecclesiocentrism, constitutive christocentrism; normative christocentrism, Christ above the religions; dialogic theocentrism, different religions as partners in God. The various categories partially coincide with Schineller's four members.

24. Among the authors who take account of the various positions, the following two adopt this nomenclature: Alan Race, *Christians and Religious Pluralism: Patterns in the Christian Theology of Religions* (Maryknoll, N.Y.: Orbis Books, 1982; London, SCM Press, 1983); Harold Coward, *Pluralism: Challenge of Other Religions* (Maryknoll, N.Y.: Orbis Books, 1985; Oxford: Basil Blackwell, 1986). Aloysius Pieris, "Speaking of the Son of God," *Concilium* 153 (1982/3, *Jesus, Son of God?*): 65–70, makes an equivalent distinction: Christ against the religions, the Christ of the religions, Christ among the religions.

25. Hendrick Kraemer, *The Christian Message in a Non-Christian World* (London: Edinburgh House Press, 1947); idem, *Religion and the Christian Faith* (London: Lutterworth, 1956); idem, *Why Christianity of All Religions?* (London: Lutterworth, 1962).

26. See the letter of the Holy Office to the Archbishop of Boston (August 8, 1949) condemning the rigid interpretation of the axiom, *Extra ecclesiam nulla salus* proposed by Leonard Feeney, according to which explicit membership in the church or the explicit desire to enter it are absolutely required for individual salvation. A relationship with the church *in desiderio,* even merely implicit, can suffice for the salvation of the person *(DS* 3866–73); Neuner-Dupuis, *Christian Faith,* nos. 854–57.

27. See, for example, Richard P. McBrien, *Catholicism,* vol. 2 (Minneapolis: Winston, 1980), pp. 691–729. In order to account for these two different views of the role of the church, Schineller introduces a subdistinction under the heading, "christocentric universe, inclusive christology": (a) Jesus Christ and the church as

constitutive, but not exclusive, means of salvation; (b) Jesus Christ as constitutive means of salvation, the church as a nonconstitutive means. See the schema in *Why the Church?* p. 6.

28. See Ernst Troeltsch, *The Absoluteness of Christianity and the History of Religions* (Richmond: John Knox Press, 1971); Paul Tillich, *Systematic Theology*, vol. 2 (Chicago: University of Chicago Press, 1957); idem, *Christianity and the Encounter of World Religions* (New York: Columbia, 1963).

29. Race, *Christians and Religious Pluralism*, pp. 106–48.

30. Knitter, *No Other Name?*, pp. 169–231.

31. See especially John Hick, *God and the Universe of Faiths: Essays in the Philosophy of Religion* (London: Macmillan, 1973); idem, *The Centre of Christianity* (London: SCM Press, 1977); idem, *The Second Christianity* (London: SCM Press, 1983); idem, *God Has Many Names: Britain's New Religious Pluralism* (London: Macmillan, 1980); idem, *Problems of Religious Pluralism* (London: Macmillan, 1985).

32. In his youth, Hick published a book entitled *Christianity at the Centre* (London: Macmillan, 1968), before he himself underwent the Copernican christological revolution. This was transformed into a second edition, *The Centre of Christianity*, to become, in turn, in a third edition, *The Second Christianity*.

33. See Karl Rahner, various essays in *Theological Investigations* (New York: Crossroad, 1961–1988) (esp. vols. 5ff.); also Rahner, *Foundations of Christian Faith* (New York: Crossroad, 1978).

34. See Leonard Swidler, ed., *Toward a Universal Theology of Religions* (Maryknoll, N.Y.: Orbis Books, 1987), esp. pp. 227–30. See also John Hick and Paul F. Knitter, eds., *The Myth of Christian Uniqueness: Toward a Pluralistic Theology of Religions* (Maryknoll, N.Y.: Orbis Books, 1987).

35. See, for example, J. J. Lipner, "Does Copernicus Help?" in Richard W. Rousseau, ed., *Inter-Religious Dialogue: Facing the Next Frontier* (Scranton, Penn.: Ridge Row Press, 1981), pp. 154–74, who accuses John Hick of a naive relativism and a historical idealism.

36. Gavin D'Costa, *Theology and Religious Pluralism: The Challenge of Other Religions* (Oxford: Basil Blackwell, 1986).

37. Ibid., p. 136.

5. SALVATION HISTORY AND DIVINE COVENANTS

1. For the theology of history, the reader may refer, for example, to Jean Daniélou, *Lord of History* (London: Longmans, 1958); Hans Urs von Balthasar, *A Theology of History* (London: Sheed and Ward, 1964); Oscar Cullmann, *Salvation in History* (London: SCM, 1967); Wolfhart Pannenberg, *Revelation as History* (London: Macmillan, 1969).

2. Oscar Cullmann, *Immortalité de l'âme ou résurrection des morts?* (Neuchâtel and Paris: Delachaux et Niestlé, 1956).

3. On the contrast between the biblical concept of history and the Greek concept, see Claude Tresmontant, *Etudes de métaphysique biblique* (Paris: Gabalda, 1955); idem, *Essai sur la pensée hébraique* (Paris: Cerf, 1953); also Oscar Cullmann, *Christ and Time* (London: SCM, 1965); A. H. Armstrong and R. A. Markus, *Christian Faith and Greek Philosophy* (London: Darton, Longman and Todd, 1960).

4. See Duraisamy S. Amalorpavadass, *Foundations of Mission Theology* (Bangalore: NBCLC), pp. 68–69; Robert Smet, *Essai sur la pensée de Raimundo Panikkar*

(Louvain-la-Neuve: Centre d'histoire des religions, 1986), pp. 84–86.

5. See Samuel Rayan, "Indian Theology and the Problem of History," in Richard W. Taylor, ed., *Society and Religion* (Madras: Christian Literature Society, 1976); also in Douglas J. Elwood, ed., *Asian Christian Theology: Emerging Themes* (Philadelphia: Westminster Press, 1980), pp. 125–32.

6. Samuel Rayan, "Models of History," *Jeevadhara* 73 (January–February 1983): 3–26; here, pp. 19–21.

7. Joachim Gnilka, "Réflexions d'un chrétien sur l'image de Jésus tracée par un contemporain juif," in *Bible et christologie,* by Commission Biblique Pontificale (Paris: Cerf, 1984), pp. 212–13.

8. Cullmann, *Christ and Time.*

9. Irenaeus of Lyon, *Adversus Haereses,* 3, 11, 8; in *Sources chrétiennes* 211: 169–71. Cf. *Demonstrations of Aphraates,* 11, 11: "The law and the covenant have been completely transformed. God transformed the first covenant, granted to Adam, and gave another to Noah; yet another to Abraham, which he transformed in order to give another to Moses. And as the Mosaic covenant was not observed, he gave another, in these latter days, which is not to be transformed. ... All of these covenants were different from one another. ..." See *Patrologia Syriaca,* 1, 1, pp. 498–502. Text cited in the Roman Office of readings, in the second reading for Wednesday of the First Week of Lent.

10. See, for example, Heinz R. Schlette, *Towards a Theology of Religions* (New York: Herder & Herder, 1966).

11. Dermot A. Lane, "Jesus in Jewish-Christian-Muslim Dialogue," *Journal of Ecumenical Studies* (Summer 1977): 464. On the Jewish-Christian dialogue, see, for example, John T. Pawlikowski, *What Are They Saying about Christian-Jewish Relations?* (New York: Paulist Press, 1982); idem, *Christ in the Light of Christian-Jewish Dialogue* (New York: Paulist Press, 1982); Joseph E. Monti, *Who Do You Say that I Am? The Christian Understanding of Christ and Antisemitism* (Ramsey, N.J.: Paulist Press, 1984); Franz Mussner, *Tractate on the Jews: The Significance of Judaism for Christian Faith* (London: SPCK, 1984); Michel Remaud, *Chrétiens devant Israel serviteur de Dieu* (Paris: Cerf, 1983).

12. Bull, *Cantate Domino* (*DS* 1348). See Neuner-Dupuis, *The Christian Faith,* no. 1003.

13. Karl Rahner, "Christianity and the Non-Christian Religions," *Theological Investigations,* vol. 5, pp. 115–34.

14. Text published in *Documentation Catholique* 70 (1973):419–22.

15. Ibid., p. 420.

16. Ibid.

17. Ibid., p. 421.

18. Text in *Origins* 4 (1974–1975):463–64.

19. Text in ibid., 15 (1985–1986):102-107.

20. Ibid., p. 463. We may observe, however, that the permanent validity of the old covenant was stated more clearly in a working document presented to the plenary assembly of the Secretariat for Christian Unity in November 1969 (from which "Orientations" borrows a great deal). The working document stated: "An effort should be made in favor of a better understanding of the fact that the Old Testament retains its proper validity (*Dei Verbum*). This must not be denied in virtue of the subsequent interpretation of the New Testament. The Old Testament must not be understood exclusively in reference to the New, or be reduced to an

allegorical sense, as so often occurs in the Christian liturgy." The text is cited in Helga Croner, ed., *Stepping Stones to Further Jewish-Christian Relations: An Unabridged Collection of Christian Documents* (London and New York: Stimulus, 1977), p. 8.

21. See Thomas Michel, "Islamo-Christian Dialogue: Reflections on the Recent Teachings of the Church," *Bulletin* 20 (1985/2):172–93.

22. *Osservatore Romano,* December 3, 1979.

23. Ibid., February 23, 1981.

6. SALVATION WITHOUT THE GOSPEL

1. See, for example, Karl Rahner, *Zur Theologie des Todes,* Quaestiones Disputatae, no. 2 (Freiburg: Herder, 1958); Ladislas Boros, *The Mystery of Death* (New York: Crossroad, 1973); Roger Troisfontaines, *Je ne meurs pas* (Paris: Editions Universitaires, 1960).

2. It is on this implicit faith that the "baptism of desire," of which the Council of Trent speaks is based. See "Decree on Justification," Neuner-Dupuis, *The Christian Faith,* no. 1928; *DS* 1524.

3. Schineller, as well, distinguishes, under the rubric, "christocentric universe, inclusive christology," two differing opinions. According to the first, not only Christ, but the church itself is "constitutive mediator of grace"; according to the second, while Christ is the constitutive mediator of grace, the church represents and points to the constitutive mediation of Christ. See Burghardt and Thompson, *Why the Church?,* pp. 10–11. This subdistinction coincides only partially with the one with which we are concerned here, its formal object—the function of the church—being narrower.

4. John N. Farquhar, *The Crown of Hinduism* (London: Oxford University Press, 1915); Pierre Johanns, *Vers le Christ par le Vedanta,* 2 vols. (Louvain: Museum Lessianum, 1932–1933).

5. See Jean Daniélou, *The Salvation of the Nations* (Notre Dame, Ind.: UND Press, 1962); Henri de Lubac, *Paradoxe et mystère de l'Eglise* (Paris: Aubier-Montaigne, 1967); Hans Urs von Balthasar, *The Moment of Christian Witness* (New York: Newman Press, 1969).

6. Text in *Acta Apostolicae Sedis* 68 (1976):41–42.

7. See the interventions published in D. S. Amalorpavadass, ed., *Evangelisation of the Modern World* (Bangalore: NBCLC, 1975). See also our chapter ten, below.

8. See de Lubac, *Paradoxe et mystère,* pp. 148–49.

9. Pierre Teilhard de Chardin, *Science et Christ* (Paris: Seuil, 1965), pp. 60–61.

10. Panikkar, *The Unknown Christ.*

11. Karl Rahner, *Foundations of Christian Faith,* p. 306.

12. Idem, "Christianity and Non-Christian Religions," pp. 115–34.

13. Ibid., pp. 131–32.

14. See Bernard Sesboüé, "Karl Rahner et les chrétiens anonymes," *Etudes* 361 (1984):521–36.

15. On the prophetic literature, see, for example, Angelo Penna, "Civiltà e religioni delle nazioni nei libri profetici," in *Foi et culture à la lumière de la Bible: Actes de la session plénière 1979 de la Commission Biblique Pontificale* (Turin: Elle Di Ci, 1981), pp. 93–115.

16. See Jean Daniélou, *Holy Pagans in the Old Testament* (London: Longmans, Green and Co., 1957).

17. See, for example, Jean Daniélou, "Christianity and Non-Christian Religions," in T. Patrick Burke, ed., *The Word in History* (New York: Sheed and Ward, 1966), pp. 86ff.

18. See Gustave Thils, *Propos et problèmes de la théologie des religions non chrétiennes* (Tournai: Casterman, 1966), pp. 67–78.

19. On this subject, see Jacques Dupuis, "The Kingdom of God and World Religions," *Vidyajyoti* 51 (1987):530–44.

20. See François X. Durrwell, "Le salut par l'évangile," *Spiritus* 32 (1967):380–95.

21. On the problems raised by the discourse in the Areopagus, see Jacques Dupont, "La rencontre entre Christianisme et Hellénisme dans le discours à l'Aréopage," in *Foi et culture à la lumière de la Bible,* pp. 261–86; idem, *Etudes sur les Actes des Apôtres* (Paris: Cerf, 1967), pp. 157–260; idem, *Nouvelles études sur les Actes des Apôtres* (Paris: Cerf, 1984). See also Lucien Legrand, "The Missionary Significance of the Areopagus Speech," in G. Gispert-Sauch, ed., *God's Word among Men* (Delhi: Vidyajyoti Institute of Religious Studies, 1974), pp. 59–71; idem, "The Unknown God of Athens," *Vidyajyoti* 45 (1981):222–31; idem, "Aratos est-il aussi parmi les prophètes?" in *La vie de la parole: De l'Ancien au Nouveau Testament. Etudes d'exégèse et d'herméneutique bibliques offertes à Pierre Grelot* (Paris: Desclée, 1987), pp. 241–58.

22. Heinz R. Schlette, "Religions," in *Encyclopédie de la foi* 4 (Paris: Cerf, 1967), p. 64.

23. The citation is from John Paul II, *Dominum et Vivificantem,* no. 53. For a fuller development of the same subject, see Jacques Dupuis, *Jesus Christ and His Spirit* (Bangalore: Theological Publications in India, 1977), pp. 3–19. The reader may also consult Jean Daniélou, *Gospel Message and Hellenistic Culture,* vol. 2 (London: Darton, Longman and Todd, 1973); Chrys Saldhanha, *Divine Pedagogy: A Patristic View of Non-Christian Religions* (Rome: LAS, 1984).

24. Thus, we leave aside Justin's reductive interpretation, proposed by Paul Hacker, *Theological Foundations of Evangelization* (St. Augustin: Steyler Verlag, 1980), pp. 35–40.

25. See Yves Congar, "Ecclesia ab Abel," in *Abhandlungen über Theologie und Kirche: Festschrift für Karl Adam* (Düsseldorf: Patmos, 1952), pp. 79–108.

26. We cannot survey the post-patristic tradition here, in which we should find negative opinions, as well, to abound. For a general view through the centuries, consult Julien Ries, *Les chrétiens parmi les religions: Des Actes des Apôtres à Vatican II,* Le Christianisme et la foi chrétienne, no. 5 (Paris: Desclée, 1987). Let us cite in passing the surprisingly positive opinion of Cardinal Nicholas of Cusa, a member of the papal court in the fifteenth century. In his *De pace fidei*—on peace among the various forms of faith—he apprises the reader of the "dialogue of saints" held by the representatives of the great religions, and writes: "There is but one religion, there is but one worship—that of all who live according to the principles of the *Logos*-reason. This one religion underlies the various religious practices. ... All worship of the gods testifies in behalf of the Divinity." Thus, agreement among the religions is realized by the operative presence of the *Logos* in each of them (cited by Paul Tillich, *Le Christianisme et les religions* [Paris: Aubier-Montaigne, 1968], p. 107). See *De Pace Fidei,* 10–12, 16–18, 68.

27. Karl Rahner, "Current Problems in Christology," in idem, *Theological Investigations,* vol. 1 (London: Darton, Longman and Todd, 1961), p. 189.

28. See Kurien Kunnumpuram, *Ways of Salvation: The Salvific Meaning of non-Christian Religions according to the Teaching of Vatican II* (Poona: Pontifical Athenaeum, 1971), which answers the question in the affirmative.

29. Pietro Rossano, "Christ's Lordship and Religious Pluralism in Roman Catholic Perspective," in G. H. Anderson and T. F. Stransky, eds., *Christ's Lordship and Religious Pluralism* (Maryknoll, N.Y.: Orbis Books, 1981), p. 193; Paul F. Knitter, *No Other Name?* p. 124.

30. Hans Küng, "The World Religions in God's Plan of Salvation," in Neuner, *Christian Revelation and World Religions,* pp. 51–53.

31. Text in *Acta Apostolicae Sedis* 68 (1976):74.

32. Typis Polyglottis Vaticanis, 1984, pp. 16–17. The text is likewise given in *Bulletin, Secretariatus pro non Christianis* 56 (1984/2):135–36.

33. See, for example, the collection by Johannes Feiner and Magnus Löhrer, eds., *Mysterium Salutis: Grundriss Heilsgeschichtlicher Dogmatik,* 5 vols. (Einseideln: Benziger, 1965–1976).

34. Oscar Cullmann, *Christ and Time* (London: SCM Press, 1965).

35. Heinz R. Schlette, *Towards a Theology of Religions* (New York: Herder and Herder, 1966).

36. See Henri Limet and Julien Ries, eds., *L'expérience de la prière dans les grandes religions* (Louvain-la-Neuve: Centre d'histoire des religions, 1980).

37. The reader may consult, for example: Louis Gardet and Olivier Lacombe, *L'expérience du soi: Etude de mystique comparée* (Paris: Desclée de Brouwer, 1981); Robert C. Zaehner, *Mysticism Sacred and Profane: An Inquiry into Some Varieties of Praeternatural Experience* (Oxford: Clarendon Press, 1957); Louis Gardet, *Expériences mystiques en terres non chrétiennes* (Paris: Alsatia, 1953); Joseph Maréchal, *Studies in the Psychology of the Mystics* (Albany, N.Y.: Magi Books, 1964); A. Ravier, ed., *La mystique et les mystiques* (Paris: Desclée de Brouwer, 1965).

38. Durrwell, "Le salut par l'Evangile," pp. 387ff, regards the proposition that, even before the Christian Era, grace implies God's communication of the Spirit as having its roots in a "juridical" approach to the mystery of grace. In a recent book entitled *Holy Spirit of God* (London: Chapman, 1986), the same author resumes his earlier opinion. According to him, the indwelling of the Spirit is limited to salvation in the church. To deny this would be to obscure the novelty of Christianity, as occurs with the theory of "anonymous Christianity." One must ask, however: if, as Durrwell is correct in insisting, grace consists in God's self-communication, will it not therefore entail, necessarily and in all situations, the immanent gift of the Spirit? What can be the meaning of the proposition that, while in the Old Testament the Spirit was present by its activity (for example, with the prophets), its presence is "personal" only in the New Testament, as it was in Jesus himself? In order to explain salvation before Christ and outside the church today, Durrwell is forced to have recourse to a personal encounter with Christ at the moment of death. This means re-adopting an abandoned interpretation of the descent of Christ to the dead, in order to apply it to salvation outside the church today.

39. See Rahner, "Christianity and the Non-Christian Religions," p. 121.

40. See Hans Küng, "World Religions in God's Plan," p. 46.

41. De Lubac, *Paradoxe et mystère de l'Eglise,* p. 34.

42. We shall not enter into the distinctions that must be made regarding the manner in which the mystery of salvation is present and active in the Catholic Church, on the one hand, and in the other churches and ecclesial communities on

the other. On this point we may refer to Francis A. Sullivan, "The Significance of the Vatican II Declaration that the Church of Christ 'Subsists in' the Roman Catholic Church," in *Vatican II: Assessment on Perspectives Twenty-five Years Later (1962–1987)*, ed., René Latourelle (Rahwah, N.J.: Paulist Press, 1989), 2:272–87.

43. On the subject of sacramental rites, see Nihal Abeyasingha, *A Theological Evaluation of Non-Christian Rites* (Bangalore: Theological Publications in India, 1984).

44. See, for example, Hans Küng, *On Being a Christian*, pp. 97–98; von Balthasar, *The Moment of Christian Witness*.

45. Rahner, "Observations on the Problem of the 'Anonymous Christian,' " *Theological Investigations*, vol. 14 (London: Darton, Longman and Todd, 1976), pp. 280–98.

46. See D'Costa, *Theology of Religious Pluralism*.

7. ECONOMY OF THE SPIRIT, WORD OF GOD, AND HOLY SCRIPTURES

1. Charles Davis, *The Study of Theology* (London: Sheed & Ward, 1962), p. 145.

2. See René Laurentin, *L'enjeu du synode: Suite du Concile* (Paris: Seuil, 1967), pp. 81–82.

3. See Jacques Dupuis, "Western Christocentrism and Eastern Pneumatology," in *Jesus Christ and His Spirit*, pp. 21–31.

4. Ibid., pp. 99–110.

5. We may refer to Peggy Starkey, "Agape: A Christian Criterion for Truth in the Other World Religions," *International Review of Mission* 74 (1985):425–63; and our response, "The Practice of Agape Is the Reality of Salvation," ibid., pp. 472–77.

6. Oscar Cullmann, *Christ and Time*, p. 188.

7. On the universal economy of the Spirit in the Old and New Testaments, we may likewise refer to: Pietro Rossano, "Sulla presenza e attività dello Spirito Santo nelle religioni e nelle culture non cristiane," in Mariasusai Dhavamony, *Prospettive di missiologia, oggi* (Rome: Università Gregoriana Editrice, 1982), pp. 59–71, esp. pp. 64–69; also idem, "Lo Spirito Santo nelle religioni e nelle culture non cristiane," in *Credo in Spiritum Sanctum: Atti del Congresso Teologico Internazionale di Pneumatologia* (Rome: Libreria Editrice Vaticana, 1983), 2:1393–1403. Kenneth Cracknell, *Towards a New Relationship: Christians and People of Other Faiths* (London: Epworth Press, 1986), studies certain biblical passages, often the subject of controversy, dealing with the activity of God outside of Israel and the church. He concludes that the biblical evidence contradicts the "exclusivistic" thesis.

8. Albert Greiner, "L'Esprit Saint dans le Nouveau Testament," in Henri Cazelles, Paul Evdokimov, Albert Greiner, eds., *Le mystère de l'Esprit-Saint* (Paris: Mame, 1968), p. 68.

9. Cited in Olivier Clément, *Dialogues avec le Patriarche Athénagoras* (Paris: Fayard, 1969), p. 496.

10. On the presence of the Holy Spirit in the religions of the world according to Vatican II, see Rossano, "Presenza e attività dello Spirito Santo," pp. 59–63; Yves Congar, *Je crois en l'Esprit Saint*, vol. 2 (Paris: Cerf, 1979), pp. 279–84.

11. See Nikos A. Nissiotis, "The Main Ecclesiological Problem of the Second Vatican Council," *Journal of Ecumenical Studies* 2 (1965):31–62.

12. See Yves Congar, "Pneumatologie ou Christomonisme dans la tradition

latine," *Ecclesia a Spiritu Sancto Edocta: Lumen Gentium,* no. 53: *Mélanges théologiques, hommage a Mgr Gérard Philips* (Gembloux: J. Duculot, 1970), pp. 42–63; idem, *The Word and the Spirit* (London: Chapman, 1986), pp. 101–21, esp. 113–14.

13. Congar, *The Word and the Spirit,* p. 79. John D. Zizioulas, for his part, prefers to make a distinction between Christ "instituting" the church and the Spirit "constituting" it. See also Jacques Guillet, *Entre Jésus et l'Eglise* (Paris: Seuil, 1984).

14. See Jacques Dupuis, "Apostolic Exhortation *Evangelii Nuntiandi*," *Vidyajyoti* 40 (1976):218–30.

15. Text in *Acta Apostolicae Sedis* 68 (1976):66.

16. Text in *Origins* 8 (1978-1979): 629–30, 632.

17. Text in *Documentation Catholique* 78 (1981):281–82.

18. Text in ibid., p. 321.

19. Text in *The Pope Speaks to India* (Bombay: St. Paul Publications, 1986):83–85.

20. All of the texts from this Day of Prayer have been published in *Assise: Journée mondiale de prière pour la paix (27 Octobre 1986)* (Commission Pontificale "Justitia et Pax," 1987), with the text of the Pope's address to the Roman Curia on pp. 147–55.

21. See Jacques Dupuis, "World Religions in God's Salvific Design in Pope John Paul II's Discourse to the Roman Curia (22 December 1986)," *Seminarium* 27 (1987):29–41.

22. Text in *Osservatore Romano* (English ed.), 5 January 1987.

23. Text in *Origins* 16 (1986-1987):93–94.

24. Part of this section has already appeared as part of our "L'économie cosmique de l'Esprit et les saintes Ecritures des traditions religieuses," *Vie Spirituelle* 130 (1976):729–46.

25. Hans Urs von Balthasar, "Der Zugang zur Wirklichkeit Gottes," p. 39 in *Mysterium Salutis,* vol. 3.

26. On this entire question, the reader may consult Duraisamy S. Amalorpavadass, ed., *Research Seminar on Non-Biblical Scriptures* (Bangalore: NBCLC, 1975); Mariasusai Dhavamony, ed., *Revelation in Christianity and Other Religions,* Studia Missionalia, no. 20 (Rome: Università Gregoriana Editrice, 1971); Ishanand Vempeny, *Inspiration in Non-Biblical Scriptures* (Bangalore: Theological Publications in India, 1973); Pietro Rossano, "Y a-t-il une révélation authentique en dehors de la révélation judéo-chrétienne?" *Bulletin, Secretariatus pro non Christianis* 3 (1968):82–84; A. M. Aagaard, "The Holy Spirit in the Word," *Studia Theologica* 28 (1974):53–171; Michael Amaladoss, "Other Scriptures and the Christian," *East Asian Pastoral Review* 22 (1985):104–15. Apropos of the Qur'an in particular: GRIC (Muslim-Christian Research Group), *The Challenge of the Scriptures* (Maryknoll, N.Y.: Orbis Books, 1989); K. Cragg, *Muhammad and the Christian: A Question of Response* (London: Darton, Longman and Todd, 1984). With regard to the holy books of Hinduism: G. Chemparathy, *Bible et Véda comme parole de Dieu,* Homo Religiosus, no. 7 (Louvain-la-neuve: Centre d'histoire des religions, to appear).

27. On the theology of revelation, see especially René Latourelle, *Theology of Revelation* (Staten Island: Alba House, 1987); Gabriel Moran, *Theology of Revelation* (New York: Herder and Herder, 1966); idem, *The Present Revelation* (New York: Herder and Herder, 1972); Aylward Shorter, *Revelation and Its Interpretation* (London: G. Chapman, 1983); Avery Dulles, *Models of Revelation* (Garden City, N.Y.: Doubleday, 1983).

28. Cf. André Neher, *L'essence du prophétisme* (Paris: Calmann-Lévy, 1972).

29. "Introduction to the Prophets," in *The New Jerusalem Bible* (London: Darton, Longman and Todd, 1985), p. 1159.

30. Robert C. Zaehner, *Concordant Discord* (Oxford: Clarendon Press, 1970), pp. 23–29.

31. See especially: Cragg, *Muhammad and the Christian*, pp. 92–93; Claude Geffré, "Le Coran, une parole de Dieu différente?" *Lumière et Vie* 32 (1983):21–32; Robert Caspar, "La rencontre des théologies," ibid., pp. 63–80; Michael Lelong, "Mohammed, prophète de l'islam," in Mariasusai Dhavamony, ed., *Founders of Religions*, Studia Missionalia, no. 33 (Rome: Università Gregoriana Editrice, 1984), pp. 251–76; GRIC, *The Challenge of the Scriptures*, pp. 44–86; W. Montgomery Watt, *Islamic Revelation in the Modern World* (Edinburgh: Edinburgh University Press, 1969).

32. We might also mention, on the subject of the Buddha, the enlightened and inspired one, mystic and prophet, Michael Fuss, "A Sacred Drama on the Lord's Enlightenment," in Dhavamony, *Founders of Religions*, pp. 101–26.

33. See the creed of Constantinople (381): The Holy Spirit "has spoken through the prophets." Text in Neuner-Dupuis, *The Christian Faith*, no. 12.

34. Karl Rahner, *Inspiration in the Bible*, Quaestiones Disputatae, 1 (New York: Herder, 1961); see also idem and J. Ratzinger, *Revelation and Tradition*, Quaestiones Disputatae 17 (New York: Herder, 1966).

35. Geoffrey Parrinder, "Revelation in Other Scriptures," in Dhavamony, *Revelation in Christianity and Other Religions*, pp. 101–13, distinguishes the Qur'an as word of God from the scriptures of the other religious traditions; in Hinduism itself he distinguishes among the Vedas, the Upanishads, and the *Bhagavad-Gita*.

36. See Ignace de la Potterie, "Jésus-Christ, plénitude de la vérité, lumière du monde et sommet de la révélation d'après Saint Jean," in Dhavamony, *Founders of Religions*, pp. 305–24.

37. Geffré, "Le Coran, une parole de Dieu différente?" pp. 28–29. See also Lelong, "Mohammed, prophète de l'islam," esp. p. 274; GRIC, *The Challenge of the Scriptures*, pp. 44–86.

38. Wilfred C. Smith, *Questions of Religious Truth* (London: Gollanez, 1967), asserts it in the case of the Qur'an; see also Parrinder, "Revelation in Other Scriptures," pp. 105–107; GRIC, *The Challenge of the Scriptures*, pp. 44–86, esp. 68. More broadly, on the subject of the nonbiblical scriptures in general, and those of Hinduism in particular, Michael Amaladoss, "Other Scriptures and the Christian," *East Asian Pastoral Review* 22 (1985):104–115; Parrinder, "Revelation in Other Scriptures," pp. 107–13.

39. See Kees Abel, "Non-Christian Revelation and Christian Worship," in G. Gispert-Sauch, ed., *God's Word among Men* (Delhi: Vidyajyoti Institute of Religious Studies, 1974), pp. 257–303; idem, "Non-Biblical Readings in the Church's Worship," *Bijdragen* 30 (1969):350–80; 31 (1970):137–71; Michael Amaladoss, "Textes hindous dans la prière chrétienne," *Christus* 17 (1970):424–32; idem, "Non-Biblical Scriptures in Christian Life and Worship," *Vidyajyoti* 39 (1975):194–209; Abhishiktananda, "Hindu Scriptures and Christian Worship," *Word and Worship* 4 (1973), pp. 187–95; 5 (1974):245–53; Amalorpavadass, *Research Seminar on Non-Biblical Scriptures*.

40. The Research Seminar on Non-Biblical Scriptures, held at Bangalore in December 1974, shows how they can be fitted into the liturgy of the word in such

a way as to respect the various stages of revelation and indicates the unique place that the revelation in Jesus Christ should have there. See the final declaration, "Statement of the Seminar," in Amalorpavadass, *Research Seminar on Non-Biblical Scriptures*, pp. 681–95, esp. nos. 55–62 (pp. 685–89).

41. I have shown some concrete applications in an article entitled, "The Use of Non-Christian Scriptures in Christian Worship in India," in Mariasusai Dhavamony, ed., *Worship and Rituals in Christianity and Other Religions* (Rome: Università Gregoriana Editrice, 1974), pp. 127–143.

42. See Abhishiktananda, *Hindu-Christian Meeting-Point* (Delhi: ISPCK, 1976).

8. THE CHRIST OF FAITH AND THE HISTORICAL JESUS IN THE ENCOUNTER OF RELIGIONS

1. See Ernst Käsemann, "Das Problem des historischen Jesus," *Theologie und Kirche* 51 (1954):125–53.

2. We may cite, for example: Charles H. Dodd, *The Founder of Christianity* (London: Macmillan, 1970); Günther Bornkamm, *Jesus of Nazareth* (London: Hodder and Stoughton, 1960); Edward Schweizer, *Jesus* (London: SCM, 1978); Hans Conzelmann, *Jesus* (Philadelphia: Fortress, 1973); Xavier Léon-Dufour, *Les Evangiles et l'histoire de Jesus* (Paris: Seuil, 1963). See also the works of Joachim Jeremias, for example *New Testament Theology*, vol. 1 (London: SCM, 1971); likewise Charles Perrot, *Jésus et l'histoire* (Paris: Desclée, 1979).

3. On Jesus' consciousness, see especially: Jacques Guillet, *Jésus devant sa vie et sa mort* (Paris: Aubier-Montaigne, 1971); Xavier Léon-Dufour, *Face à la mort Jésus et Paul* (Paris: Seuil, 1979). On the development of the explicit christology of the New Testament from a point of departure in the implicit pre-Paschal christology, the reader may consult, for example: Charles F. D. Moule, *The Origin of Christology* (Cambridge: Cambridge University Press, 1977); Martin Hengel, *The Son of God* (Philadelphia: Fortress, 1976); Jacques Dupont, ed., *Jésus aux origines de la christologie* (Gembloux: Duculot, 1975); Ignace de la Potterie, ed., *De Jésus aux Evangiles: Tradition et rédaction dans les évangiles* (Gembloux: Duculot, 1967); Reginald H. Fuller, *The Foundations of New Testament Christology* (London: Collins, 1965); I. Howard Marshall, *The Origins of New Testament Christology* (Downers Grove, Ill., 1976); James D. G. Dunn, *Christology in the Making: An Inquiry into the Origins of the Doctrine of the Incarnation* (London: SCM Press, 1980); Albert Dondeyne et al., *Jésus-Christ, Fils de Dieu* (Brussels: Facultés Universitaires Saint Louis, 1981); Pontifical Biblical Commission, *Bible et christologie* (Paris: Cerf, 1984).

4. See Oscar Cullmann, *Les premières confessions de foi chrétiennes* (Paris: Presses Universitaires de France, 1948).

5. It will be enough to mention, without entering into the discussions occasioned by them, the following works: Hans Küng, *On Being a Christian*; Edward Schillebeeckx, *Jesus: An Experiment in Christology*.

6. See especially: Leonardo Boff, *Jesus Christ Liberator: A Critical Christology for Our Time* (Maryknoll, N.Y.: Orbis Books, 1978); idem, *Jesucristo y la liberación del hombre* (Madrid: Cristiandad, 1981), containing various christological essays; Jon Sobrino, *Christology at the Crossroads: A Latin American Approach* (Maryknoll, N.Y.: Orbis Books, 1978); idem, *Jesus in Latin America* (Maryknoll, N.Y.: Orbis Books, 1987); Juan Luis Segundo, *Jesus of Nazareth Yesterday and Today*, 5 vols. (Maryknoll, N.Y.: Orbis Books, 1984-88), esp. vol. 2, *The Historical Jesus and the*

Synoptics and vol. 3, *The Humanistic Christology of Paul*; Hugo Echegaray, *La pratique de Jésus: Essai de christologie* (Paris: Centurion, 1980); Ignacio Ellacuría, *Freedom Made Flesh* (Maryknoll, N.Y.: Orbis Books, 1976). See also J. van Nieuwenhove, ed., *Jésus et la libération en Amérique Latine* (Paris: Desclée, 1986).

7. Thus, in the Asian context, Sebastian Kappen, *Jesus and Freedom* (Maryknoll, N.Y.: Orbis Books, 1977); Tissa Balasuriya, *Jesus Christ and Human Liberation* (Colombo: Centre for Society and Religion, 1976). In the African context, Albert Nolan, *Jesus before Christianity: The Gospel of Liberation* (Maryknoll, N.Y.: Orbis Books, 1976).

8. See Samuel Rayan, "Models of History," *Jeevadhara* 73 (January–February 1983), 3–26; Troeltsch, *The Absoluteness of Christianity*. On Troeltsch's "historical relativism," see Paul F. Knitter, *No Other Name?* (Maryknoll, N.Y.: Orbis Books, 1985), pp. 23–36.

9. Felix Wilfred, "A Matter of Theological Education: Some Critical Reflections on the Suitability of 'Salvation History' as a Theological Model for India," *Vidyajyoti* 48 (1984), pp. 538–56.

10. This seems to be the position of, for example, Paul Tillich, *Christianity and the Encounter of World Religions* (New York: Columbia, 1963). Likewise, see Troeltsch, *Absoluteness of Christianity*; Paul F. Knitter, "Jesus—Buddha—Krishna: Still Present," *Journal of Ecumenical Studies* 16 (1979): 651–71.

11. This is the position of, among other authors, John Hick, as already described in chapter 4, to which we shall have to respond in the following chapter. See also: Arnold Toynbee, "What Should Be the Christian Approach to the Contemporary Non-Christian Faiths?" in *Christianity among the Religions of the World* (New York: Scribner's, 1957); Alan Race, *Christians and Religious Pluralism*.

12. See Mariasusai Dhavamony, ed., *Evangelization, Dialogue and Development*, Documenta Missionalia 5 (Rome: Università Gregoriana Editrice, 1972); the declaration of the conference appears pp. 1–15. See also Joseph Pathrapankal, ed., *Service and Salvation* (Bangalore: Theological Publications in India, 1973); the declaration appears pp. 1–16.

13. Dhavamony, loc. cit., p. 4.

14. Ibid., p. 5.

15. London: Darton, Longman and Todd, 1964.

16. Paris: Centurion, 1972.

17. Jacques Dupuis, "The Unknown Christ of Hinduism," *Clergy Monthly Supplement* 7 (1964–65):278–82; text p. 280.

18. Especially in the 1981 "revised and enlarged" edition of *The Unknown Christ of Hinduism: Towards an Ecumenical Christophany* (London: Darton, Longman and Todd, 1981); *The Intra-Religious Dialogue* (New York and Ramsey, N.J.: Paulist Press, 1978); *Salvation in Christ: Concreteness and Universality. The Supername* (Santa Barbara, Calif., 1972).

19. See n. 18, above.

20. Raimundo Panikkar, *Unknown Christ of Hinduism* (1981), pp. 2–30.

21. Ibid., pp. 19–20.

22. Ibid., p. 22.

23. Ibid., pp. 23, 26–27.

24. Ibid., p. 27.

25. Ibid., p. 29.

26. Ibid., p. 30.

27. New York and Ramsey, N.J.: Paulist Press, 1978.

28. This seems to be related to the concept of "faith" as found in Wilfred C. Smith, *The Meaning and the End of Religion* (New York: New American Library, 1964). The "faith" he distinguishes from "cumulative tradition" is the living experience, common to all religions, of a transcendence. See Knitter, *No Other Name?* p. 45.

29. In a letter to the author dated November 8, 1983.

30. Panikkar had already moved in this direction in *Salvation in Christ*, where he had asked: "Is there any way of understanding Jesus Christ in a universal way without diluting his concreteness?" (p. 45). That "Christ is the universal savior is certainly the most traditional Christian interpretation" (p. 51); but "Christ the Savior is . . . not to be restricted to the merely historical figure of Jesus of Nazareth. Or . . . the identity of Jesus is not to be confused with historical identification. To say 'Jesus Christ is Lord' may be considered as the epitome of the Christian confession of faith, but this sentence is not reversible without qualifications . . ." (pp. 51–52). "Christ the Lord and Savior is for the Christian the symbol of that mystery which is unveiled in or through Jesus" (p. 59).

31. Robert Smet, *Essai sur la pensée de Raimundo Panikkar: Une contribution indienne à la théologie des religions et à la christologie* (Louvain-la-Neuve: Centre d'histoire des religions, 1981). See also idem, *Le problème d'une théologie hindoue-chrétienne selon Raymond Panikkar* (Louvain-la-Neuve: Centre d'histoire des religions, 1983).

32. Smet, *Essai sur la pensée de Raimundo Panikkar*, p. 105.

33. Ibid., pp. 46–47. See also p. 79, where, commenting on Panikkar's thought, Smet writes: "While the *Logos* is manifested in Jesus the Christ for Christians, one must open oneself to a Christ at once universally revealed and hidden. Christ belongs to no one but God, and he gives himself to all. For Christian faith, the Christ historically incarnate in Jesus is logically the basic criterion, but one must open oneself to a Christ acting also in all of the religions of the world. . . ." Seeking to determine what Christ is for Panikkar, Smet likewise writes: "Marked by Hinduism, he wishes to believe in a Christ who is not 'only' Jesus Christ. 'His' Christ is the *Logos* present in creation, directive principle of the world (*Pantocrator*), inner guide (*antaryamin*) in the heart of each human being, active in all religions" (p. 104).

34. Paul Lamarche, *Christ vivant: Essai sur la christologie du Nouveau Testament* (Paris: Cerf, 1966), pp. 135–36.

35. Ibid., pp. 60–61.

36. Ibid., p. 67.

9. UNICITY AND UNIVERSALITY OF JESUS CHRIST

1. Walter Kasper, *Jesus the Christ* (New York: Paulist, 1976), pp. 267–68. See also Yves M.-J. Congar, *The World and the Spirit* (London: Chapman, 1986), pp. 123–24, who cites Kasper on this subject (pp. 127–28).

2. For the state of the question, the reader may refer to the excellent article by Felipe Gomez, "The Uniqueness and Universality of Christ," *East Asian Pastoral Review* 20 (1983/1):4–30; also Carl E. Braaten, "The Uniqueness and Universality of Jesus Christ," in G. H. Anderson and T. F. Stransky, eds., *Faith Meets Faith*, Mission Trends 5 (New York and Ramsey, N.J.: Paulist Press, 1981), pp. 69–89.

3. However, see Karl Rahner, *Foundations of Christian Faith* (New York: Seabury, 1978; London: Darton, Longman and Todd, 1978), pp. 153-61. Gerald O'Collins, *Interpreting Jesus* (London: Geoffrey Chapman, 1983), devotes a short chapter to "Christ beyond Christianity" (pp. 202–208). Coming at the end of the book, this rapid treatment of other religions serves only imperfectly to situate the mystery of Christ in the broader context of the religious pluralism of humanity.

4. Hans Küng, *On Being a Christian*.

5. Ibid., p. 110.

6. For a more adequate evaluation of Islam, Hinduism, and Buddhism in dialogue with Christianity, see Küng's more recent *Christianity and World Religions*.

7. Küng, *On Being a Christian*, p. 123.

8. As in the original German: see Küng, *Christ sein* (Munich: Piper, 1974), p. 117.

9. Küng, *On Being a Christian*, p. 265.

10. Ibid., pp. 409–10.

11. Ibid., pp. 381–410.

12. Ibid., p. 444.

13. Ibid., p. 390; cf. p. 449.

14. Paul F. Knitter, "World Religions and the Finality of Christ: A Critique of Hans Küng's 'On Being a Christian,' " in Rousseau, *Inter-religious Dialogue*, pp. 202–21, regards Küng's claims of a uniqueness for Jesus Christ as arbitrary. For Knitter, such pretensions are necessary neither for the Christian commitment to Christ, nor for fidelity to Christian tradition; furthermore, it scouts other religions and obstructs the interreligious dialogue; finally, the "norms of the theological and historical-critical method" invalidate this claim.

15. See Paul F. Knitter, "Hans Küng's Theological Rubicon," in Swidler, *Toward a Universal Theology of Religions*, pp. 224–30; idem, "Toward a Liberation Theology of Religions," in Hick and Knitter, *The Myth of Christian Uniqueness*, pp. 178–200; here, pp. 194–95.

16. Hans Küng, "What Is True Religion? Toward an Ecumenical Criteriology," in Swidler, *Toward a Universal Theology*, pp. 230–50; here, pp. 246–47.

17. See chapter 4. For an extended presentation and detailed critique of the position of John Hick, see Gregory H. Carruthers's doctoral dissertation, *The Uniqueness of Jesus Christ in the Theocentric Model of the Christian Theology of Religions: An Elaboration and Evaluation of the Position of John Hick* (Lanham, N.Y. and London: University Press of America, 1990).

18. Alan Race, *Christians and Religious Pluralism*, pp. 106–48.

19. Knitter, *No Other Name?*, pp. 169–231. Along the same lines, see Harold Coward, *Pluralism: Challenge to World Religions* (Maryknoll, N.Y.: Orbis Books, 1985).

20. Race, *Christians and Religious Pluralism*.

21. See John Hick, *God and the Universe of Faiths*; idem, *Problems of Religious Pluralism* (London: Macmillan, 1985); Leonard Swidler, "Interreligious and Inter-ideological Dialogue: The Matrix for All Systematic Reflection Today," in *Toward a Universal Theology*, pp. 5–50.

22. See Wilfred C. Smith, *Towards a World Theology*; idem, "Theology and the World's Religious History," in Swidler, *Toward a Universal Theology*, pp. 51–72; Swidler, "Interreligious and Interideological Dialogue," ibid., 5–50. In the same direction, see Clifford G. Hospital, *Breakthrough*, where he envisages not a "super-

religion" or syncretistic mixture, but a "metatheology that arises out of . . . the wide-ranging history of human religiousness" (p. 167 and n. 76).

23. Knitter, *No Other Name?* pp. 182–86. See also David Tracy, *Blessed Rage for Order: The New Pluralism in Theology* (New York: Seabury Press, 1975), pp. 72–79, 131–36.

24. See, for example, Don Cupitt, "The Finality of Christ," *Theology* 78 (1975), pp. 618–22; Hick, *God and the Universe of Faiths*, pp. 108–19.

25. See Hick, *God and the Universe of Faiths*, pp. 148–79; idem, ed., *The Myth of God Incarnate* (London: SCM Press, 1977); Thomas McFadden, ed., *Does Jesus Make a Difference?* (New York: Seabury Press, 1974); John A. T. Robinson, *The Human Face of God* (London: SCM Press, 1973); Hick and Knitter, *Myth of Christian Uniqueness*.

26. See Gregory Baum, "Is There a Missionary Message?" in Gerald H. Anderson and Thomas F. Stransky, eds., *Crucial Issues in Mission Today*, Mission Trends 1, (New York: Paulist Press, 1974), pp. 81–86.

27. Oscar Cullmann, *Christ and Time*.

28. Pierre Benoit, "L'aspect physique et cosmique du salut dans les écrits pauliniens," in *Bible et christologie*, by Commission Biblique Pontificale (Paris: Cerf, 1984), pp. 253–69; here, 265.

29. See Karl Rahner, "On the Theology of the Incarnation," *Theological Investigations*, vol. 4 (London: Longman and Todd, 1966), pp. 105–20.

30. See, in response to Hick, *The Myth of God Incarnate*: Michael Green, ed., *The Truth of God Incarnate* (London: Hodder and Stoughton, 1977); Anthony E. Harvey, ed., *God Incarnate: Story and Belief* (London: SPCK, 1981); Thomas V. Morris, *The Logic of God Incarnate* (London: Cornell University Press, 1986); Brian Hebblethwaite, *The Incarnation: Collected Essays in Christology* (Cambridge: Cambridge University Press, 1987).

31. See, for example, James D. G. Dunn, *Christology in the Making: An Inquiry into the Origins of the Doctrine of the Incarnation* (London: SCM Press, 1980).

32. See the creed of Nicaea (325): ". . . For us human beings and for our salvation he came down, was incarnated, became a human being . . ." Text in Neuner-Dupuis, *The Christian Faith*, no. 7, p. 6. See also the creed of Constantinople I (381), ibid., no. 12.

33. See Jacques Dupuis, "The Uniqueness of Jesus Christ in the Early Christian Tradition," *Jeevadhara* 47 (September–October, 1978), pp. 393–408.

34. See Jon Sobrino, *Christology at the Crossroads* (Maryknoll, N.Y.: Orbis Books, 1978).

35. See Pierre Rousselot, "Les yeux de la foi," *Recherches de Science Religieuse* 1 (1910):241–59, 444–75.

36. See Leslie Dewart, *The Foundation of Belief* (London: Burns and Oates, 1969); idem, *The Future of Belief: Theism in a World Come of Age* (New York: Herder and Herder, 1966).

37. See Bernard Lonergan, "The De-Hellenization of Dogma," *Theological Studies* 28 (1967):336–50; Aloys Grillmeier, "De Jésus de Nazareth, dans l'ombre du Fils de Dieu, au Christ, image de Dieu," in *Comment être chrétien? La réponse de Hans Küng* (Paris: Desclée de Brouwer, 1979); idem, *Christ in Christian Tradition*, vol. 1.

38. Bernard Lonergan, *The Way to Nicea* (London: Darton, Longman and Todd, 1964).

39. Ernst Troeltsch, *The Absoluteness of Christianity*, p. 121.

40. Schubert M. Ogden, *Christ without Myth* (New York: Harper and Brothers, 1961).

41. Eugene TeSelle, *Christ in Context: Divine Purpose and Human Possibility* (Philadelphia: Fortress Press, 1975).

42. Paul Tillich, *Systematic Theology* 2 (Chicago: University of Chicago Press, 1957), pp. 167–68.

43. See chapter 4 on Alan Race, Paul F. Knitter, and others. See also Hick and Knitter, *Myth of Christian Uniqueness*.

44. Toynbee, "What Should Be the Christian Approach to the Contemporary Non-Christian Faiths?" in *Christianity among the Religions of the World*, pp. 83–112.

45. See Coward, *Pluralism*.

46. Translation based on that of Robert C. Zaehner, *Hindu Scriptures* (London: Dent, 1966), p. 288.

47. Paul F. Knitter, "Horizons on Christianity's New Dialogue with Buddhism," *Horizons* 8 (1981):40-61; idem, "Jesus-Buddha-Krishna: Still Present," *Journal of Ecumenical Studies* 16 (1979):651–71.

48. See William Johnston, *The Inner Eye of Love: Mysticism and Religion* (New York: Harper and Row, 1978). A specialist in the dialogue with Buddhism, Johnston acknowledges "an inner revelation, a gift of faith, an interior word, offered to all human beings." Notwithstanding, he professes his faith in the uniqueness of Jesus Christ as universal savior: "I also believe that this inner grace is offered to all, thanks to the death and resurrection of Jesus Christ, who is 'the true light that enlightens every person' (John 1:9). In other words, the inner light of faith is not unrelated to Christ but is his gift to all human beings. . . . I give to Jesus Christ a unique role, which I cannot accord the founders of other religions, even when I esteem them profoundly. . . . Perhaps the matter could be stated more positively by saying that the Risen Christ who sits at the right hand of the Father belongs to all human beings and to all religions" (p. 70).

49. See Carruthers, *Uniqueness of Jesus Christ*.

50. See, for example, Coward, *Pluralism*, pp. 94–109.

51. See Knitter, *No Other Name?* pp. 68–69.

52. See ibid., pp. 205–231.

53. Ibid., p. 231.

54. See Michael Amaladoss, "Evangelisation in India: A New Focus," *Vidyajyoti* 51 (1987):7–28; idem, "Dialogue and Mission," *Vidyajyoti* 50 (1986):62–86; idem, "Faith Meets Faith," *Vidyajyoti* 49 (1985):6–15.

55. See Jacques Dupuis, "The Kingdom of God and World Religions," *Vidyajyoti* 51 (1987):530–44.

56. See Ursula King, *Towards a New Mysticism: Teilhard de Chardin and Eastern Religions* (London: Collins, 1980).

57. See William M. Thompson, *The Jesus Debate: A Survey and Synthesis* (New York, Mahwah, N.J.: Paulist Press, 1985), p. 388.

58. See Stanislas Breton, *Unicité et monothéisme* (Paris: Cerf, 1981), pp. 149–59. The author writes: "The good Christian usage of uniqueness . . . reduces the intransigence of the unique and contests its property of excellence and establishment only in order to lead it back, by the detour of a more austere fidelity, to the Biblical God of perpetual passage" (p. 158).

59. See, for example: Hans Urs von Balthasar, *Qui est chrétien?* (Mulhouse:

Salvador, 1967); idem, *L'amour seul est digne de foi* (Paris: Aubier, 1966); idem, *Retour au centre* (Paris: Desclée de Brouwer, 1971); René Marlé, *La singularité chrétienne* (Tournai: Casterman, 1970); André Manaranche, *Je crois en Jésus-Christ aujourd'hui* (Paris: Seuil, 1968); Karl Rahner, *Ich Glaube an Jesus Christus* (Eisielden: Benziger, 1968). See also Jacques Dupuis, "Knowing Christ through the Christian Experience," *Indian Journal of Theology* 18 (1969):54–64.

10. INTERRELIGIOUS DIALOGUE IN THE EVANGELIZING MISSION OF THE CHURCH

1. We here include (and update) René Latourelle, ed., *Vatican II*, vol. 3, pp. 237–63.

2. Adam Wolanin, "Il concetto della missione nei decreti Ad Gentes e Apostolicam Actuositatem e nella Evangelii Nuntiandi," in M. Dhavamony, *Prospettive di missiologia, oggi*, pp. 89–105.

3. Domenico Grasso, "Evangelizzazione: Senso di un termine," in Mariasusai Dhavamony, *Evangelisation*, Documenta Missionalia 9 (Rome: Università Gregoriana Editrice, 1975), pp. 21–47; here, p. 43.

4. See Yves M. J. Congar, "Commentaire sur le Décret: Principes doctrinaux," in Johannes Schütte, ed., *Vatican II: L'action missionnaire de l'Eglise* (Paris: Cerf, 1967), pp. 198–208.

5. The Latin text of the encyclical constantly uses *colloquium*, and not *dialogus*.

6. See Pietro Rossano, "Sulla presenza e attività dello Spirito Santo nelle religioni e nelle culture non cristiane," in Dhavamony, *Prospettive di missiologia, oggi*, pp. 59–71; Kurien Kunnumpuram, *Ways of Salvation*.

7. For evangelization, see Grasso, "Evangelizzazione: Senso di un termine," esp. pp. 29–30.

8. The debates of the symposium have been published in "Salut et développement," *Spiritus* 10 (1969):321–521 (conclusions: pp. 518–521). The symposium has been translated into English as *Foundations of Mission Theology* (Maryknoll, N.Y.: Orbis Books, 1972). The conclusions, to which our numbers in the text refer, are found on pp. 165–68.

9. The debates of the Nagpur Conference appear in Dhavamony, *Evangelization, Dialogue and Development*. The final declaration appears on pp. 1–15. Our numerals refer to those of the declaration.

10. Text quoted in its entirety in chapter 8.

11. Still less is this asserted in the Report of the Special Committee on Evangelization, Dialogue, and Development, which makes an effort to define these three terms. In this text, for which the members of the committee alone take responsibility, evangelization and dialogue are distinguished even more radically. Evangelization "is the proclamation of the good news of salvation in Jesus Christ to persons who do not know him, in order to bring them to the faith and to fellowship in him." In this definition, whatever the positive value of the interreligious dialogue, the latter is foreign to evangelization. (See the text of the report in Dhavamony, *Evangelization, Dialogue and Development*, pp. 17–20).

12. By way of example, we may cite the communication of the Catholic Bishops' Conference of India, which appears in *Report of the General Meeting of the Catholic Bishops' Conference of India: Calcutta, January 6–14, 1974* (New Delhi: Catholic Bishops' Conference of India Centre, 1974), pp. 124–43.

13. *Evangelization in Modern Day Asia: The First Plenary Assembly of the Federation of Asian Bishops' Conferences (FABC)* (Hong Kong: FABC Secretariat, 1974). The same document is found in *For All the Peoples of Asia. The Church in Asia: Asian Bishops' Statements on Mission, Community and Ministry 1970-1983*, vol. 1, *Texts and Documents* (Manila: IMC, 1984) (= FAPA), pp. 25–47. Numerals cited are those of the Declaration.

14. Characteristic of this tendency are the interventions of Archbishop Lawrence T. Picachy, President of the Indian Bishops' Conference, and Archbishop Angelo I. Fernandes—both speaking in the name of the conference. The complete text of their interventions is found in D. S. Amalorpavadass, ed., *Evangelization of the Modern World* (Bangalore: NBCLC, 1975), pp. 124–34. "The church in India," states Archbishop Picachy, "regards the inter-faith dialogue as a normal expression of evangelisation" (p. 125); and Archbishop Fernandes: "Evangelisation . . . embraces the entire mission of the church. . . . Inter-faith dialogue and development work . . . must be considered as authentic dimensions of the church's work of evangelisation" (pp. 129–30). A summary of the interventions in Italian is found in Giovanni Caprile, *Il Sinodo dei Vescovi: Terza Assemblea Generale* (Rome: Civiltà Cattolica, 1975), pp. 214–16, 432–35.

15. *De Evangelizatione Mundi Huius Temporis*, part 1: *Mutua Communicatio Experientiarum, Synthesis Relationum et Interventionum Patrum* (Vatican: Typis Polyglottis Vaticanis, 1974). References are to page numbers.

16. *De Evangelizatione Mundi Huius Temporis*, part 2: *Themata Quaedam Theologica cum Experientiis Connexa Clarificantur: Synthesis Relationum et Interventionum Patrum* (Vatican: Typis Polyglottis Vaticanis, 1974). References are to page numbers.

17. For a brief account of the Synod, see Jacques Dupuis, "Synod of Bishops 1974," *Doctrine and Life* 25 (1975):323–48.

18. *Suffragatio circa Argumentum de Evangelizatione Mundi Huius Temporis* (Vatican: Typis Polyglottis Vaticanis, 1974).

19. Latin text in Caprile, *Sinodo dei Vescovi*, pp. 1011–16; English translation in Duraisamy S. Amalorpavadass, ed., *Evangelization of the Modern World*, pp. 96–101.

20. Text in *Acta Apostolicae Sedis* 68 (1976): 5–76.

21. The oft-quoted text reads as follows: "Activity in behalf of justice, and participation in the transformation of the world, fully appear to us as a constitutive dimension (*ratio constitutiva*) of the preaching of the Gospel, or in other words, of the mission of the Church for the redemption of the human race and its liberation from every oppressive situation" (*AAS* 63 (1971):924.

22. The reader may consult our commentary on the apostolic exhortation in *Vidyajyoti* 40 (1976):218–30.

23. The reader may see Pier G. Falciola, *"L'Evangelizzazione nel pensiero di Paolo VI* (Rome: Pontificia Unione Missionaria, 1980); idem, *Sulle vie della evangelizzazione con Giovanni Paolo II* (Rome: Pontificia Unione Missionaria, 1981).

24. Text in *Origins* 8 (1978-1979): 625–644.

25. Text in *Documentation Catholique* 78 (1981):203–206.

26. See chapter 7. We may also refer to the article by Thomas Michel, "Islamo-Christian Dialogue: Reflections on the Recent Teaching of the Church," *Bulletin, Secretariatus pro non Christianis* 20 (1985/2):172–93, for a review of the teaching of Paul VI and John Paul II on the relations of the church with Islam in particular. The author calls attention to a growing openness to Islam and a more pressing call

for dialogue. Here see our chapter 5. Among the more recent documents on the same subject, see especially John Paul II's address on the occasion of his meeting with Muslim youth at Casablanca, Morocco, August 19, 1985, in *Islamochristiana* 11 (1985):193–200; also in *Documentation Catholique* 82 (1985):17.

27. The Secretariat for Non-Christians already had a number of publications to its credit on the dialogue with specific religions: Hinduism, Buddhism, Islam, the African religions. The new document, however, besides being addressed to the other religions in general, has the benefit of the experience of the Secretariat's twenty years, and is more theological. It is the fruit of a long-term project, begun in 1979: The text had seen four successive redactions before its current formulation, which was presented and approved by the plenary assembly in February and March 1984.

28. The text of the document and that of the Pope's address are published in several languages in *Bulletin, Secretariatus pro non Christianis* 56, 19 (1984/2):117–242. Numerals in our text are those of the Pope's address and the document.

29. A colloquium was held at Lyon-Francheville, September 15–23, 1983, in preparation for the Mission Congress of Lisieu (April 1984), organized by the French Bishops' Commission for Foreign Missions, and Oeuvres Pontificales Missionaires. See "Un colloque de théologie missionaire," *Spiritus* 94, 25 (1984):1–110. In part two of its report on this "Colloquium on Mission in Action in the Local Church," the commission lists, in its conclusions, the "constitutive elements of evangelization," namely: "A silent presence in the midst of human beings, the testimonial of a life in Christ, activity in behalf of the promotion and liberation of the human being and all human beings, the absolute of the contemplative life, and so on, are an integral part of evangelization, on an equal footing with the Word. It is not a matter of a stage in the course of the journey of salvation history. These are *constitutive elements* of evangelization, because, each in its own way, they are all the expression and revelation of the one Love of the Father" ("Colloque de théologie missionaire," p. 101). This text is comparable to that of the Secretariat for Non-Christians.

30. The word *finally* does not occur in the original Italian text ("... vi è l'annunzio e la catechesi...."). However, as mission is first described as a "single, but complex and *articulated* reality," it seems clear that the document regards it as a dynamic reality and a process. In the apostolic exhortation *Evangelii Nuntiandi*, Paul VI had likewise described evangelization as a "rich, complex, and dynamic reality" (no. 17); see *Acta Apostolicae Sedis* 68 (1976): 17.

31. On the various forms of dialogue according to the document, see Jacques Dupuis, "Forms of Inter-religious Dialogue," *Bulletin, Secretariatus pro non Christianis* 59 (1985/2):164–71; also in *Portare Cristo all'uomo: Congresso del ventennio dal Concilio Vaticano II, 18-21 Febbraio 1985*, vol. 1: *Dialogo* (Rome: Pontificia Università Urbaniana, 1985), pp. 175–83.

32. Text in *The Pope Speaks to India* (Bombay: St. Paul, 1986), p. 29.

33. See Jacques Dupuis, "World Religions in God's Salvific Design in Pope John Paul II's Discourse to the Roman Curia (22 December 1986)," *Seminarium* 27 (1987):29–41.

34. English text in *Osservatore Romano*, 5 January 1987 (English Edition); French text in Pontifical Justice and Peace Commission, *Assise: Journée mondiale de prière pour la paix (27 octobre 1986)*, 1987, pp. 147–55.

35. There is no need to take up the encyclical *Dominum et Vivificantem*, on the Holy Spirit (1986). We have shown above (chapter seven) that it is the most explicit

text on the presence of the Holy Spirit outside the church. However, the encyclical does not speak of the universal economy of the Spirit as theological foundation of the interreligious dialogue.

36. Abridged text in Giovanni Caprile, *Il Sinodo straordinario 1985* (Rome: Civiltà Cattolica, 1986), pp. 215–17.

37. Text in *Origins* 15 (1985-1986):444–50.

38. Ibid., p. 450.

39. *De Vocatione et Missione Laicorum in Ecclesia et in Mundo Viginti Annis a Concilio Vaticano II Elapsis: Elenchus Unicus Propositionum* (Vatican City, 1987).

40. *De Vocatione et Missione Laicorum in Ecclesia et in Mundo Viginti Annis a Concilio Vaticano II Elapsis: Elenchus Definitivus Propositionum* (Vatican City, 1987). See proposition 30 (pp. 28–29), where the dialogue is included under the heading, "Strength of the Missionary Witness."

41. *De Vocatione et Missione Laicorum in Ecclesia et in Mundo Viginti Annis a Concilio Vaticano II Elapsis: Elenchus Ultimus Propositionum* (Vatican City, 1987). The French text has been published in *Documentation Catholique* 84 (1987):1088–1100.

42. *Documentation Catholique* 84 (1987):1095.

43. The last sentence in Proposition 30-bis reads: "The Synod thanks the Christian laity for all that they have contributed, and continue to contribute, to the evangelization of the world" (ibid.). May we conclude, then, that the dialogue is regarded as evangelization in the proper sense? This is actually unclear. The sentence cited has been added as a conclusion to Proposition 30, which dealt with "the power of the missionary witness," in the *Elenchus Definitivus Propositionum*. This proposition spoke both of a commitment to justice and peace, characterized as an "integral part of evangelization," and of the interreligious dialogue, to which a "primary importance" was attributed ("partem habet praeeminentem"), without any explicit statement to the effect that it would be part of evangelization properly speaking (*Elenchus Definitivus*, pp. 28–29). Indeed, proposition 29, even in the *Elenchus Finalis*, seems to identify "missionary evangelization" with the proclamation of the gospel (*Documentation Catholique* 84 [1987]:1095).

44. Certain authors still speak of evangelization and the interreligious dialogue as two entirely distinct tasks of the church's mission. Mission is then broadly understood to include these two tasks, but evangelization remains strictly identified with the proclamation of the gospel. A few examples will suffice. Mariasusai Dhavamony, "Evangelisation and Inter-religious Dialogue," in *Evangelisation*, Documenta Missionalia, no. 9 (Rome: Università Gregoriana Editrice, 1975), pp. 245–272, adopts this viewpoint. Domenico Grasso, *Foundations of Mission Theology*, pp. 104–10, identifies evangelization with the proclamation of the gospel, and distinguishes it from pre-evangelization. In an article entitled, "Meeting of Religions: Indian Perspectives," in Thomas A. Aykara, ed., *Meeting of Religions: New Orientations and Perspectives* (Bangalore: Dharmaram Publications, 1978), pp. 7–24, Archbishop D. Simon Lourdusamy, then Secretary of the Congregration for the Evangelization of Peoples, regards evangelization (identifed with proclamation) and dialogue as "two functions of the Christian existence," to which there correspond two distinct documents of Vatican II, *Ad Gentes* and *Nostra Aetate*, and in the Vatican, two distinct offices, the Congregation for the Evangelization of Peoples, and the Secretariat for Non-Christians. Bishop Pietro Rossano, "Theology of Religions: A Contemporary Problem," in René Latourelle and Gerald O'Collins, eds., *Problems and Perspectives*

of Fundamental Theology (New York: Paulist, 1982), pp. 292–308, however, offers a different interpretation: "The presence of both documents in the conciliar corpus is enough to show how specious the claim is that mission and dialogue in the church are mutually exclusive. It should also be noted that whenever *Ad Gentes* speaks of mission it always associates with it the word dialogue, while *Nostra Aetate*, regarded as the Magna Carta of dialogue, does not hestitate to speak of the church's duty to 'ever proclaim Christ,' who is 'the way, the truth, and the life' (no. 2)" (p. 303). The dialogue is "an element and necessary aspect" of the church's missionary engagement (ibid.)—without mission and evangelization being explicitly identified here. In "Sulla presenza e attività dello Spirito," Bishop Rossano pursues the same line: "The two attitudes, of dialogue and of proclamation, of listening and announcing, do not cancel one another, but actually meet, in the space of the Spirit, who is at the root of both" (p. 70). In "Dialogue in the Mission of the Church," *Bulletin, Secretariatus pro non Christianis* 57, 19 (1984/3):265–69, Marcello Zago, then Secretary of the Secretariat for Non-Christians, writes, in his presentation of the Secretariat's new document: "Dialogue was established to be intrinsic to mission, included within mission in the broad sense, as is the whole of the church's activity, which springs from the command of Christ. . . ." Unfortunately he adds: "In this sense, dialogue is clearly distinguished from evangelization," the latter being identified once more with proclamation (p. 268). By contrast, in an allocution at the meeting of the Committees for Interreligious Affairs of the Federation of Asian Bishops' Conferences, held at Sampran, Thailand, October 23–30, 1984, Archbishop Francis A. Arinze, then Pro-Prefect of the Secretariat for Non-Christians, forthrightly declared: "We share the mystery of Christ by the work of mission, and mission includes dialogue with those who do not believe in Christ. Interreligious dialogue between Christians and non-Christians is one of the ways in which we Christians bear witness to Christ, *in which we evangelize*, in which we live our faith, and in which we work for the coming of God's Kingdom" (unpublished; emphasis ours). Here, beyond the shadow of a doubt, the interreligious dialogue is regarded as an expression of mission, which in turn is identified with evangelization.

45. We prescind here from the discussion whether the 1971 Synod of Bishops ought to have spoken of an "integral part" rather than of a "constitutive dimension."

46. The distinction between pre-evangelization and evangelization should not be over-hastily attributed to Pope Paul VI himself in his message for the World Mission Day of 1970, in which he explains the relationship between evangelization and development. The Pope asserts that, while evangelization always maintains its "essential and intentional priority," development, in particular circumstances, can receive a "pastoral priority." The original Italian text continues: "Si parla di pre-evangelizzazione, cioè dell'accostamento dei futuri cristiani per via di carità . . ." (*AAS* 62 [1970]:538). The English text reads: "There is first *what some refer to as* pre-evangelization . . ." (emphasis ours). And the French: "On parle de pré-évangélisation" (*Documentation Catholique* 67 [1970]:811).

47. On the Holy Spirit and the evangelizing mission of the church, see Jacques Dupuis, *Jesus Christ and His Spirit* (Bangalore: Theological Publications in India, 1977), pp. 245–58; also Archbishop D. Simon Lourdusamy, "The Holy Spirit and the Missionary Activity of the Church," in Dhavamony, *Prospettive di missiologia, oggi*, pp. 45–58; Bishop Pietro Rossano, "Sulla presenza e attività dello Spirito," ibid., pp. 59–72; "Esprit et évangelisation," *Spiritus* 75, 20 (1979): 115–83.

11. TOWARD A THEOLOGY OF DIALOGUE

1. On the foundation of dialogue, the reader may refer to the document of the Secretariat for Non-Christians, "The Attitude of the Church Towards the Followers of Other Religions," nos. 20–27; text in *Bulletin, Secretariatus pro non Christianis* 56, 19 (1984/2):133–36.

2. The expression is borrowed from the document of the Secretariat, "The Attitude of the Church," no. 13; text in *Bulletin*, ibid., p. 130. The Italian original reads: ". . . per camminare insieme verso la verità" (ibid., p. 170). The French translation, ". . . Pour marcher ensemble á la recherche de la vérité," is incorrect (ibid., p. 150).

3. The reader may see Leonard Swidler, "The Dialogue Decalogue," *Journal of Ecumenical Studies* 20 (1983), pp. 1–4; also Raimundo Panikkar, "The Rules of the Game," in Anderson and Stransky, eds., *Faith Meets Faith*, pp. 111–122.

4. See Raimundo Panikkar, *The Intra-Religious Dialogue.*

5. Frank Whaling, *Christian Theology and World Religions: A Global Approach* (London: Marshall Pickering, 1986), pp. 130–31.

6. See Knitter, *No Other Name?* pp. 205–231.

7. See John V. Taylor, "The Theological Basis of Interfaith Dialogue," in John Hick and Brian Hebblethwaite, eds., *Christianity and Other Religions* (London: Collins, 1980), pp. 212–33; also in Anderson and Stransky, eds., *Faith Meets Faith*, pp. 93–110.

8. See the Declaration, *Mysterium Ecclesiae*, of the Congregation for the Doctrine of the Faith (May 11, 1973); text in *AAS* 65 (1973):402–404. Also Karl Rahner, "Mysterium Ecclesiae," *Theological Investigations*, vol. 17 (London: Darton, Longman and Todd, 1981), pp. 139–55.

9. *The Challenge of the Scriptures* by GRIC (Groupe de Recherches Islamo-Chrétien or Muslim-Christian Research Group), approaches the question in a very honest and sincere way, keeping account of the relative aspects of Christian revelation.

10. The reader may also see, on the subject of Hinduism: Michael Amaladoss, "Qui suis-je? Un catholique hindou," *Christus*, no. 86, 22 (1975):159–71; for Buddhism: John B. Cobb, Jr., "Christianity and Eastern Wisdom," *Japanese Journal of Religious Studies*, 1978, pp. 285–98; idem, "Can a Buddhist Be a Christian Too?", ibid., 1980, pp. 35–55.

11. This is the explanation proposed by Hans Staffner, *The Open Door* (Bangalore: Asian Trading Corporation, 1978). See also Claude Geffré, *The Risk of Interpretation* (Mahwah, N.J.: Paulist, 1987), pp. 170–71; idem, ed., *Théologie et choc des cultures: Colloque de l'Institut Catholique de Paris* (Paris: Cerf, 1984).

12. This is the solution proposed more recently for the problem of the Hindu-Christian by Staffner, *The Significance of Jesus Christ in Asia*; for the Islamo-Christian, see Kenneth Cragg, *Muhammad and the Christian: A Question of Response* (Maryknoll, N.Y.: Orbis Books, 1984).

13. Abhishiktananda, "The Depth-Dimension of Religious Dialogue," *Vidyajyoti* 45 (1981):202–21; here, p. 214. See idem, *Hindu-Christian Meeting Point* (Delhi: ISPCK, 1976). See also Whaling, *Christian Theology and World Religions*, pp. 130–31; Panikkar, *Intra-Religious Dialogue*; Arnulf Camps, *Partners in Dialogue: Christianity and Other World Religions* (Maryknoll, N.Y.: Orbis Books, 1983); Stanley J.

Samartha, *Courage for Dialogue: Ecumenical Issues in Inter-Religious Relationships* (Maryknoll, N.Y.: Orbis Books, 1982).

14. Text in *Bulletin, Secretariatus pro non Christianis* 56, 19 (1984/2):136–38.

15. See Jacques Dupuis, "The Forms of Inter-religious Dialogue," ibid. 59 (1985/2):164–71; likewise in *Portare Cristo all'uomo: Congresso del ventennio del Concilio Vaticano II, 18–21 Febbraio 1985*, vol. 1: *Dialogo* (Rome: Pontificia Università Urbaniana, 1985), pp. 175–83.

16. See Dhavamony, ed., *Evangelisation, Dialogue and Development*, p. 7; also Pathrapankal, *Service and Salvation*, p. 7.

17. Abhishiktananda, "Depth-Dimension of Religious Dialogue," pp. 220–21.

18. Raimundo Panikkar, *Maya e apocalisse: L'incontro dell'Induismo e del Cristianesimo* (Rome: Edizione Abete, 1966), pp. 136–41; here, p. 137. Also idem, *The Unknown Christ of Hinduism*.

19. Johnston, *The Inner Eye of Love*, pp. 43–52; esp. 51–52.

20. The Constitution, *Gaudium et Spes* says: "What is man? What is this sense of sorrow, of evil, of death, which continues to exist despite so much progress? What is the purpose of these victories, purchased at so high a cost? What can man offer to society, what can he expect from it? What follows this earthly life?" (no. 10).

21. See also the call to "dialogue and collaboration with those who follow other religions" in *Nostra Aetate*, no. 2.

22. See Secretariat for Non-Christians, "The Attitude of the Church," no. 13; text in *Bulletin, Secretariatus pro non Christianis* 19 (1984/2), p. 130.

23. See Jules Monchanin, "L'Inde et la contemplation," *Dieu Vivant* 3, 1 (1945):11–49, esp. 46.

24. Abhishiktananda, *Saccidananda: A Christian Approach to Advaitic Experience* (Delhi: ISPCK, 1984), pp. 121–22.

CONCLUSION

1. See, for example, Smith, *Towards a World Theology*; idem, "Theology and the World's Religious History," in Swidler, *Toward a Universal Theology of Religion*, pp. 51–72; also Leonard Swidler, "Interreligious and Interideological Dialogue," ibid., pp. 5–50.

2. Smith, *Towards a World Theology*, pp. 124–28.

3. For a critique of W. C. Smith's universal theology, see Whaling, *Christian Theology and World Religions*, pp. 106–10.

4. Tissa Balasuriya, *Planetary Theology* (London: SCM Press, 1984), p. 189.

5. See Whaling, *Christian Theology and World Religions*, pp. 53, 64, 67.

6. Ibid., p. 29.

7. Ibid., p. 94.

8. See Charles H. Kraft, *Christianity in Culture: A Study in Dynamic Biblical Theologizing in Cross-Cultural Perspective* (Maryknoll, N.Y.: Orbis Books, 1979).

9. See Thomas Dean, "Universal Theology and Dialogical Dialogue," in Swidler, *Toward a Universal Theology of Religion*, pp. 162–74.

10. Raimundo Panikkar, "The Invisible Harmony: A Universal Theory of Religion or a Cosmic Confidence in Reality?" in Swidler, ibid., pp. 118–53.

11. See Jacques Dupuis, "Auf dem Wege zu ortsgebundenen Theologien," *Internationale katholische Zeitschrift Communio* 16 (1987), pp. 409–19.

12. Claude Geffré, *The Risk of Interpretation*, p. 50.

13. Ibid., p. 53.

14. See Smet, *Le problème d'une théologie hindoue-chrétienne selon Raymond Panikkar*; idem, *Essai sur la pensée de Raimundo Panikkar*.

15. See Smet, *Problème d'une théologie hindoue-chrétienne*, p. 5.

16. See Smet, *Essai sur la pensée*, p. 55.

17. Raimundo Panikkar, "Le sujet de l'infaillibilité: Solipsisme et vérification," in *L'infaillibilité: Son aspect philosophique et théologique* (Paris: Aubier-Montaigne, 1970), pp. 423–45, and discussion 447–53, esp. 452.

18. See John B. Cobb, "Toward a Christocentric Theology," in Swidler, *Toward a Universal Theology of Religion*, pp. 86–100.

Select Bibliography

This select bibliography mentions only books treating the themes studied in the work. Some thematic issues of periodicals have been added. The bibliography has been adapted, amplified, and updated for the English edition.

Abeyasingha, Nihal. *A Theological Evaluation of Non-Christian Rites.* Bangalore: Theological Publications in India, 1984.

Akhilananda, Swami. *The Hindu View of Christ.* New York: Philosophical Library, 1949.

Aldwinckle, Russell F. *Jesus — A Savior or the Savior? Religious Pluralism in Christian Perspective.* Macon: Mercer University Press, 1982.

Amaladoss, Michael. *Faith, Culture and Inter-religious Dialogue.* New Delhi: Indian Social Institute, 1985.

———. *Mission Today: Reflections from an Ignatian Perspective.* Anand: Gujarat Sahitya Prakash, 1989.

———. *Making All Things New.* Maryknoll, N.Y.: Orbis Books, 1990.

Amaladoss, Michael et al., eds. *Theologising in India Today.* Bangalore: Theological Publications in India, 1983.

Amalorpavadass, Duraisamy Simon. *Approach, Meaning and Horizon of Evangelization.* Bangalore: NBCLC, 1973.

———. *Theology of Evangelization in the Indian Context.* Bangalore: NBCLC, 1984.

Amalorpavadass, Duraisamy Simon, ed. *Research Seminar on Non-Biblical Scriptures.* Bangalore: NBCLC, 1975.

Anderson, Gerald H., and Thomas F. Stransky, eds. *Christ's Lordship and Religious Pluralism.* Maryknoll, N. Y.: Orbis Books, 1981.

———. *Faith Meets Faith* (Mission Trends 5). New York and Ramsey, N.J.: Paulist Press, 1981.

Anderson, J.N. *Christianity and World Religions.* Leicester: Inter-Varsity Press, 1984.

Animananda, B. *The Blade.* Calcutta: Roy and Son, 1947.

Arai, Tosh, and S. Wesley Ariarajah. *Spirituality in Interfaith Dialogue.* Geneva: WCC, 1989.

Ariarajah, S. Wesley. *The Bible and People of Other Faiths.* Geneva: WCC, 1985.

Arnaldez, Roger. *Mohamet, la prédication prophétique.* Paris: 1970.

———. *Jésus, Fils de Marie, prophète de l'Islam.* Paris: Desclée, 1980.

———. *Trois messagers pour un seul Dieu.* Paris: Alba Michel, 1983.

———. *Jésus dans la pensée musulmane.* Paris: Desclée, 1988.

Aykara, Thomas A., ed. *Meeting of Religions: New Orientations and Perspectives.* Bangalore: Dharmaram Publications, 1978.

Balasuriya, Tissa. *Planetary Theology.* London: SCM Press, 1984.

Balchand, Asandas. *The Salvific Value of Non-Christian Religions according to Asian*

Christian Theologians Writing in Asian-Published Journals, 1965–1970. Manila: East Asian Pastoral Institute, 1973.

Balthasar von, Hans Urs. *A Theology of History.* London: Sheed and Ward, 1964.

———. *L'amour seul est digne de foi.* Paris: Aubier, 1966.

———. *Qui est chrétien?* Mulhouse: Salvador, 1967.

———. *The Moment of Christian Witness.* New York: Newman Press, 1969.

———. *Retour au centre.* Paris: Desclée de Brouwer, 1971.

———. *Das Christentum und die Weltreligionen.* 1979.

Barlage, Heinrich. *Christ Saviour of Mankind. A Christian Appreciation of Swami Akhilananda.* St. Augustin: Steyler Verlag, 1977.

Barnes, Michael. *Christian Identity and Religious Pluralism: Religions in Conversation.* Nashville: Abingdon Press, 1989.

Barzel, Bernard. *Mystique de l'ineffable dans l'hindouisme et le christianisme: Çankara et Eckhart.* Paris: Cerf, 1982.

Bassuk, D.E. *Incarnation in Hinduism and Christianity: The Myth of the God-Man.* London: Macmillan, 1987.

Borrmans, Maurice. *Guidelines for Dialogue between Christians and Muslims,* 2d ed. New York: Paulist Press, 1990.

Boublik, Vladimir. *Teologia delle religioni.* Roma: Editrice Studium, 1973.

Boyd, Robin H. S. *Manilal C. Parekh, Dhanjibhai Fakirbhai.* Madras: Christian Literature Society, 1974.

———. *India and the Latin Captivity of the Church: The Cultural Context of the Gospel.* Cambridge: Cambridge University Press, 1974.

———. *An Introduction to Indian Christian Theology,* 2d ed. Madras: Christian Literature Society, 1975.

———. *Kristadvaita. A Theology for India.* Madras: Christian Literature Society, 1977.

Braswell, G.W. *Understanding World Religions.* Nashville: Broadman Press, 1983.

Brauer, Jerald C., ed. *The Future of Religions.* New York: Harper and Row, 1966.

Braybrooke, Marcus. *The Undiscovered Christ: A Review of Recent Developments in the Christian Approaches to Hinduism.* Madras: Christian Literature Society, 1973.

———. *Time to Meet: Towards a Deeper Relationship between Jews and Christians.* London: SCM Press, 1990.

Breton, Stanislas. *Unicité et monothéisme.* Paris: Cerf, 1981.

Bühlmann, Walbert. *The Coming of the Third Church.* Maryknoll, N.Y.: Orbis Books and Slough: St Paul Publications, 1976.

———. *All Have the Same God.* Slough: St Paul Publications, 1982.

———. *The Chosen Peoples.* Maryknoll, N.Y.: Orbis Books and Slough: St Paul Publications, 1982.

Bultmann, Rudolf. *History and Eschatology.* Edinburgh: The University Press, 1957.

Buren, Paul Matthews van. *A Theology of the Jewish-Christian Reality.* 3 vols. San Francisco: Harper and Row, 1987–1988.

———. *Christ in Context.* San Francisco: Harper & Row, 1988.

Burghardt, Walter J. and William G. Thompson, eds. *Why the Church?* New York: Paulist Press, 1977.

Camps, Arnulf. *Partners in Dialogue: Christianity and Other World Religions.* Maryknoll, N. Y.: Orbis Books, 1983.

Cangh van, Jean-Marie, ed. *Salut universel et regard pluraliste.* Paris: Desclée, 1986.

Cantone, Carlo, ed. *Le scienze della religione oggi.* Roma: LAS, 1981.

Carmody, Denise Lardner. *What Are They Saying about Non-Christian Faith?* New York: Paulist Press, 1981.

Carruthers, Gregory H. *The Uniqueness of Jesus Christ in the Theocentric Model of the Christian Theology of Religions. An Elaboration and Evaluation of the Position of John Hick.* Lanham, New York and London: University Press of America, 1990.

Caspar, Robert. *Traité de théologie musulmane.* Vol.1. Rome: PISAI, 1987.

CBCI Commmission for Dialogue and Ecumenism. *Guidelines for Inter-Religious Dialogue,* 2d rev. ed. New Delhi: CBCI Centre, 1989.

Chemparathy, G. *Bible et Veda comme parole de Dieu.* Louvain-la Neuve (à paraître).

Chenu, Bruno. *Théologies chrétiennes des tiers mondes.* Paris: Centurion, 1987.

Chethimattam, John B. *Unique and Universal: Fundamental Problems of an Indian Theology.* Bangalore: Dharmaram Publications, 1972.

Christianity among the Religions of the World. New York: Scribner's, 1957.

Clasper, Paul. *Eastern Paths and the Christian Way.* Maryknoll, N. Y.: Orbis Books, 1980.

Clayton, J.P., ed. *Ernst Troeltsch and the Future of Theology.* Cambridge: Cambridge University Press, 1976.

Clévenot, Michel, ed. *L'état des religions dans le monde.* Paris: Cerf, 1987.

Coakley, Sarah. *Christ without Absolutes. A Study of Ernst Troeltsch.* Oxford: Clarendon, 1989.

Cobb, John B. *Christ in a Pluralistic Age.* Philadelphia: Westminster Press, 1975.

———. *Beyond Dialogue: Towards a Mutual Transformation of Christianity and Buddhism.* Philadelphia: Fortress Press, 1982.

Cobb, John B. and Ives, Christopher, eds. *The Self-Emptying God: A Buddhist-Jewish-Christian Conversation.* Maryknoll, N.Y.: Orbis Books, 1990.

Cobb, John B. et al., eds. *Death or Dialogue? From the Age of Monologue to the Age of Dialogue.* London: SCM Press, 1990.

Cocagnac, A.M. *Ces pierres qui attendent.* Paris: Desclée, 1979.

Comment être chrétien? La réponse de Hans Küng. Paris: Desclée de Brouwer, 1979.

Commission Biblique Pontificale. *Bible et christologie.* Paris: Cerf, 1984.

Congar, Yves. *I Believe in the Holy Spirit.* 3 vols. London: G. Chapman, 1983.

———. *The Word and the Spirit.* London: G. Chapman, 1986.

Corless, Roger, and Paul F. Knitter, eds. *Buddhist Emptiness and Christian Trinity.* Mahwah, N.J.: Paulist Press, 1990.

Cornelis, Etienne. *Valeurs chrétiennes des religions non chrétiennes.* Paris: Cerf, 1965.

Covell, Ralph R. *Confucius, the Buddha and Christ.* Maryknoll, N. Y.: Orbis Books, 1986.

Coward, Harold. *Pluralism: Challenge to World Religions.* Maryknoll, N. Y.: Orbis Books 1985.

———. *Sacred Word and Sacred Text: Scripture in World Religions.* Maryknoll, N. Y.: Orbis Books, 1988.

Coward, Harold, ed. *Hindu-Christian Dialogue: Perspectives and Encounters.* Maryknoll, N. Y.: Orbis Books, 1989.

Cox, Harvey. *Turning East.* New York: Simon and Schuster, 1977.

———. *Many Mansions: A Christian's Encounter with Other Faiths.* Boston: Beacon Press, 1988.

Cracknell, Kenneth. *Towards a New Relationship: Christians and People of Other Faiths.* London: Epworth Press, 1986.

Cragg, Kenneth. *Sandals of the Mosque.* London: SCM Press, 1959.

——. *The Call of the Minaret.* New York: Oxford University Press, 1964. 2nd ed., revised and enlarged, Maryknoll, N.Y.: Orbis Books, 1985.

——. *Christianity in World Perspective.* London: 1968.

——. *The Christian and the Other Religions.* London: Mowbrays, 1977.

——. *Muhammad and the Christian: A Question of Response.* Maryknoll, N.Y.: Orbis Books, and London: Darton, Longman and Todd, 1984.

——. *Jesus and the Muslim: An Exploration.* London: Allen and Unwin, 1985.

——. *The Christ and the Faiths: Theology in Cross-Reference.* London: SPCK, 1986.

Cullmann, Oscar. *Christ and Time.* London: SCM Press, 1965.

——. *Salvation in History.* London: SCM Press, 1967.

Cuttat, Jacques-Albert. *La rencontre des religions.* Paris: Aubier-Montaigne, 1957.

——. *Le dialogue spirituel Orient-Occident.* Louvain: Eglise vivante, 1964.

——. *Expérience chrétienne et spiritualité orientale.* Bruges: Desclée de Brouwer, 1967.

Cyriac, M.V. *Meeting of Religions.* Madras: Dialogue Series, 1983.

D'Costa, Gavin. *Theology and Religious Pluralism: The Challenge of Other Religions.* Oxford: Basil Blackwell, 1986.

——. *John Hick's Theology of Religions: A Critical Evaluation.* New York and London: University Press of America, 1987.

——. *Faith Meets Faith: A Volume of Inter-Faith Essays.* London: West London Institute of Higher Education, 1988.

D'Costa, Gavin, ed. *Christian Uniqueness Reconsidered: The Myth of a Pluralistic Theology of Religions.* Maryknoll, N.Y.: Orbis Books, 1990.

dal Covolo, Antonio. *Missioni e religioni non cristiane.* Roma: Città Nuova, 1981.

Dalmais, Irénée-Henri, ed. *Shalom: Chrétiens à l'écoute des grandes religions.* Bruges: Desclée de Brouwer, 1972.

Damboriena, Prudencio. *La salvación en las religiones no cristianas.* Madrid: La Editorial Católica, 1973.

Daniélou, Jean. *Holy Pagans in the Old Testament.* London: Longmans, Green and Co., 1957.

——. *The Lord of History. Reflections on the Inner Meaning of History.* London: Longmans, 1958.

——. *The Salvation of the Nations.* Notre Dame: University of Notre Dame Press, 1962.

——. *Mythes païens, mystère chrétien.* Paris: Seuil, 1966.

Davis, Charles. *Christ and World Religions.* London: Collins, 1970.

Davy, Marie-Madeleine. *Henri Le Saux: Swami Abhishiktananda. Le passeur entre deux rives.* Paris: Cerf, 1981.

Dawe, Donald G., and John B. Carman, eds. *Christian Faith in a Religiously Plural World.* Maryknoll, N. Y.: Orbis Books, 1978.

Devanandan, Paul D. *Preparation for Dialogue.* Bangalore: CISRS, 1964.

Dhavamony, Mariasusai, ed. *Revelation in Christianity and Other Religions.* Studia Missionalia 20. Rome: Gregorian University Press, 1971.

——. *Evangelization, Dialogue and Development.* Documenta Missionalia 5. Roma: Università Gregoriana Editrice, 1972.

——. *Mediation in Christianity and Other Religions.* Studia Missionalia 21. Rome: Gregorian University Press, 1972.

——. *Worship and Ritual in Christianity and Other Religions.* Studia Missionalia 23. Rome: Gregorian University Press, 1974.

——. *Evangelisation.* Documenta Missionalia 9. Roma: Università Gregoriana Editrice, 1975.

——. *Mysticism in Christianity and Other Religions.* Studia Missionalia 26. Rome: Gregorian University Press, 1977.

——. *Salvation in Christianity and Other Religions.* Studia Missionalia 29. Rome: Gregorian University Press, 1980.

——. *Ways of Salvation in Christianity and Other Religions.* Studia Missionalia 30. Rome: Gregorian University Press, 1981.

——. *Prospettive di missiologia, oggi.* Documenta Missionalia 16. Roma: Università Gregoriana Editrice, 1982.

——. *Founders of Religions: Christianity and Other Religions.* Studia Missionalia 33. Rome: Gregorian University Press, 1984.

Donovan, Vincent. *Christianity Rediscovered: An Epistle from the Masai.* London: SCM Press, 1978.

Dournes, Jacques. *God in Vietnam.* London: G. Chapman, 1966.

——. *L'offrande des peuples.* Paris: Cerf, 1967.

Drummond, Richard Henry. *Gautama the Buddha: An Essay in Religious Understanding.* Grand Rapids, Mich.: Eerdmans, 1974.

——. *Towards a New Age in Christian Theology.* Maryknoll, N. Y.: Orbis Books, 1985.

Dulles, Avery. *Models of the Church.* Garden City, N.Y.: Doubleday, 1974.

——. *Models of Revelation.* Garden City, N.Y.: Doubleday, 1983.

——. *The Catholicity of the Church.* Oxford: Oxford University Press, 1985.

Dupont, Jacques. *The Salvation of the Gentiles.* New York: Paulist Press, 1979.

Dupuis, Jacques. *Jesus Christ and His Spirit.* Bangalore: Theological Publications in India, 1977.

Edwards, Denis. *What Are They Saying about Salvation?* New York: Paulist Press, 1986.

Elwood, Douglas J. *Asian Christian Theology: Emerging Themes.* Philadelphia: Westminster Press, 1980.

Eminyan, Maurice. *The Theology of Salvation.* Boston: St. Paul's Publications, 1960.

Emprayil, Thomas. *The Emergent Theology of Religions.* Padra: Vincentian Ashram, 1980.

Eterovic, Nikola. *Cristianesimo e religioni secondo H. de Lubac.* Roma: Città Nuova, 1981.

Falaturi, Abdoldjavad, Jacob J. Petuchowski, and Walter Strolz. *Three Ways to the One God: The Faith Experience in Judaism, Christianity and Islam.* New York: Crossroad, 1987.

Farquhar, John Nicol. *The Crown of Hinduism.* London: Oxford University Press, 1915.

Fédou, Michel. *Christianisme et religions païennes dans le Contre Celse d'Origène.* Paris: Beauchesne, 1988.

Fernando, Antony. *Buddhism and Christianity: Their Inner Affinity.* Colombo: Ecumenical Institute for Study and Dialogue, 1983.

Fitzmyer, Joseph A. *Scripture and Christology: A Statement of the Biblical Commission with a Commentary.* New York and Mahwah, N.J.: Paulist Press, 1986.

Fries, Heinrich. *Das Christentum und die Weltreligionen.* Würzburg: 1965.

Fries, Heinrich et al. *Jesus in den Weltreligionen.* St. Ottilien: Eos Verlag, 1981.

Gandhi, Mohandas K. *Christian Missions.* Ahmedabad: Navajivan Publishing House, 1941.

——. *The Message of Jesus Christ.* Bombay: Bharatiya Vidya Bhavan, 1963.

Gardet, Louis. *Expériences mystiques en terres non chrétiennes.* Paris: Alsatia, 1953.

——. *Regards chrétiens sur l'Islam.* Paris: Desclée de Brouwer, 1986.

——, and Olivier Lacombe. *L'expérience du soi. Etude de mystique comparée.* Paris: Desclée de Brouwer, 1981.

Gatti, Vincenzio. *Il discorso di Paolo ad Atene.* Brescia: Paideia, 1982.

Geffré, Claude. *Révélation de Dieu et langage des hommes.* Paris: Cerf, 1972.

——. *The Risk of Interpretation. On Being Faithful to the Christian Tradition in a Non-Christian Age.* New York and Mahwah, N.J.: Paulist Press, 1987.

Geffré, Claude, ed. *Théologie et choc des cultures: Colloque de l'Institut Catholique de Paris.* Paris: Cerf, 1984.

Gillis, Chester. *A Question of Final Belief. J. Hick's Pluralistic Theology of Salvation.* London: Macmillan, 1989.

Gispert-Sauch, George, ed. *God's Word among Men.* Delhi: Vidyajyoti, 1974.

Gort, Jerald et al., eds. *Dialogue and Syncretism.* Grand Rapids, Mich.: William B. Eerdmans, 1989.

Gounelle, André. *Le Christ et Jésus.* Paris: Desclée, 1990.

Gozier, André. *Le Père Henri Le Saux à la rencontre de l'hindouisme.* Paris: Centurion, 1989.

Green, Michael, ed. *The Truth of God Incarnate.* London: Hodder and Stoughton, 1977.

Griffiths, Bede. *Vedanta and Christian Faith.* London: Dawn Horse Press, 1973.

——. *Return to the Centre.* London: Collins, 1976.

——. *The Marriage of East and West.* London: Collins, 1982.

——. *The Cosmic Revelation.* Bangalore: Asian Trading Corporation, 1985.

——. *Christ in India.* Bangalore: Asian Trading Corporation, 1986.

——. *A New Vision of Reality: Western Science, Eastern Mysticism and Christian Faith.* London: Collins, 1989.

Griffiths, Paul, ed. *Christianity through Non-Christian Eyes.* Maryknoll, N.Y.: Orbis Books, 1990.

Grillmeier, Aloys. *Christ in Christian Tradition,* vol. 1: *From the Apostolic Age to Chalcedon (451),* 2d ed. London: Mowbrays, 1975.

Guidelines on Dialogue with People of Living Faiths and Ideologies. Geneva: WCC, 1979.

Hacker, Paul. *Theological Foundations of Evangelization.* St. Augustin: Steyler Verlag, 1980.

Hallencreutz, Carl F. *New Approaches to Men of Other Faiths (1938–1968).* Geneva: WCC, 1970.

Hamnett, I., ed. *Religious Pluralism and Unbelief.* London: Routledge, 1990.

Harvey, Anthony E., ed. *God Incarnate: Story and Belief.* London: SPCK, 1981.

Hayek, Michel. *Le Christ et l'Islam.* Paris: Seuil, 1959.

Hebblethwaite, Brian. *The Incarnation. Collected Essays in Christology.* Cambridge: Cambridge University Press, 1987.

Heiler, Friedrich. *Die Religionen der Menschheit in Vergangenheit und Gegenwart.* Stuttgart: Reclam-Verlag, 1959.

Heim, S.M. *Is Christ the Only Way? Christian Faith in a Pluralistic World.* Valley Forge: Judson Press, 1986.

Hellwig, Monika K. *Jesus the Compassion of God.* Wilmington, Del.: Michael Glazier, 1983.

Henry, Antonin-Marcel, ed. *Les relations de l'Eglise avec les religions non chrétiennes.* Paris: Cerf, 1966.

Hick, John. *God and the Universe of Faiths: Essays in the Philosophy of Religion.* London: Macmillan, 1973.

————. *The Centre of Christianity.* London: SCM Press, 1977.

————. *God Has Many Names.* London: Macmillan, 1980.

————. *The Second Christianity.* London: SCM Press, 1983.

————. *Problems of Religious Pluralism.* London: Macmillan, 1985.

————. *An Interpretation of Religion: Human Responses to the Transcendant.* London: Macmillan, 1989.

Hick, John, ed. *Truth and Dialogue: The Relationship between World Religions.* London: Sheldon Press, 1975.

————. *The Myth of God Incarnate.* London: SCM Press, 1977.

Hick, John, and Brian Hebblethwaite, eds. *Christianity and Other Religions: Selected Readings.* London: Collins, 1980.

Hick, John, and Hasan Askari, eds. *The Experience of Religious Diversity.* Aldershot: Gower Publishers, 1985.

Hick, John, and Paul F. Knitter, eds. *The Myth of Christian Uniqueness: Toward a Pluralistic Theology of Religions.* Maryknoll, N. Y.: Orbis Books, 1987.

Hillman, Eugene. *The Wider Ecumenism: Anonymous Christianity and the Church.* New York: Herder and Herder, 1968.

————. *Many Paths: A Catholic Approach to Religious Pluralism.* Maryknoll, N. Y.: Orbis Books, 1988.

Holzner, G. *San Paolo e la storia delle religioni.* Roma: Paoline, 1956.

Hooker, Roger. *Themes in Hinduism and Christianity: A Comparative Study.* Frankfurt am Main: Verlag Peter Lang, 1989.

Hooker, Roger, and Christopher Lamb, eds. *Love the Stranger: Christian Ministry in Multi-Faith Areas.* London, SPCK, 1986.

Hospital, Clifford G. *Breakthrough: Insights of the Great Religious Discoverers.* Maryknoll, N. Y.: Orbis Books, 1985.

Howe, Reuel L. *The Miracle of Dialogue.* New York: Seabury Press, 1963.

Incontro tra le religioni. Milano: A. Mondadori, 1968.

Ingram, Paul O., and Fredrick J. Streng. *Christian-Buddhist Dialogue: Mutual Renewal and Transformation.* Honolulu: University of Hawaii Press, 1986.

Jamier, J. *Bible et Coran.* Paris: Cerf, 1959.

Jathanna, Constantine D., ed. *Dialogue in Community. Essays in Honour of Stanley J. Samartha.* Mangalore: The Karnataka Theological Research Institute, 1982.

Jathanna, Origen Vasantha. *The Decisiveness of the Christ-Event and the Universality of Christianity in a World Religious Plurality.* Bern: Lang, 1981.

Jeremias, Joachim. *Jesus' Promise to the Nations.* London: SCM Press, 1958.

Jesudasan, Ignatius. *A Gandhian Theology of Liberation.* Maryknoll, N. Y.: Orbis Books, 1984.

Johanns, Pierre. *Vers le Christ par le Vedanta.* 2 vols. Louvain: Museum Lessianum, 1932–1933.

————. *La pensée religieuse de l'Inde.* Namur: Facultés Universitaires, 1952.

Johnston, William. *The Inner Eye of Love: Mysticism and Religion.* New York: Harper and Row, 1978.

Jones, E. Stanley. *Mahatma Gandhi: An Interpretation.* London: Hodder and Stoughton, 1948.

Keenan, John P. *The Meaning of Christ: A Mahayana Theology.* Maryknoll, N. Y.: Orbis Books, 1989.

King, Ursula. *Towards a New Mysticism: Teilhard de Chardin and Eastern Religions.* London: Collins, 1980.

Klostermaier, Klaus K. *Hindu and Christian in Vrindaban.* London: SCM Press, 1969.

Knitter, Paul F. *Towards a Protestant Theology of Religions.* Marburg: Eelwert, 1974.

———. *No Other Name? A Critical Survey of Christian Attitudes toward the World Religions.* Maryknoll, N. Y.: Orbis Books, 1985.

Koyama, Kosuke. *Mount Fuji and Mount Sinai.* London: SCM Press, 1984.

Kraemer, Hendrik. *The Christian Message in a Non-Christian World.* London: Edinburgh House Press, 1947.

———. *Religion and the Christian Faith.* London: Lutterworth, 1956.

———. *The Communication of the Christian Faith.* London: Lutterworth, 1957.

———. *World Cultures and World Religions.* London: Lutterworth, 1960.

———. *Why Christianity of All Religions?* London: Lutterworth, 1962.

Kraft, Charles H. *Christianity in Culture: A Study in Dynamic Biblical Theologizing in Cross-Cultural Perspective.* Maryknoll, N. Y.: Orbis Books, 1979.

Kramer, Kenneth. *World Scriptures: An Introduction to Comparative Religions.* New York: Paulist Press, 1987.

Küng, Hans. *On Being a Christian.* New York: Doubleday, 1976; London: Collins, 1977.

Küng, Hans et al. *Christianity and World Religions: Paths of Dialogue with Islam, Hinduism and Buddhism.* New York: Doubleday, 1986; London: Collins, 1987.

Küng, Hans, and Julia Ching. *Christianity and Chinese Religions.* New York: Doubleday, 1989.

Kunnumpuram, Kurien. *Ways of Salvation: The Salvific Meaning of Non-Christian Religions according to the Teaching of Vatican II.* Poona: Pontifical Athenaeum, 1971.

Lacombe, Olivier. *L'absolu selon le Vedanta.* Paris: Geuthner, 1937.

———. *Chemins de l'Inde et philosophie chrétienne.* Paris: Alsatia, 1956.

———. *L'élan spirituel de l'hindouisme.* Paris: Oeil, 1986.

Latourelle, René. *Theology of Revelation.* Staten Island, N.Y.: Alba House, 1987.

Ledit, Charles J. *Mahomet, Israel et le Christ.* Paris: La Colombe, 1956.

Legrand, Lucien. *Le Dieu qui vient. La mission dans la Bible.* Paris: Desclée, 1988.

Lelong, Michel. *J'ai rencontré l'Islam.* Paris: Cerf, 1979.

Le Saux, Henri (Abhishiktananda). *Prayer.* Delhi: ISPCK, 1972.

———. *Guru and Disciple.* London: SPCK, 1974.

———. *Saccidananda: A Christian Approach to Advaitic Experience.* Delhi: ISPCK, 1974 (revised edition: 1984).

———. *Hindu-Christian Meeting-Point.* Delhi: ISPCK, 1976.

———. *The Secret of Arunachala.* Delhi: ISPCK, 1979.

———. *Intériorité et révélation: Essais théologiques.* Sisteron: Editions Présence, 1982.

———. *The Eyes of Light.* Denville, N. J.: Dimension Books, 1983.

———. *The Further Shore,* 2d ed. Delhi: ISPCK, 1984.

————. *La montée au fond du coeur: Le journal intime du moine chrétien-sannyasi hindou.* Paris: Oeil, 1986.

Limet, Henri, and Julien Ries, eds. *L'expérience de la prière dans les grandes religions.* Louvain-la-Neuve: 1980.

Lochhead, David. *The Dialogical Imperative: A Christian Reflection on Interfaith Encounter.* Maryknoll, N. Y.: Orbis Books, 1988.

Lubac, Henri de. *La rencontre du Bouddhisme et de l'Occident.* Paris: Aubier, 1952.

————. *Aspects du Bouddhisme.* 2 vol. Paris: Seuil, 1951–1955.

————. *Paradoxe et mystère de l'Eglise.* Paris: Aubier-Montaigne, 1967.

————. *Théologies d'occasion.* Paris: Desclée de Brouwer, 1984.

Lyonnet, Stanislas. *Les étapes de l'histoire du salut selon l'épître aux Romains.* Paris: Cerf, 1969.

Mampra, Thomas, ed. *Religious Experience: Its Unity and Diversity.* Bangalore: Dharmaram Publications, 1981.

Manaranche, André. *Je crois en Jésus-Christ aujourd'hui.* Paris: Seuil, 1968.

Maréchal, Joseph. *Studies in the Psychology of the Mystics.* Albany, N. Y.: Magi Books, 1964.

Marlé, René. *La singularité chrétienne.* Tournai: Casterman, 1970.

Martin-Achard, Robert. *Israël et les nations: La perspective missionnaire de l'Ancient Testament.* Neuchâtel: Delachaux et Niestlé, 1959.

Masson, Denise. *Le Coran et la révélation Judéo-chrétienne. Etudes comparées.* 2 vol. Paris: Adrien Maisonneuve, 1958.

————. *Monothéisme coranique et monothéisme biblique. Doctrines comparées.* Paris: Desclée de Brouwer, 1976.

Mattam, Joseph. *Land of the Trinity: A Study of Modern Christian Approaches to Hinduism.* Bangalore: Theological Publications in India, 1975.

Matus, Thomas. *Yoga and the Jesus Prayer Tradition: An Experiment in Faith.* Ramsey, N. J.: Paulist Press, 1984.

Maupilier, Maurice. *Les mystiques hindous-chrétiens (1830–1967).* Paris: Oeil, 1985.

Maurier, Henri. *Essai d'une théologie du paganisme.* Paris: Orante, 1965.

McFadden, Thomas, ed. *Does Jesus Make a Difference?* New York: Seabury Press, 1974.

Monchanin, Jules. *Mystique de l'Inde, mystère chrétien.* Paris: Fayard, 1974.

————. *Théologie et spiritualité missionnaire.* Paris: Beauchesne, 1985.

Monti, Joseph E. *Who Do You Say that I Am? The Christian Understanding of Christ and Antisemitism.* Ramsey, N. J.: Paulist Press, 1984.

Moran, Gabriel. *Theology of Revelation.* New York: Herder and Herder, 1966.

————. *The Present Revelation.* New York: Herder and Herder, 1972.

Morris, Thomas V. *The Logic of God Incarnate.* London: Cornell University Press, 1986.

Mundadan, A. Matthias. *Hindu-Christian Dialogue: Past Twenty-Five Years.* Bangalore: Dharmaram Publications, 1981.

Muslim-Christian Research Group. *The Challenge of the Scriptures: The Bible and the Qur'an.* Maryknoll, N. Y.: Orbis Books, 1989.

Mussner, Franz. *Tractate on the Jews: The Significance of Judaism for Christian Faith.* London: SPCK, 1984.

My Neighbour's Faith and Mine: Theological Discoveries through Inter-Faith Dialogue. Geneva: WCC, 1986.

Neher, André. *L'essence du prophétisme.* Paris: Calmann-Lévy, 1972.

Neill, Stephen. *Christian Faith and Other Faiths: The Christian Dialogue with Other Religions.* Oxford: Oxford University Press, 1965.

――――. *The Supremacy of Jesus.* London: Hodder and Stoughton, 1984.

――――. *Crisis of Belief: The Christian Dialogue with Faith and No Faith.* London: Hodder and Stoughton, 1984.

Neuner, Josef. "Das Christus-Mysterium und die indische Lehre von den Avataras." In Aloys Grillmeier and Heinrich Bacht, eds. *Das Konzil von Chalkedon: Geschichte und Gegenwart,* vol.3. Würzburg: Echter-Verlag, 1954, pp.785-824.

Neuner, Joseph, ed. *Christian Revelation and World Religions.* London: Burns and Oates, 1967.

Newbigin, Lesslie. *L'universalisme de la foi chrétienne.* Geneva: Labor and Fides, 1965.

――――. *The Finality of Christ.* London: SCM Press, 1969.

――――. *The Gospel in a Pluralistic Society.* Grand Rapids, Mich.: Eerdmans, 1990.

Niebuhr, H. Richard. *Christ and Culture.* New York: Harper and Brothers, 1951.

Nys, Hendrik. *Le salut sans l'évangile.* Paris: Cerf, 1966.

Ogden, Schubert M. *Christ without Myth.* New York: Harper and Brothers, 1961.

Osten-Sacken von der, Peter. *Christian-Jewish Dialogue: Theological Foundations.* Philadelphia: Fortress Press, 1986.

Oxtoby, Williard G. *The Meaning of Other Faiths.* Philadelphia: Westminster Press, 1985.

Panikkar, Raymond. *The Unknown Christ of Hinduism.* London: Darton, Longman and Todd, 1964.

――――. *Religionen und die Religion.* München: Hüber Verlag, 1965.

――――. *Maya e apocalisse.* Roma: Edizione Abete, 1966.

――――. *L'homme qui devient Dieu.* Paris: Aubier, 1969.

――――. *Le mystère du culte dans l'hindouisme et le christianisme.* Paris: Cerf, 1970.

――――. *Salvation in Christ: Concreteness and Universality. The Supername.* Santa Barbara, California, 1972.

――――. *The Trinity and the Religious Experience of Man.* London: Darton, Longman and Todd, 1973.

――――. *The Intra-Religious Dialogue.* New York: Paulist Press, 1978.

――――. *Myth, Faith and Hermeneutics: Cross-Cultural Studies.* New York: Paulist Press, 1979.

――――. *The Unknown Christ of Hinduism: Towards an Ecumenical Christophany.* Revised enlarged edition, Maryknoll, N.Y.: Orbis Books, 1981. London: Darton, Longman and Todd, 1981.

――――. *The Silence of God: The Answer of the Buddha.* Maryknoll, N.Y.: Orbis Books, 1989.

Pannenberg, Wolfhart. *Basic Questions in Theology. Collected Essays,* vol.2. Philadelphia: Fortress Press, 1971.

Pannenberg, Wolfhart, ed. *Revelation as History.* London: Macmillan, 1969.

Paranilam, Z. *Christian Openness to the World Religions.* Alwaye: Pontifical Institute Publications, 1988.

Parekh, Manilal C. *Brahmarsi Keshub Chunder Sen.* Rajkot: 1931.

――――. *A Hindu's Portrait of Jesus.* Rajkot: 1953.

Parichha, Cassian. *Revelation in Other Religions according to Asian Christian Theologians 1970–1980.* Manila: East Asian Pastoral Institute.

Parrinder, Geoffrey. *The Christian Debate: Light from the East.* London: 1964.

——. *Avatar and Incarnation.* London: Faber and Faber, 1970.

——. *Jesus and the Qur'an.* London: Sheldon Press, 1977.

——. *Encountering World Religions: Questions of Religious Truth.* New York: Crossroad, 1987.

Pathrapankal Joseph, ed. *Service and Salvation.* Bangalore: Theological Publications in India, 1973.

Pawlikowski, John T. *Christ in the Light of Christian-Jewish Dialogue.* New York: Paulist Press, 1982.

——. *What Are They Saying about Christian-Jewish Relations?* New York: Paulist Press, 1980.

Pieris, Aloysius. *An Asian Theology of Liberation.* Maryknoll, N. Y.: Orbis Books, 1988.

——. *Love Meets Wisdom: A Christian Experience of Buddhism.* Maryknoll, N. Y.: Orbis Books, 1988.

Pinto, Joseph Prasad. *Inculturation through Basic Communities: An Indian Perspective.* Bangalore: Asian Trading Corporation, 1985.

Pontifical Council for Inter-religious Dialogue. *Guidelines for Dialogue between Christians and Muslims*, 2d ed. New York: Paulist Press, 1990.

Portare Cristo all'uomo. Congresso del ventennio dal Concilio Vaticano II. Vol. 1: *Dialogo.* Roma: Pontificia Università Urbaniana, 1985.

Puthanangady, Paul, ed. *Sharing Worship.* Bangalore: NBCLC, 1988.

Race, Alan. *Christians and Religious Pluralism: Patterns in the Christian Theology of Religions.* Maryknoll, N.Y.: Orbis Books, 1982; London: SCM Press, 1983.

Radhakrishnan, Sarvepalli. *The Hindu View of Life.* London: Allen and Unwin, 1926.

——. *An Idealist View of Life.* London: Allen and Unwin, 1937.

——. *Eastern Religions and Western Thought.* London: Allen and Unwin, 1939.

Raguin, Yves. *Bouddhisme-Christianisme.* Paris: Epi, 1973.

——. *The Depth of God.* St. Meinard: Abbey Press, 1975.

——. *La source.* Paris: Desclée, 1989.

Rahner, Karl, *Inspiration in the Bible*, Quaestiones Disputatae 1. New York: Herder, 1961.

——. *Ich glaube an Jesus Christus.* Eiselden: Benziger, 1968.

——. *Foundations of Christian Faith. An Introduction to the Idea of Christianity.* London: Darton, Longman and Todd, 1978; New York: Herder, 1978.

——. "Current Problems in Christology." *Theological Investigations*, vol. 1. London: Darton, Longman and Todd, 1961, pp. 149–200.

——. "Membership of the Church According to the Teaching of Pius XII's Encyclical 'Mystici Corporis Christi'." Ibid., vol. 2, 1963, pp. 1–88.

——. "On the Theology of the Incarnation." Ibid., vol. 4, 1966, pp. 105–120.

——. "History of the World and Salvation History." Ibid, vol. 5, 1966, pp. 97–114.

——. "Christianity and the Non-Christian Religions." Ibid., vol. 5, 1966, pp. 115–134.

——. "The Man of Today and Religion." Ibid., vol. 6, 1969, pp. 3–20.

——. "Anonymous Christians." Ibid., vol. 6, 1969, pp. 390–398.

——. "Atheism and Implicit Christianity." Ibid., vol. 9, 1972, pp. 145–164.

——. "One Mediator and Many Mediations." Ibid., vol. 9, 1972, pp. 169–186.

——. "Church, Churches and Religions." Ibid., vol. 10, 1973, pp. 30–49.

——. "Anonymous Christianity and the Missionary Task of the Church." Ibid., vol. 12, 1974, pp. 161–178.

——. "Observations on the Problem of the 'Anonymous Christian'." Ibid., vol. 14, 1976, pp. 280–298.

——. "Anonymous and Explicit Faith." Ibid., vol. 16, 1979, pp. 52–59.

——. "The One Christ and the Universality of Salvation." Ibid., vol. 16, 1979, pp. 199–224.

——. "Jesus Christ in the Non-Christian Religions." Ibid., vol. 17, 1981, pp. 39–50.

——. "On the Importance of the Non-Christian Religions for Salvation." Ibid., vol. 18, 1984, pp. 288–295.

——. "Profane History and Salvation History." Ibid., vol. 21, 1988, pp. 3–15.

——. "Christianity's Absolute Claim." Ibid., vol. 21, 1988, pp. 171–184.

Rahner, Karl, and Josef Ratzinger. *Revelation and Tradition.* Quaestiones Disputatae 17. New York: Herder, 1966.

Ratansekara, Leopold. *Christianity and the World Religions.* Kandy: Lake House Printers, 1982.

Ravier, A., ed. *La mystique et les mystiques.* Paris: Desclée de Brouwer, 1965.

Remaud, Michel. *Chrétiens devant Israel serviteur de Dieu.* Paris: Cerf, 1983.

Richard, Lucien. *What Are They Saying about Christ and World Religions?* New York: Paulist Press, 1981.

Richards, Glyn. *Towards a Theology of Religions.* London: Routledge, 1989.

Ricoeur, Paul et al. *La révélation.* Bruxelles: Facultés Universitaires Saint-Louis, 1977.

Ries, Julien. *Les chemins du sacré dans l'histoire.* Paris: Aubier-Montaigne, 1985.

——. *Les chrétiens parmi les religions.* Paris: Desclée, 1987.

Robinson, John A. T. *Truth Is Two-Eyed.* London: SCM Press, 1979.

Röper, Anita. *The Anonymous Christian.* New York: Sheed and Ward, 1966.

Rossano, Piero. *Il problema teologico delle religioni.* Catania: Paoline, 1975.

Rouner, Leroy S., ed. *Religious Pluralism.* Notre Dame, Ind.: University of Notre Dame Press, 1984.

Rousseau, Richard W., ed. *Inter-Religious Dialogue: Facing the Next Frontier.* Scranton: Ridge Row Press, 1981.

——. *Christianity and the Religions of the East: Models for a Dynamic Relationship.* Scranton: Ridge Row Press, 1982.

Rupp, George. *Christologies and Cultures.* The Hague: Mouton, 1974.

Saldanha, Crys. *Divine Pedagogy: A Patristic View of Non-Christian Religions.* Roma: LAS, 1984.

Samartha, Stanley J. *Living Faiths and the Ecumenical Movement.* Geneva: WCC, 1971.

——. *The Hindu Response to the Unbound Christ.* Madras: Christian Literature Society, 1974.

——. *Courage for Dialogue: Ecumenical Issues in Inter-Religious Relationships.* Maryknoll, N. Y.: Orbis Books, 1982.

——, ed. *Dialogue between Men of Living Faiths.* Geneva: WCC, 1971.

——. *Living Faiths and Ultimate Goals: A Continuing Dialogue.* Maryknoll, N. Y.: Orbis Books, 1975.

——. *Faith in the Midst of Faiths: Reflections on Dialogue in Community.* Geneva: WCC, 1977.

Sanneh, L. *Translating the Message: The Missionary Impact on Culture.* Maryknoll, N. Y.: Orbis Books, 1990.

Schilpp, Paul Arthur. *The Philosophy of Sarvepalli Radhakrishnan.* New York: Tudor, 1952.

Schlette, Heinz Robert. *Towards a Theology of Religions.* New York: Herder and Herder, 1966.

——. *Epiphany as History.* New York: Herder and Herder, 1969.

Schreiter, Robert J. *Constructing Local Theologies.* Maryknoll, N. Y.: Orbis Books, 1985.

Schütte, Johannes., ed. *Vatican II: L'action missionnaire de l'Eglise.* Paris: Cerf, 1967.

Scott, David C. *Keshub Chunder Sen.* Madras: Christian Literature Society, 1979.

Secretariatus pro non christianis. *Towards the Meeting of Religions: Suggestions for Dialogue.* Vatican: Polyglot Press, 1967.

——. *Meeting the African Religions.* Roma: Ancora, 1969.

——. *Religions: Fundamental Themes for a Dialogical Understanding.* Roma: Ancora, 1970.

——. *Towards the Meeting with Buddhism.* 2 vol. Roma: Ancora, 1970.

——. *For a Dialogue with Hinduism.* Roma: Ancora, n.d..

——. *Religions in the World.* Vatican: Polyglot Press: n.d..

——. *The Attitude of the Church towards the Followers of Other Religions: Reflections and Orientations on Dialogue and Mission.* Vatican: Typis Poliglottis Vaticanis, 1984.

Sen, Keshub Chunder. *Lectures in India*, 2 vols. London: Cassell, 1901–1904.

Senior, Donald and Carroll Stuhlmueller. *The Biblical Foundations for Mission.* London: SCM Press, 1983.

Sharpe, Eric J. *Comparative Religion.* London: Duckworth, 1975.

——. *Faith Meets Faith: Some Christian Attitudes to Hinduism in the 19th and 20th Centuries.* London: SCM Press, 1977.

Sheth, Noel. *The Divinity of Krishna.* New Delhi: Munshiram Manoharlal, 1984.

Shorter, Aylward. *Revelation and Its Interpretation.* London: G. Chapman, 1983.

——. *Toward a Theology of Inculturation.* Maryknoll, N. Y.: Orbis Books, 1988.

Singh, Herbert Jai, ed. *Inter-religious Dialogue.* Bangalore: CISRS, 1967.

Slater, R. L. *World Religions and World Community.* New York: 1963.

Smart, Ninian. *The Yogi and the Devotee.* London: Allen and Unwin, 1968.

——. *Beyond Ideology: Religion and the Future of Western Civilization.* London: Collins, 1981.

——. *The World Religions: Old Traditions and Modern Transformations.* Cambridge: Cambridge University Press, 1989.

Smet, Robert. *Essai sur la pensée de Raimundo Panikkar: Une contribution indienne à la théologie des religions et à la christologie.* Louvain-la-Neuve, 1981.

——. *Le problème d'une théologie hindoue-chrétienne selon Raymond Panikkar.* Louvain-la-Neuve: 1983.

Smith, Wilfred Cantwell. *The Faith of Other Men.* New York: Harper and Row, 1962.

——. *The Meaning and the End of Religion.* New York: Macmillan, 1962.

——. *Questions of Religious Truth.* London: Gollanez, 1967.

——. *Faith and Belief.* Princeton, N. J.: Princeton University Press, 1979.

——. *Towards a World Theology: Faith and the Comparative History of Religion.* Philadelphia: Westminster Press, 1981; Maryknoll, N.Y.: Orbis, 1989.

——. *Religious Diversity.* New York: Crossroad, 1982.

Soares-Prabhu, George. *Inculturation, Liberation, Dialogue.* Pune: Jnanadeepa, 1984.

Song, Choan-Seng. *The Compassionate God: An Exercise in the Theology of Transposition.* Maryknoll, N. Y.: Orbis Books, 1982.

——. *Tell Us Our Names: Theology from an Asian Perspective.* Maryknoll, N.Y.: Orbis Books, 1984.

——. *Christology and Other Faiths: Some Theological Reflections.* Toronto: Ecumenical Forum of Canada, 1985.

Spink, Kathryn. *A Sense of the Sacred: A Biography of Bede Griffiths.* Maryknoll, N.Y.: Orbis Books, 1989.

Staffner, Hans. *The Open Door.* Bangalore: Asian Trading Corporation, 1978.

——. *The Significance of Jesus Christ in Asia.* Anand: Gujarat Sahitya Prakash, 1985.

——. *Jesus Christ and the Hindu Community: Is a Synthesis of Hinduism and Christianity Possible?* Anand: Gujarat Sahitya Prakash, 1988.

Straelen van, Henry. *The Catholic Encounter with World Religions.* London: Burns and Oates, 1965.

Strolz, Walter. *Heilswege der Weltreligionen,* 4 vol. Freiburg: Herder, 1984–1987.

Strolz, Walter, and Hans Waldenfelds. *Christliche Grundlagen des Dialogs mit den Weltreligionen.* Freiburg: Herder, 1983.

Stuart, James D.M. *Swami Abhishiktananda: His Life Told through His Letters.* Delhi: ISPCK, 1989.

Swearer, Donald. *Dialogue: The Key to Understanding Other Religions.* Philadelphia: Westminster Press, 1977.

Swidler, Leonard, ed. *Toward a Universal Theology of Religion.* Maryknoll, N. Y.: Orbis Books, 1987.

——. et al. *Death or Dialogue? From the Age of Monologue to the Age of Dialogue.* London: SCM, 1990.

——. et al. *Bursting the Bonds? A Jewish-Christian Dialogue on Jesus and Paul.* Maryknoll, N.Y.: Orbis Books, 1990.

Teasdale, Wayne Robert. *Toward a Christian Vedanta.* Bangalore: Asian Trading Corporation, 1987.

Teissier, Henri. *Eglise en Islam. Méditation sur l'existence chrétienne en Algérie.* Paris: Le Centurion, 1984.

——. *La mission de l'Eglise.* Paris: Desclée, 1985.

Terrin, Aldo Natale et al. *Le scienze della religione oggi.* Bologna: Centro Ed. Dehoniano, 1983.

TeSelle, Eugene. *Christ in Context.* Philadelphia: Fortress Press, 1975.

Thandy, Z.P., K. Pathil, and F. Podgorski. *Religion in Dialogue: East and West Meet.* Lanham: UPA, 1985.

Théologie d'aujourd'hui et de demain. Paris: Cerf, 1967.

Thils, Gustave. *Propos et problèmes de la théologie des religions non chrétiennes.* Tournai: Casterman, 1966.

——. *Pour une théologie de structure planétaire.* Louvain-la-Neuve, 1983.

——. *Présence et salut de Dieu chez les non chrétiens.* Louvain-la-Neuve, 1987.

Thomas, M. M. *The Acknowledged Christ of the Indian Renaissance.* London: SCM Press, 1969.

——. *Man and the Universe of Faiths.* Bangalore: Christian Literature Society, 1975.

——. *Risking Christ for Christ's Sake: Towards an Ecumenical Theology of Pluralism.* Geneva: WCC, 1987.

Thomas, Owen C. *Attitudes towards Other Religions.* London: SCM Press, 1969.

Thompson, William M. *The Jesus Debate: A Survey and Synthesis.* New York: Paulist Press, 1985.

Thottakara, Augustine, ed. *Self and Consciousness: Indian Interpretations.* Bangalore: Dharmaram Publications, 1989.

Tillich, Paul. *Christianity and the Encounter of World Religions.* New York: Columbia, 1963.

——. *The Future of Religions.* New York: Harper and Row, 1966.

——. *The Kingdom of God and History.* Chicago: 1983.

Toynbee, Arnold J. *Christianity among the Religions of the World.* New York: Scribner's, 1957.

Tracy, David. *Blessed Rage for Order.* New York: Seabury Press, 1975.

——. *The Analogical Imagination: Christian Theology and the Culture of Pluralism.* New York: Crossroad, 1981.

——. *Plurality and Ambiguity: Hermeneutics, Religion, Hope.* San Francisco: Harper and Row, 1987.

Tracy, David, and John B. Cobb, eds. *Talking about God: Doing Theology in the Context of Modern Pluralism.* New York: Seabury Press, 1983.

Troeltsch, Ernst. *The Absoluteness of Christianity and the History of Religions.* Richmond: John Knox Press, 1971.

Vandana, ed. *Swami Abhishiktananda: The Man and His Teachings.* Delhi: ISPCK, 1986.

Vattakuzhy, Emmanuel. *Indian Christian Sannyasa and Swami Abhishiktananda.* Bangalore: Theological Publications in India, 1981.

Veliath, Dominic. *Theological Approach and Understanding of Religions. Jean Daniélou and Raimundo Panikkar: A Study in Contrast.* Bangalore: Kristu Jyoti College, 1988.

Vempeny, Ishanand. *Inspiration in Non-Biblical Scriptures.* Bangalore: Theological Publications in India, 1973.

——. *Krsna and Christ.* Anand: Gujarat Sahitya Prakash, 1988.

Walgrave, Jan-Hendrik. *Un salut aux dimensions du monde.* Paris: Cerf, 1970.

Wandelfelds, Hans. *Absolutes Nichts. Zur Grundlegung des Dialogs zwischen Buddhismus und Christentum.* Freiburg: Herder, 1980.

——. *La méditation en Orient et en Occident.* Paris: Seuil, 1981.

——. *Faszination des Buddhismus. Zum christlich-buddhistischen Dialog.* Mainz: Mathias Grudewald, 1982.

Watt, W. Montgomery. *Islamic Revelation in the Modern World.* Edinburgh: University Press, 1969.

——. *Islam and Christianity Today.* London: Routledge and Kegan Paul, 1983.

Weber, J. G., ed. *In Quest of the Absolute: The Life and Work of Jules Monchanin.* London: Mowbray, 1977.

Whaling, Frank. *Christian Theology and World Religions: A Global Approach.* London: Marshall Pickering, 1986.

——, ed. *Contemporary Approaches to the Study of Religion,* 2 vols. Berlin: Mouton, 1983–1985.

——. *The World's Religious Traditions: Current Perspectives in Religious Studies.* Edinburgh: T. & T. Clark, 1984.

——. *Religion in Today's World.* Edinburgh: T. & T. Clark, 1987.

Whitson, R. H. *The Coming Convergence of World Religions.* Westminster: Newman Press, 1971.

Winslow, J. C. *The Christian Approach to the Hindu.* London: 1966.

Zaehner, Robert Charles. *Mysticism Sacred and Profane.* Oxford: Clarendon Press, 1957.

——. *The Convergent Spirit: Towards a Dialectics of Religion.* London: Routledge and Kegan Paul, 1963.

——. *The Catholic Church and World Religions.* London: Burns and Oates, 1964.

——. *Inde, Israel, Islam: Religions mystiques et révélations prophétiques.* Bruges: Desclée de Brouwer, 1965.

——. *Concordant Discord.* Oxford: Clarendon Press, 1970.

Zago, Marcello. *Buddhismo e Cristianesimo in dialogo.* Roma: Città Nuova, 1985.

——. *Il dialogo inter-religioso a 20 anni dal Concilio.* Roma: Piemme, 1986.

Zuidema, Willem. *God's Partner: An Encounter with Judaism.* London: SCM Press, 1987.

Periodicals

Communio. Vol. 13 (1988/4). "Oriental Religions and Christianity."

Concilium. No. 112 (1976/3). "Utilisation des écritures hindoues, bouddhiques et islamiques dans le culte chrétien."

Concilium. No. 116 (1976/6). "Chrétiens et musulmans."

Concilium. No. 116 (1978/6). "Buddhism and Christianity."

Concilium. No. 135 (1980/5). "True and False Universality of Christianity."

Concilium. No. 136 (1980/6). "What Is Religion? An Inquiry for Christian Theology."

Concilium. No. 183 (1986/1). "Christianity among World Religions."

Concilium. No. 208 (1990/2). "Ethics in the Great Religions and Human Rights."

Cross Currents. Vol. 38 (1989/3), pp. 268–351: "The One, the Christian and the Many."

Indian Journal of Theology. Vol. 30 (1981/3-4), pp. 115–217: "World Religions and the Economy of Salvation."

Jeevadhara. No. 47, vol. 8 (1978), pp. 353–408: "Religious Pluralism."

Jeevadhara. No. 65, vol.11 (1981), pp. 317–394: "Inter-religious Dialogue Today."

Jeevadhara. No. 77, vol. 13 (1983), pp. 309–366: "Christian Existence in a World of Inter-religious Dialogue."

Journal of Ecumenical Studies. Vol. 24 (1987/1), pp. 1–52: "Thinking about Theocentric Christology."

Journal of Ecumenical Studies. Vol. 26 (1989/1), pp. 1–216; "Universality and Uniqueness in the Context of Religious Pluralism."

Pro Mundi Vita, Bulletin. No. 88 (1982/1), pp. 1–30: "Hindu Christian Dialogue in India."

Spiritus No. 39, vol.10 (1969), pp.321–521: "Salut et développement."

Spiritus. No. 75, vol. 20 (1979), pp. 115–183; "Esprit et évangélisation."

Spiritus. No. 94, vol. 25 (1984), pp. 1–110: "Un colloque de théologie missionnaire."

Spiritus. No. 106, vol. 28 (1987), pp. 3–88: "Un autre regard."

Index

Also in the Faith Meets Faith Series

THE NEW UNIVERSALISM
Foundations for a Global Theology
by David J. Krieger
Within today's global horizon every religion and worldview has as much right to answer the basic questions of human existence as any other. The task confronting theology, therefore, lies in the integration and mutual appropriation of many seemingly conflicting revelations. Drawing upon the work of Panikkar and Wittgenstein, Krieger constructs a method and a philosophical foundation for resolving ideological conflicts and carrying out a theological appropriation of non-Christian religions.

"Krieger has in this volume pursued with learning and with care the philosophical issues latent in plurality, and explored the possibility of communicative discourse across deep cultural and religious differences. This is a ground-breaking work in an area of the very greatest theological and cultural concern." — **Langdon Gilkey, Professor Emeritus, University of Chicago Divinity School**

200pp. Index. ISBN 0-88344-727-4 Paperback
ISBN 0-88344-728-2 Clothbound

WOMEN SPEAKING, WOMEN LISTENING
Women in Interreligious Dialogue
by Maura O'Neill
Is gender an issue in interreligious dialogue? *Women Speaking, Women Listening* explores this question and its impact on the central issues of interfaith dialogue. O'Neill argues that current interreligious dialogue is crippled because its purported base in religious pluralism is not sufficiently critical in regard to sexism, and therefore insufficiently plural. Inasmuch as religion and faith fail to struggle with issues of gender (sexuality, inequality, liberation) women in dialogue must raise these considerations and force them to the center of current debate. O'Neill also discusses issues unique to women's dialogue and suggests a practical agenda to bring women from different traditions into dialogue with each other and with men. *Women Speaking, Women Listening* is a helpful first step to an interreligious dialogue — of both women and men — that will result in mutual understanding not only across religious and cultural lines, but across gender as well.

"This is an important book which opens up a major new dimension of interfaith dialogue." — **John Hick, Claremont Graduate School**

142pp. Notes, index. ISBN 0-88344-697-9 Paperback
ISBN 0-88344-698-7 Clothbound

THE EMPTYING GOD
A Buddhist-Jewish-Christian Conversation
edited by John B. Cobb, Jr., and Christopher Ives
Seven eminent scholars respond to the challenge of Masao Abe's seminal essay, "Kenotic God and Dynamic Sunyata" which demonstrates powerfully the dynamism of the Buddhist appreciation of the divine Emptiness at the heart of Being. From perspectives as diverse as American feminism, post-Holocaust Judaism, process thought, and hermeneutics, Thomas J.J. Altizer, Eugene Borowitz, Catherine Keller, Schubert M. Ogden, Jurgen Moltmann, and David Tracy reply to Abe's proposal for considering God to be intrinsically "self-emptying." Including a final response from Abe, this provocative and illuminating work shows how interfaith dialogue at its very best provides materials for the mutual transformation of all traditions.

"This book is an event. . . . Professor Abe's work, deeply rooted in the Zen philosophy and at the same time open for dialogue, is a real challenge for Jewish-Christian thinking. . . ." — **Hans Kung**

232pp. Bibliography, index. ISBN 0-88344-670-7 Paperback
ISBN 0-88344-671-5 Clothbound

THE CHALLENGE OF THE SCRIPTURES
The Bible and the Qur'ān
by Muslim-Christian Research Group (GRIC)
The culmination of a unique, long-range project of interfaith encounter, here Muslim and Christian scholars from Europe and North Africa report on five years of research and discussion. Experts in their own areas, they met independently and as individual representatives of their faith traditions — and as friends, with neither political nor religious agendas. The development of their search for common ground in sacred texts involved the defining of scripture, its role and meaning in both traditions, and methods for its study and dissemination both to the individual and the faith community. Concludes with two "assessments" — Islamic scholars commenting on the Bible and Christian scholars on the Qur'ān — *The Challenge of the Scriptures* demonstrates clearly how interreligious dialogue must be done: carefully, thoughtfully, respectfully, with knowledge and with faith.

". . . This mutual exploration of [scriptures] bearings on each other in Islam and Christianity is a thorough and patient venture of mind and spirit which deserves to be warmly welcomed and carefully weighed." — **Bishop Kenneth Cragg**

112pp. Notes. ISBN 0-88344-650-2 Paperback
ISBN 0-88344-651-0 Clothbound

MANY PATHS
A Catholic Approach to Religious Pluralism
by Eugene Hillman
The author, a pioneer in the area of interreligious dialogue and Catholic thought, argues that the wide ecumenism to which Christians were summoned by Vatican II may be the most radically demanding of the Council's many calls. By exploring religion's historico-cultural dimensions, examining the Church's tradition and practice, and the challenges of post-Vatican II ministry, *Many Paths* makes a vital contribution to the development of interfaith dialogue.

"This work is an obvious choice for those grappling with Christian theological approaches to religious diversity and pluralism. . . . I consider it essential for courses on theology and world religions." — **James M. Kroeger, Loyola School of Theology, Manila**

110pp. Notes, references, index. ISBN 0-88344-548-4 Paperback
ISBN 0-88344-547-6 Clothbound